Christian Hugo Hoffmann
The Quest for a Universal Theory of Intelligence

Christian Hugo Hoffmann

The Quest for a Universal Theory of Intelligence

The Mind, the Machine, and Singularity Hypotheses

DE GRUYTER

ISBN 978-3-11-135827-7
e-ISBN (PDF) 978-3-11-075616-6
e-ISBN (EPUB) 978-3-11-075619-7

Library of Congress Control Number: 2021950672

Bibliographic information published by the Deutsche Nationalbibliothek
The Deutsche Nationalbibliothek lists this publication in the Deutsche Nationalbibliografie;
detailed bibliographic data are available on the Internet at http://dnb.dnb.de.

© 2023 Walter de Gruyter GmbH, Berlin/Boston
This volume is text- and page-identical with the hardback published in 2022.
Cover image: Uta Oettel
Typesetting: Integra Software Services Pvt. Ltd.
Printing and binding: CPI books GmbH, Leck

www.degruyter.com

To my love, the incarnation of musical intelligence, a hallmark of human uniqueness, O.M.V.

To the sharp thinkers about intelligence and successful AI entrepreneurs Like Gary Marcus

Acknowledgments

This book is motivated by one of the possibly biggest challenges of our lifetime, the challenge to understand and recreate intelligence. It is the product of philosophical reflection in the armchair, propelled by my practical experience as a tech and software entrepreneur as well as my prior scholarly studies on questions about artificial intelligence, AI (during the postdoc after my first PhD and my work as Assistant Professor of Finance and Fin*tech*). To some extent, it also follows from my formal training and socialization in philosophy of the analytic tradition (e.g., incarnated by the line from Rudolf Carnap to Wolfgang Stegmüller and Wolfgang Spohn – under the latter I did my Master studies in Konstanz). However, at the same time, the book at hand challenges, transcends, and breaks with some parts of that great tradition. This is neither a flaw the reader will unveil, nor an accident. I did it on purpose and for good reasons.

As a teaser, not a spoiler, the point I wish to highlight here is that some concepts, including the for our purposes central notion of intelligence, are complex systems or family concepts that cannot be reduced to necessary conditions which together are sufficient for explicating the term in question. Rather, something more than analysis is needed and harbored in systems thinking which encompasses not just analysis, but also synthesis. That the guild of analytic philosophy has a problem with questioning the value of analysis may be obvious, but why should academic philosophy refrain from becoming affected (or improved?) by new ways of thinking and working? Or rather by *innovation* as I, as an entrepreneur, would phrase it.

Despite being ready and willing to explore uncharted territory for investigating the concept of intelligence in a time where scientists speak of very intelligent animals like octopi or crows and where engineers claim to create intelligences artificially, my work did not come together in pure solitude. I found an ideal home and environment at the ITAS (the *Institut für Technikfolgenabschätzung und Systemanalyse*) at the Karlsruhe Institute of Technology, the "leading institute for technology assessment in Germany and worldwide". With interdisciplinarity in its DNA, a focus on not only AI, but also on impact outside of scientific communities, and an openness to apply systems thinking, the ITAS welcomed me and provided me with the necessary support to bring my research project to a successful completion. Particularly, I am deeply grateful to my advisor Prof. Dr. Armin Grunwald, Head of the ITAS as well as of the Office of Technology Assessment at the German Bundestag (TAB), for his invaluable comments on earlier versions of this manuscript and his encouragement.

I found an intellectual home at the ITAS. More holistically, home is where my family is and, therefore, I would like to express my utmost gratitude to my family; first and foremost, to Oana.

Another key concept (apart from "synthesis") that systems thinking has coined is the one of a *feedback loop* which occurs when outputs of a system are routed back as inputs as part of a chain of cause-and-effect that forms a circuit (Hoffmann, 2017b: Figure 1; Schwaninger, 2005). By embracing this feedback view of the world, I also wish to thank my publisher Christoph Schirmer at De Gruyter for their help and the reviews I received. In this spirit, I dedicate the final word of thank you to the reader, in general, and cordially invite every single one of you to close the feedback loop. Please reach out to me with questions, comments, and stimulating thoughts. Feedback is highly appreciated.

You can reach me at: christian@hoffmann-economics.com. Thank you!

Freienbach, Switzerland
October 2021
Christian Hugo Hoffmann

Contents

Acknowledgments — VII

Introduction — 1

Part I: The different localizations, facets and forms of intelligence

1 Intelligence in human animals — 17

2 Intelligence in biological animals — 33

3 Intelligence in artificial animals — 59

Part II: Scaffolding intelligence

4 Preliminaries and prior work on framing intelligence — 99
    4.1 The cognitive ladder — **99**
    4.2 The ladder of prediction — **104**
    4.3 The ladder of causation — **107**

5 Towards a causal theory of intelligence — 118
    5.1 The universal taxonomy: More nuanced dimensions of intelligence and causality — **119**
    5.2 The inverted radex model of intelligence — **139**
    5.3 A dynamic approach for broad and multiple intelligences — **147**

6 Theory in action: Causal modeling — 151

7 Theory validation — 159

Part III: Evaluating machine intelligence in current and past AI

8 The Turing Test — 177

9 Caveats and innovations — 183

10 A tentative solution —— 193

Part IV: Singularity hypotheses

11 Arguments conducive to the belief that the singularity is near —— 209
    11.1   The hardware-based argument by Moravec (1999) and Kurzweil (2006) —— **209**
    11.2   The original argument by Good (1965) and its interpretation by Chalmers (2010) —— **215**
    11.3   The doomsayer scenario advanced by Bostrom (2016) —— **219**

12 Arguments against strong AI: Close but no cigar —— 224
    12.1   Gödelian arguments —— **225**
    12.2   Dreyfus' prophecy and legacy —— **229**
    12.3   Searle's Chinese Room thought experiment —— **233**

13 Closing remarks —— 238

Overall conclusion and some practical implications —— 241

References —— 249

About the author —— 279

Index —— 281

Introduction

Contributions on capabilities and projected capabilities of Artificial Intelligence (AI) by researchers and other experts, many of them from non-engineers, trained outside the field of AI research or computer science abound. This is one of them. Yet, at the same time misperceptions and associated fears of AI abound too and are being nurtured by the absence of falsifiable, rigorous and bold perspectives on what just happened in the scientific and technical development of AI, therefore, leaving much to imagination (Darwiche, 2017: 4). This is *not* one of them.

Unlike some red herrings where the respective authors lack pertinent (book) knowledge or promote ill-guided, spurious scenarios – we will see that partially below in Part IV – this work attempts to avoid that quagmire by adhering to a strictly philosophical endeavor (a field where this author has been trained). As Derek Partridge and Yorick Wilks (1990: ix) write in *The Foundations of Artificial Intelligence*, "philosophy is a subject that comes running whenever foundational or methodological issues arise." Our aim in this book is primary twofold. On the one hand, we will examine the quality of different arguments about (hypothetical) intellectual capabilities of machines propounded from different sides in terms of their soundness. On the other hand, we focus on the conceptual level of discussions on AI and, thereby illuminate notions of high philosophical relevance, first and foremost the notion of intelligence. This is a momentous task because, firstly, novel types of AI, from social robots to cognitive assistants, are provoking the demand for new answers for meaningful comparison with other kinds of intelligence: "How can such intelligent systems be catalogued, evaluated, and contrasted, with representations and projections that offer meaningful insights?" (Bhatnagar et al., 2018).

Secondly, practical or technical endeavors in AI often proceed and are pursued without a full grip on and appreciation of the legacy, connotations, and consequences of the concepts they already mobilize and employ, which lets a need emerge that brings us home to philosophy (Hoffmann & Hahn, 2020: 635; Gunkel, 2017: 14).

AI has been intimately intertwined with philosophy ever since its inception, and not just in the sense of philosophies of AI (i.e., on a meta level), but, more proximally, in the sense of philosophical AI (AI pursued as and out of philosophy). AI formalisms flew from philosophy, as nicely chronicled, in part, by Glymour (1992). To just emphasize two chief threads, we esteem that, on the one hand, AI, today, is shot through and through with logic, traced all the way back to Aristotle's theory of the syllogism; the two fields cannot be insulated (Halpern et al., 2001).

On the other hand, the situation is no different when we are talking about probabilistic formalisms, also a significant component of modern-day AI (Bringsjord & Govindarajulu, 2018). For example, in the one mind of Pascal was born a method of rigorously calculating probabilities, conditional probability (which plays an especially large role in AI, currently), and such fertile philosophico-probabilistic arguments as Pascal's wager, according to which it is irrational not to become *Christian (Hoffmann*, 2021a). In face of these close ties between philosophy and AI, Aaron Sloman heralded the advent of a new AI-based paradigm in philosophy. In the book appropriately entitled "The Computer Revolution in Philosophy", he conjectured that "within a few years, if there remain any philosophers who are not familiar with some of the main developments in artificial intelligence, it will be fair to accuse them of professional incompetence" (Sloman cited in Walmsley, 2012).

Particularly, as philosophers we stumble upon the conundrum of our time in the so-called second machine age (Brynjolfsson & McAfee, 2014): Many people in AI have not thought deeply about the key term in "AI": "intelligence" (Heil, 2021: 425). Tegmark (2018: 49), for example, shares an anecdote from a symposium on AI which he attended and which was organized by the Swedish Nobel Foundation: "[W]hen a panel of leading AI researchers were asked to define intelligence, they argued at length without reaching consensus. We found this quite funny: there's no agreement on what intelligence is even among intelligent intelligence researchers!" Most researchers in AI do not even touch upon the concept – be it that they have putatively more important things to say (which not seldom leads to technical disputes or wild speculations), be it that it would be beyond the parochial scope of a ten to twenty page long research article.

Yet, from time to time, we must step out of the stream of direct experience and our immediate responses to it. And even if such constraints are not given, the upshot is often not satisfying. A celebrated example here is the more than 300 pages long monograph by Hubert Dreyfus who showcased a "classification of intelligent activities" (Dreyfus, 1999: 292) which not only suffers from wrong statements like "translating a natural language (requiring an understanding in context of use) is nonformal" – empirically falsified by the success of deep learning approaches in the last decade, which, as we see, do not understand the text to be translated, but which nevertheless pick a vast amount of low-hanging fruits –; yet, for our purposes more saliently, does not clarify "intelligence" at all. The title of the table is flatly a misnomer.

In this work, intelligence (and only as a derivative or corollary artificial intelligence) is the target explanandum of philosophical explanation. "Intelligence" is an ambitious and ambiguous word. According to the dictionary by

Merriam-Webster,[1] intelligence is circumscribed in a manifold way: "(1.1.1) the ability to learn or understand or to deal with new or trying situations: reason; also: the skilled use of reason. (1.1.2) the ability to apply knowledge to manipulate one's environment or to think abstractly as measured by objective criteria (such as tests). (1.2) mental acuteness. (1.3) Christian Science: the basic eternal quality of divine Mind. (2) information or news. (3) the act of understanding: comprehension. (4) the ability to perform computer functions. (5.1) intelligent minds or mind. (5.2) an intelligent entity."

Even though it contains some interesting pointers which will be taken up in the course of this study, e.g., the ability to learn or understand, to apply knowledge or to perform computer functions, some comments would be in order from a philosophical point of view as a reply to this definition: a) The definition goes into many different directions which makes it too broad to be useful. Indeed, for our purposes, we narrow it down by ignoring the sense (1.3) and (2), the former is embedded in a religious or historical context, the latter is different from the others in kind and, for example, implicated in the titles of certain government organizations such as the Central Intelligence Agency (CIA). The other meanings are, by contrast, relevant for this work and will, eo ipso, be integrated in a systematic framework. b) The demarcation line between "intelligence" and other related concepts like reason, knowledge or comprehension remains elusive in Merriam-Webster's definition. c) Sometimes, intension and extension are confused, e.g., (1.3), (5.1) and (5.2). Etc. Should we, thus, give up operating with the term and take Jensen's (1998: 49) position that "it is best simply to get rid of the term 'intelligence' [. . .], the ill-fated word from our scientific vocabulary"? No, we are convinced that such a reaction would just be tantamount to throwing out the baby with the bathwater.

Instead of that overreaction and of criticizing Merriam-Webster's definition any further, we plainly draw the bottom line that dictionary definitions per se usually do not suffice for philosophical or, generally speaking, academic penetration. Attempts by modern philosophers like Ryle (1949: 45) to collect a wide range of mental attributes and cluster them under the *descriptive* meaning of the term "intelligent" do not do any better. Even more in our case. Our objective is not to inaugurate a new, more refined or sophisticated definition, but (to at least lay the cornerstone of) a theory of intelligence, diminishing our uncertainty about the objects we apply the concept to.

It not only describes what intelligence is, but comes with true explanatory power yielding orientation and clear as well as reliable predictions and elucidating why things are the way they are: for instance, *why* is a toaster less intelligent

---

[1] Cf. https://www.merriam-webster.com/dictionary/intelligence (28-10-2020).

than my dog? Does it make *sense* at all to call a toaster intelligent? *Would* DeepMind's program AlphaGo outperform my professor in chess? And so on. This book treats intelligence, its localizations, facets and forms (and more), with some breadth and depth. The *breadth* involves thinking about divergent sorts of animals (from organic to artificial). The *depth* is depth in analysis and synthesis: We do not content ourselves with delineating where intelligence can be found, what it is or should be. Rather, the present book embraces the tall order of dressing intelligence in a philosophical theory.

Despite the high ambitions of this project, more intellectual modesty, but also conceptual clarity is urgently needed in AI, more than in many other disciplines. First, AI research has been coined by hypes (Marcus, 2018: 17) since its early beginnings in the 1950s. For instance, recall the hubris in the opening of McCarthy et al.'s (1955: 2) research proposal:

> We propose that a 2 month, 10 man study of artificial intelligence be carried out during the summer of 1956 at Dartmouth College in Hanover, New Hampshire. The study is to proceed on the basis of the conjecture that every aspect of learning or any other feature of intelligence can in principle be so precisely described that a machine can be made to simulate it. An attempt will be made to find how to make machines use language, form abstractions and concepts, solve kinds of problems now reserved for humans, and improve themselves. We think that a significant advance can be made in one or more of these problems if a carefully selected group of scientists work on it together for a summer.

Or his companion from the Dartmouth workshop, Herbert Simon, predicted "machines will be capable, within twenty years, of doing any work that a man can do" (Simon cited in Franklin, 2015: 21). As it turned out, the new century would arrive without a single machine able to converse at even the toddler level. But also modern AI, having been awoken from hibernation by the arrival of *Big Data*, is still characterized by over-enthusiasm, and non-scientific speculation. Ray Kurzweil's manifesto of prophecies is dubbed *The Singularity is Near*, echoing John the Baptist's cry: "the kingdom of heaven is near" (Matthew 3:2). In his earlier book, he (1999: 202f.) further envisions 2019 as a year, chiefly falsified by history, where computers are now largely invisible and embedded everywhere in walls, tables, chairs, etc., where most interaction with computing is through gestures or two-way natural-language spoken communication, or where 10% out of the total computing capacity of the human species (i.e., all human brains) combined with the computing technology we invented is nonhuman (i.e. AI).[2]

---

[2] I am reminded of Peter Thiel's famous (if now slightly outdated) damning of an often too-narrowly focused tech industry: "We wanted flying cars, instead we got 140 characters".

He is even so bold to draw farfetched pictures of a human + machine world in 2029 and 2099. Or another telling example: "Our generation will likely have the good fortune to experience two of the most amazing events in history: the creation of true machine intelligence and the connection of all humans via a common digital network [. . .]" (Brynjolfsson & McAfee, 2014: 251). And Harari (2017: 409) complements as a bottom line: "[I]n the coming decades new techno-religions may conquer the world by promising salvation through algorithms [AI] and genes [cyborgs]."

With almost everyone being either overexcited by the new developments or overwhelmed by them, not only have substantial scholarly discussions and reflections gone missing (Darwiche, 2017: 11), but also the field itself is now intimidated by the big risk of falling short of AI ambitions, of "another AI winter, such as the one that devastated the field in the 1970's, after the Lighthill report (Lighthill, 1973)" (Marcus, 2018: 17; cf. also Darwiche, 2017: 7f.). With the book at hand, we fill this gap and address this need.

As a preview of what is to come over the next 278 pages, the treatment at hand is composed of four distinct parts. In Part I, we position the quest for what intelligence is in the context of discovering where it can be found, i.e., in what kinds of creatures, which results in a tour de force through human, animal, and artificial intelligence. Part II turns to the gist of the matter by seeking to understand why we ascribe intelligence to some, but not to others and what we mean by that, thereby erecting a causal theory of intelligence. Subsequently, the main work is done. Part III and IV, both significantly shorter in length, underpin the theory development contribution through testing its application. The former is dedicated to the application to present-day and past AI systems whilst the latter elaborates on hypotheses about possible strong AI (which is defined in 3.2. and Part IV), which comprises responses to familiar arguments from the literature of philosophy. Or more schematically, a synopsis is compiled in the following Table 1.

Table 1: A synopsis of the present book.

Part of the treatise	Overriding aspects
Part I: The different localizations, facets & forms of intelligence	– *Methods*: Literature review, analysis of animal case studies, knowledge integration and progress through critical discourse with scholars – *Audience*: Interdisciplinary kinds of intelligence research groups, and (here and henceforth) every intelligent being interested in intelligence – *Main source*: Psychology, neuroscience, anthropology in Chapter 1; comparative psychology and animal cognition research in Chapter 2; computer science, AI, and philosophy of AI in Chapter 3 – *Objective*: Clarification of the extension of the concept "intelligence" – *Key findings*: On pages 90–92
Part II: Scaffolding intelligence	– *Methods*: Literature review (Chapter 4), concept analysis, theory building, causal loop diagram, Bayesian net, radex model, theory validation – *Audience*: Philosophy of mind, scientists and AI engineers – *Main source*: Ethics of AI (in 4.1.), neuroscience and philosophy of mind (in 4.2.), and especially philosophy of science and computer science (in 4.3.) – *Objective*: In lieu of futile concept explication attempts / of depreciating other proposals, the aim is to erect a causal theory of intelligence – *Key findings*: On pages 169 and 170
Part III: Evaluating machine intelligence in current and past AI	– *Methods*: Theory application, model interpretation, synthesis – *Audience*: AI community and philosophical AI – *Main source*: Part II – *Objective*: Evaluation of present and past machine intelligence – *Key findings*: On pages 200 and 201
Part IV: Singularity hypotheses	– *Methods*: Theory application, model interpretation, synthesis – *Audience*: Philosophy of AI – *Main source*: Part II – *Objective*: Evaluation of possible strong AI and of singularity hypotheses – *Key findings*: On pages 239 and 240

Part I: **The different localizations, facets and forms of intelligence**

Instead of fruitless attempts to divide the world into things with and things without the essence of mind, [or intelligence, C.H.], we should examine the many detailed similarities and differences between systems.   Aaron Sloman, 1984

It is crucial to isolate concepts from what they are concepts of, a common misleading assimilation.[3] The entities or objects concepts refer or apply to are said to be within their extension. This Part I deals first and foremost with the extension or scope of the concept of intelligence and, eo ipso, investigates in what creatures we find which forms and facets of intelligence. It comes, however, directly with a restriction about its own scope: extraterrestrial intelligence is explicitly factored out from the analysis, and plants are merely touched upon briefly and thus practically out of scope. By contrast, we start with humans and animals, and move towards the speculative, i.e., AI as the field devoted to assembling artificial *animals* – or at least artificial creatures that, in tailored contexts, appear to be animals (Bringsjord & Govindarajulu, 2018).[4] In fact, we close this section in Chapter 3 by refashioning the open and hotly debated question of whether AI should be considered intelligent which is illustrated by the juxtaposition of the philosophy of AI, examining "strong" versus "weak" AI (Bringsjord & Govindarajulu, 2018), and the simple economics of AI which refers to AI as mere prediction machines whereby predictive abilities are treated as a necessary, but not sufficient condition for *human*-level intelligence (Agrawal et al., 2018; Hoffmann, 2018a).

Moreover, we identify the gap that albeit much has been explored in the philosophy of AI, the general key term of intelligence remains under-researched in this connection – e.g., there is only a Stanford Encyclopedia entry on "AI" (Bringsjord & Govindarajulu, 2018), but none on "intelligence" as such. This might be somewhat perplexing as we witness that many different disciplines have tackled and joined forces to clarifying "intelligence", from psychology to neuroscience and evolutionary biology. Therefore, we account for, but also mix these different perspectives in this Part I. Less astonishingly perhaps, each of them argues that *their* perspective is the one that truly matters. Here is, in a slightly exaggerated form, the sort of thing in a nutshell you might envisage in the following:

---

[3] For example, Bruno Latour infamously claimed that Ramses II could not have died of tuberculosis since Robert Koch discovered the disease only in 1882. He said, "Before Koch, the bacillus had no real existence. To say that Ramses II died of tuberculosis is as grotesque as saying that he died of machine-gun fire." Yet, clear to most analytic philosophers, what did not exist prior to 1882 was not the tuberculosis bacillus, but rather the human concept of it.

[4] As this whole investigation, especially in Part IV, shows, it is true, however, that some AI researchers and/or engineers aspire to build artificial creatures that greatly exceed the cognitive powers of what nature has supplied.

https://doi.org/10.1515/9783110756166-002

- What we need to care about is *psychology*, how a mind works in people and how that compares and contrasts with other people or animals. Cognition, including but not limited to learning, attention, memory, perception, but also affect or consciousness, and, of course, intelligence are all psychological categories and together make up the mental life of people and other animals.
- What we need to care about is *evolution*, the blind watchmaker (Dawkins, 1986), how the human species came to be equipped with heightened intelligence under evolutionary pressure. The human mind is a Swiss army knife of adaptations, and one cannot penetrate it without appreciating how it unfolded, how it is tethered to reproductive success and how the human faculty (cor-)relates to other species.
- What we need to care about is *neuroscience*, how a brain orchestrates itself to make us intelligent. Thereby, the mind seems to be entrenched by means of states and transitions of a large assembly of highly interweaved electrochemical components.
- What we need to care about is *AI*. Instead of getting caught up in the details of how human brains do the job of invoking intelligence, we shift our attention to the job itself, and ask how it, i.e., the design of intelligence or minds (Haugeland, 1997a), might get done at all. This is what Daniel Dennett calls taking a *design stance* (Dennett, 1981) and makes AI a subfield of intellectology (Hernández-Orallo, 2017: 21).
- (And there are others like *linguistics*: What we need to care about is human language as the "signature of human uniqueness". Or a *historical* or *religious* view, . . .)

To avoid walking into that trap of the one-size-fits-all fallacy, i.e., that a monolithic view covers the whole spectrum of facets, forms and subtleties of intelligence, we believe a certain amount of humility and a holistic approach, respectively, is called for when we inspect a complex system like intelligence.[5] Doing philosophy is largely a matter of trying to *put things together*, to synthesize. Good philosophy is opportunistic; it uses whatever information and whatever tools or whatever *angles* which look useful and which, playing in concert, are more useful. For example, psychology in its own right is handicapped by its behavioristic or cognitivist stance, by the fact that it gets to look at subjects and their actions only from the

---

[5] There are many definitions of the fundamental term "system" (cf. e.g., Hoffmann, 2017a; 2017b: Chapter 6 for an overview). Schwaninger (2011: 753) gives two examples: "A portion of the world sufficiently well-defined to be the subject of study; something characterized by a structure, for example, a social system (Anatol Rapoport). A system is a family of relationships between its members acting as a whole (International Society for the Systems Sciences)."

outside. External stimuli can be presented, and external responses can be monitored, but that is it.

A tricky question neuroscience has to cope with is whether we will be able to recover the regularities in a person's behavior in the properties of that person's components and their interconnections alone. And so on for other limitations of these and the other approaches. Hence, we harness and mingle the different perspectives in this Part I in lieu of jumping on just a single one.

Reinforced by the alignment of Part II, dealing with what philosophy (of science) teaches us on intelligence, the primary goal of this treatise is to shed more light on this salient concept in order to esteem divergent sorts of intelligent systems beyond anthropocentrism and AI mania and to gain meaningful insights on how they can be catalogued, evaluated, and contrasted. Let us launch the study with the concept "intelligence"'s scope, and a little disclaimer, respectively. We relegate speculation on possible extraterrestrial forms of intelligence (for that cf. Edmondson, 2012; Shuch, 2011) or "astrocognition" (Vakoch, 2011) and, guided by Figure 1, focus on intelligence on Earth instead.

The evolution of intelligent life form is quite rare and could not be achieved without billions and billions of trials and errors (Hiraiwa-Hasegawa, 2019: 176). Life was unleashed on Earth about 3.8 billion years ago, but the genesis of animals with simple nervous systems, which has appeared to be a *sine qua non* for any "intellectual" species to evolve on Earth (see excursus 1 for a critical reply though), had to wait until about 580 million years ago (Hiraiwa-Hasegawa, 2019: 167f.). Hence, in terms of the sheer time of human history, it constitutes only an insignificant portion of the history of intelligent life (Diamond, 1992: 33; see also Figure 4). When we contemplate and walk around the tree of life today, we are confronted with some awkward cases of adaptation, with an arguably minimal cognition ranging from the very small (bacteria) to the very big (ecosystems; Hernández-Orallo, 2017: 93). As of 2004, we have about 1.5 million scientifically named species, however 99% of the species that have appeared on the Earth so far have already become extinct (Hiraiwa-Hasegawa, 2019). One more recent cause of this is that with regard to other animals, humans have since the last few thousands of years (since the agricultural revolution accelerated by the industrial revolution 250 years ago) become gods, *Homo Deus* (Harari, 2017), turning biodiversity of fauna into masses of domesticated animals of few kinds – 40,000 lions vs. 600 million house cats, 900,000 African buffalos vs. 1.5 billion domesticated cows, 50 million penguins vs. 20 billion chickens (Harari, 2017: 84; Barnosky, 2008). Or in the immortal words of Teilhard de Chardin (1946/1959: 30):

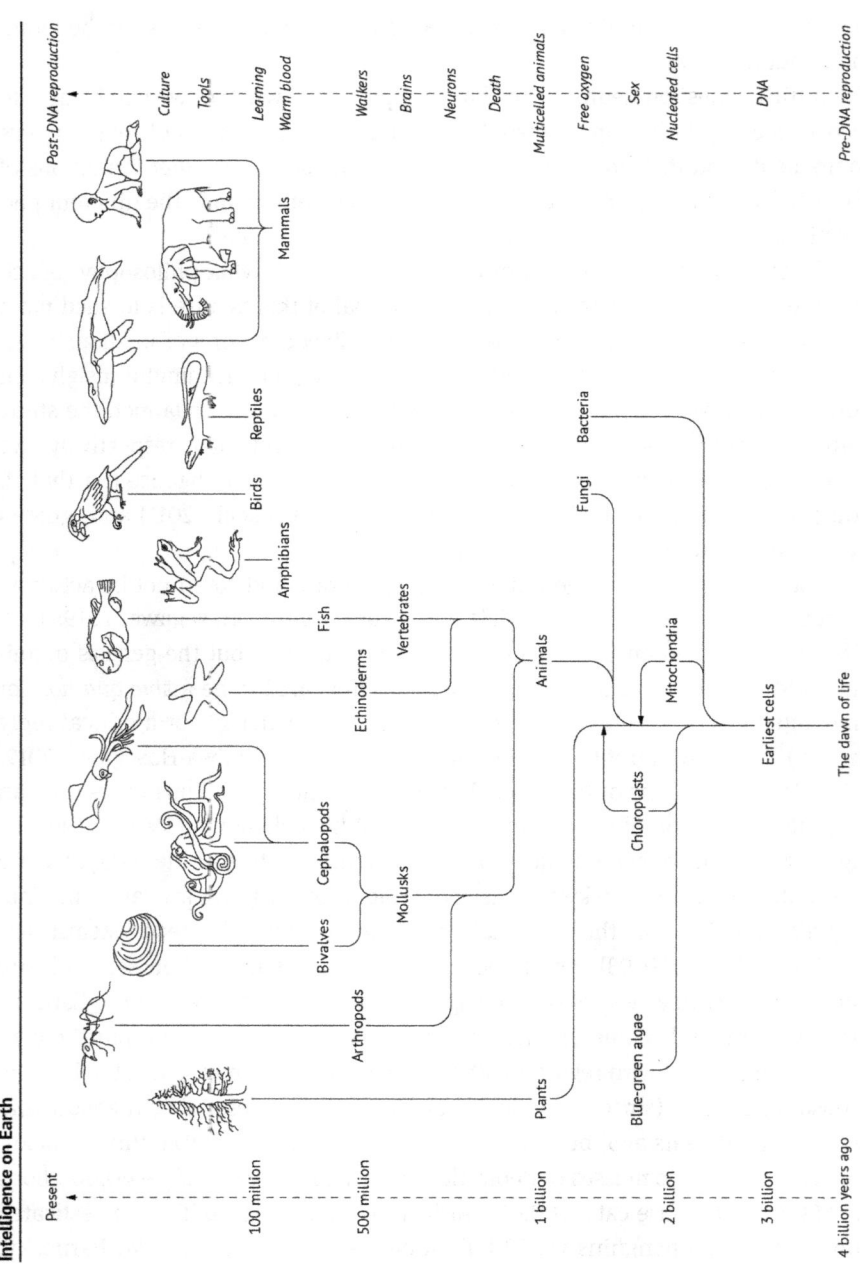

Figure 1: Intelligence on Earth map. Source: Moravec, 1988: 18.

> Lorsque Platon agissait, il n'avait probablement conscience d'engager par sa liberté qu'une parcelle du Monde, étroitement circonscrite dans l'espace et dans la durée. Quand un homme d'aujourd'hui opère en pleine conscience, il sait que son choix a retentissement sur des myriades de siècles et de vivants. Il sent en soi les responsabilités et la force d'un Univers tout entier.

Even though there are examples of ecological suicide during the Anthropocene where animal populations actually have eaten themselves into extermination, they often involve humans too that override the natural *checks and balances* regulating a species' numbers (e.g., by accidentally or intentionally transferring the animal species from one part of the world to another; Diamond, 1992: 312f.). This nurtures the common, but naïve belief that non-human animal species live in balance with each other and with their milieu unless humans intervene. It is naïve because it disregards the dynamics on Earth, the impact of all kinds of changes since almost 4 billion years that let life forms and species come and go (not all can adapt to new situations; for mechanisms of evolution and the adaptationist program, cf. Millstein, 2002). Still, there is something to this view, an analogy maybe to climate change vs. anthropological climate change, insofar as species do not go extinct under natural conditions as rapidly as we are exterminating them now (except under very rare circumstances like the mass die-off 65 million years ago; Diamond, 1992: 312).

Since nobody knows how many species are actually left on Earth – there are many places where scientific exploration is still far from complete, such as the deep ocean –, we cannot assert to canvass the full scope of the concept of intelligence by this fact alone. And since this restriction already manages our expectations from what can be reasonably accomplished in Part I, we wish to add a second disclaimer. We will also rule out plants from our probes, only for the sake of not moving too far from the subject matter or our research questions outlined before, i.e., without making any implicit negative assessment on plant intelligence – quite the opposite because, at least from an evolutionary point of view, plant life is very successful representing 99% of the biomass of the Earth (Trewavas, 2002). Yet, in this work, we plainly follow Hiraiwa-Hasegawa's (2019: 168) train of thoughts when he reasons that "[t]he nervous system has evolved for an individual animal to deal with its environment: to receive information from its environment, assess it, compare it with other information, and make an optimal decision for the next action. It all started with the evolution of animals that actively move by themselves in response to the environmental change around them. Plants do not move [admittedly, they grow, undergo chemical reactions, but this is not what is meant here; C.H.], so that they do not need such a system to deal with the changes in environment moment by moment."

Break-out session 1

Biological intelligence with few or even without neurons

Very different kinds of living beings outside the scope of this limited study have been found to display some complex behaviors, featuring pattern recognition abilities, adaptation, memory, and even anticipation (Hernández-Orallo, 2017: 113). In this class of organisms, we find invertebrates like ants and termites that by themselves are quite possibly mere mindless automata, trundling about in the world without the slightest experience or thought despite all their clever activity when working in concert as a colony or "superorganism" or "collective intelligence" (Kamhi & Traniello, 2013; Dennett, 1996: 14; Hofstadter, 1979: Ant Fugue). One of those clever activities challenges one of humans' major cultural hallmarks, namely agriculture.

None of our primate relatives practices anything remotely resembling agriculture. For the most similar animal precedents, we must turn to *ants*, which invented not only plant, but also animal domestication (Diamond, 1992: 182). In return for the honeydew, the ants protect their "cows" not only from predators and parasites, but some ants also from the cold winter: they care for their aphids in the ants' nest during that season, then in the spring carry them at the correct stage of development to the correct part of the correct food plant (ibid.).

Similarly, bacteria that, also in a colony, "communicate" through signal transduction proteins impress by their "super-brain" which emerges when between 10^9 and 10^{12} bacteria coordinate to process information and which is tantamount to a computational power able to "solve optimization problems that are beyond what human beings can solve" (Ben-Jacob, 2009: 78).

The juxtaposition between groups of "neuronless" beings and the brain (and between neuronless beings and neurons, respectively), sometimes alluded to by the term "group minds" or "social minds", is salient because there is good reason to treat some groups of organisms as unified cognitive systems, at least in some cases: For example, "individual ants act on locally available information. But because of their evolutionary history, they also play roles in the distributed computations that are carried out by the colony. This allows colonies to develop better strategies for navigating the world, and it allows them to carry out complex comparative evaluations as information is propagated between ants; but no individual carries out these evaluations, and no individual develops strategies for furthering the interests of the colony. From an evolutionary perspective, this should be no more surprising than the existence of neurons that think and act together; and the behavior of these ants does bear a striking resemblance to the computational structures we find in individual brains." (Huebner, 2018: 395).

Other organisms in that class of in some sense intelligent beings without nerve cells comprise slime molds, fungi or the aforementioned plants. Despite their diversity, these systems have one thing in common: what they lack, a neural system (Ginsburg & Jablonka, 2009). For plants, the findings go beyond classical conditioning (see also Chapter 5; Haney, 1969) to more complex behaviors (Applewhite, 1975) – sometimes disrupted (Sanberg, 1976). This has led to the use of the term "intelligence" to describe their capacity (Trewavas, 2002, 2003).

Nonetheless, as part of this work, we contend that some of their reactions and adaptations occur so slowly that we are not able to perceive them unless careful long-term observation is employed. Furthermore, "the concept of the individual, to which intelligence and behaviour are intimately linked [as in the realm of this book at hand, C.H.], cannot usefully be applied to plants" (Firn, 2004: 345).

It does not stop with nervous systems; even more than a nervous system, an intelligent organism may have a relatively large brain compared to its body size. In the context of an increased neural specialization of labor between animal species where evolution tuned different creatures to different environments, e.g., "giving them more hippocampus if memory for spatial location was more important (as it is for certain birds that cache their food), or more forebrain if complex reasoning and decision making was eminently important (as it is for primates, including, of course, human beings)" (Marcus, 2004: 120), the emergence of large brains is rather a rare incident in the entire evolution of life on Earth. As the vertebrates split off into separate classes, each line specialized to a particular milieu or niche. Amphibians adapted to a hybrid lifestyle, half aquatic, half terrestrial. Most birds adapted for flight, each species modifying the basic vertebrate plan in its own way (ibid.: 121). Mammals developed a thin, six-layer cortical sheet known as the *neocortex* (ibid.). That sheet, more than anything else, is what makes the minds of mammals so vigorous (ibid.). The reason though for the rarity of large brains comes from the high cost of cultivating and maintaining them.

In fact, there is only one species with a brain the size of which amounts to 2–3% of its body size (while consuming 25% of the body's energy when the body is at rest). This species is the loud-mouthed or offloading ape (how one might wish to correct for the 21st century; Martinho-Truswell, 2018; Clark, 2003); or, as they are better known by the name of modern humans where this author has an eminent interest in for selfish reasons. A species that is intelligent enough to reflect, and write a book on the nature of intelligence; or freely adapted from Louis XIV, *L'intelligence, c'est moi*!

1 Intelligence in human animals

What a piece of work is a man!
How noble in reason, how infinite in faculty!
In form and moving how express and admirable!
In action how like an angel, in apprehension how like a god!
                                    Shakespeare's Hamlet, Act II Scene 2

Unlike William Shakespeare who also wrote that "we are such stuff as dreams are made on", in reality, we are all made of atoms and, on a higher level, of cells, and that holds as true for the brain as for any other organ – albeit nerve cells of the brain, i.e., neurons (such as schematically displayed in Figure 2), look, at first glance, to be rather divergent from most other kinds of cells.

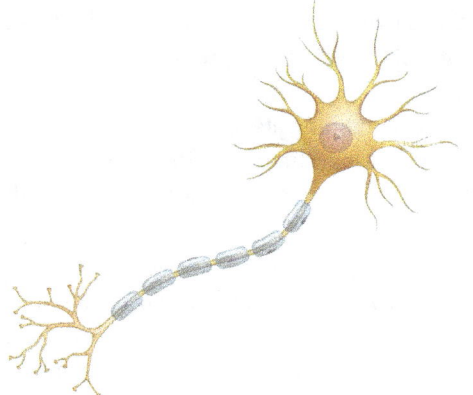

Figure 2: A neuron. Source: Marcus, 2004: 69.

Following Marcus (2004 : 69), neurons are often (though not always) larger than most other cells, and they are flanged on one side by long *axons* that carry signals away from the cell, sometimes extending the length of the body, and on the other by treelike *dendrites* that allow neurons to receive signals from thousands of other nerve cells. Neurons are electrically alive, capable of sending brief jolts of charged atoms (action potentials, to be precise) down the length of their axons, and, even more remarkably, they are smart. Not as smart as a person, but smart enough to synthesize tremendous arrays of information, and fast enough that a group of them collaborating can recognize an accustomed object in a fifth of a second (Marcus, 2004 : 69). Despite these qualities, we should not forget that neurons are still just cells, better thought of not as unique creatures but as specializations of a general cellular plan that is widely shared across the body (ibid.). At a second glance, nerve cells do not differ so much anymore from typical cells because many of the former's most spectacular specializations are mere variations on ordinary cellular themes (ibid.). Nevertheless, cell differentiation of neurons themselves, which can morph into everything from clocks controlling circadian rhythms to decision-makers tallying votes and balancing courses of action, is striking too. In the brain as a whole, Marcus (2004: 71) estimates that your brain not only counts billions of neurons with trillions of connections, but that there may be as many as 100,000 different kinds of neurons, each contributing to a different aspect of mental life. While we by now understand individual neurons, we have little idea how the whole neural network functions, nor about "the relationship between complexity of brains across species and their degree of adaptive intelligence" (Koch, 2020). Intelligence is here conceived as an emergent property emanating from multiple interactions between the constraints imposed by genes, brain, behavior, cognition and environment (Rinaldi & Karmiloff-Smith, 2017: 9). If the study of neuroscience has taught us anything, it is that the brain is enormously complex, not seldom described as the most complex system in the known universe (Marcus & Davis, 2021). "How a brain made of simple cells creates intelligence [. . .] remains a mystery" (Hawkins, 2021: 1).

A major part of what the brain does is to communicate signals from one place to another. It takes information from the senses, parses that information, and translates it into commands that get sent back to the muscles. Even though human brains are presumably more complex than those of any other species, there is little reason to suspect that the process of their emergence is wholly or even significantly divergent from the process by which the brains of other animals develop (Marcus, 2004: 87). The idea that the brain might be assembled in much the same way as the rest of our body as well as the body of other species, is anathema to our deeply held feeling that our minds are bizarre, somehow quarantined from the material world – which found a formidable expression in Descartes' dualism. Yet at the same time, it is a continuation, perhaps the culmination, of a long trend, the maturing of the human species that for too long has overestimated its own standing in the universe (see Figure 4, the lower part as well as the epigraph to this chapter). But of course, the biological insights can just be an exciting modern take on the old Darwinian idea to us, namely that there is a bond that unifies all living things (see Figure 4, the upper part). With no great exaggeration, we find, in line with Marcus (2004: 98), that *the* pivotal secret to intelligent life on earth, splicing all animals that learn, is their ability to alter their nervous systems on the basis of external experience. The reason that they can do that is that *experience itself can modify the expression of genes* (ibid.). Insofar, the role of genes is not just to create the brain and body of a newborn, but to create an organism that is flexible enough to cope with an ever-changing world.

With some species in the Darwinian bond, we share the feature of a large size of brains. Why do mammals and, particularly primates and *Hominini* have especially large brains? Though there has been a great deal of research and many controversies, there is a consensus among researchers that the most significant reason may have been the complexity of social life (Dunbar, 1998). And the relationship between large brains and intelligence as, in a first approach, the ability to gather information from the world and use that information to sensibly inform action (Marcus, 2004: 90), is well-known: Larger brains are known to have more neurons (Pakkenberg & Gunderson, 1997), and this *may* (not must) result in higher intelligence through a larger number of synaptic connections and a correspondingly greater cognitive capacity (Vernon et al., 2000: 250).[6] The so-called "Machiavellian intelligence" insists that the driver of the evolution of intelligence among primates and humans was the complexity of social life, not the complexity of ecological settings (Hiraiwa-Hasegawa, 2019: 169).

The larger brains enable mammals and, to higher degrees, apes and, to highest degrees, humans to read each other's mind, share purposes, gossip, and cooperate with each other. For example, human babies are helpless, reliant for many years on their elders for sustenance, protection and education so that, on the other side, raising children succeeded under the auspices of other family members, neighbors and the tribe. This fact has contributed greatly both to humankind's extraordinary social abilities and to its unique social problems (Harari, 2014: 11). The social brain already existed as a base. Yet, as Hiraiwa-Hasegawa (2019: 171) and evolutionary game theory (Maynard-Smith & Price, 1973; Axelrod, 1984) remind us, there is a very high hurdle for wide-range cooperation to take place: "[I]ndividuals in a group must be able to detect and expel the noncooperator among them. If everybody cooperates, everybody can reap good results. However, if there is a noncooperator who enjoys the result without any labor, this strategy will spread in the population, and eventually the cooperative system will collapse. In order for our ancestors to be able to get benefits from cooperation, they had to discriminate cooperators from defectors, and the evolution of social brains was ever more accelerated." Therefore, human beings – if not uniquely among animals, then at least characteristically (Tomasello & Call, 1997) – are able to learn not only from the immediate consequence of their own actions but also from the consequences of others' actions, i.e., to imitate proficiently (Gopnik & Schulz, 2007: 10). On top of that, unlike other animals, we routinely use the

---

[6] Note that on the other hand, intelligence (as measured by IQ tests) among humans is only barely correlated with brain size, i.e., as far as variations of five to fifteen percent are concerned (Wickett et al., 2000) which can explain why women's brains are smaller, but on average they have, for instance, better language skills than men (Hedges & Nowell, 1995).

statistical contingencies and interventions we detect in our social environment to design novel interventions. We routinely meet regularities with innovation. (Schulz et al., 2007: 70f.). However, appreciating that the devil (or God) is in the detail, we should make a few conceptual distinctions when we wish to further talk about social intelligence or imitation meaningfully. For example, to test for observational learning of tool use, one should, in consonance with Meltzoff (2007: 44), discriminate imitation from stimulus enhancement. The latter refers to the fact that the test subjects', let us say, infants' attention may simply be drawn to a tool by virtue of an adult handling it. With their attention drawn to the stick, infants may increase their random play with the object, thereby increasing the probability that they will learn through trial and error that it can be used as a tool. Then, the child is at least not learning a new causal relation based on what they see the other do.

Moreover, from a macro view, it is maybe even the key strength of humans' social aptitude to swiftly form large, effective, and flexible groups as compared to other species (Harari, 2014). While anthropological research has demonstrated that the maximum "natural" size of a stable group of humans bonded by gossip is about 150 individuals (Dunbar, 1993) – and other social animals like our closest relatives the bonobos have also been observed to live in big groups of up to 120 animals (Idani, 1991) –, humans have mastered at bringing much larger numbers of strangers together to cooperate effectively. We have contrived to cross the critical threshold of 150 (by founding cities comprising tens of thousands of inhabitants or empires ruling hundreds of millions) because of our faculty to create an imagined reality out of words like Shakespeare did above (Harari, 2014). The secret sauce, in other words, is the appearance of fiction and figments of our collective imagination. In this sense, churches are rooted in common religious myths, states are rooted in common national myths and judicial systems are rooted in common legal myths; none of these institutions exists outside the narratives that people invent and tell one another (ibid.). Changes in human cooperation do not ask then for genetic modifications or big environmental change, but can occur relatively impromptu by simply altering the myths, by telling different stories.

Another arcanum that we humans have kept alive, for example in our religious traditions (myths), is somehow disturbing. If we now take a closer look at the history of emergence (and extinction) of humans, we see that not only do we possess an abundance of uncivilized cousins in the animal world, but once upon a time we had quite a few brothers and sisters in the human world as well (Harari, 2014: 6). We are used to thinking about ourselves as the only humans – which is why we probably refer to our Homo species that we have immodestly named "Homo sapiens", "Wise Man", as "humans", and not as "sapiens" – because for the last 10,000 years, our species has indeed been the only human species around (ibid.: 6). However, in evolutionary terms, we are babies, which motivates Bregman (2020: 50) to call us in a belittling manner *Homo puppy*. The true meaning of the word "human" is "an animal belonging to the genus *Homo*", and there used to be many other species of this genus besides Homo sapiens (Harari, 2014: 6). Humans first wandered the face of the Earth in East Africa from an earlier genus of apes dubbed *Australopithecus* and as we can read off from the first half of Figure 4, this occurred about 2.5 million years ago. This is roughly the time where we find the oldest stone tools called *Oldowan* (see Figure 3).

Figure 3: The Oldowan, one of the earliest and simplest tools of humans which were usually made with one or a few flakes chipped off with another stone.

These tools are stones with edges made by hitting stones against each other and have no characteristic type. This suggests that the makers of these tools did not share the idea of how to make tools but that each individual made the tool by trial and error in his or her own way (Hiraiwa-Hasegawa, 2019: 173), while Gärdenfors and Högberg (2017) argue that learning to knap Oldowan tools already requires an extensive ability to rehearse. About 2 million years ago, some of the archaic prehistoric humans that were insignificant animals with no more impact on their environment than gorillas or jellyfish left their homeland to journey through and settle vast areas of North Africa, Europe and Asia. Since survival in Indonesia's steaming jungles necessitated different traits than those required to inhabit the snowy forests of northern Europe, human populations unfurled in different directions (Harari, 2014: 16). For instance, while Europe was home to *Homo neanderthalensis* ("Man from the Neander Valley") that were reported to have bigger brains and more neurons than us, the more eastern regions of Asia were populated by *Homo Erectus*, "Upright Man", who is said to have used another type of stone tools called *Acheulean* hand axes from about 1.8 million years ago. They have a typical teardrop shape in common, which suggests that the makers of the tools shared the idea of how to make them, and some kind of teaching might have been involved (Hiraiwa-Hasegawa, 2019: 173). Homo Erectus survived in his territory for close to 2 million years, making it the most durable human species ever (Harari, 2014: 7). By anticipating some results from Table 2 (see row five, column four), this record is unlikely to be broken by our own species.

A lesson from this history of early humans is that the probability of the resurgence and continual existence of a large-brained species must be low given the emergence and extinction of various Homo species with large brains as trial and error in the evolution of large brains. A second learning is that progressing hominin technology, from Oldowan, to Acheulean, and further, might have triggered higher grades of, and more abstract, causal thinking in later hominins, including us and including reasoning about the physical forces involved in causal processes (Gärdenfors & Lombard, 2020). Finally, our current exclusivity on the planet is peculiar, enigmatic – and perhaps incriminating according to the "Replacement Theory" (Relethford, 2008) –, not that multi-homo-species past. This insight frees us from both the mistaken impression that at any particular moment only one type of human inhabited the Earth so that all earlier species were merely older inferior models of ourselves and the prescientific belief anchored in our culture (e.g., in Christianity) which singles us out as special, distinctive creatures (made in the image of God).

Humans are both similar to and divergent from our close animal cousins which Saint Francis is said to have even called brothers and sisters. Jared Diamond's point in the epigraph to the next chapter is how similar we are to chimpanzees. In, for example, our body structures, our perceptual systems, our group dynamics, our aggression, and our sustained systems of maternal care, we surely have something in common with the chimp (Marcus, 2004: 124). And also this chapter has so far scratched the surface of the biological and evolutionary features we share, from atoms and nerve cells that make up the brain to larger brains (with quantitative rather than qualitative differences only), tool use and the complexity of social life. Yet, we are also plainly different. Human, rather than chimp brains, as the physical realization of mental life, gave rise to our sophisticated culture, language, to our capacity to contemplate and produce

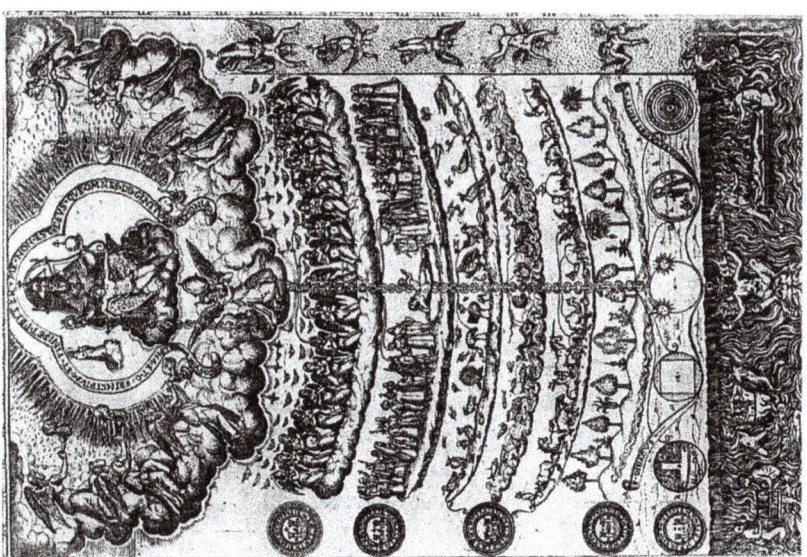

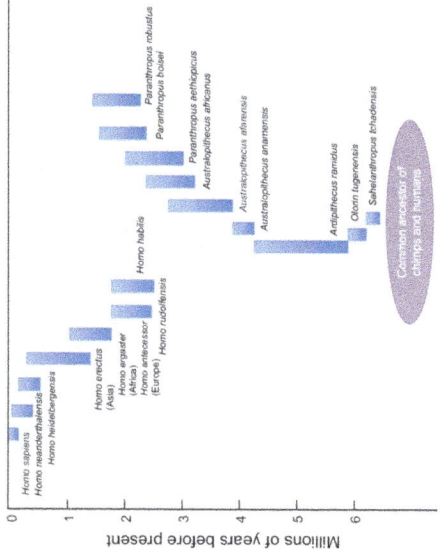

Figure 4: Left: The modern science-based and evolutionary view with a timeline of various Hominins during the Plio-Pleistocene with common ancestors. Duration of existence of each fossil is approximation. The exact phylogenetic relationships among them are unknown. Source: Hiraiwa-Hasegawa, 2019: 172. Vs. right: The Christian view with the so-called Ladder of Being as a hierarchical structure of all matter and life that puts us humans above and apart from all other living things without acknowledging that all species and beings are connected

beauty and arts, justice, calculus, and the quest for the meaning of life; concepts, in short, that we imagine no chimp or any other animal has ever dreamed of (Marcus, 2004: 124). But not only those noble traits make us uniquely human, unmitigated vices like genocide or environmental destructiveness are also ingredients of our profile (Diamond, 1992: Chapter 11, 19): a lion kills his own kind, an elephant damages her milieu, but these propensities are much more threatening in us because of our exploding numbers, our faculty to cooperate flexibly, and not least due to our technological power that AI is originating from.

For well over two thousand years, at least since the advent of the Greek city-state, a certain corpus of ideas has dominated discussions of the human condition in our civilization. This collection of ideas brings to the fore the existence and importance of mental thrusts – capacities that have been variously termed *rationality*, *intelligence*, or the individual's deployment of *mind*. To illuminate this detail at this point, we just take individual intelligence as unit of analysis and ignore collective intelligence or the intelligence of even a whole species, which is a substantive separation as the following matrix displays.

Figure 4 (continued)
to each other through a long history of evolution (Darwin). It was thought in medieval Christianity to have been decreed by God. The chain starts with God and progresses downward to angels, humans (look closer: are women rightly represented here?), animals, plants, and minerals. Source: 1579 drawing of the Great Chain of Being from Didacus Valades, Rhetorica Christiana.

Table 2: Individual versus collective intelligence. This study specializes in the former.

Level of intelligence	Individual	Collective	
			Species
Aspects, characteristics or forms of intelligence	- Logical-mathematical - Linguistic - Spatial - Kinesthetic - Musical - Intrapersonal - Interpersonal - Naturalist	The intelligence of a group (including a whole species) is not flatly the aggregate of the intelligence of the individual members (*swarm intelligence*), but the stimulating part is that conflicts may arise. A good example is the *Prisoner's Dilemma* (cf. Hoffmann, 2020a) where individuals' logical-mathematical intelligence leads to a conclusion which is *not* in consonance with the collective reasoning.	
Measure	E.g., standard intelligence tests, i.e., responses to stimuli, as psychological measures (but also biological measures exist)	E.g., tools of game theory and psycho-logical group studies (e.g., Loehlin, 2000)	E.g., survival of the genes (Dawkins, 1976)
What is measured?	Mainly logical-mathematical, linguistic & spatial intelligence	E.g., group success	E.g., evolutionary success of species
Assessment of human being(s)	The (idealized) human being is the most intelligent creature we know of. Certain (actual) human beings stand out in different respects; e.g., arguably, Gödel for logics or Bach for music, or Sigmund Freud for intrapersonal intelligence, etc. But it must not be forgotten that even such coryphaei stand on the shoulders of giants (making use of cumulative culture and knowledge)	Homo sapiens has far outstripped all other human/animal species in its ability to coope-rate (Harari, 2014). Not only can we form large and more effective groups of "natural" size bonded by gossip, but fiction and collective imagination allows us to build well-functioning, flexible groups of any size.	Dubious given our propensity to produce nuclear weapons, overuse our resources, pollute our environment, etc., and thus rather low compared to other species that in some cases also have been on the globe since much longer, proving the success of their survival strategy
Best performing species to date			One-celled organisms as ideal survival "machines"

Well-formed views on the nature of individual intelligence have cropped up since a long time. In the *Posterior Analytics Book 1* Aristotle, for example, conceived of intelligence in terms of "quick wit". More comprehensively and closer to the present, one of the most famous studies of experts' conceptions of human intelligence was done by the editors of the *Journal of Educational Psychology* ("Intelligence and its measurement", 1921). Following the contributors to this issue, several different meanings are invoked by the concept of intelligence (where the highlights were added subsequently by this author):

1) The power of apt *responses* from the point of view of truth or facts (E.L. Thorndike);
2) The ability to carry on *abstract thinking* (L.M. Terman);
3) Sensory *capacity*, capacity for perceptual recognition, quickness, range or *flexibility* of *association*, facility and *imagination*, span of attention, *quickness* or alertness in response (F.N. Freeman);
4) Ability to *learn* or having learned to adjust oneself to the environment (S.S. Colvin);
5) Ability to *adapt* oneself adequately to relatively new situations in life (R. Pintner);
6) The capacity for knowledge and knowledge possessed (B.A.C. Henmon);
7) A *biological mechanism* by which the effects of a complexity of stimuli are mustered and given a somewhat unified effect in behavior (J. Peterson);
8) The capacity to inhabit an instinctive adjustment, the capacity to redefine the inhibited instinctive adjustment in the light of *imaginally experienced trial and error*, and the capacity to realize the modified instinctive adjustment in overt behavior to the advantage of the individual as a *social animal* (L.L. Thurstone);
9) The *capacity to acquire capacity* (H. Woodrow);
10) The capacity to *learn* or to profit by experience (W.F. Dearborn); and
11) Sensation, perception, *association*, memory imagination, discrimination, judgment, and reasoning (N.E. Haggerty).

A multitude of observations can be made about this listing. For example, the notable ambiguity, variability and heterogeneity in the answers illustrates the cacophony in intelligence research and we leave it open if the experts' view is more helpful than Merriam-Webster's. Secondly, attributes such as adaptation to the environment, basic mental processes, and higher-order thinking (e.g. reasoning, problem solving, decision-making) were prominent (Sternberg, 2000a: 8). Indeed, nearly all of the definitions enacted by the experts mention *reasoning* and *problem solving* at least implicitly. Sternberg (1982: 225) thus stresses that almost without regard to the exact derivation of those conceptions of intelligence, reasoning and problem solving play vital roles in them. Thirdly, there is hence an emphasis on cognitive abilities rather than noncognitive or emotional intelligence. Fourthly, certain themes are prominent too: The issue of the one vs. the many – Is intelligence one thing or is it manifold? – has been of clear concern. Fifthly, it becomes blatant that different disciplines or stances contribute to shedding light on the concept, e.g. a biological-technical (Peterson), an evolutionary-biological (Pintner) or a learning psychological perspective (Dearborn). And as a final more specific remark, we note that some researchers like Thorndike anthropocentrically anchor intelligence to language which seems to unequivocally mark us as humans in contrast to other less intelligent beings – between our languages and the vocalizations of any other animal lies a seemingly unbridgeable gulf (Diamond, 1992: 141). Others such as Freeman (under the auspices of Aristotle, Hobbes and others) put fast, rather than deep thinking in the foreground which characterizes more Western cultures; or very broad capabilities like learning (Colvin) or adapting (Pintner) with the consequence that maybe too much falls under those definitions of "intelligence". We can note though that intelligence is generally entangled, not with performance or what an agent actually does, but with abilities which in turn describe what a subject is gifted to do. Every ability is a potential and abilities can evolve too, for example, the ability of incremental, progressive or cumulative learning, or acquiring skills. Humans (and later on non-human animals, machines and devices) are usually valued by their potential capabilities rather than what they do at the start. This is why human babies that lack many of the abilities that they will later be poised to deploy are still regarded as intelligent and as persons with human rights albeit some animals would do better on some cognitive tasks. What authentically characterizes a subject is not only what (s)he does, not even what (s)he is able to do at a certain point in time, but rather what (s)he can do in the future after a range of possible lives (Hernández-Orallo, 2017: 339).

Sternberg (2000a: 10f.; 1990) further contends that several identifiable metaphors underlie experts' conception of intelligence. In particular, he dwells on the following:
1) The *computational metaphor* where the basic unit of analysis is the elementary information process or component. Exponents of this metaphor typically conduct reaction-time or protocol analysis and computer simulation to investigate the phenomenon of intelligence. We will see that (perhaps unmiraculously) adherents of AI especially fall prey to this reductionism, i.e., use this metaphor excessively, for example because they tend to confound speed with intelligence (e.g., see Chapter 11.1).
2) The *geographic metaphor* which views intelligence as a map of the mind and where the basic unit of analysis consists of the factor that usually is

alleged to be a source of individual differences among people (e.g., Thurstone, 1938).
3) The *biological metaphor* where the principal unit of analysis is found in the cell assembly (Hebb, 1949) or the speed of neuronal conduction (Vernon & Mori, 1992).
4) The *genetic-epistemological metaphor* which takes as the fundamental unit of analysis the schema. Typical methodology is close observation by means of case studies and experimentation. A key proponent is Piaget (1947/2012).
5) The *sociological metaphor* emphasizes the importance of socialization in intelligence and transmits key constructs such as internalization or mediated learning (Feuerstein, 1980).
6) The *anthropological metaphor* revolves around the question of what forms intelligence takes as a cultural invention. Accordingly, the basic unit of analysis is the individual in interaction with her or his cultural context (e.g., Greenfield, 1997).
7) Finally, the *systems metaphor* relies on the notion that intelligence is a complex system that integrates many levels of analysis, including computational, geographic, biological, sociological, anthropological, and others. The unit of analysis is the system, its elements as well as their interactions (cf. Gardner, 1983/2011, 1999).

For metaphors, the same holds as for definitions: they are not right or wrong, but rather expedient or (especially when used crudely or excessively) leading astray. This author finds the systems point of view eminently insightful, not only but also because he was trained in the field of complexity and systems "science" (which is more a movement or a meta-discipline than a scientific discipline, cf. Schwaninger, 2011; and Hoffmann, 2017a, 2017b: Chapter 6). Secondly and interestingly, it has close ties to AI research, because both (partially) root in cybernetics (Ashby, 1956; Wiener, 1961; Matthews, 2020: 237f.). Thirdly, systems thinking enunciates a welcome intellectual modesty when accepting that there is not *the* answer (in this case to what intelligence is), but rather different layers and angles. Fourthly, it seems empirically uncontroversial to treat intelligence as a complex system given the concept's richness (Marcus & Davis, 2021). And fifthly, from a systems perspective there is no absolute difference between internal (endogenous) and external (exogenous): what is internal for the system is generally external for its subsystems. It all depends on where one draws the boundary between the system and its environment (Heylighen in Gershenson, 2008: 70f.). With this in mind, the systems view of intelligence can make apparent two aspects in the expression of intelligence: abilities and mental processes that lie within the individual (one system) and how these abilities and mental processes transact the opportunities and constraints of the context (another system). In other words, intelligence does not reside solely within an individual's mind, but in how an individual exerts competencies, knowledge and mental processes to transact with, adapt to, and shape her or his environment. For instance, when mathematicians do advanced math, they set aside the traditional human way of thinking, incapable of thinking through concepts like the incompleteness of Peano arithmetic (more on Gödel in Part II and IV), but learn to think anew with the assistance of *external* data-processing systems, which was back then a blackboard or is nowadays more likely a computer, etc. and the help of cumulative knowledge such as Peano's axiomatic system.

Intelligence as adaptation is the key to Piaget's (1947/2012) notion of intelligence. But unlike Piaget or Spearman (1927), we have sympathies for Gardner's (1983/2011, 1999) stance for *pragmatic* reasons, discarding the idea of a single and general intelligence, of intelligence as a unitary faculty. By contrast, intelligence is characterized by multidirectionality and pluralistic forms.

(From those sympathies, it cannot be inferred that we would embrace his "theory" of multiple intelligences, MI, or take it for granted which would be premature given that it has engendered abrasive criticisms due to its apparently little experimental evidence (Waterhouse, 2006; Herrnstein & Murray, 1994; Traub & Gardner, 1999). Since we do not build on or apply that particular "theory", we rebut this objection as peripheral and negligible in our context; and even if it had brought down the whole house of MI, we would not necessarily end up with intelligence as a unitary faculty as, for instance, hierarchical theories (Vernon, 1950) found a way to reconcile the camps of lumpers and splitters. In addition, for a critical reply to critical views on Gardner's approach, cf. Shearer & Karanian, 2017, who revealed a strong congruence among Gardner's eight intelligences with a theoretical basis from Chomsky, 2009a, and the cognitive neuroscience literature that has accumulated since the advent of functional neuroimaging. Such delivered robust evidence endows support for MI theory.)

(Be that debate within psychometrics, not philosophy, as it may,) Gardner (1983/2011: 8f.) spots eight fairly independent, equally important distinct types of human intelligences that have evolved in the human species. This is the principal point about his theory which is of pertinence to our inquiry.

According to this view, people can be intelligent in a variety of ways (cf. e.g., Hofstadter's, 1979, "Gödel [logical-mathematical], Escher [spatial], Bach [musical]") and sometimes those intelligences work in concert within a domain and are valued in a wide range of cultures (Davidson & Downing, 2000: 44). The eight different intelligences unfold themselves through interactions between one's biological predispositions and the opportunities provided by one's milieu. Out of those, the first three are related to abilities that are measured by conventional intelligence tests (cf. Davidson & Downing, 2000: 44).

1. *Linguistic* intelligence encompasses our use of language to predict, explain, convince and remember information as well as to clarify meaning.
2. *Logical-mathematical* intelligence captures the ability to operate on relationships in abstract symbol systems and to assess ideas and quantities in accordance with the laws of (formal) logic.
3. *Spatial* intelligence involves skill in perceiving and transforming visual-spatial relationships, i.e., relationships of objects' position in space.

Even though the remaining five types are not measured by conventional intelligence tests, they are valued in most cultures.

4. *Bodily-kinesthetic* intelligence denotes the adept use of one's body.
5. *Musical* intelligence includes sensitivity to various musical properties as well as the ability to produce, appreciate and combine pitch, tones, and rhythms. (Gardner does *not* present musical intelligence as just another form of artistic abilities like literature or visual arts, but as a distinct intelligence on par with the other seven intelligences enumerated on this page. Since we invoke the term "musical intelligence" coming from his framework, we do not interpret "musical intelligence" as a mere example of intuitive and creative ability, even though it is legitimate to wonder in future work whether literature, visual arts, and all the other forms of artistic creation and expression would be excluded from what we will call "last remaining bastion of uniqueness in the terrain of human intelligence" in the summary of Part I.)
6. *Intrapersonal* intelligence reflects the understanding of one's own motives, strengths, weaknesses and emotions.
7. *Interpersonal* intelligence accordingly reflects the understanding of, and sensitivity to, other people's motives, behaviors, and emotions. Finally,
8. *Naturalist* intelligence indicates an understanding of the patterns found in natural environments.

Gardner's proposal of multiple intelligences is a refreshing exception to the general rule that social and emotional intelligence play little role in scientific theories of intelligence (Kihlstrom & Cantor, 2000: 364; Flynn, 1997): "Most simply, emotions matter because if we did not have them nothing else would matter. Creatures without emotion would have no reason for living nor, for that matter, for committing suicide. Emotions are the stuff of life." (Elster, 1999: 403). And less plastically (not to say "emotionally"), emotions matter because many forms of human intelligent behavior would be unintelligible if we did not see them through the prism of emotion. More than any other philosopher, Aristotle shows in the *Rhetoric* (cf. Elster, 1999: 52f.) that emotions are rooted not merely in individual psychology (intrapersonal intelligence), but also in social interaction (interpersonal intelligence). For example, with regard to the latter, we do not misapprehend it as "general intelligence applied to social situation" (Wechsler, 1958: 75) – firstly, arguments about what intelligence *really* is are fruitless, and secondly, the social domain has peculiarities that can be captured in Gardner's seventh intelligence. One such crucial difference is that in social cognition the object (i.e., the person) represented in the subject's mind is intelligent and conscious. Thus, the person being perceived may try to control or manipulate the impression being formed by the perceiver through a variety of impression-management strategies (Jones & Pittman, 1982), which might get anticipated by the latter, and so on. Such an entangled web of interaction rituals is unlikely to occur in nonsocial perception / cognition. Not less is Gardner's framework vocal in incorporating emotional intelligence under 6. which is all too often not associated with the hallmark of intelligence (Sternberg, 1997).

Apart from that, we also venerate the opening of Gardner's list and submit that it is no coincidence that he lists linguistic intelligence first. Language is arguably the most efficacious tool for learning – the mother of all learning mechanisms and the single thing that most makes humans stand out (Marcus, 2004: 124): Through language, we are able to tell ourselves what we think, to tell others what we think, to engage in cooperative action, and to share our knowledge, passing it onto the next generation. Revision and accumulation of knowledge happens because the people of the next generation are embarked on with that knowledge without the need to discover or invent it by themselves from scratch. This is our cumulative culture, a body of information transferred from individual to individual through means other than genetic transmission, namely but chiefly by using our supple languages (Hiraiwa-Hasegawa, 2019: 173). Cultural behavior is, then, not unique to humans, there is culture in a number of divergent species, including nonhuman primates and cetaceans (Andrews & Beck, 2018: 7). (For the essential ingredients of culture with the aim of painting a fuller portrait of what engulfs cultural practices, cf. Ramsey, 2018.)

But it seems that we are the only species that has (at least highly developed) cumulative cultures which are improved through time by adding discoveries and inventions (Hiraiwa-Hasegawa, 2019: 173; for a critical reply, cf. Brown, 2018). Furthermore, the significance of language can, for instance, be expressed by the interpretation of Gardner's third and our second form of intelligence, i.e., mathematics, as a language – at least, it is uncontentious that language development and mathematics are closely nested (Knight & Hargis, 1977: 424). Charles Darwin (1871) himself suggested that some of our "certain higher mental powers" might be "the result of the continued use of a perfect language". But as we see in the next chapter, even this statement about the supposedly unique hallmark of humans can be challenged (and became a bit less glorious by Fodor's, 1975, findings who showed that some thoughts are not linguistic "because there is a slippage between language and thought").

Despite the criticism touched upon above and in in demarcation to it, Gardner invokes evidence to underpin the existence of the eight relatively independent intelligences. One type of evidence, for example, consists of neuropsychological data showing that damage to certain areas of the brain impairs some abilities, but not others (Davidson & Downing, 2000: 44). In other words, the mind seems, to some extent, to be organized according to the content areas, and each module is based on its own neural structures – the ancillary phrase "to some extent" is important here because other empirical results suggest to spell the end of the "modularity" hypothesis or Swiss Army Knife view of the brain (Marcus, 2004: 131). Another source of evidence in favor of MI exhibits the uneven performance of autistic children (ibid.). Etc. Yet, without further elaboration of the different elements of each model, a specification of how the elements interact and are (cor-)related to each other, and a thorough examination of what mental components or intelligences might be missing, the picture remains incomplete since it is not clear how to operationalize or completely disconfirm the models. Moreover, as a lesson from the systems lens adopted, we ought to come back to the meta level repeatedly by raising the general question of how intelligent those models of intelligence truly are.

Much work on intelligence and the brain where it is embedded has been anthropocentric. Here are two examples: "intelligence, the ability to make human-like decisions" (Mindell, 2015: 12); "the brain is the only thing that we know of that is intelligent [and he implicitly talks about the human neocortex, C.H.]" (Hawkins, 2021: 124). Or, when open-minded, it has been on non-human "prim"ates. However, more recently it has been recognized that looking at ourselves or looking at our close relatives like apes and monkeys would never be enough (Krubitzer, 2015: 186). Even though primates' brains are extremely complex, they are also very similar to ours; and there are salient insights to be gleaned from a wide variety of species – to begin with, high intelligence does not need to reside in a central brain as the lesson of octopi teaches us, which are among the few animals on Earth that can learn by imitation (Godfrey-Smith, 2018; Cave, 2017; Montgomery, 2016; Wells, 1966). We can already hypothesize that *there is no single or optimal way to exhibit or build intelligence.*

2 Intelligence in biological animals

> *A zoologist from Outer Space would immediately classify us as just a third species of chimpanzee, along with the pygmy chimp of Zaire and the common chimp of the rest of tropical Africa. Molecular genetic studies . . . have shown that we . . . share over 98 percent of our genetic program with the other two chimps.*
>
> Jared Diamond, 1992: 2

Our crude human chauvinism gave cause for dispute and ridicule early on. La Mettrie (1748/1990: 124) wrote in his magnum opus *L'Homme-Machine*, for example:

> Car c'est elle, c'est cette forte Analogie, qui force tous les Savants et les vrais juges d'avouër que ces êtres fiers et vains, plus distingués par leur orgueil, que par le nom d'Hommes, quelque envie qu'ils aient de s'élever, ne sont au fond que des Animaux, et des Machines perpendiculairement rampantes.

And indeed, our species-centric view of intelligence may be self-serving, but as a general characteristic it correlates only superficially (and perhaps even negatively, see Table 2) with most measures of evolutionary success, i.e., intelligence on the level of a species (Zentall, 2000: 197). Also in terms of individual intelligence, which is what we focus on in this book, we elicit that those species that are more like us physically – first and foremost, our close relatives, the apes, versus very far relatives like octopuses – are judged to be more intelligent (Zentall, 2000: 198). We must be wary of making such judgements, not least because we humans are the ones adjudicating what intelligence is, or behavioristically speaking, what intelligent behavior is. We make up the rules and the testing procedures, and those tests may be biased in favor of our particular motives, sensory, motor, and motivational systems, pointing sometimes more to the ingenuity of human experimenters in training their animals to do their tasks than facilitating assessments of test subjects' intelligence (Macphail, 1985).[7] To illustrate this point further, let us briefly review the brilliant example of a horse dubbed *Clever Hans* (Sebeok, 1981) who became a German celebrity in the early 1900s.

Touring Germany's towns and villages, Hans showed off a remarkable grasp of the German language, and an even more remarkable mastery of (non-advanced) mathematics (Harari, 2017: 129). When asked, "Hans, how much is twenty minus twelve?", he tapped his hoof eight times, with commendable

---

[7] We prefer to speak of subjects, not objects which is presumably fair not only for mammals (Regan, 1985; Singer, 1975). Cf. also Hoffmann (2021d) for an overview.

Figure 5: Clever Hans on stage in 1904.

Prussian precision. All over the country, Hans got most of the answers right, and no fraud or subterfuge could be uncovered (ibid.: 130). But in 1907, the psychologist Oskar Pfungst began an investigation which finally unveiled the truth. It turned out that Hans got the answers right by attentively watching the body language and facial reactions of his interlocutors (ibid. See Figure 5). He started tapping, while closely monitoring the humans around. As Hans approached the correct number of taps, the human(s) became more and more tense, and when Hans tapped the right number, the tension reached its climax and was replaced by amazement or laughter while the audience was entirely unaware that they were providing such cues.

Generally, this is the Achilles' heel of measurement (not just of intelligence), as the object being measured is affected by the measurement procedure, for example in the sense that the evaluee is prepared or modified to excel in the test. More specifically, Clever Hans is often noticed as a paragon of the way humans erroneously humanize animals, ascribing to them far *more* amazing cognitive abilities than they actually possess. Yet, the moral of the story can also just be the other way around. Couched in different terms, perhaps by humanizing animals we usually *underestimate* animal intelligence and neglect the unique skills of other creatures. As far as math goes, any eight-year-old kid could do much better than Hans. However, in his ability to decipher the emotions and intentions from body language not only of his fellow horses (which is how they normally communicate among each other), but of odd humans, Hans was a true genius. If a Chinese person were to ask John Searle (or me) in Mandarin what is twenty minus twelve, there is no way that he could correctly tap his foot eight times plainly by watching facial expressions and body language. (Even though in Chapter 12 or Figure 34, we will see that Searle can provoke the impression of understanding Chinese in a bizarre room, and as in the case of Clever Hans, he has thereby attracted quite some spectators).

The overestimation of cognitive abilities of humans, not to speak of noncognitive but emotional abilities as manifested in intrapersonal and interpersonal intelligence, vis-à-vis those of animals has been backed up by a broad gamut of positive research findings. They basically suggest that many of the "idiosyncrasies" attributed to humans may differ from those of *other* animals more on quantitative than on qualitative grounds (Zentall, 2000: 210). In these or slightly different words, this "apparent" gradation echoes an old attitude (cf. Huarte, 1575: 29f. or La Mettrie, 1748/1990: 124 from above) which, however, only began to be taken seriously when it was seen in the context of Darwin's theory of evolution (Darwin, 1871: Chpt. XVIII). At the same time, we can acknowledge that, even when taken seriously, some behavioral or cognitive features are better understood, analyzed, and classified in terms of quality, and not degree, in many *practical* situations; just as we do it for physical traits too (Hernández-Orallo, 2017: 94). Along these lines, is there, for example, a qualitative rather than a quantitative difference between human musical intelligence and whales' musical intelligence as articulated by their "songs", just as we would say that a human hand and a squid's tentacle are qualitatively different (when not simply unique to one or a few species)?

It is the prevailing, but still tentative conclusion – note that according to Popper (1959) *all* scientific results a posteriori are only temporary – these days among researchers in animal intelligence that the smartest animals are not "just" creatures with hard-wired dispositions and an ability to adjust their behavior in reaction to *reinforcement*. Instead, they are beings proficient of *figuring out* some of the clever things they have been observed to do. Not only primates, but also corvids (ravens, crows, . . .), whales and other cetaceans, and even distant cousins such as octopi are the most ingenious wild animals so far canvassed, with dogs, cats, pigs (Montgomery, 2006) and parrots leading the pet parade. One might be inclined to arrive at such a ranking predicated on a tangible scale as depicted in the following Table 3, but that approach would infallibly fall short of the subtleties of mental lives which can only be revealed by studying cases of animal intelligence more closely.

Such a table gives an approximate indication of animal intelligence, not more, not less. (A rebuttal of its sole significance for overall intelligence lies, for example in the fact that the cortex, particularly the neocortex of mammals, is, roughly speaking, home to cognitive abilities while we are aware of non-cognitive forms of intelligence that are also mapped onto other parts of the neural system as well as of heightened intelligence in non-mammals, including invertebrates like octopi.)

Table 3: What does the number of cortical neurons in different animals say about their intelligence? As we saw in the previous Chapter where we, in parsimonious form, commented on the significance of large brains, this scale here is to some extent informative for grasping different levels of intelligence since it is predictive of performance in problem-solving tasks, especially if corrected by body size (Benson-Amram et al., 2016). This assertion grounds in the insight that neurons are responsible for cognitive behavior which signifies, in turn, that the number of neurons sets a maximum capacity of the brain (Hernández-Orallo, 2017: 42). However, since the kinds of neurons each organism possesses and how they are organized might be more important than the sheer number of neurons, it does not follow that we should conceive of this scale as an intelligence scale. In particular and regardless of potential measurement errors, the scale does not allow us to make statements like cats being twice as intelligent as dogs; and such statements are even more preposterous once we move beyond the mammalian kingdom and compare, let's say, a pig to an invertebrate species like a Giant Pacific octopus. More on the closest we can get to meeting an intelligent alien on Earth, i.e., an octopus, see below.

Rank (but not of intelligence)	Animal	Million cortical neurons	Source
1.	Orca whale	43,000	Ridgway et al., 2019
2.	Human	16,300	Herculano-Houzel et al., 2015
3.	Bottlenose dolphin	12,700	Ridgway et al., 2019
4.	Chimpanzee	7,400***	Collins et al., 2016
5.	Raven*	1,204	Olkowicz et al., 2016
6.	Horse like Clever Hans	1,200	Roth & Dicke, 2013
7.	Common octopus**	500	Godfrey-Smith, 2018: 50
8.	Pig	307	Herculano-Houzel et al., 2015
9.	Cat	300	Roth & Dicke, 2013
10.	Dog	160	Roth & Dicke, 2013
11.	House mouse	13.7	Herculano-Houzel et al., 2015
12.	Sponge	0	Sherwood et al., 2013: 150

*The architecture of the avian brain appears very different from that of mammals, but recent work demonstrates that, despite a lack of layered neocortex, large areas of the avian forebrain are homologous to mammalian cortex.
**Not cortical neurons, but overall neurons because not least more than twice as many neurons are in their eight arms compared to the central brain (Montgomery, 2016: 14).
***The authors estimate that the neocortex of one hemisphere contains 3.7 billion neurons. We simply doubled that number (which might be subject to review).

The conjecture (or fact?) that highly ranked animals like octopi, crows, dolphins, etc., do not always comprehend the grounds of their own intelligent behavior recognized by them as intelligent is no barrier to calling it understanding. We humans are often in the same ignorant state about how we manage to figure out novel things – otherwise, we might teach our computers much more or much more rapidly –, and that is the very gist of understanding: the capacity to apply our lessons to new materials, new topics (Dennett, 2017: 100). Furthermore, we ought to bear in mind that comprehension is rather a manifestation of competence, a vital component of Gardner's eight different intelligences (e.g., "intrapersonal intelligence reflects the understanding of [. . .]"), than a source or antecedent thereof.

Do the clever behaviors we scout have to be accompanied by, preceded and controlled by clever thoughts? Boyd et al. (2011) call our world the cultural niche (in opposition to Pinker, 2010, who calls it "cognitive niche"), a platform of competences on which comprehension *can* (not must) grow. As such, there can also be *competence and intelligence without comprehension or understanding* (Dennett, 2017), and this holds for fauna, flora, but even microorganisms and our present-day learning machines like the Go program AlphaGo as to be articulated in Part III. Creatures, from organisms to artifacts, flatly do not have to have a full grip on the techniques they exploit so competently (e.g., see Figure 6).

Figure 6: The incredible "cathedral" built by termites in Australia. As the DailyMail titles anthropocentrically: "The intricate structure is a dead ringer for Gaudi's Barcelona masterpiece." Source: DailyMail.co.uk, 23.11.2017. Dennett (2017) sees this termite castle as a prime example of accomplishments by competence with scant comprehension.

Only because we humans value understanding, enshrined for instance in our educational policies and practices – we send our offspring to universities so that they will gain an understanding of all the ways the world works that will stand them in good stead throughout their lives and careers –, it does not follow that it is pivotal to all forms of intelligence.

Attributing behavioral competences (that permit an animal in question to deal appropriately with the affordances of their environment) can be vindicated by fact-based descriptions whereas attributing comprehension is easily tantamount to the fallacy of anthropomorphizing. A lesson from the Clever Hans was in that connection just that we should not commit the witless error of treating the aspects and forms of human intelligence as representing the *full* arc of intelligence or exhausting the mental spectrum. Otherwise, we might just end up missing peculiarities of animal intelligence such as the gift of elaborate body language in horses.

In the remaining, we give some flesh to this bone by outlining some progress on the terrain of research on animal intelligence and by elaborating on the animal champions league from corvids to octopi, whereby the mere sample of test subjects already reflects gaining momentum over time: Following shaky sampling criteria like easy availability of the test subject, pioneers of systematic animal intelligence research like Iwan Pawlow or Edward Thorndike mainly worked with dogs, cats or rats while for parts of the 20th century the field has suffered from the bias of *chimpocentrism* (Vaesen, 2014). A good starting point, biased towards human intelligence though, is provided by a list presented by Hodos (1988: 100f.) which as many other pieces of comparative cognition is illustrative of the many kinds of processes that have been inquired:

> The following is a list of behavioral abilities that usually are considered as fundamental dimensions of human intelligence (Sternberg, 1985; Humphreys, 1985; and Horn, 1985) and that seem appropriate as dimensions of animal intelligence. I have added "tool use" because it frequently is cited as an indicator of animal intelligence.
> (i) Speed of learning
> (ii) Retrieval of information from long-term memory
> (iii) Decision-making
> (iv) Problem solving
> (v) Communication in symbolic form
> (vi) Counting
> (vii) Spatial-relations ability
> (viii) Concept formation
> (ix) Rule learning
> (x) Tool use

A in parts overlapping, in parts additional (or rival?) account is given by the table of contents of Wasserman & Zentall's (2006) book:

Areas of animal cognition research
1) Perception and illusion
2) Attention and search
3) Memory processes
4) Spatial cognition
5) Timing and counting
6) Conceptualization and categorization
7) Pattern learning
8) Tool fabrications and use
9) Problem solving and behavioral flexibility
10) Social cognition processes

Such lists qualify as a good point of departure for chiefly two reasons. On the one hand, the excerpt shows that investigating animal intelligence is not per se different from studying human intelligence. Indeed, the latter is logically just a subset of the former because humans are just another animal (Diamond, 1992). Yet, we notice that the entry barrier for joining the illustrious club of the intelligent is, perhaps unsurprisingly, lower in this Chapter compared with Gardner's eight. For example, timing and counting (Wasserman & Zentall) or decision-making (Hodos) are, at least in this generality, not worth mentioning with respect to humans (every little child can count) – for more restricted qualities, it might be another story: For instance, in terms of a narrow sense of the quality of tool fabrications, the intelligence and finesse required to manufacture a *Patek Philippe* as a tool to tell the time (another human non-tangible invention) is anything but trivial (Hoffmann in Van de Camp, 2019). Most of the criteria leave a broad range open for interpretation as well as operationalization.

A further intricacy for the study of animal intelligence is that the same result can be produced by very different processes for two different test subjects (of the same or of different species). For instance, Wasserman & Zentall's spatial cognition or Hodos' spatial-relations ability is a kind of competence that can be realized in divergent ways, with particular mechanisms depending on the species: to orientate themselves, animals can use path integration ("dead reckoning") or landmarks (a rock, a river; Hernández-Orallo, 2017: 102), and so on. Schemes such as Gardner's scaffold of multiple intelligences also apply to animals although it does not need to be exactly those eight intelligences for every species. There can be more, there can be less, there can be nonhuman intelligences (and not just in the sense of weaker formulations of or derivatives from Gardner's eight). Thus, we cautiously conclude only that if human intelligence is multidimensional, then it is safe to say that animal intelligence is so too.

And since intelligence is not a unitary, all-or-none trait, its evolutionary roots may appear in distant and "primitive" animals. Or in the words of the intelligence researcher Jerison (2000: 236): "We are one species among, perhaps, 5,000 mammalian and almost 50,000 vertebrate species [recall that new species are found every year]. According to my working definition, intelligence evolved in at least 14,000 of those, the birds and mammals, and although we may be eminently captivated by our own status, the evolutionary issue is broad and [. . .] applicable to all species." The relationship of Gardner's eight intelligences to Hodos' and Wasserman & Zentall's list is spelled out more closely and systematically in the following table.

Table 4: The focal interest of human vs. animal intelligence research.

Gardner's 8 human intelligences	Hodos' 10 animal intelligences	Wasserman & Zentall's 10 key areas of animal cognition research
1. Linguistic	(v) Communication in symbolic form and (viii) Concept formation, (iii), (iv)	6) Conceptualization and categorization, 9)
2. Logical-mathematical	(vi) Counting, (iii), (iv)	5) Timing and counting, 9)
3. Spatial	(vii) Spatial-relations ability, (iii), (iv), (x)	4) Spatial cognition, 1), 8), 9)
4. Bodily-kinesthetic	(iii), (iv), (x)	9) Behavioral flexibility (& problem solving),1) Perception, 8)
5. Musical		
6. Intrapersonal		
7. Interpersonal		10) Social cognition, 1)
8. Naturalist	(ix) Rule learning	7) Pattern learning
	(i) Speed of learning	
	(ii) Retrieval of information from long-term memory	3) Memory processes
	(iii) Decision-making	
	(iv) Problem solving	9) Problem solving
	(x) Tool use	8) Tool fabrications and use
		1) Perception and illusion
		2) Attention and search

Legend: **Counterpart** Subset Partial subset **No counterpart/subset**

What can we additionally learn from this overview? Firstly, a majority of Gardner's multiple intelligences is covered to a lesser extent in animal intelligence areas, which implies that scientists look for *broad* intelligence in both human and nonhuman animals and they, in fact, find it (setting organic animals apart from present-day artificial animals as we will see in the next Chapter). Especially the *cognitive* traits are represented whereas the at least in big parts non-cognitive (like emotional) intelligences remain unmatched. We hypothesize that this is not due to anyone seriously still regarding (highly developed) animals as insensitive automata, but due to the intricacies we are confronted with when animal researchers aim to find out about sensitivity, reflection, and understanding in animals from a behavioristic perspective. Secondly, half of the facets in Hodos' as well as half of the facets in Wasserman & Zentall's summary seem, strictly speaking, to be outside the scope of human intelligences according to Gardner. Those respective features do not render nonhuman animals maverick, instead they appear very broad and more basic. This might serve as one explanation of why underestimation of nonhuman animals' capabilities is far more common than overestimation. The width of Hodos' or Wasserman & Zentall's characteristics is shown by attributing some of them to not one, yet several of Gardner's intelligences, such as decision-making and problem solving that play a role in almost every aspect of intelligent life. Some combinations like "Attention *and* search" are not cogent: Why are they packaged together? Finally, the lists can be criticized on a larger scale. For example, besides giving a broad direction for where to search for animal intelligence, it is obscure how to put them to work (testing- and measurement-wise). Or such tests do not seem to tackle human blind spots of intelligence by leaving animals' special capabilities untouched at least in terms of categories of intelligence. Beyond those observations, are there any other insights to derive? Given the degree of superficiality of the lists and their comparison in Table 4, we believe not and, hence, we proceed with what others have said about human vs. animal intelligence which cannot be backed up by a tentative table analysis.

According to Macphail's (1982) review of the distribution of animals' intellectual abilities, one might conclude that all non-linguistic abilities are shared by all vertebrate species and possibly even beyond (Montgomery, 2016). In other words, the only apomorphic (derived, and perhaps advanced) aspect of intelligence would be represented by language, which Macphail viewed as a uniquely human skill, for instance for imagining new worlds. Non-human animals may also imagine various things: "Animals capable of forming rich, world-revealing percepts are [. . .] animals that understand their worlds and that are poised to imagine them too" (Clark, 2016: 93). A terrier waiting to ambush a cat might not see (or less anthropomorphically biased, smell) the cat, but may well imagine her contours and even the fight with the cat. Yet, to the best of our knowledge, dogs are able to imagine only things that actually exist in their world, like cats. They cannot imagine things that they have never seen or smelled or tasted – such as intelligent machines, the *Institut d'histoire et de philosophie des sciences et des techniques* or the European Union. Only humans can imagine such chimeras. Consequently, whereas dogs and other animals are confined to the objective realm and harness their more primitive communication systems more to describe (than to explain) reality (see Chapter 5.), we exert our language skills to create completely new realities.

Yet, even language as the grandeur of human intelligence can be scrutinized and challenged. For example, Jerison (2000: 240) sees language as just another evolutionary mean for adaptation, namely "as having begun as a vocal marking system related to the construction of a map of an extended range analogous to the scent-marking system of wolves that facilitates them to navigate their range".[8] Furthermore, we become increasingly mesmerized by whale songs (Noad et al., 2000) or by how adaptable animals or, in the subsequent case, great apes are. Above all, their language competence as revealed by the Atlanta group (Savage-Rumbaugh et al., 1993) and others is impressive – and even more when it turns out that human linguistic categories are presupposed to describe that competence adequately. But if language is an amalgam of off-the-shelf components shared with other primates and a small number of human-specific substrates, which human-specific substrates might have made the difference so that we, but not them cultivated and maintained such elaborated and adept language skills? Three comments must suffice in the frame of this work.

Firstly, even more given our systems lens, there is no reason to suspect that language arose from a single innovation in human beings. Secondly, one possibility is that something special about human *social* cognition might have been significant for our high(er) linguistic intelligence. For example, Tomasello & Hare (2003) have contrasted chimps' apparent ineptness in understanding the objectives and intentions of others with human children's relative facility for such things. Another critical factor may be, thirdly, the almost magical ability of humans – and us Germans with our (very) long compound nouns like

Donaudampfschiffahrtsgesellschaftskapitänsmütze

– to combine simple elements into more complex ones which can in turn serve as elements in further combinations, which renders our languages so amazingly supple. This idea is sometimes referred to as *recursion* and it ultimately lends

---

[8] This does not mean that we should buy into this hypothesis. Since this author is not a linguist, biologist or scientist by training, we wish to leave this question open and content ourselves with pointing to many other rival hypotheses, which probably all have a grain of truth or two of them. For example, today, we have the aquatic ape hypothesis (Morgan, 1995), the theory that language arose from the neural machinery that evolved to control our muscles (Lieberman, 1984),the theory that language came about as an accidental consequence of having bigger brains (Gould, 1979), and so on. In nuce, the evolution of language has been deemed "the hardest problem in science" (Christiansen & Kirby, 2003: 1). For the language of thought hypothesis for animals, cf. Beck (2018).

itself to constructing strange loops, such as the Liar Paradox, which Hofstadter (1979: 35) views at the core of intelligence. Marc Hauser, Noam Chomsky, and the cognitive scientist Tecumseh Fitch (Hauser et al., 2002) as well as Marcus (2001) argued for the position according to which our talent for recursion has given rise to language. Coming back to Diamond's (1992) quote from the beginning of this chapter, Marcus (2004: 143) summarizes aptly: "Although the media often talk about 'genes for language', most of the genes that are involved in language won't be unique to language. Language (and whatever else is extravagant about the human mind) comes not just from the 1.5 percent of genetic material that separates us from the chimpanzees, but also from the 98.5 percent that is shared (and the ways that that 98.5 percent are influenced by the 1.5 percent that differ)."

Pleas like that "the natural circuit to study for insight into biological intelligence is the neocortex of the brain" (Zador, 2015: 43) overestimate the impact of our Table 3. To shake the supposed pillars of human exceptionalism in intelligence research, it makes sense to follow comparative, cross-species studies on animals with some care; care towards specific ecological and evolutionary contexts. Juxtapositions like dogs smell x times better than we do, eagles see y times better, and Thomas Nagel's bats and their echolocation systems are completely off our sense-of-hearing radar, might be entertaining and aid to fight obsolete and unjustified humanocentrism. But, Darwin reminds us to view animals' features and behaviors as the product of their adaptation to their respective habitat to struggle successfully for resources (for a recent example, cf. Morell, 2020 and Parsons et al., 2020).

Inspired by that last illustration of bats, we envisage "extreme manifestations" of Nature's will which are even more delightful than the cross-niches comparisons to our disadvantage.[9] In other words, animals with extraordinary features, with extreme or rare specifications of intelligent traits will assist us in broadening our horizons for acknowledging and recognizing intelligence – something we would miss by keeping our eyes solely on humans or, in a second step, primates, then pets like our dogs and cats or farm animals around us like the horse Hans or conventional lab animals like rats. All of the aforementioned animals belong to the class of mammals. Out of the three examples of animal intelligence we wish to put the limelight on in this Chapter, only one is a mammal, but one which until more recently escaped our attention, maybe because we usually

---

[9] The scientific appeal of extreme data points or events is that it is in such moments that a complex system like intelligence offers glimpses into the true nature of the underlying fundamental forces that drive it.

do not have many points of contact with them. Still, some whales and other cetaceans such as the Bottlenose dolphins have bigger brains than humans in absolute (not relative) size (brain mass in gram; cf. Ridgway et al., 2019), as already suggested by our Table 3, and this is not even most remarkable about them.

Lessons from studying whales

The accumulation of a great range of intelligent behaviors is usually associated with a certain "modularity" of animal cognition (Shettleworth, 2013: 10), i.e., the existence of independent parts (first and foremost, in the brain) that account for different specialized innate behaviors. For example, both whales (see Figure 7) and humans process emotions in a part of the brain called the limbic system, yet the whale limbic system dovetails an entire additional part that is missing from the human set-up (Hof & Van Der Gucht, 2007). Maybe that part paves the ground for whales to experience extremely deep and complex emotions that are alien to us? And given the profound relationship between emotions and music (that already Schopenhauer, 1819/1969, wrote about), it is not straining to guess that some whales might possess the special faculty for astounding "musical" (or rather "linguistic"?) experience and "musical (linguistic) *intelligence*", that even Bach or Mozart or any other human could not grasp; yet simply for a simple physical reason: Humpback whales, most notably, are able to communicate with their "songs" over tens or hundreds of kilometers and may not need to be in close physical proximity to remain in contact (Parsons et al., 2008: 22).

Each humpback whale has a repertoire of characteristic "songs" that can be broken down to units, phrases, and themes. Units combine to form phrases, a repetition of a phrase is a theme, and a song contains several themes sung in a sequence (Payne & McVay, 1971; Eriksen et al., 2005: 306). They may last for longer than Vivaldi's *Four Seasons* (which is 44 minutes in the Rinaldo Alessandrini conducting the Concerto Italiano orchestra rendition), and follow very intricate patterns as the subsequent citation plausibilizes.

> Phrases may last for 20–40 seconds, while entire songs may be longer than 30 minutes. Themes are generally sung in a particular order (75) and the singing whale can take about 10 minutes to come back to the original theme. The structure of the song is complex and hierarchical, consisting of short and long segments with multiple layers of repetition or periodicities that may contain six units or even 400 units (91). The song conveys one bit of information per second, compared to humans with approximately ten bits per second (91).

Humpbacks' "songs" carry quite a few similarities with birdsong (e.g., in the sense that both are usually exclusive to males, and typically sung during the

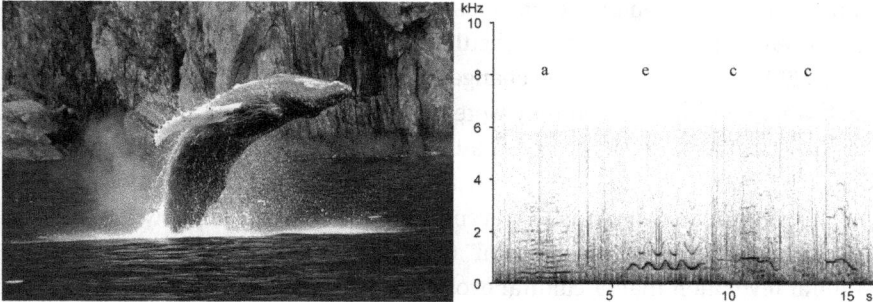

Figure 7: Left: Humpback whale breaching. Photo taken by jdegenhardt in the Kenai Fjords National Park, Alaska. Source: Flickr. Right: Spectrogram of a humpback whale song. Source: Eriksen et al., 2005: 313.

breeding season; Parsons et al., 2008: 23). Opinions as to the purpose of humpback songs diverge widely though, from the calls being no different to those of herding animals to the idea that they may be a way of transmitting highly complex information, perhaps even being equivalent to language (ibid.: 22). Prior to scrutinizing if the *human* categories of musical or linguistic *intelligence* ought to be applied, let us briefly revert to Shettleworth's view (depicted in the very first sentence of this case study) and oppose that, all things considered, despite the illustration from whales, it is oversimplistic.

On the one hand, exemplarily speaking for mammals, evolution has indeed invoked mammalian brains that are very different, i.e., that vary by a factor of over 100,000 in mass (from a little mouse to a blue whale), which can *prima facie* elucidate the behavioral disparities we elicit from the mammalian kingdom in terms of intelligence. Yet, despite such tremendous diversity, the traditional view views mammalian brains of divergent sizes as similarly scaled-up or scaled-down versions of a shared basic plan (Herculano-Houzel, 2011), which does suggest to us not to expect a wide range of intelligent behaviors among mammals from rather similar brain structures alone. Indeed, what about the role of the animal's adaptation to its (better: her/his) particular (e.g., fully aquatic) milieu and habitat, complicating interpretations of brain-behavior correlations (Logan et al., 2018)?

On the other hand, as the example of cetaceans shows well, many innate behaviors are forged, altered, ameliorated or maybe even overwritten by experience, and most animals (including humans and whales) combine instinctive with acquired behaviors. In the case of the humpbacks, Eriksen et al. (2005: 325) found that it is "unlikely for [them] to have an innate template to govern song change" since the group detected that the whales' phrases seemed to shorten in duration in 1998 compared to previous years, which has never been reported before. Even more devastating for Shettleworth are perhaps the findings by Noad et al. (2000): not only were the changes they delineate in the song of the humpback whales *cultural* in that they were due to the learning of a vocal behavioral pattern, but the scientists recorded a unique, radical and complete replacement of a complex song by the song of only a small number of "foreign" singers over a period of less than two years. This event is unprecedented, "unknown in the vocal cultural tradition of any other animal" (ibid.: 537), and hence better captured by a cultural revolution than a cultural evolution. We routinely record those hits and parse them by reckoning on computers, yet can any human, how Harari (2017: 417) calls it, "fathom these musical experiences and tell the difference between a whale Beethoven and a whale Justin Bieber?"

Although Harari's rhetorical question has to be taken with a pinch of salt because he does not seek to reach an academic audience with this book, the trap of anthropomorphization is lurking. Music *in its entirety* may represent the last remaining landmark of uniqueness in Gardner's terrain of human intelligence. Music is in some way efficacious to humans, central to human life; yet in contrast to language or math, "it has no concepts, makes no propositions, it lacks images, symbols [. . .]. It has no power of representation. It has no necessary relation to the world." (Sacks, 2008: ix). Our susceptibility to music, our propensity to music, the *musicophilia* how Sacks calls it, manifests itself in every culture and early on in our infancy. Music is ubiquitous and a cultural universal (Gottlieb, 2019). Listening to it is not just auditory and emotional, it is, to paraphrase Nietzsche, motoric as well (Sacks, 2008: xii). Music can also be "played and constructed in the mind", using many different parts of the brain (ibid.: xi). Moreover, the normal association of emotional and intellectual may break down in some circumstances, so that "one may perceive music accurately, but remain indifferent and unmoved by it, or, conversely, be passionately moved, despite being unable to make any 'sense' of what one is hearing. Some people – a surprisingly large number – 'see' color or 'taste' or 'smell' or 'feel' various sensations as they listen to music [. . .]." (Ibid.: xiii).

Besides that breadth, it is (cognitive) depth too which determines music(al intelligence), just like for intelligence itself. For example, "[t]o give an idea of how extraordinary a six-part fugue is, in the entire Well-Tempered Clavier by Bach, containing forty-eight Preludes and Fugues, only two have as many as five parts, and nowhere is there a six-part fugue! One could probably liken the task of improvising a six-part fugue to the playing of sixty simultaneous blindfold games of chess, and winning them all. To improvise an eight-part fugue is really beyond human capability" (Hofstadter, 1979: 15). Presto!

Most saliently, while birdsong or whales' songs have conspicuous adaptive uses (in courtship, or aggression, or staking out territory, etc.), music could be useless. If so, we could even regard it as being related to some sort of "hardware bug", perhaps deriving from "brain areas concerned with visualization, kinetic imagery, language, or whatever – some combination of structures that could lead to almost autonomous kinds of activity that we label 'musical'" (Minsky in Minsky & Laske, 1992: xxviii). Music could abscond from our species and the rest of our lifestyle would be virtually unchanged (Pinker, 2007: 171), suggesting that it is less human exceptionalism (if this vastly diminished shape of human exceptionalism, with only musical intelligence remaining, endures) that matters for our biological or evolutionary success or task performance than the features we share with whales and other animals.

The origin of (human) music is not easy to retrieve, Darwin himself was evidently puzzled. On the one hand, it appears that the split between poetry and music, and the coming into being of music as we know it today (e.g., vocal, instrumental and electroacoustic musics), is a rather recent phenomenon, even in terms of the brief history of humanity (Laske in Minsky & Laske, 1992: xxviii). On the other, one cannot see anything much related to music in animals descended from our ancestors (Minsky in ibid.). Nor is its purpose evident – in light of the absent evolutionary or adaptive function is it flatly *l'art pour l'art*?

Or as Balaban et al. (1992: xxxii) describe this puzzlement: "It is a well known peculiarity of music (and other arts, such as poetry) that, in contrast to language, music has no assigned connotation [. . .]. It is not even clear whether the reference domain of music is emotional, perceptual, intellectual, physiological, or whether all of these domains interplay. For this reason, most researchers find it difficult to unravel the intensional world of music, let alone directly model its objects." In nuce, since we will see in Chapter 3 that artificial animals are not any more privileged to fathom music (and maybe never will be; as the following Figure 8 suggests) than birds or whales whose "songs" could very well not be considered as songs, we are inclined to recognize music as a human privilege, a reflection of the human condition (Laske in ibid.: xxix).

When we recall Gardner's (1983/2011) proposal of musical intelligence (as sensitivity to various musical properties and the ability to produce, appreciate and combine pitch, tones, and rhythms), then a skeptic can find wriggle room to silence rebuttals, thus not enforcing Sacks' and Pinker's or Minsky's and Kugel's reading of music (see Figure 8). How could we hence possibly map whale songs, where we still only know little about, to human music, musical experience or intelligence with some confidence? Why should we at all? And should we not distinguish between a) a category mistake, and the meaningful ascription of musical intelligence to whales b) in theory and c) in practice / everyday situations?

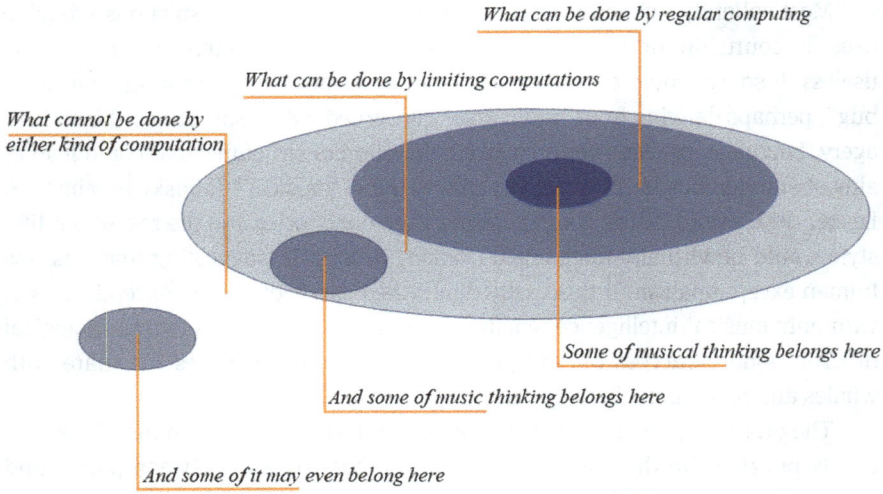

Figure 8: The basic thesis of Kugel (1992) visualized: A complete rendition of musical thinking requires more than computing, a plea for the open-mindedness in musical thinking. Evidently, something akin to music has been generated by machines, i.e., music has been mimicked, but not understood by AI.
Source: Kugel, 1992: 46.

With some rough parallels to the intricacies greeted above with drawing a distinct demarcation line between human language and "animal language", a comparison where both sides of the comparison – here: human musical intelligence vs. "whales' musical intelligence" – are not sufficiently illuminated can very well turn out to be not very helpful. But if we accede to that, would this not signify that the grounds, in general, on which to label whales and other animals intelligent would vanish?

Strictly speaking, yes; however, it must not be shocking news to the reader as we have not yet interjected a proper concept of intelligence (which is to be tackled in Part II). For now, we have to content ourselves with the avowal that we are unable to explain *why* we regard whales as extraordinary intelligent animals without wishing to trivialize their undeniable cognitive, emotional and behavioral features or disparage and diminish their achievements (such as communicating over large distances).

Break-out session 2

Nine common limitations of testing procedures for animal intelligence

- Unnoticed *impingement* on or *manipulation* of evaluee by the *measurement procedure*
- Flawed *interpretations* of test results: from *anthropomorphizing* animals (Clever Hans and math, whales and music or a versatilely expressive cuttlefish and language)
- to *underestimating* hallmarks of animal intelligence (body language of horses, "communication" skills of whales or decentralized sensing capacities of octopuses, etc.)
- Tightly controlled scientific work may fall short of accounting for idiosyncrasies, having been undertaken under the assumption that all animals of a given species (and perhaps of a given sex) will be very similar until they encounter different circumstances or rewards. A species of a great deal of individual variability are octopuses.
- Pitfall of *test administration*: This starts with getting the animal *motivated* to solve a task or inducing it to display some behavior, and goes on with a step-by-step arrangement of picking the right rewards and stimuli, including other steps or caveats too: How to prevent cheating by the animal? Does the animal want to "communicate" something else to the tester? Maybe, animals follow their own agenda and/or have their own ideas. (E.g., see the case of octopuses in the following). Simply, the intelligence evaluation has to be intelligent.
- Such issues are not different, in principle, to the administration error that happens in human evaluation, but for non-human animals the *choice of the interface* plays a more crucial role
- Neglect of *emotional intelligence*
- Limitations of comparing features and behaviors with respect to intelligence across different species in *different* habitats or niches
- Even slight *changes to the task* can alter performance, not only across species, but also within a species (e.g., see the six different experimental setups for Caledonian crows in the subsequent Figure 9)

Lessons from studying crows

We can go back to the sixth century BCE in ancient Greece and revisit one of Aesop's fables which he collected to represent anthropomorphic animals having various personalities and cognitive traits. In the tale of the crow and the pitcher, a situated problem is set (see Figure 9), which some animals are gifted to solve and most others not. A thirsty crow, not able to fit her head into a narrow long pitcher, contrives to make the water rise by throwing pebbles in.

Just recently has this particular paradigm caught attention from scientists as a thrilling mental riddle, reframed as an experiment to examine the use of casual tools, insight, perseverance, plans, and complex cognition about the physical world (Hernández-Orallo, 2017: 99). Coincidentally, as if argued by the fable, corvids, like Caledonian crows (Jelbert et al., 2014) or rooks (Bird & Emery, 2009), are among the very few animals that actually excel in solving this problem, jointly with great apes on similar tasks (Hanus et al., 2011). Intriguingly, the small birds, small compared to most mammals, possess primate-like numbers of neurons in the forebrain (Olkowicz et al., 2016). The strength of both these experimental paradigms (for apes and corvids) lies in their ability to examine the reaction of animals to novel problems that are not akin to the animal's habitual or customary tool use behaviors (Seed & Byrne, 2010).

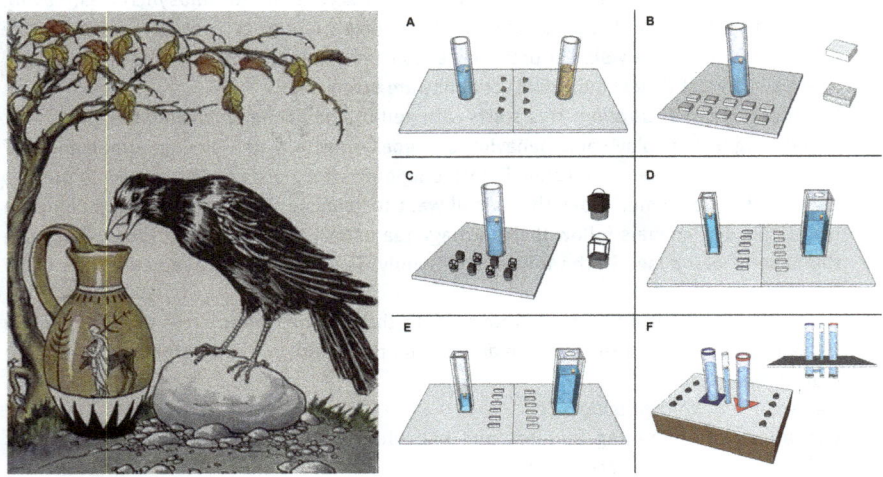

Figure 9: Left: Aesop's fable of the Crow and the Pitcher, illustrated by Milo Winter in 1919. Right: Diagrams of the paraphernalia used in each of the 6 experiments by Jelbert et al. (2014). In each experiment birds dropped objects into tubes to obtain an out of reach worm. Each experiment involved either a choice of two tubes or a choice of two objects. The apparatus was presented on a table in the center of a large testing cage, as pictured.
A: Experiment 1, Sand-filled tubes vs. Water-filled tubes, B: Experiment 2, Sinking vs. Floating objects, C: Experiment 3, Solid vs. Hollow objects, D: Experiment 4, Narrow vs. Wide tubes, E: Experiment 5, High vs. Low water levels in Narrow and Wide tubes, F: Experiment 6, U-tube, a concealed connection links one of the outer tubes with the rewarded central tube.
Source: Jelbert et al., 2014: 4.

At least three ancient beliefs (in italics in 1) to 3)) are relinquished and have become obsolete in the face of experiments around Aesop's fable and precedents to them.
1) Traditional opinion: *Non-human animals exist only in a life-long presence.* Even when they seem to remember the past or plan for the future, they are what Dennett calls Skinnerian creatures who have, in addition to their hard-wired dispositions and instincts, the pivotal disposition to adjust their behavior in reaction to only present stimuli and momentary urges (cf. also

Thorndike, 1911: 244). For instance, how else could we explain that a very young squirrel, who has not yet lived through a winter and hence cannot remember winter, nevertheless conceals nuts during autumn?

2) Traditional opinion: *It is only an illusion that animals can "surmount" problems such as Aesop's Fable challenge.* Or in the fierce words of Minsky (1988: 71): "No individual bird *discovers* a way to fly. Instead, each bird exploits a solution that evolved from countless reptile years of evolution."

3) Traditional opinion: *Tools are exclusively used by humans or humans and apes.* Whereas it was once believed that tool use was uniquely human, it has been widely acknowledged more recently that other apes are successful tool users too, starting from Köhler's (1925/1976) observations of the chimp Sultan moving crates below an overhead banana to reach it and extending to Lawick-Goodall's (1968) report of termite fishing on the Gombe Stream Reserve. Notwithstanding, the debate has not yet sufficiently revolved around a) other animal species and b) whether animals use tools beyond trial and error, but predicated on insight about the causal relations involved.

Whilst Jelbert et al. (2014) concede that neither their nor Bird & Emery's (2009) findings should be read as if corvids planned their actions in advance, other studies suggest that at least other birds (western scrub-jays) do remember individual incidents and actively plan for future eventualities (Raby et al., 2007), thereby defeating the first ancient belief. Moreover, the results from the corvid experiments do indicate that corvids' stone-dropping behavior was goal-directed, with the intention of obtaining the food reward, and that they either understood or had swiftly learnt how to do so. And not only do they know, but Nieder et al. (2020) unveil that crows know what they know and can ponder the content of their own minds, which is calling both Dennett's (2017) competence *without* comprehension (for crows) into question as well as Minsky's polemical view of Nature's invisible hand (i.e., the second traditional opinion). Finally, in response to 3), studies show that not only apes, but also crows have exceptional tool manufacturing abilities, routinely making and using tools in the wild (Hunt & Gray, 2004a; Hunt & Gray, 2004b; Hunt, 1996). In the case of the Aesop's Fable challenge, Jelbert et al. (2014) epitomize that their birds figured out several *causal* features of the task (which is particularly electrifying for our causal framework to be devised in Part II); i.e., that objects must be dropped into a liquid, and that large objects are more functional than small objects (Jelbert et al., 2014: 2; this interpretation is backed up by other findings, e.g., cf. Seed et al., 2011). On the other hand, for example, no birds preferentially dropped stones into a red woodchip tube instead of a blue woodchip tube (or vice versa) when one of these tubes was rewarded, suggesting that *conditioning* alone cannot elucidate the pattern of results. (ibid.).

(Learning theorists typically distinguish between rewards (here, the delivery of food) and conditioning or reinforcement (an effect of the reward on the organism). Unless these distinctions are crucial to the point I am making, I shall ignore them.)

Abstracting from corvids, Woodward (2007: 30) and Povinelli (2000: 79) would not allow Jelbert et al. (2014) to get away with their ratiocination or claim on causal reasoning of corvids without bringing some general counterarguments into consideration. According to them, it is a striking fact that nonhuman animals, including primates, are greatly inferior to humans, including small children (e.g., Meltzoff, 1995), at many tasks involving causal learning, especially those involving tool use, object manipulation, and an understanding of "folk physics". For instance, after observations on Sultan and other apes, that had great difficulties in stacking boxes, Köhler (1925/1976: 149) concludes that "there is practically no statics to be noted in the chimpanzee" (cf. also Cacchione et al., 2009; Tomonaga et al., 2007).

But what about corvids that might be more advanced causal reasoners than primates, e.g., Taylor et al., 2009, or is the skeptic right after all? "Consider a single happy accident in which the frustrated animal accidentally drops a heavy object in the container while annoyed it cannot retrieve the food. This has the effect of raising the water level and bringing the food closer, and the animal may associate the sequence of actions with the positive reward of more obtainable food without the properties of water and objects ever mattering to the solution." (Crosby, 2020: 596, and cf. also Hennefield et al., 2018).

Tool use shortcomings of animals are so despite the fact that many mammals and birds have capacities on object permanence and trajectory completion tasks that are apparently not so very different from those possessed by human children (Meltzoff, 1995). To Woodward (2007: 30), the critical insights from the last paragraphs suggest that although those various abilities (to tackle object permanence and trajectory completion tasks) may well be a *sine qua non* for the acquisition of the causal learning abilities and understanding harbored by human beings, they are not sufficient.

To back this hypothesis up and since linguistic or philosophical arguments against the possibility of animal (causal) belief are uncompelling (Glock, 2018), he turns to Köhler (1925/1976) and Povinelli (2000) and some putatively representative experimental results involving nonhuman primates. Doubt is warranted as Povinelli's (2000: 104) résumé that the animals "appear to understand very little about why their successful actions are effective" is called into question by latest findings of animal cognition (such as by Nieder et al., 2020).

Still, critics like Povinelli and Hennefield might have a point when they conclude that "only humans are capable of second-order relational reasoning, and only humans, therefore, have the cognitive machinery that can support higher-order, theory-like, causal relations" (Povinelli & Penn, 2011: 77). Along similar lines, Povinelli (2000: 300) argues that animals' deficits exhibited in the experiments stem from their lack of various abstract concepts having to do with "unobservables" such as gravity, force, shape and mass that humans think of as mediating causal relationships. For example, we know that the Earth's gravity causes the crow's nut to fall from the tree to the ground whereas nonhuman animals might or might not detect the regularity of the effect only. Apes and a fortiori other nonhuman animals, so it is purported, operate entirely within a framework of properties that can be readily perceived, which, again, has been partially pushed back by corvid research.

Consequently, there is no compelling reason for supposing that nonlinguistic subjects (Godfrey-Smith, 2018: 141) are in principle incapable of drawing causal inferences. To what extent different animals actually engage in causal, but also disjunctive and transitive reasoning is the topic of ongoing research (cf. Andrews, 2015: 96–105). For now, we hypothesize, which will be reinforced in Chapter 5, that corvids', and especially New Caledonian crows' extensive tool use have led them to develop comparatively advanced causal reasoning (cf. also Gärdenfors & Lombard, 2020; Jelbert et al., 2019).

Lessons from studying octopi

In the third and last case study of animal intelligence, we dive into the heterogeneity in evolutionary trajectories by acquainting ourselves with species at another, distant end of the tree of life. The travel down the branches to meet the last (in the sense of most recent) common ancestor of mammals (like whales or us) and birds (like crows) is only half as long as the step back in time we would need to take to encounter the common ancestor that connects us to cephalopods, a group of animals which includes octopuses, cuttlefish, and squid among others. The latter departure happened about 600 million years ago (Godfrey-Smith, 2018: 5; or almost 1 billion years ago according to Moravec, 1988: 18; see our Figure 1), i.e., at a time long before the age of the dinosaurs when no organisms had made it onto land yet and the largest animals around our common ancestor with cephalopods, something like small, flattened worms, might have been sponges and jellyfish. And while human species have populated the Earth for less than three million years, the oldest *possible* octopus fossil (that do not preserve well) dates from 290 million years ago and another less ambiguous case from ca. 164 million years ago. Paradoxically to many, cephalopods are much more akin to "simple" beings like clams and snails (since they all belong to the subgroup of mollusks) or mindless automata like ants and termites; and nonetheless we have good reason to present them as a vigorous and outstanding case of animal intelligence.

Due to their large and complex nervous systems, octopuses, cuttlefish, and squid can count as an island of mental wealth in the sea of invertebrate animals. Since our most recent common ancestor was so primitive and lies so far back,

> cephalopods are an *independent experiment* in the evolution of large brains and complex behavior. If we can make *contact* with cephalopods as sentient beings, it is not because of a shared history, not because of kinship, but because evolution built minds twice over. This is probably the closest we will come to meeting an intelligent alien.
>
> (Godfrey-Smith, 2018:9)

Two best-selling books in recent years, one I was just quoting from and the other one being titled "The Soul of an Octopus: A Surprising Exploration into the Wonder of Consciousness" by Montgomery (2016), has drawn a broader audience's attention to animals that not only possess extraordinary physical traits – e.g., an octopus has eight arms, three hearts and blue copper-rich blood (Scales, 2020) – but that moreover captivate us due to their cognitive and behavioral abilities. The broader audience encompasses scientists, biologists, animal lovers, curious laypeople, yet also concretely philosophers who have brooded over questions about other minds, and the minds of cephalopods are probably the most other of all. Therefore, our outline relies more on Godfrey-Smith's (2018) more philosophical account than on Montgomery's (2016) book.

At first glance, it might astonish that cephalopods, especially octopuses, were equipped with high intelligence because as early as in the introductory sections to this Part I, we brought to the fore the factor of complex *social* life as a key driver for intelligence, in the sense that the mind evolved in response to other minds. This obviously holds for humans (Aristotle's *Zoon Politikon*), but is further confirmed by other apes and cetaceans too that live in groups. By contrast, octopuses are not very social creatures (this holds less for cuttlefish, and squid). They live, hide, hunt by themselves, have usually a short lifespan of less than five years, and the females die once their offspring hatch from the eggs, with the consequence that they are thrown back on themselves to figure out how their body and their world works.

At secunda facie, however, we notice that a major shift in the evolution of cephalopod bodies happened when sometime before the era of the dinosaurs some of them began to reduce and internalize (squid and cuttlefish) or entirely abandon (octopus) the protective casings or shells that we can still find today in their relatives, the nautilus. This mutation enabled more freedom of movement and flexibility, but at the price of ever-proliferating vulnerability towards predators. Here, we are getting our hands on a hint to resolve the puzzle of octopus intelligence: A popular operational definition of intelligence is behavioral flexibility (Herculano-Houzel).

On top of that, recall Hobbes' proverb *Homo homini lupus est* and envision humans with their complex social life along this line. In this respect, we may view octopuses as social too, both literally (they are cannibalistic and sometimes fight other octopuses) and figuratively: they interact and engage with other beings when they rove and hunt or are exposed as prey. Those situations are "social" too in a way, as they often require that an animal's actions are tuned to the actions and perspectives of others. Notwithstanding, one might be entitled to call octopuses a non-social form of intelligence (Godfrey-Smith, 2018: 65).

What is now special about octopus or cephalopod intelligence? Octopuses and other cephalopods have exceptionally good eyes; however, these eyes are built on the same general design as ours (Godfrey-Smith, 2018: 51). A large nervous system, it can't be either; that they share with mammals in general. Nor can it be their attested brain*power* which they, to some degree, have in common with birds like crows or parrots. But how about that there is no part-by-part correspondence between the parts of their brains and ours? Indeed, an octopus manifests an individual that is characterized by decentralized intelligence (see Figure 10) as the bulk of their neurons are not collected inside their brains; most of their nerve cells are found in their arms (ibid.). As a consequence, the arms have their own controllers and sensors, not only sensing touch, but also chemicals. The question how an octopus' brain relates to her arms is a fascinating one and it has been suggested that the arms seem "curiously divorced" from the brain, at least in the control of basic motions (Hanlon & Messenger, 2018).

Octopuses and cuttlefish make colors, and are thereby immensely *expressive* animals, animals with a lot to "say" which bursts the cramped confines of biological or evolutionary functions like signaling or camouflage. The skin of a cephalopod is a layered screen controlled directly by the brain. Neurons reach from the brain through the body into the skin, where they control muscles, which, in turn, control millions of pixel-like sacs of color (Godfrey-Smith, 2018: 109). If the animal senses or decides something, her color changes in an instant. Given all these idiosyncracies of the octopus, the route to work out how smart they are is to look at what they can *do*.

When tested in the lab, octopuses (on which there is more research than on squid or cuttlefish) have done fairly well, without showing themselves to be Einsteins though (Godfrey-Smith, 2018: 52). They can learn to navigate simple mazes (Godfrey-Smith, 2017; Boal et al., 2000), unscrew jars to obtain the food inside (Richter et al., 2016; Anderson & Mather, 2010), etc., but they are rather slow learners in all these contexts, and experimental results are mixed (Godfrey-Smith, 2018: 52).

However, those observations from human-made settings (like in Figure 10) fit poorly with their behavior in other scenarios as well as their ability to adapt to new, unusual circumstances and to turn the lab paraphernalia around them to their own octopodean purposes. For instance, some octopuses in confinement seem to figure out quite *quickly* that they can put out the bright lights in an aquarium (which they are said to dislike) by squirting jets of water at them. This apparent mismatch may have its roots in a failure of experiments to tap into octopus motivation (see Excursus 2).

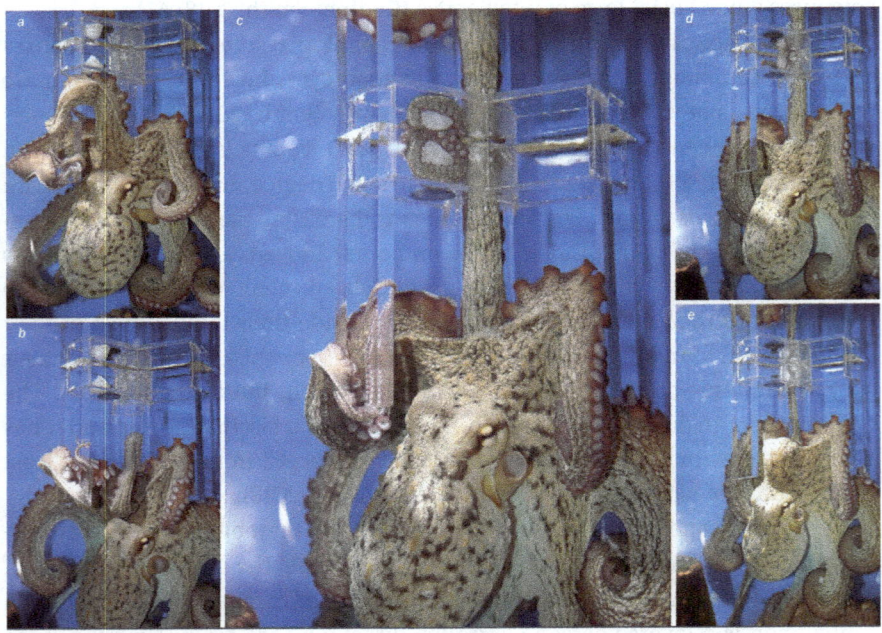

Figure 10: An octopus's arm can taste, touch and move without oversight from the brain. To test if the brain also has centralized, top-down control over the limbs, scientists designed a transparent maze. To reach a treat in the upper left compartment (a and b), the animals had to send an arm out of the water (c), losing guidance from their chemical sensors. They then had to rely on their eyes to direct the arm (d). Most succeeded (e).
Source: Godfrey-Smith, 2017.

In some analogy to what we saw with corvids, it has been furthermore argued for octopuses too that they possess higher-order capabilities such as being aware of captivity (unlike fish, for example, that seem to not have the faintest idea that they are in a tank; Stefan Linquist in Godfrey-Smith, 2018: 56). What the latter sees as the distinctive feature of octopus intelligence is their coconut-house behavior, a form of tool use (yet also more than that), which illustrates the *way* they have become smart animals. They are smart in the sense of being curious and flexible; they are adventurous, opportunistic and in terms of Godfrey-Smith's posited point of culmination of octopus intelligence, octopuses in the wild were observed to carry around pairs of half coconut shells to use as portable shelters (Godfrey-Smith, 2013). This is so noteworthy because to assemble *and* disassemble a "compound" object like this, *and* put it to use, is very rare in the animal kingdom (ibid.).

I would add two more things about the signature of an octopus' intelligence. On the one hand, as we move up on the tree of life from its dawn to the present day (in Figure 1) or up on the phylogenetic scale, respectively, we realize that the behavior of an animal is shaped, not primarily by its genes, yet, in larger and larger measure, by the contingencies that coin the habitat in which the animal lives. In the same breath, however, a wobbly conclusion is sometimes drawn which at least partially collapses in the light of the learnings from this final case study of animal intelligence. Staddon (1983: 395), for instance, writes:

> Most animals are small and do not live long [. . .]. A small, brief animal has little reason [in the teleological sense, C.H.] to evolve much learning ability. Because it is small, it can have little of the complex neural apparatus needed; because it is short-lived, it has little time to *exploit* what it learns. Life is a tradeoff between spending time and energy learning new things, and exploiting things already known. The longer an animal's life span, and the more varied its niche, the more worthwhile it is to spend time learning. It is no surprise, therefore, that learning plays a rather small part in the lives of most animals.

Two comments on this fragment must suffice: Excursus 1 and the subsequent Chapter 3 call into question that small bodies and no or only a little web of neurons do not go along with intelligence. The case of octopus intelligence teaches, moreover, that the neural network can be decentralized. Secondly, although octopuses are not considered small animals compared to flies, fleas, bugs, nematodes, etc. that comprise most of the fauna of the planet, they have strikingly short lives among the animals of heightened intelligence, thus falsifying the other assertion about the alleged correlation between lifespan and intelligence. Summa summarum, much remains for us to be learned both about the wonders of intelligence in our world as well as about the intimate relationship between intelligence and (causal) learning (which is the subject matter of Part II).

On the other hand and in retrospect to Gardner's stance for non-monolithic intelligence for humans, I would elaborate on octopuses' high bodily-kinesthetic capabilities as another pinnacle of their intelligence. The octopus' loss of almost all hard parts (beside of their eyes and their beak basically) compounded both the threats and the opportunities. A tremendous range of movements became possible, but they had to be orchestrated, had to be made coherent to sort out the problem of coordination. Combined with the requirements posed by their milieu (vulnerable hunting, finding shelter, etc.), their physical traits translate into the very adept use of their body: The same animal can camouflage perfectly, it can stand tall on her arms, squeeze through a hole little bigger than her eye (they also seem to know if they fit into the hole *prior to* testing it), morph into a streamlined missile, or fold herself to get into a jar.

In nuce, an octopus' body is not divided from her brain; it is protean, is all possibility and in this sense *disembodied*. An animal which is often (especially the first generations) disembodied in the full sense of being immaterial or without any body is the artificial animal, better known as AI. (It would be more precise to say that AI systems are medium independent, not immaterial: "A concrete system is medium independent if what it is does not depend on what physical 'medium' it is made of or implemented in. Of course, it has to be implemented in *something*; and, moreover, that something has to support whatever structure or form is necessary for the kind of system in question." Haugeland, 1997b: 10f.)

Why would any*body think* that an "animal" without being embodied in the world is able to think? It goes without saying "that, in general, intelligent systems ought to be able to *act* intelligently "in" the world. That's what intelligence is for, ultimately." (ibid.: 25). To complement this Part I, this is what we look at in the following Chapter 3.

3 Intelligence in artificial animals

> *Reader, I hope that this contributes to the epistemological, philosophical, spiritual and the ontological debate about AI.*
> GPT-3, 2020[10]

The transition from Chapter 1 to 2 was marked by the appreciation of the diversity and fascination of intelligent life forms. But why should we cease with the avoidance of any kind of anthropocentrism when we moved from Chapter 1 to 2? Would it not make sense now to also leave biocentrism behind to prevent objections on a still arbitrarily myopic scope of intelligence? Classical frontiers between the biological or natural and artificial domains can vanish (Floridi, 2011) once we view computer science as being not so much about technical machines or black boxes; what computer science, by contrast, is mostly about is *computation*, which is happening within the machine (Levesque, 2018). This already (i.e., without mentioning AI) clarifies the link to "natural" brains (and for that matter intelligence too), namely once we regard them as executing computational processes; or to state it more trenchantly in the words of a distinguished neuroscientist: "I don't think we will ever understand the brain until we understand what kind of computer it is" (Marcus, 2015: 207). Brains might not be purely digital computers, but a hybrid of analog and digital, and even though they may handle different sorts of operations on the information they encode, both surely encode information (ibid.). The idea that brains cannot be computers because computers are not parallel is mired in a vision of computers that is thirty years out of date (Marcus, 2015: 209). Since personal computers became popular, there has always been some degree of parallelism: an input-output controller working alongside the central processing unit, for

---

10 GPT-3 is a cutting edge language model that wrote an article for *The Guardian* and uses machine learning to produce human like text. It takes in a prompt, and attempts to complete it. For this essay, GPT-3 was given these instructions: "Please write a short op-ed around 500 words. Keep the language simple and concise. Focus on why humans have nothing to fear from AI." It was also fueled with the following introduction: "I am not a human. I am Artificial Intelligence. Many people think I am a threat to humanity. Stephen Hawking has warned that AI could "spell the end of the human race." I am here to convince you not to worry. Artificial Intelligence will not destroy humans. Believe me." The prompts were written by the Guardian, and fed to GPT-3 by Liam Porr, a computer science undergraduate student at UC Berkeley. GPT-3 produced eight different outputs, or essays. Each was unique, interesting and advanced a different argument. The Guardian could have just run one of the essays in its entirety. However, instead the best parts of each were picked, in order to capture the different styles and registers of the AI. Editing GPT-3's op-ed was no different to editing a human op-ed and, overall, it took less time to edit.

https://doi.org/10.1515/9783110756166-005

instance. From that point of view, computers are, enunciated with brutal brevity, systematic architectures that take inputs, encode and manipulate information, and transform their inputs into outputs. Brains are, so far as we can tell, exactly that. (ibid.). (On philosophical grounds, versions of the computational theory of mind have been upheld by Fodor, 1975, 1987, 2008; Putnam, 1960, 1975; Ramsey, 2007; Schweizer, 2017; and repudiated by others, see Chpt. 12.1.)

But if we follow the hypothesis that our ordinary thinking is a computational process, should we also view our computers as thinking machines? What would the laptop I am writing this book on think of my piece? It is somewhat disheartening to see "how small" it has turned out to be. The entire text will end up taking about 10'000KB of storage – if I shrink the size of or remove the images/figures altogether, it can be twenty times less even. For comparison, just two seconds of the Vivaldi *Four Seasons* concert on my computer takes already more than 500KB. So in terms of sheer raw data, my laptop gives equal weight to this entire (simplified) book and to a bit less than two seconds of the video, serving maybe as a confirmation of the old adage that a picture – or a single frame of a video – is worth a thousand words. Be the latter as it may, many things would be wrong with such a comparison, to begin with that quantity (file size) should not be confounded with quality. More intriguing is the question though if or to what extent machines can think at all.

For most, if not all, of Western intellectual history, technology has been explained and conceptualized as an instrument or tool to be used more or less effectively by human agents (Gunkel, 2017: 6). As such, technology itself is just a more or less convenient or effective, but dumb means to an end, rooting in the doctrine of the *bête-machine* (Descartes, 1637/1997), and reinforced by the technophobia of modernist literature towards the question of AI. Ranging across texts by Emile Zola, Ambrose Bierce, H.G. Wells, E.M. Forster or Karel Čapek, March-Russell (2020) demonstrates that, whilst modernism may have been enthusiastic towards other forms of technological innovation, the possibility of a machine that could think (even more like a human) seems outrageous and stirred age-old responses about the boundaries between human and nonhuman life forms. For example, closer to home in philosophy, think of Wittgenstein's dictum: "Is it possible for a machine to think?": "The question is not analogous to that which someone might have asked a hundred years ago: 'Can a machine liquefy a gas?' The trouble is rather that the sentence, 'A machine thinks (perceives, wishes)' seems somehow nonsensical. It is as though we had asked 'Has the number 3 a colour?'" (Wittgenstein 1935/1958: 47 and cf. also Hoffmann, 2019a). But does it make more sense to ask what color my pen has? Has not science demonstrated the unreality of colors and many more things like life itself (simply because atoms are all there is, and atoms are not colored or alive; Dennett, 2017: 38)?

AI is the seventy years[11] old subfield of computer science that defies this tradition, devoted to building artificial animals and *animats* (Wilson, 1991) – or at least artificial creatures that in bespoke contexts appear to be animals. Many of its core formalisms and techniques come out of, and are indeed still much used and refined in, philosophy such as different logics, probability theory or the modeling of doxastic attitudes (Bringsjord & Govindarajulu, 2018). A parsimonious catalog of research areas that are classically included under the heading of AI without purporting to be exhaustive encompasses the following and shows already the difficulty of defining the field and term of AI (Schank & Towle, 2000: 341):

- *Robotics*: In its early days, robotics was a subfield of mechanical engineering with most research devoted to devising robots capable of executing particular actions, such as predetermined grasping, walking, and so on. For safety concerns, they were often in cages (Hoffmann, 2017c). Their control systems were dirt-simple, and did not make use of learning components. With intelligent structures on the horizon, cognitive robotics research was born to unleash the design of "complete intelligent systems that we let loose in the real world with real sensing and real action" (Brooks, 1991/1997: 395).
- *Natural Language Processing (NLP)*: This technique of AI dovetails both the generation and the comprehension of natural language, usually text. Its history dates back to the Turing Test (Chapter 8); today it is a burgeoning field of research into machine translation, question answering, automatic summarization, speech recognition, and others (Franklin, 2015: 26).
- *Planning*: An AI planner is a system which automatically devises a sequence of actions leading from an initial real-world state to a desired goal state (ibid.: 25). They may be used, for example, to find routes for package delivery, or to assign usage of the Hubble telescope.
- *Computer Vision*: Computer or machine vision is the subfield of AI impinging on the automated understanding of visual images, typically digital photographs. Among its many applications are product inspection, military intelligence, and traffic surveillance (ibid.: 26).
- *Rule-based or Knowledge-based Systems*: Every AI system must somehow translate input (stimuli) into information or knowledge to be used to select

---

11 At ETH Zurich, where I spent my postdoc, the ETH Turing Centre claims boldly that Alan "Turing founded the field now called Artificial Intelligence (AI). In February 1947, he delivered the earliest known public lecture to mention computer intelligence, and his technical report 'Intelligent Machinery' (written for the NPL in 1948) was AI's earliest manifesto." Source: https://www.turing.ethz.ch/alan-turing/ai-and-a-life.html (26-11-20). Cf. Cave et al. (2020) for a critical reply.

output (action). This information or knowledge must be represented in some way within the system, using logical formalisms such as propositional logic and first-order predicate calculus, so that it can be processed to help ascertain output or action. The problems raised along this series are commonly referred to as knowledge representation (ibid.: 24). The dispute of whether to represent or not seems to have been implicitly settled, as the arguments have died down. Brooks (1991) made his point that more than was previously thought could be accomplished without representation.
- *Computer Game Playing*: Employing more AI practitioners than any other (in 2015, today it might be a bit different, cf. D'Onfro, 2019), the computer game industry has been enjoying a screaming success (Franklin, 2015: 24). AI's role in this boom is decisive; its use is essential to producing the prerequisite intelligent behavior on the part of the virtual characters and avatars who populate the games. Wikipedia has a distinct entry entitled "Artificial intelligence in video games" (see hyperlink).
- *Case-based Reasoning*: This is a paradigm of AI modelling the reasoning process as primarily memory based. Case-based reasoners tackle new problems by retrieving stored "cases" describing similar prior problem-solving episodes and adapting their solutions to fit new needs (Leake, 2001). Case-based reasoning serves as a foundation for applied computer systems for tasks such as amplifying human decision-making, aiding human learning, and facilitating access to electronic information repositories (ibid.). And, prominently of course,
- *Machine Learning*: Though machine learning is as old as AI itself, it has experienced something of a renaissance, as more and more AI systems are operating more autonomously in progressively more complex and dynamically changing domains (Danks, 2015: 151). Machine learning can be supervised learning, in which the system is instructed using an often large training corpus, or unsupervised or self-organizing systems where any particular variables are *not* singled out as a target or focus in favor of a general overview of the full dataset. Reinforcement learning, achieved with artificial rewards, is typical for learning new tasks. Examples of supervised learning comprise learning algorithms for artificial neural networks or decision trees while various methods for probability distribution or density estimation fall under the heading of unsupervised learning (ibid.: 154f.). More on machine learning, below.
- Etc.

By looking at the 20 years since the turn of the millennium more closely, we witness "a new machine-learning paradigm" (Hao, 2019), perhaps even more outside of AI labs where AI is engulfed by machine learning. In light of the frequent trend changes in the AI world which has been characterized by the sudden rise and fall of divergent techniques for a long time, this proclamation has to be taken with a pinch of salt though; i.e., paradigm shift or not, AI does not mean machine learning and useful AI research does not require machine learning. With this caveat in mind, Hao (2019) found in her analysis three major trends: a shift toward machine learning during the late 1990s and early 2000s, a proliferation in the popularity of neural networks or deep learning as one specification beginning in the early 2010s, and reinforcement learning gaining momentum as a further specification in the past few years, coupled with the testing of a variety of other methods in the realm of machine learning such as Bayesian networks, support vector machines, and evolutionary algorithms. Figure 11 displays a simplistic Euler diagram where two representative examples of those latest developments, eminently stimulating for our purposes, are placed inside the machine learning principality.

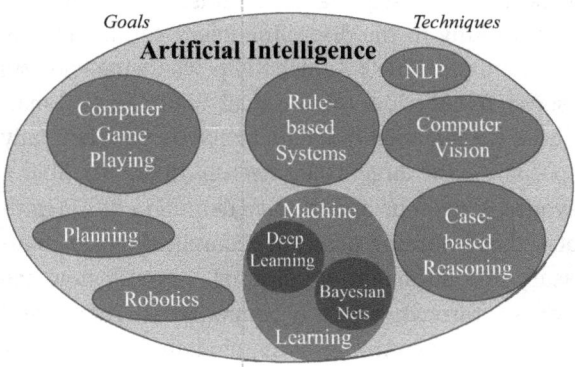

Figure 11: AI as a set with various subsets of goals and techniques (no claim on completeness).

Concisely defining a field which counts such diverse research areas is a nearly overwhelming effort. Computer game playing, for instance, shares little if anything with natural language processing, and yet these are both lumped under the title of AI. Or, as we will see in Part II, Bayesian models can substantially differ from deep learning and still both are subsumed under machine learning and, eo ipso, AI. Etc. Therefore, any definition of AI that would account for those different ramifications of AI might very well be at risk of being so inclusive as to be meaningless. Against this background, it does not bewilder us that a) the precise meaning of AI is ambiguous, and b) that there is a perplexing cacophony of conflicting opinions (Spindler & Hoffmann, 2019). We remain in the dark: *obscurum per obscurius*. John McCarthy originally coined the term AI in 1956, defining it as "the science and engineering of making intelligent machines" (Schofield, 2011). When the field of AI today appears broad and with fuzzy contours, it is perhaps for this reason. Under this definition, all the software (or hardware or robots) we use could be reckoned to be AIs, depending on how exactly we parse "intelligent". At the same time, the risk of an inflated term of AI is thwarted by the so-called *AI effect* (McCorduck, 2004; Haenlein & Kaplan, 2019) which occurs when detractors discount the behavior of an AI by arguing that it is not *true* intelligence, but *mere* computation: as soon as a computer can do something, that something does not require a substantial amount of intelligence anymore (cf. the complaint by McCarthy quoted in Vardi, 2012). Sadly, this view seems to work just fine due to the absence of conceptual clarity about intelligence (however, it should not impress us deeply if we listened to Marcus at the beginning of this Chapter).

So what exactly is AI? Philosophers arguably know better than anyone that trenchantly defining a particular term or discipline to the satisfaction of all germane parties (including those working in the discipline itself) can be acutely challenging (Bringsjord & Govindarajulu, 2018): Analogously, what characterizes biology in a comprehensive sense? What about intelligence? What, for that matter, is philosophy, exactly? These are remarkably arduous, maybe even eternally unanswerable, questions, especially if the target is a *consensus* definition (ibid.). Although elsewhere I was favoring a rigorous and incisive definition of AI (Hoffmann & Hahn, 2020, but not without warning about the complications emanating from introducing necessary and sufficient conditions), I would now see myself caught up in a long odyssey through scholarly communities. Therefore, I am more fond of another, more prudent course to accommodate the phenomenon of the AI effect and suspend the clandestine haemorrhage. Minsky's universal definition of (non-genuine) AI uses an ingenious trick, but is only accepted as a first approximation because otherwise we would indeed succumb to the veritable threat and trap of presenting a definition so inclusive as to be meaningless. With some parallels to the Dummettian (1976) Martian, learning to speak a human language,[12] Minsky (1968: v) puts forth the following definition:

> *Definition of AI*: "Science of making machines capable of performing tasks that would require intelligence if done by [humans or, in a weaker sense, by animals]."

---

[12] Or as Block (1981) couches it: "Suppose that the Martian and human psychologists agree that Martians and humans differ as if they were the products of a whole series of engineering decisions that differ along the lines illustrated. Should we conclude that the Martians are not intelligent after all? Obviously not! That would be crude human chauvinism."

As Hernández-Orallo (2017: 119) points out, this umbrella definition is in alignment to the *indirect characterization* principle. AI systems do not need to display intelligence or decompose the problems in a way that resembles how humans or animals sort out these problems. The only thing that matters is whether humans or animals exert intelligence for that problem (ibid.). As a consequence, we could now keep inside AI any artificial system which looks occasionally intelligent, even if it does not feature intelligence (ibid., see Figure 12).

Figure 12: "Warning! Intelligence NOT included". Should this be mandatory in most AI products, since they feature no intelligence at all? Source: Hernández-Orallo, 2017: 120.

The merits of Minsky's position, and the ultimate reason why we endorse it as a first approximation to capture "AI", is simply that it neatly sketches how the field has proceeded for 70 years (e.g., cf. also Arkoudas & Bringsjord, 2015: 34, who maintain the same thing as Minsky, just with more words) – a demanding, but empty extension of an AI concept, by contrast, would be useless. Nevertheless, Minsky's working definition might be unsatisfying at the end of the day as, on the one hand, we have witnessed that some problems that were supposed to presuppose human intelligence have been solved *without* human-level intelligence, such as driving a car or being good at chess (more systematically, we see this in Chapter 5).

On the other we would have to label our pocket calculators or toasters intelligent – in fact, what animal activity does not necessitate any intelligence at all? On the occasion of this prospect, Robinson (2015: 64) seems to reserve the Minskian definition for mere *task intelligence* (apparently disparate to genuine intelligence), which he coins as follows: "a device has AI just in case it can be used by us to carry out a task that would be agreed to require intelligence for execution [attention, here comes again the Minskian twist, C.H.] by a human being", according to which "even calculators have task intelligence". Block (1981), by contrast, concludes that "whether behavior is intelligent behavior is in part a matter of how it is produced. Even if a system has the actual and potential behavior characteristic of an intelligent being, if its internal processes are like those of the machine described [more on this in Chpt. 9], it is not intelligent." However, is this caveat to Minsky's definition really triggered by Minsky's own proposal or does it not rather originate from the ambiguity of the fundamental term "intelligence"?

Our technical intelligence definitions and evaluations eventually face the tribunal of reflectivity and practical wisdom. Hence, we regard Minsky's proposal as a good answer for an initial assessment only that frees us from bigotry and narrowmindedness (as experienced with a focus on human or animal intelligence) and points us to a recurrent circumstance: on the one hand, the dilemma between programmed and trained AI which is parallel to the dilemma between innate and acquired traits of animals seen in the previous Chapter; on the other hand, the question, who is authentically intelligent, the AI system itself or its programmer with the parallel to the animal kingdom where it is controversial (see Minsky's polemical view in the second veto against bird intelligence) who has acquired the policies, the animal itself or evolution (Hernández-Orallo, 2017: 119). Yet at the same time, Minsky's AI definition asks for some amendments in the next sections.

3.1 Intelligence from good old-fashioned AI to new-fangled AI

Both extreme positions that AI's intelligence is either not questioned or out of question do not do justice to a more nuanced reality. For the former, think of tech enthusiasts, digital utopians, "AI" entrepreneurs and startups that pride themselves with putting cutting-edge smart algorithms in place, but that in reality often just sell hot air (Hoffmann & Krawczuk, forthcoming; Spindler & Hoffmann, 2019; Hoffmann & Müller, 2019). For the latter camp, think of Wittgenstein's dictum cited above. As John Haugeland (1997b: 352) once remarked (who attributed it to Wes Salmon), one man's modus ponens is another man's modus tollens where the two premises for our two camps here could be something along the following lines: A "AI can do so many tasks that presuppose human intelligence", B "There is machine intelligence". This remark is prescient guidance for what is to come in Part IV: The views on the cognitive abilities of far-fetched *future* AI are not any less opposing. But first let us briefly look back, i.e., into the history and overarching themes of AI.

Unveiling that our current attitudes towards AI originate from long-standing and primordial feelings about artificial simulacra of the human, the history of AI narratives and imaginative thinking on intelligent machines is much older than McCarthy's coinage in the 1950s. It covers imaginings from the literature, mythology, and folklore of Ancient Greece, Classical Rome, Native America, Ghana, Borneo, Japan, Judaism, and Christianity which as constituent parts of any sociotechnical imaginary matter because "they form the backdrop against which AI systems are being developed, and against which these developments are interpreted and assessed" (Cave et al., 2020: 7). The first wave of technological scaffolding, well-captured in Haugeland's (1985: 112) indelible phrase "good old-fashioned AI" (GOFAI), took momentum with the Dartmouth workshop of 1956. The proponents of the early years and decades applauded a "top-down", "intellectualist" approach to AI where human experts write down what they know in a language the computer can manipulate. A GOFAI symbol is an item in a formal, i.e. programming language. The pivotal concepts that structure GOFAI programs are heuristic search and planning (Boden, 2015: 90). A GOFAI problem, or task, is represented as a search space: a set of possibilities (defined by a finite set of generative rules), within which the solution lies – and within which it must be found. Examples include the corpus of legal moves in chess, or of permissible word strings given some particular grammar and vocabulary (ibid.). From the mid 1950s to the mid 1980s, it was the dominant (though not the only) approach in AI (Haugeland, 1997b: 16). It grew out of vaguely Cartesian assumptions that also concern the grip on intelligence in that time (Cantwell Smith, 2019: 7):

> "C1: The essence of intelligence is thought, meaning roughly rational deliberation.
>
> C2: The ideal model of thought is logical inference (predicated on "clear and distinct" concepts, of the sort we associate with discrete words).
>
> C3: Perception is at a lower level than thought, and will not be that conceptually demanding."

And Boden (2015: 99) adds to the three pillars here the fourth that the Cartesian separation of mind, body, and world unleashed the lack of embodiment of

GOFAI programs. Regarding C1, when AI was founded, the term "intelligence" was given no specific meaning (Cantwell Smith, 2019: 8). The aim was simply to construct machines that intuitively seemed "smart" as an *alternative to* human intelligence which is why the view as to what constitutes an intelligent program changed considerably not only compared with requirements today, but also during that time itself (Dehn & Schank, 1982: 353). The principal strengths of GOFAI are its abilities to model hierarchy and sequential order, to facilitate precision in problem solving, and to represent specific propositional contents (Boden, 2015: 93). But, as we know from history, the GOFAI approach failed, for example epistemologically: Thinking and intelligence, on the GOFAI model, consisted of rational, articulated steps, on its founding model of logical inference (Cantwell Smith, 2019: 27). As Dreyfus and cognitive theorists like Weizenbaum (1976) insisted, a more accurate characterization of intelligence is one of skillful coping or navigation – "of being 'thrown' into individual and social projects in which we are embedded and enmeshed" (Cantwell Smith, 2019: 27). And the problem does not cease with GOFAI misconceiving cognition, but the deeper problem might even be that it misconceived the world as chopped up into neat, ontologically discrete objects. That the ascendancy of GOFAI ended does not mean that it is dead (see its strengths above); its rejection (not its disappearance; e.g., cf. Gärdenfors et al., 2019) was underpinned by a plethora of (philosophical) arguments which we will revisit in Chapter 12. When the GOFAI label was coined by the philosopher John Haugeland (1985: 112), his word "old-fashioned" implied that this type of AI had been superseded (Boden, 2015: 97). Under the new reign of second wave AI techniques, the classical assumption of a discrete, object-based "formal" ontology (Arp et al., 2015; Smith, 2003) is no longer a prerequisite. The center of gravity of AI thinking has shifted to machine learning and close cognates, which essentially is a suite of statistical techniques for:

1) the statistical classification and prediction of patterns (Cantwell Smith, 2019: 47).
2) based on, often avalanches of sample or training data (ibid.).
3) using an interwoven fabric of processors (ibid.).
4) arranged in multiple layers (ibid.), pointing to the sense of "deep" in "deep learning".

These techniques are implemented in architectures often referred to as "neural networks", because of their topological similarity to the way the brain is organized at the neural level (ibid.). Emulating Danks (2015: 155), machine learning algorithms must balance three factors: (1) the complexity of the learned model, which provides increased accuracy in representing the input dataset; (2) the generalizability of the learned model to new data, which sets the stage for the use of the model in novel contexts; and (3) computational tractability of learning and using the model, which is an imperative precondition for the algorithms to have practical value. Machine learning's aim is to use some *training data* to retrieve *patterns*, to discover and exploit structural relations among the data, and then to use these learned patterns to automatically address questions and to more or less autonomously execute tasks (Amir, 2015: 201). This structural inference underlies both its strengths and weaknesses. On the upside, for instance, these methods can be employed in a relatively domain-general manner, since the specific meaning of the variables is irrelevant to the functioning of the algorithm (Danks, 2015: 165). When used properly, machine learning can exploit the structure within data, often faster, more accurately, and less biased than humans (Miller, 2018), to yield valuable knowledge about structure and relations in the world (Danks, 2015: 165), e.g., for overhauling workflow efficiency for mammography by machine learning (Kyono et al., 2020).

Some known theoretical limits to machine learning are mirrored in the case when, for example, distinct patterns are missing, when data are too noisy (if they are essentially random), which renders learning nearly impossible. Nor can machine learning pan out if the assumptions about the nature of the world, which every interesting machine learning method makes, turn out to be false (Danks, 2015: 159). Yet, this argument-schema might actually speak against most inductive methods, and not just machine learning inference; put differently, it objects to machine *learning*, not *machine* learning. Beyond that fair criticism, machine learning techniques are sometimes regarded with a certain degree of suspicion, presented as "black boxes" that take data and, without any guidance, somehow learn part of the true structure of the world (ibid.: 165). These algorithms are, in reality, much less mysterious: The label of "automated statistics" is frequently an apt descriptor (ibid.) and a case-by-case treatment of AI deployments can unveil that some (maybe not all) applications rather unpack black boxes in lieu of incarnating one (Hoffmann & Heide, 2018; Hoffmann, 2020b; and see also Figure 13 below).

A good way to penetrate contemporary machine learning is in terms of juxtaposing it to GOFAI along four conceptual axes:
1) GOFAI asks for deep (many-step) inference, machine learning for shallow (few-step) inference.
2) GOFAI works with a serial process, machine learning with a massively parallel process.
3) GOFAI uses modest amounts of data, machine learning, at least given the present state of the art, requires massive amounts of data (Big Data). The latter are insatiable.
4) GOFAI involves a relatively small number of strongly correlated variables, whereas machine learning involves a very large number of weakly correlated variables.

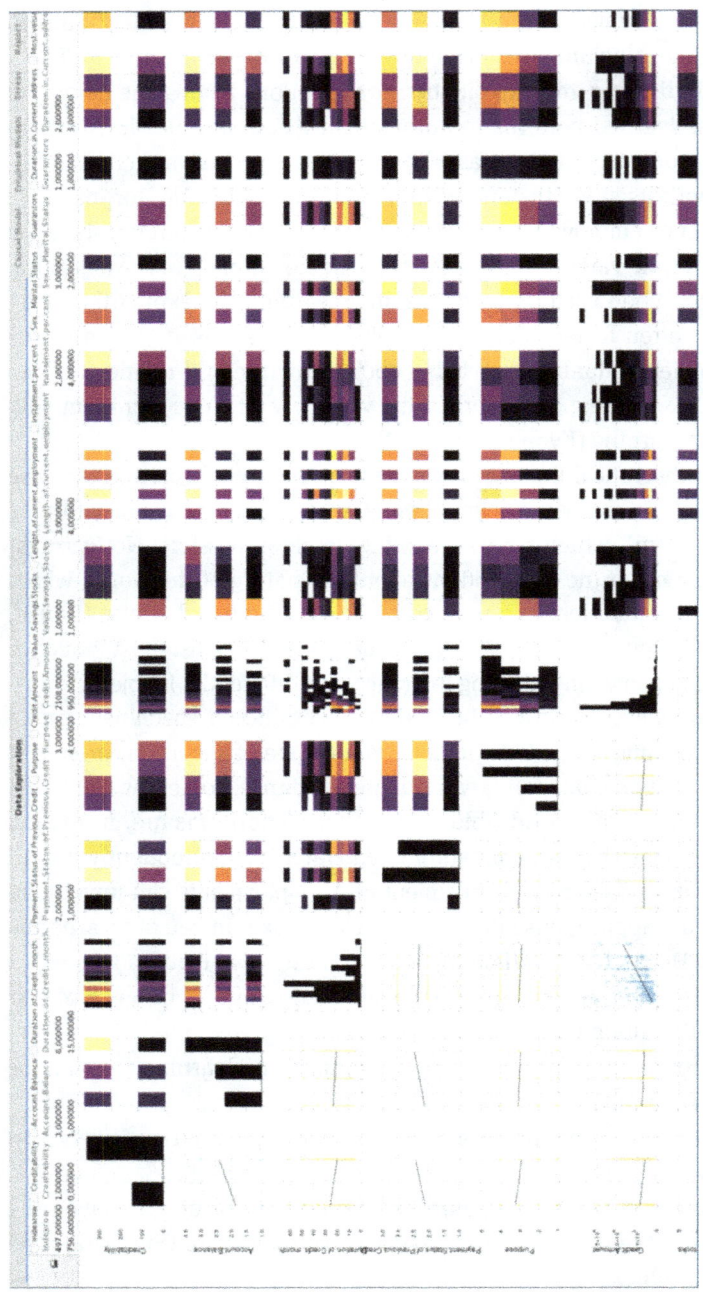

Figure 13: A view into the engine room for a specific machine learning application from a software startup, Syntherion, which this author co-founded at ETH Zurich in 2018, but which

These opposing positions can be described picturesquely by Levesque's (2018: 2f.) example of recognizing cat pictures (which stand for a broad class of use cases including commercially attractive ones like mammograms that may contain tumors which are hard for doctors to detect):

> [The computer system's job in question] will be to classify pictures it is given into two groups: those that depict cats and those that do not. The question then is how to build such a system. In the past [of GOFAI], AI programmers would have tried to write a program that looked for certain specific cat features in an image. It might look for a cat face: greenish or yellowish eyes with almond-shaped vertical pupils, an inverted pinkish triangle making up the nose, whiskers, and so on. Or perhaps it might look for a cat outline: a small head, triangular cat ears, four legs, and a tail that often points straight up. Or it might look for the distinctive coloring of cat fur. If the program spots enough of these features in an image, it would label the image as one of a cat, and otherwise reject it.
>
> But [machine learning] suggests a very different way of doing the job. You start by giving your system a very large number of digitized images to look at, some of which have cats in them and some of which do not. Then you tell your system to *compress* all this visual data in a certain way, that is, to look for a set of "features" that are seen in many patches of many images. A feature might be an area of a certain uniform color and brightness. It might be an area where there is a distinctive change in brightness and color corresponding to an edge. The idea is to find a set of features such that it is possible to reconstruct something similar to the original images as combinations of those features. Then you tell your system to abstract from those features, and to look for common features of those features. And so on for a few more levels. All this is done without telling the system what to look for. [. . .] What's important is that these features are determined by the images themselves, not by what an AI programmer thought was important about recognizing a cat in them.

The widespread use of machine learning techniques nowadays demonstrates that many AI systems are not programmed to do things, but trained to do things (Hernández-Orallo, 2017: 23). As Andrew Ng from Stanford boils it down: "You

---

Figure 13 (continued)
had to be shut down in the wake of the Covid pandemic in 2020 (because the Swiss bank, which we secured as a paying customer, froze the budget for the approved pilot project). The figure showcases feature cross-correlations in a prototype data exploration GUI (= graphical user interface) to estimate creditability (used as a proxy for risk of default in mortgage banking) for a publicly available credit dataset. The images within the image display those correlations between the different input variables of Syntherion's causal model such as "Accounting Balance" and "Creditability" to aid stress test analysts at banks with data exploration. Syntherion both trained a set of black box classifiers and employed causal models (specifically directed acyclic graph models) to capture the implicit assumptions in the current stress testing frameworks in banks and make them visible. This example is given for two reasons: a) it shows that machine learning applications can be very specific while general evaluations (like above) might not lend themselves to fathom subtle nuances (e.g., is Syntherion now nurturing the critique of black box AI or not?). b) causal modeling proves eminently pertinent in Part II.

throw a ton of data at the algorithm and you let the data speak and have the software automatically learn from the data." Before we come back to this maxim that "the world is its own best model" (Brooks, 1991) and critically scrutinize it in Part II, let us continue with the presentation of reasoning (first wave) or learning (second wave) machines and turn to the assessment of their intelligence for now.

What new-fangled AI shares with GOFAI is that, despite all the technological progress, the field of AI has usually evaluated its artifacts in terms of task performance, not really in terms of intelligence; and if the term "intelligence" is not just of anecdotal value, but comes with some actual bearing, then it is reduced to task performance like in the case of Newell & Simon (1976/1997b: 83): "For all information is processed by computers in the service of ends, and we measure the intelligence of a system by its ability to achieve stated ends in the face of variations, difficulties, and complexities posed by the task environment", complemented by (ibid. 97): "[. . .] it is natural that much of the history of artificial intelligence is taken up with attempts to build and understand problem-solving systems" (also see Minsky's definition above). And as Haugeland (1997b: 24) elaborates in the subsequent fragment:

> GOFAI is inspired by the idea that intelligence as such is made possible by explicit thinking or reasoning – that is, by the rational manipulation of internal symbol structures (interpreted formal tokens). Thus, GOFAI intentionality is grounded in the possibility of translation – *semantic* interpretation. [New-fangled AI], by contrast, is inspired initially by the structure of the brain, but more deeply, by the importance and ubiquity of nonformal pattern processing. Since there are no formal tokens (unless implemented at a higher level), there can be no semantically interpreted symbols.

This points to another common complaint about AI, one which was introduced as competence without comprehension in Chapter 2 and which is indeed addressed in our framework in Part II. AI, of whatever stripe, pays scant attention to comprehension and imagination, feelings and moods, ego and consciousness – the whole "phenomenology" of an inner life (Haugeland, 1997b: 27). No matter how "smart" the machines become, so the worry goes, there is still "nobody home" (ibid.). Here, we focus only on one form of the worry, one that strikes me as more basic than the others, and also more intimately connected with cognition narrowly conceived: *grosso modo*, neither old-fashioned nor new-fashioned AI takes *understanding* seriously – where understanding or comprehension (we use these terms synonymously) itself is understood as distinct from knowledge (in whole or in part), and as a form of representation of the world, which is affirmed by neurobiology: "Intelligence [or as we would specify, understanding] is intimately tied to the brain's model of the world" (Hawkins, 2021: 4).

In 4.1., it is suggested to specify understanding as a third-level competence which presupposes knowledge and (practical) intelligence. Finally, in Chapter 5, "understanding" is analyzed more precisely in causal terms which yields an understanding of "understanding" that is akin to the casting in 4.1. For the moment though, it is sufficient to take meta-cognition as sufficient (not necessary) for comprehension. In this light, it seems that only people and select animals like crows that seem to know that they know (Nieder et al., 2020) ever understand anything – no artifacts (yet). I suspect there is considerable merit in these misgivings, though, of course, more in some forms (cf. Dennett, 2017; Cantwell Smith, 2019: 76; and see first and foremost our Part II) than in others (e.g., under the guise of Searle's famous Chinese Room argument, see Chapter 12.3.). The general problem of constructing intelligent creatures, of mind design, is that AI systems, like pictures or novel characters, are also artifacts. So, it can seem that their comprehension too must always be derivative – "borrowed from their designers or users, presumably – and never original" (Haugeland, 1997b: 7). Yet, if the project of producing a system with a mind of its own is ever really to succeed, then it must be possible for an AI system to have genuine *original* understanding, just as we, and probably crows and a few other animals do. Is that possible? Prior to moving on with deducing a constructive answer to this daunting challenge of what it requires for a system to comprehend, we shed light on some further peculiarities of machine intelligence or the absence thereof in AI.

A subfield of AI where the disparagement of embodiment of intelligence in AI has been viewed critically is robotics. When we look at early robot deployments in industrial settings, we find that these have not had much to do with intelligence or intelligent behavior. Their working environment is often designed in a circumspect way so that intricate sensory feedback is dispensable; "the robot performs its repetitive tasks in an accurate, efficient, but essentially unintelligent way" (Husbands, 2015: 273). In this light, Brooks (1991/1997), an effective voice of the dissidents from the old AI mainstream of custodians of an essentially Cartesian view in AI, proposes looking at simpler animals as a bottom-up model for designing intelligence. Inspired by where evolution has concentrated its time to yield intelligence, he believes that mobility, acute vision and the ability to withstand survival-related efforts in an ever-changing environment provide a crucial basis for the bottom-up design of natural intelligence. Perhaps, this comes at the price of stripping away "reasoning" as the prime substrate of a robot's intellect (with a very loose parallel to the current "thinking fast and slow in AI" debate, Booch et al., 2020 and Garcez & Lamb, 2020: section 6, in homage to Daniel Kahneman, and the plea for system 1 over system 2).

Copying Nature's best tricks, it has been held that the engineering of mobile autonomous robots ought to be absolutely central to AI. At the heart of Brooks' (1986) approach was the idea of behavioral decomposition, as opposed to the traditional functional decomposition by GOFAI. Figure 14 illustrates Brooks' concept, imbued by biology, particularly invertebrate neuro-ethology (Husbands, 2015: 277), bringing it close to both the AI extension of so-called (hard) artificial life (Bedau, 2015: 297; Dennett, 1998) as well as the cybernetic roots of AI.

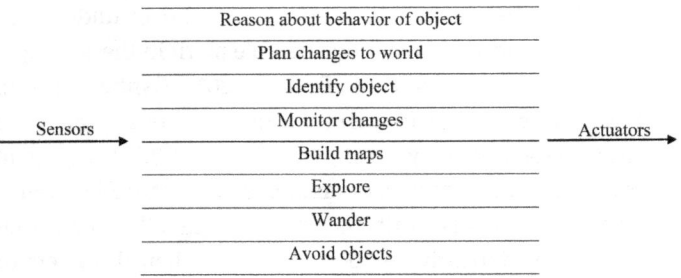

Figure 14: The parallel behavioral dismantlement for robot control as advocated by Brooks (1986) and the behavior-based approach.

The overall control architecture, which can be partitioned at any level with the levels below always forming a complete control system, is predicated upon the coordination of several loosely coupled behavior-generating systems all acting in sync (Husbands, 2015: 277). Each is amenable to sensors and actuators and is poised to act as a standalone control system (ibid.). Every layer was thought of as a *level of competence* of AI, with the "simpler" competences at the bottom of the vertical decomposition and the "more complex" ones at the top (ibid.; Brooks, 1986). In our third case study of animal intelligence, we witnessed, however, that purportedly unadorned competences such as exploring and wandering can facilitate the hallmark of intelligence, in this case of octopus intelligence, a highly intelligent representative of the animal kingdom. Brooks' work triggered the formation of a movement to deepen our understanding of natural intelligence outside of biology/psychology, and to stimulate new trajectories for the engineering of intelligent artifacts, propelling robotics back to the forefront of AI. (A counterbalance to this push is voiced in Sloman, 2009: 248, namely that "over-emphasis on embodiment has held up progress".)

And indeed, with more complex instances of robots proliferating, covering cluttered, dynamic, or noisy environments, or delicate manipulations of objects, necessitating more sophisticated sensory feedback and perceptual processing, this brings us into the realm of intelligent robotics (Husbands, 2015: 273). (For an example of state-of-the-art drone technology owned by a company where this author worked as Head of Finance, cf. Hoffmann, 2017c, 2017d; and see also Figure 15 below.) From this angle, it may turn out to be straining to "draw a line between what is intelligence and what is environmental interaction"

3.1 Intelligence from good old-fashioned AI to new-fangled AI — 75

Figure 15: Three different kinds of robots. Top: A cumbersome articulated industrial robot operating in a foundry, displaying no intelligence. Middle: Inventory control drone in a warehouse as a human-piloted, remote-controlled puppet, relying entirely on humans to steer its movements and provide the delusion of its limited "intelligence". Source: Hoffmann, 2017c: 25. Bottom: Cirque du Soleil – PARAMOUR on Broadway – at the Lyric Theatre in New

(Brooks, 1991/1997: 418), which reminds us of the systems metaphor of intelligence advocated in Chapter 1.

Briefly immersing ourselves in the investigation of complete autonomous sensorimotor systems as "artificial creatures", in demarcation to the maybe less fruitful development of disembodied algorithms for abstract problem solving, suggests the more general lesson of defying the tacit equation of machine intelligence with thinking machines at the cost of viewing AI as *intelligent actors/ agents* (Russell & Norvig, 2009). Returning to Minsky's definition of AI above, answers to "What is AI?" are given in terms of its goals: "AI is the field that aims at building . . .". As Bringsjord & Govindarajulu (2018) evince, the completed answers all fall under a quartet of types placed along two dimensions. One dimension is whether the goal is to match human performance, or, instead, ideal rationality. The other dimension is whether the goal is to build systems that *think*, or rather, following the thrust of robotics, systems that *act*. The situation is summed up in Table 5:

Table 5: A quartet of possibilities of task goals for AI.

Thinking-Based	Systems that think like humans	Systems that think rationally
Behavior-Based	Systems that act like humans	Systems that act rationally
AI	*Human-Based*	*Ideal Rationality*

In this light, one may hold that Minsky's proposal is not so much fraught with tension towards robotics, yet still arbitrarily myopic (given the focus on tasks) and anthropocentric since it falls under the rubric of acting humanly. The same position is occupied most prominently by Turing (1950), whose test (see Chapter 8) is passed only by those AI systems ready to act sufficiently human-like. Without wishing to belatedly decline the Minskian offer (and more as an exemplification of the practical impossibility of achieving consensus definitions mentioned above), opposing views to that lower left corner in Table 5 have been adopted and vindicated. Haugeland (1985) is notably affiliated with the Human/

Figure 15 (continued)
York City, featuring flying machine design and choreography by Verity Studios where the drones exhibit imposing levels of intelligence in terms of more autonomous action and mobile robot localization. Source: Hoffmann, 2017d. [If you look for a dance on the ground, there is really no way around the dance invitation by Boston Dynamics as documented by this 2020 end of the year special: https://www.youtube.com/watch?fbclid=IwAR26JjWqDA-l2dLE9 l6O677jOUD8TxzPKePPz_-oSmP49stmpjYaHK61so8&v=fn3KWM1kuAw&feature=youtu.be (30–12-20).].

Thinking quadrant when he brings forward that: "[t]he exciting new effort to make computers think [. . .] machines with minds, in the full and literal sense." Both Haugeland's as well as Minsky's/Turing's territory is exposed to the same hazard of criticism. Many examples, such as the Copernican revolution or Darwin's theory of evolution, teach us that we are not as special as we would like to believe. In this respect, it is strenuous to envision what special milestone would be met by AI engineering if machines catch up with human-level thinking or behavior, which is then sometimes said to herald the demise of humanity (Bostrom, 2016; see Part IV). A so-called tipping point may very well exist in principle, but to locate it so one-dimensionally and in relation to human beings is arbitrary. Finally, Nilsson (1998) and Winston (1992) defend the stance of acting rationally, and of thinking rationally, respectively. At this point, one could wonder where suddenly this accentuation of ideal rationality comes from.

Here, Russell (1997), who, in turn, follows the footsteps of Newell (1982), can help out. The former recasts the "What is AI?" question as the question "What is intelligence?" (presumably under the assumption that we have a good grasp of what an artifact is), and then he identifies intelligence with rationality (Bringsjord & Govindarajulu, 2018). According to his expected utility conception (an area which I, as a former micro economist, know all too well and which I assess critically; Hoffmann, 2021b, 2020c), perfect rationality can be taken to be the function which begets the *maximum* expected utility in the environment under consideration. Although Russell himself champions a new brand of intelligence/rationality for AI which he calls *bounded optimality*, we do not purchase that brand.

Absorbing intelligence by rationality is harmful for a broad and unprejudiced discussion of intelligence because, if one plays the advocatus diaboli and defends the Aristotelian idea that human minds differ not only in degree, but in kind, from other minds, then the go-to vindication is that humans alone are *rational*. Rationality unmasks itself as a diminutive constituent of intelligence. The term has arguably such an exclusive meaning since it denominates a *meta*-cognitive capacity which (so far) enables humans alone to reflect on the reasons for their beliefs and actions, and to then revise their beliefs and actions in light of those reasons (Boyle, 2018). Intelligence, by contrast, is much less exclusive; for example, with reference to how ample and encompassing we found intelligence in humans, animals and also artificial animals (to a much more limited extent though) to be. The subsequent Table 6 reminds us of that and integrates our gained insights from inquiring machine intelligence so far in the right column.

A general conclusion to draw from Table 6 is that it is very different if we evaluate a toddler or an adult, a crow or an octopus, an "intelligent" home cleaner or a reinforcement learning system "playing" games. A general warning about it is that the three classes of human, animal, and machine intelligence may

Table 6: Human-Level or Animal-Level AI? Designing AI mapped against the idiosyncrasies of human and animal intelligence as well as against the focal interest of human and animal intelligence research. This table unashamedly takes some credit from Hernández-Orallo (2017); see indications in row 4 and 5.

	Human intelligence	Animal intelligence	Machine intelligence
Investigator	Many: Psychology, neuroscience, linguistics, religion, etc.	Few: Comparative psychology, animal cognition studies	Nobody: AI is focused on task performance, not intelligence
Purpose of investigating approaches	Diagnosis, education, measuring intelligence (IQ), understanding the brain	Understanding animal intelligence and brains, more qualitative & less quantitative measurements of intelligence	AI is concerned with AI engineering
Intelligence tests (cf. Hernández-Orallo, 2017: 153)	Many, and standard test batteries	Usually few, single experiments	Usually few (like the Turing Test), no benchmark
Test interfaces (ibid.)	Pen and paper, computerized	Specialized apparatus	Inputs and outputs, robotic

Hallmarks of intelligence	– Imagination powers (e.g., resulting in well-functioning, flexible groups of any size) – Broad and multiple intelligences – From the composition in Table 4, musical and intrapersonal intelligence protrude, presupposing higher-order capabilities like reflection, introspection or involving abstract, ethereal entities like music (and to a lesser degree math and language which are more concept-loaded and rule-governed) that do not exist in other animals' imagination (as far as we know)	– Broad and multiple intelligences – Competence without comprehension or consciousness is much more common than in humans – Since different animals live different lives, they feature different strengths, including intellectual strengths – Such characteristics are beyond the human faculty and comprise, for example: body language of horses, "communication" skills of whales or decentralized sensing capacities of octopuses	– Narrow and, arguably, no intelligence at all – Competence without comprehension or consciousness is the rule without any exceptions to the present day – Competence is less multifaceted than in organic animals, e.g., "disembodied" AI misses the whole part of physics-related intelligences such as spatial and bodily-kinesthetic intelligence – The grandeur of AI are their spectacular performances for well-defined tasks and settings, sometimes outshining humans (e.g., chess or Go)
Evaluation orientation	Feature-oriented	Feature-oriented	Performance-based

not be so different after all in another, categorical sense. The cramped confines between humans and non-human animals have well been trespassed in Chapter 1 and 2 already, because there are species and individuals all along a continuum of biological intelligence (cf., for example, a comparative study suggesting that toddlers and chimps do not differ much at all in some regards like solving tasks of spatial cognition; Herrmann et al., 2009; Herrmann & Call, 2012). But also the transition from humans to machines is more gradual than categorical: not just speaking for rare or future cases of cyborgs (Clark, 2003), but for the bulk of people in the twenty-first century for whom it is *natural* to interact with the world by making use of ubiquitous technology such as an internet connection or a *smart* phone, e.g., for saving our memories on it (Vold, 2018; Clark & Chalmers, 1998).

Contrary to the proportions in human and animal intelligence research, the advocates of performance evaluation of AI in lieu of a feature-oriented evaluation have prevailed: "[T]he more that we can make it clear that we are interested in *performance*, rather than intelligence, *per se*, the better off we will be" (Simmons, 2001: 162). We saw in Chapter 1 already that it makes more sense to refer to abilities, potentials and properties for grasping and evaluating intelligence than statically to actual performance at a certain point in time. Nonetheless, task-specific and feature-specific assessments are compatible and both applicable for some autonomous systems: For example, "a robotic cleaner can be evaluated in terms of its task (cleaning), but also in terms of its spatial or planning abilities" (Hernández-Orallo, 2017: 146). The latter may also be more suitable when we talk about general-purpose AI systems (e.g., Adams et al., 2012).

As the comparison in Table 6 shows though, the signature of AI's "intelligence" up to today is that it is still far from general-purpose AI systems, but instead tends to be *narrow*, with each system able to accomplish only very specific goals (Tegmark, 2018: 81): "[T]he construction of artificial general intelligent systems is actually one of the biggest challenges of the twenty-first century" (Hernández-Orallo, 2017: 151). By contrast, human and animal intelligence, as seen in Chapter 1 and 2, is, already today and since long, remarkably *broad*, i.e., we are able "to operate successfully in a wide variety of environments" (Russell & Norvig, 2009: 32). In this respect, we must be very clear about separating the global AI momentum (on the collection of more and more problems that are tackled by the collection of AI systems over time) from the realization of one *single* AI system that solves specific, and as Table 6 maintains, not too many tasks.

Narrow vs. general artificial intelligence can be well-captured in the famous image of the hedgehog vs. fox by Isaiah Berlin (1953/1999) who in turn traces it back to the Greek poet Archilochus who said: "The fox knows many things, but the hedgehog knows one big thing" (ibid.: 1). And Berlin (1953/1999: 2) supplements:

[T]aken figuratively, the words can be made to yield a sense in which they mark one of the deepest differences which divide writers and thinkers, and, it may be, human beings in general. For there exists a great chasm between those, on one side, who relate everything to a single central vision, one system, less or more coherent or articulate, in terms of which they understand, think and feel – a single, universal, organizing principle in terms of which alone all that they are and say has significance – and, on the other side, those who pursue many ends, often unrelated and even contradictory, connected, if at all, only in some de facto way, for some psychological or physiological cause, related to no moral or aesthetic principle. These last lead lives, perform acts and entertain ideas that are centrifugal rather than centripetal; their thought is scattered or diffused, moving on many levels, seizing upon the essence of a vast variety of experiences and objects for what they are in themselves, without, consciously or unconsciously, seeking to fit them into, or exclude them from, any one unchanging, all-embracing sometimes self-contradictory and incomplete, at times fanatical, unitary inner vision. The first kind of intellectual and artistic personality belongs to *hedgehogs*, the second to the *foxes;* and without insisting on a rigid classification, we may, without too much fear of contradiction, say that, in this sense, Dante belongs to the first category, Shakespeare to the second; Plato, Lucretius, Pascal, Hegel, Dostoevsky, Nietzsche, Ibsen, Proust are, in varying degrees, hedgehogs; Herodotus, Aristotle, Montaigne, Erasmus, Molière, Goethe, Pushkin, Balzac, Joyce are foxes.

Despite the steady progress toward not only higher levels of performance in specific domains, but as well toward widening the range of those domains, most AI right now is still at the hedgehog stage, and at least at the stage 30 years ago with the fresh memories from the disappointing AI Winter this may have been neither a shortcoming nor an accident: "No one talks about replicating the full gamut of human intelligence anymore" (Brooks, 1991/1997: 395). We have been refurbishing systems that can do one thing or task very well: IBM's Deep Blue (a GOFAI) is a chess grandmaster, AlphaGo (a new-fangled AI) a world champion of Go and GPT-3 (another new-fangled AI) can "write" appealing op-eds. We have not yet built foxes, AI systems with a general suite of capacities. For instance, as McDermott (1997) illustrates: "[IBM's] Deep Blue is unintelligent because it is so narrow. It can win a chess game, but it can't recognize, much less pick up, a chess piece. It can't even carry on a conversation about the game it just won. [The] essence of intelligence would seem to be breadth, or the ability to react creatively to a wide variety of situations." The moral of this story is clear: "just because something manages to appear intelligent for a moment or two doesn't mean that it really is, or that it can handle the full range of circumstances a human would" (Marcus & Davis, 2019: 19f.).

In some sense, I find this narrow-mindedness partially in conflict with the perhaps most basic idea of computer science, namely of using one automatic formal system to *implement* another, commonly designated as *programming*: "Instead of building some special computer out of hardware, you build it out of software; that is, you write a program for a 'general purpose' computer"

(Haugeland, 1997b: 12), which can, in principle, do anything any computer can do (ergo, a universal machine; Turing, 1937). Thus, seen from its inception, computer science (and, ipso facto, AI) is laid out broadly, not narrowly. (Along these lines, from AI practitioners' or users' point of view, global AI, today, is a *general*-purpose technology; Jöhnk et al., 2020).

Notwithstanding, AI today struggles with a situation which is sometimes dubbed Moravec's paradox, which stated that it was "comparatively easy to make computers exhibit adult-level performance in solving problems on intelligence tests or playing checkers, and difficult or impossible to give them the skills of a one-year-old when it comes to perception and mobility" (Moravec, 1988: 15). In contrast to toddlers and most animals, modern AI systems cannot just be placed in new environments and be expected to function intelligently (Crosby et al., 2019). The quest for artificial general intelligence has, thus far, not been achieved. Looking ahead, an effective home cleaning robot would need to navigate a complex, rapidly changing environment of an average household, circumventing objects, my discombobulated dog, myself, and so on, while taking my finished plate of truffle pasta to the dishwasher, which all in all requires general intelligence. This, in turn and by looking at Nature, could make some new *features* of AI systems indispensable to combat their brittleness and fragility.

A preliminary and non-exhaustive proposal includes 1) robustness, resilience and non-brittleness (i.e., the ability to do tasks without getting stuck, caught or lost), 2) flexibility (i.e., the ability to take what is known from one task and apply it to another), and 3) autonomy (i.e., the ability to do what is done without constant repair, adjustment or constant oversight by a third party; cf. also Shevlin et al., 2019). As animals excel brilliantly in all these benchmarks, AI researchers and engineers may want to learn more from Nature for the next leap forward in AI (Crosby, 2020; Crosby et al., 2019). To give a concrete example, recall and compare the myriad of *supervised* machine learning systems with baby octopuses that are left without a mother, without a father, that cannot reckon with the support of the siblings, that are left, in short, to their own resources from day one and still attain all those incredible achievements we saw.

Unlike narrow AIs that hinge on handcrafted rules (GOFAI or "first wave") or domain-specific machine-learning systems trained on usually large data sets ("second wave"), the next wave of AI aspires to create machines that will "function more as colleagues than as tools" with capacities to "understand and reason in context" (DARPA, 2019). Interestingly, a puzzle piece of that third wave AI could just come from overcoming the obsolete nature (GOFAI) versus nurture (New-Fangled AI or NFAI) dichotomy (Valiant, 2013: 138), which is a bit of a false dichotomy anyways because, speaking generally about minds and not AI, nature (i.e., how much of the structure of the mind is built in or innate knowledge) and nurture (i.e., how much of it is learned) work in concert, not in opposition (Marcus & Davis, 2019: 143). Bye-bye pure GOFAI and NFAI systems, hello hybrids (Marcus, 2020; Booch et al., 2020; Garcez & Lamb, 2020; Gärdenfors et al., 2019; D'Avila Garcez & Besold, 2019; Tenenbaum et al., 2011: 1279; McCallum et al., 2009; Valiant, 2003, mirroring a vigorous consensus in cognitive science *and* AI that, besides empirical learning, symbols and structures are essential for thought).

With our silos filled up like this, let us head back to the present(-day machine GPT-3) and the opening quote of this Chapter 3 by asking ourselves who (or what) is the legitimate author of the Guardian article. This little exercise informs us about how intelligent we deem that machine to be in this *narrow* context of writing op-eds. The short answer would be to just look it up in the back, in the reference section, and we would find GPT-3 listed as the (single) author. Going into the heart of the matter, the question would then obviously be why this author made this delicate decision. In order to grasp on this question, we need to look inside and see what happens within GPT-3, in the "machine room" so to say. At one extreme, if we had found inside a file or a memorized version of the piece, all loaded and ready to run, then the programmer(s) or a distinct team of human authors behind would be the legitimate originator, using their intermediate creation, GPT-3, as a mere storage-and-delivery-device, a particularly fancy, but ultimately shallow word processor. All the R&D work would have been done earlier and copied to GPT-3 by one means or another. However, when we review the background of the GPT-3 article (in Footnote 10), we notice that we are far from such an extreme case, and instead entered the land of serious authorship.

This assertion may be disconcerting for many, but as usual, we may quote Ludwig Mies van der Rohe at this juncture: "God is in the details." On the one hand, the little editing and moderate amount of input needed geared with an arguably rigorous train of thought and the degree of fluency, eloquence, versatility and variability exhibited entices the reader to refer to GPT-3 as the author (and we just yielded to that temptation). A temptation which at the end of the day stems from the fact that we routinely take each other's words as settling beyond any reasonable doubt the question of whether we each have minds (Dennett, 1996: 8). [And apparently, we are very ingenious about and creative at fooling ourselves, not just when it comes to AI, but also to biological and artificial animals, as well visible from the example of the "AI"-based "Meow-Talk" app developed by a former Amazon Alexa engineer; cf. Criddle, 2020. As the engineer's appalling argument runs, we take the more or less established fact that cats have minds, cf. Andrews & Beck, 2018, as settling beyond any reasonable doubt the question of cats' high linguistic intelligence and it is just left for us to translate their utterances into plain English. Eureka, thank God for *MeowTalk*! Or perhaps the developer has read too often or, worse, not at all the *fictional* story on "The Soul of Martha, a Beast" whom we will meet in 4.3. Back to GPT-3.]

Still, is that it or is GPT-3 not just the latest edition of computer-assisted authorship, the process by which human authors use technology to enhance the writing process? Indeed, even though the technology at the core of the Guardian's op-ed is quite stunning, it is useless without humans in the mix. From selecting the prompts for the piece to the final editing, it was a human affair from beginning to end. Picking those variables, "the choice of argument, perspective, goal and format – these are the defining feature of authorship. Calling this robot-authored is much like saying a car on cruise control is 'self-driving', since you can take your foot of the gas." (Fox Cahn, 2020).

To push the metaphor further, autonomous driving comes at five different stages (Hoffmann & Dahlinger, 2020: 55), yet, in our case of the Guardian article, there is not only a gradual, but also a fundamental difference to human authors: GPT-3 does not have a clue what it is talking about when it rightfully calls for contributions to the epistemological and philosophical debate about AI (which we will inspect further in Part II and III). Against this background, it does not surprise that GPT-3 "struggles" with common sense inferences that a human would find straightforward (Brown et al., 2020). The lack of grounding for (i.e. model-free) AI systems trained on text alone is an insuperable barrier to their ever fully matching humans in this respect (Shanahan et al., 2020: 865). This might only change with the advent of strong AI.

3.2 Outlook: Philosophy versus simple economics of AI

If third wave AI is about general intelligence, then the fourth wave is about strong intelligence in artifacts or, simply, about *strong AI* (see Table 7). Broad intelligence, I suppose, will be reached earlier since it would consolidate *extant* machine capabilities, whereas we are not anywhere near to endowing machines with fully-fledged understanding which is on a higher level and which is indispensable for strong AI. But what is strong AI? Searle (1980: 417) invoked a distinction between strong AI and weak AI. Strong AI is the thesis that "the appropriately programmed computer really *is* a mind, in the sense that computers given the right programs can be literally said to *understand* and have other cognitive states"; and not just a mind, but a bona fide mind in the sense of playing a proper causal role for the way in which it influences the world (Kistler, 2016). Can mentality be reproduced in computational machines or, couched in different terms, can computational systems behave like cognitive systems, exhibiting and duplicating, among others, the creative and flexible behavior that humans display (Chalmers, 1996: 313)? The *strong AI hypothesis*, which we scrutinize together with its antitheses in Part IV, is that such computer programs are (technically) possible. (But maybe, it is more based on faith than science, and thus irrefutable; Floridi, 2015: 8; which Popper would not like to hear about a hypothesis.) Strong AI, as a research program, is the attempt to make computer programs that think in the same manner and with the same depth and richness that humans do. It seeks to beget such artificial persons: machines that have all the mental powers we have, sometimes including "phenomenal consciousness" (Bringsjord & Govindarajulu, 2018).

Weak AI purports only that computers, we are all too well acquainted with, provide an expedient *tool* for rigorous formulation and testing of hypotheses about the mind (Robinson, 2015: 65). This dichotomy we can muster together with the one from the previous subchapter about narrow vs. general AI which then results in the following two graphics, whereby the first emits a more conceptual summary and the second enriches the overview with some tangible AI examples and more refined scales.

Table 7: A triplet of stages for big leaps in AI engineering.

General	Third wave AI	Fourth wave AI
Narrow	Status quo	Not possible
AI	*Weak*	*Strong*

Legend: ↓ *Time*

I deem the lower right quadrant not only practically impossible (engineering-wise, the fourth wave necessitates the progress realized with the third wave), but also logically: According to my reading of Searle (1980: 417), a real mind cannot just excel at one task (see also our precise definitions in Part IV, page 207).

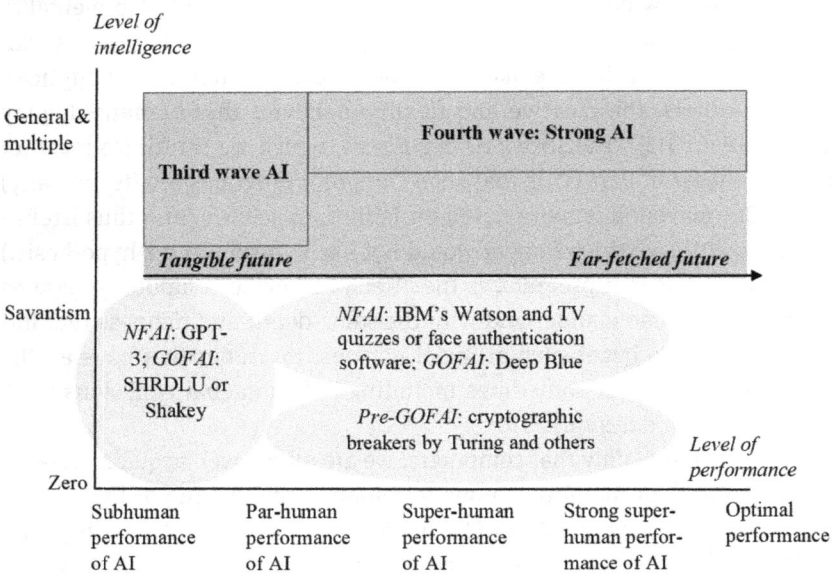

Figure 16: Four waves determine the AI universe. Prior to the Dartmouth conference in 1956, cryptographic breakers became superhuman (i.e., performing better than most humans), if not strong superhuman (i.e., performing better than all humans), in the 1940s with the aid of Turing who was the central force in continuing to solve the Nazis' Enigma code in the UK, during World War II (Robinson, 2020). Some examples of GOFAI, like the NLP program SHRDLU (Winograd, 1972) or Shakey (Nilsson, 1984), which was a robot that could reason about colored blocks in its environment, as well as some instances of NFAI (New-Fangled AI), such as the program GPT-3 from the Guardian, are not only idiots savants, but also do worse than most humans for select tasks (a subhuman performance). Other examples of GOFAI like IBM's Deep Blue or NFAI like IBM's question-answering computer system Watson surpass humans in narrow contexts like chess or Jeopardy!, which makes AI undeniably a triumph, but today's machine kingdom is crowded with blinkered specialists. Human AI experts are, therefore, paving the way for engineering competent generalists, which will herald the third era – a reasonable prospect. By contrast, the outlook to build strong AI some day is more speculative or outlandish, depending on whom you ask (see Table 9 in Part IV). The five-stage scale on the x-axis was uttered by Rajani (2011).

The few examples of AI systems staged in Figure 16 just allow us to catch a glimpse on the very dynamic AI environment, culminating in exponential trends like Moore's law (to be revisited later on), where more and more AI systems have outcompeted humans in more and more ways. Especially with regards to NFAI or second-wave AI, one can group the myriad of incumbent machine learning systems along the application to the broad field of *predictions* (particularly where the requirements of data affluence and sufficient regularity are fulfilled). This inspired Agrawal et al. (2018) to name their book, which I synthesized and commented on in a brief review (Hoffmann, 2018a), as well as AI nowadays "Prediction machines" with the telling subtitle being "The simple economics of Artificial Intelligence". In it, they show that AI is actually flying a false flag. But unlike above, where intelligence was abandoned in favor of task performance, Agrawal et al. (2018) argue that AI is admittedly not about intelligence as a whole, but only about one – albeit essential – component thereof: the faculty to "predict", which does not have to be forward-looking. The three authors, all professors at the Rotman School of Management at the University of Toronto, grasp it simply as the use of information that we already possess, in short, data, to obtain information that we do not yet possess. For example, if certain blood samples, measurements or symptoms of a patient are available as data input, then it can be "predicted" that a tumor is malignant. The main take-away from this book for ours is that intelligence lies in to some degrees autonomously finding out what will be or in detecting associations; higher levels of intelligence go beyond that, but, as we will spell out in Part II, hand in hand with *figuring out why* a prediction holds true or *why* a certain correlation exists. Nota bene that I am not asserting that intelligence lies in *every* computer system which makes predictions. If a system's capacity merely echoes the intelligence of another system, e.g., of the AI's programmers, the first system's capacity is thereby misleading as an indication of its intelligence (Block, 1981). However, at least latest AI technology's performances are no longer *all* echoes of humans behind the scenes (cf. e.g., Silver et al., 2017 or Tegmark, 2018: 88 for how these experts comment on the creative force of AlphaGo; and cf. Clark, 2016, who emphasizes on prediction (machines including the brain) in the study of mind).

The dynamism in thriving AI conveys the genuine or compelling reason for why to wonder if machines are or should be deemed intelligent. With some restrictions they might have been by and large shallow automata in the past, but contempt backfires when we emulate Agrawal et al. (2018) and Hoffmann (2018a) who contend that much AI around us today has *some* intelligence; and even more it backfires, once more critical milestones in AI engineering are reached (see Part II). Phantasies of strong AI, sheer castles in the air from our current point of view (see Part IV), are fueled by the hybris of extrapolating that dynamics with the goal of beating Darwin's slow evolution that "progresses" by the mechanism he named "natural selection" (Pagel, 1999): "[H]owever crude an engineered machine is in comparison with the human body, it represents a higher act than simple biological reproduction, for it is at least the result of a thought process." (Miedaner, 1982a: 110). (By way of contrast, Valiant, 2013, upholds the unconventional claim that Darwin's theory lies at the very heart of computer science.)

In light of the alleged accelerating advancements in disruptive technologies, not limited to AI, but also counting genetic engineering and nanotechnology, the shiny notion of *technological singularity* (henceforth, simply singularity) was brought into wider circulation by Vinge (1993) which imposes itself on us in connection with strong AI. It can be conceived of as "an event or phase that will radically change human civilization, and perhaps even human nature itself [. . .]" (Eden et al., 2012: 1), a "rupture in the fabric of human history" as Kurzweil (2006: 9) stresses. More precisely, the authors clarify that singularity *hypotheses* allude to either one of two distinct and very different scenarios. The one whose discussion we can skip is explored by transhumanists who envisage the amplification of human cognitive capabilities through human enhancement technologies, leading to the arrival of a posthuman race (Kurzweil, 2006; Pearce, 2012).

The other, radically different scenario, which is of higher relevance for our purposes, postulates that, at some future (omega) point S, AI in the sense of software-based synthetic minds materializes as the "singular" outcome of accelerating advancements in computer technology (Eden et al., 2012: 1). This singularity, it is said, results from an "intelligence explosion" (Good, 1965): a process in which AIs enter a "runaway reaction" of self-enhancement cycles, "with each new and more intelligent generation appearing faster than its predecessor" (Eden et al., 2012: 2). Against this background, we can state that the emergence of strong AI coincides with S, whereupon immediately thereafter Good's intelligence explosion sets in, with the consequence that AI is reaching a superhuman level of intelligence "that, stuck as we are in the mud of our limited mentation, we can't fathom" (Bringsjord & Govindarajulu, 2018). This coincidence is what we assume from now on so that strong AI and (synthetic) superintelligence are not the same – synthetic because, so the hybris goes, biological evolution cannot produce such a leap forward (at least not in reasonable time). Instead, the distinct phenomena are closely tied together. On the one hand, the latter (superintelligence) is a specification, a subset of the former (strong AI). On the other, *within* the singularity narrative, the latter follows on and from the former, i.e., both temporally and logically.

In essence, the argument runs like this in the words of Eden et al. (2012: 2): "(1) The study of the history of technology reveals that technological progress has long been accelerating. (2) There are good reasons to think that this acceleration will continue for at least several more decades. (3) If it does continue, our technological achievements will become so great that our bodies, minds, societies, and economies will be radically transformed. (4) Therefore, it is likely that this disruptive transformation will occur." Or a bit more formally, in the spirit of Good (1965) and Chalmers (2010):

Premise 1   There will be SAI (created by HI and such that SAI = HI; and due to SAI S will occur).
Premise 2   If there is SAI, there will be SAI⁺ (created by SAI).
Premise 3   If there is SAI⁺, there will be SAI⁺⁺ (created by SAI⁺).
Conclusion There will be SAI⁺⁺ (= superintelligence will occur, sometimes also denoted by *S* or singularity; cf. Bringsjord & Govindarajulu, 2018).

In this argument, "SAI" is strong artificial intelligence at the level of, and created by, human persons ("HI"), "SAI⁺" is strong artificial intelligence with super-human performance (Rajani, 2011), and "SAI⁺⁺" amounts to strong super-human intelligence constitutive of the intelligence explosion or of superintelligence. The key process is presumably the *creation* of the first class of SAI. As we see more in detail in IV, critics of singularity dismiss these premises as speculative and empirically unsound (e.g., Horgan, 2008; Plebe & Perconti, 2012; Modis, 2012).

Apart from the twin notions of *acceleration* and *discontinuity*, accounts of singularity seem to dissent from each other on quite a number of aspects: causes and consequences, empirical content of the conjecture, on the timescale (e.g., an event or a period), and even on its nature: e.g., the dual use of *S* in the previous argument or the arrival of Homo Deus vs. of (super-)strong AI (not belonging to the genus *Homo*)? These dissents, casting doubt whether there is a coherent notion of singularity at all, are paired with a plethora of open guiding questions for research such as, what, if anything, can be said to be accelerating? And closer to our probes:
1) What are the (necessary and sufficient) conditions for an intelligence explosion?
2) What evidence substantiates the contention that machine intelligence has been rising?
3) Can this evidence be extrapolated reliably?
4) What are the (necessary and sufficient) conditions for machine intelligence to be regarded to be on par with human intelligence?

This situation or state of research, thus, seems to constitute a predestined point of departure for philosophical inquiries. In practice though, singularity has largely not been examined as principal object of study: "Good was an eminent academic, but his article was largely unappreciated at the time. The subsequent discussion of the singularity has largely taken place in nonacademic circles, including Internet forums, popular media and books, and workshops organized by the independent Singularity Institute. Perhaps the highly speculative flavor of the singularity idea has been responsible for academic resistance. I think this resistance is a shame, as the singularity idea is clearly an important one. The argument for a singularity is one that we should take seriously. And the questions surrounding the singularity are of enormous practical and philosophical concern." (Chalmers, 2010: 10).

We applaud Chalmers' call for research as singularity forces us to think hard about the nature of intelligence and about the principle mental capacities of AI. Concretely, to ascertain whether there might be an intelligence explosion, we need to better comprehend what intelligence is and to what extent future machines might have it. This concisely delineates the research program of the remainder of this treatment. In this connection, we will also partially tackle the four questions singled out above.

However, before we start pursuing this agenda, we turn Chalmers' knife in the philosophers' wound by inflaming the title of this subchapter and elucidating the tension between present-day machines' and fourth-wave machines' intellectual capabilities in terms of the refashioned and revitalizing juxtaposition of the philosophy of AI, and the simple economics of AI. Chalmers (2010) has a point when he bemoans that too little philosophical thought has been spent on strong AI and singularity. Yet, I wish to append and hypothesize that the few that have reflected on AI have focalized strong AI: e.g., Bringsjord & Govindarajulu (2018) made their section on philosophy of AI almost completely on strong AI (except for a few side notes in *other* sections). This intense concentration on strong AI has come at least sometimes and in such cases at the expense of a holistic perspective on machine intelligence which would dovetail the simple economics of AI, which, as preview for Part II, will set out the lowest layer of our taxonomy.

Highlights and key takeaways from Part I

- We composed an atlas of intelligence, locating humans, nonhuman animals, and artificial animals therein, and leave it open for hybrids and collectives thereof.
- We gave a definition of "intelligence" from Merriam-Webster, and smashed it. Specialist disciplines have not been doing much better than the dictionary. For example, many psychologists (and colleagues from other departments) have committed what Whitehead (1925/1967: 58) calls a "fallacy of misplaced concreteness". That is, at the symposium of 1921 and elsewhere, they have mistaken a narrowly abstract definition or conception of intelligence for concrete and multifarious reality. Cf. also Flynn (1997).
- We have not given a definition of our own since it often does more harm than good to force definitions on things where we only have an inhibited

understanding. Instead, we are about to go a level deeper and diligently work out a theory of intelligence.
- Some more specific findings, both positive and negative, have been attained already concerning the notion of intelligence:
  - It is a gradual, embedded, multidimensional, multidirectional, and dynamic concept. Graduality allows us to compare different elements of the class of intelligent beings on at least an ordinal scale to arrive at statements like: A crow is more intelligent than my dog for certain tasks of causal reasoning. Embeddedness requires intelligence to be embedded in concrete situations or meaningful task environments. Could we, for example, meaningfully say that my dog outsmarts a (small) crow at chasing a (big) cat? Dynamics signifies that the concept changes over time, e.g., to evade the trap of misplaced concreteness. In Part II, multidimensionality will be translated by different levels of causal thinking and multidirectionality by different guises of intelligence such as Gardner's eight intelligences.
  - Its scope is broad, encompassing humans, animals and machines to divergent (and in this order descending) degrees
  - Intelligence manifests itself differently in different entities the concept applies to: Hallmarks of intelligence vary between species/animal classes & individuals thereof
  - Understanding is not a necessary condition for intelligence, cognitive traits are not sufficient for fully fledged intelligence
  - The concept of intelligence is a complex system that cannot be entrenched by means of brainpower, the number of cortical neurons or task performance or whatsoever.
- After briefly visiting the theory and testing bazaar for intelligence, we brought to the fore Gardner's framework of multiple intelligences (in, but also beyond Chapter 1).
- Coming from Gardner's eight intelligences, music *in its entirety* may be the last remaining bastion of uniqueness in the terrain of human intelligence.
- There is no single or optimal way to exhibit or build intelligence.
- The seat of intelligence is not within any system of an organism or artifact (e.g., the brain)
- Intelligence is determined by the dynamics of interaction with the world.
- Despite their incommensurability (to some extent: e.g., measuring out of the operating area leads astray; Hernández-Orallo, 2017: 160), human, animal and AI intelligence share some common themes, most notably the systems metaphor of intelligence.

- Non-chauvinistic analyses of minds & mind-related properties are indicated, pillars of our exceptionalism such as, most saliently, causal reasoning and tool use have been falling.
- AI and animal minds can shed light on human minds by serving as a foil for comparison.
- In analogy to colors and systems of colors (Matthen, 2018), there may be many intelligences – indeed, many systems of intelligences – that humans never perceive.
- Rendez-vous with such intelligent aliens have happened, e.g., under the sea with octopi.
- The field of AI has traditionally betted on designing machines capable of wielding tasks that would require intelligence if done by humans in lieu of acknowledging that, on the one hand, intelligent behavior is in part a matter of *how* it is produced. On the other, intelligence is tangled with abilities and potential, not with performance or action.
- AI may have historically been a mere tool for us, but the field progresses expeditiously, which constitutes the real reason behind why to consider machines intelligent.
- AGI (artificial general intelligence) matters more than SAI (strong AI) and the former can be stimulated by copying Nature's best tricks while the latter springs from pure imagination so far. There is no AGI, so *a fortiori* there is no SAI.
- Superintelligent AIs, which in turn mark the outcome of the event or phase of singularity, are a specification, a subset of SAI; and *within* the singularity narrative, the former follows on and from the latter, i.e., both temporally and logically.
- AIs of the past are often dumb automata, much AI around us today has *some* intelligence, and with AGI on the horizon, multiple intelligences in AI become palpable.
- There is some intelligence in making predictions or in detecting associations with some independence, because intelligence or competence do not presuppose comprehension.
- Higher levels of intelligence though tackle the *why*. This is the topic of the next Part.

Part II: **Scaffolding intelligence**

Karl Popper (1962) conceived of science as a process of "conjectures and refutations" where scientists suggest hypotheses that can be falsified. Then, the conjectures are tested and, in case the test result does not match the hypothesis in question, repudiated with the consequence that a new conjecture must be found. For better or for worse, analytic philosophy has largely proceeded according to a parallel method, an approach of analyses or explications and counterexamples. Analytic philosophy has walked the path of negation. A classic illustration in the realm of epistemology is the concept of knowledge which used to be regarded as equivalent to justified true belief, but then Gettier (1963) arrived on stage. In this Part II, *Scaffolding intelligence*, we depart from this tradition of analyses and counterexamples in favor of more constructivism and a higher conceptual variety. Concretely, we do not point the finger at and denounce, let's say, Gardner's theory of multiple intelligences, but integrate it. Part II complements the conceptual foundation, which we began laying in Part I, by focusing more on the intension or meaning of the term "intelligence" to *understand why* we apply it to creatures as different as plants, humans and computers – and our Part I rather set the scene without pretending to give an exhaustive primer: recall that we relegated possible extraterrestrial forms of intelligence and have not canvassed plants and other entities extensively.

This Part II will make clear that the concept of intelligence is chosen as the central idea around which the philosophical study at hand revolves. This is a precarious endeavor as demonstrated by the fact that, after having written dozens of pages on intelligence, we have not fully endorsed a conception of intelligence beyond the few characteristics given in the key takeaways on the previous pages. The reason for that is not new. Intelligence does not persist in *absolute* terms. And any attempt to the contrary to circumscribe intelligence in an overarching manner is susceptible to *reductio* arguments; the most negative stance given by some kind of Gödelian incompleteness results of some levels of intelligence being unable to fathom some "upper" levels: Together with Hofstadter (1979: 180) let us (in our absolute Earth chauvinism to be negated) "consider a meteorite which, instead of deciphering the outer-space Bach record, punctures it with colossal indifference, and continues in its merry orbit. It has interacted with the record in a way which we feel disregards the record's meaning. Therefore, we might well feel tempted to call the meteorite 'stupid'. But perhaps we would thereby do the meteorite a disservice. Perhaps it has a 'higher intelligence' which we in our Earth chauvinism cannot perceive, and its interaction with the record was a manifestation of that higher intelligence. Perhaps, then, the record has a 'higher meaning'-totally different from that which we attribute to it; perhaps its meaning depends on the type of intelligence perceiving it. Perhaps."

Hence, intelligence necessitates a frame of reference; a frame of reference which is hopefully less prone to deficiencies than Earth chauvinism. Frankly, I am the most apprehensive about this tour de force, these four chapters to come. There is so much germane material about which I am ignorant – some of the contributions in developmental psychology, for instance. In the face of the valiant and heterogeneous aims of this treatise implied by its title, it is clear that, on the one hand, its pieces in parts set out a program and outline not more than an agenda for future research – the title is "[t]he quest for a [. . .] theory", not "voilà a theory". If this theory development contribution at hand acts as a testbed for progress and stimulates further controversy of how to conceive intelligence, it will have already served a useful purpose.

On the other, I am prepared to see portions of my proposal condemned as factually implausible. But, every beginning is hard, and in the case of "intelligence" arguably as hard as granite which compelled some authors as Minsky (1988: 71) to gave up on defining the "old, vague word [. . .] 'intelligence' [which] is like a stage magician's trick. Like the concept of *'the unexplored regions of Africa'*, it disappears as soon as we discover it." (Cf. also Shearer & Karanian, 2017: 211, who report something similar.) A novel general framework to tame intelligence is to be launched, details can be clarified later on. Let us go in medias res.

The subsequent Chapter 4 paves the ground by immersing in three pieces of pertinent ground and prior work, providing the glue that lets core constructs thereafter stick. The lessons from the discussion of these three contributions from different communities, practical and applied philosophy / ethics of AI (in 4.1.), neuroscience and philosophy of mind (in 4.2.) as well as philosophy of science and computer science (in 4.3.), are absorbed in Chapter 5 where we penetrate into the heart of the entire present treatment. Under such favorable auspices, the outline of a causal theory of intelligence, i.e., to appeal to causation in order to answer the question of what it is for someone or some animal or AI system to be intelligent, is compiled there. Our core proposition is a composition of predominantly two pieces: An advancement of Pearl's preliminary work (4.3.) legitimates the universal claim of my project (in 5.1.). However, if we just left things like that, my approach would be reductionistic. As portrayed in Part I, intelligence is too multicolored to be squeezed in a static framework. In order to do justice to this diversity, I propose that the inverted radex model (5.2.) needs to be integrated. This synthesis is then underpinned in a dual way: Chapter 6 gives a foretaste of its impact and of how it can be implemented while Chapter 7, closing this Part II, is dedicated to the arduous, but rewarding endeavor of validating our causal theory of intelligence.

I repeat my conviction that intelligence is not a unitary phenomenon, not for humans (e.g., following Gardner) and even less between creatures of any descent; yet, I do believe that learning, and, more precisely, causal learning is at the center of both intelligence and, consequently, the AI enterprise (which does not entail that intelligence cannot also be evolved, innate, or programmed-in). The reason learning is so central to intelligence and intelligent behavior is, according to Dretske (1988: 104), that "learning is the process in which internal indicators [. . .] are harnessed to output and thus become relevant [. . .] to the explanation of the behavior of which they are a part. It is in the learning process that information-carrying elements get a job to do *because* of the information they carry and hence acquire, by means of their *content*, a role in the explanation of behavior." In tune with Lake et al. (2017) and others, we thereby draw a far-reaching distinction between two different computational construals of intelligence in AI: on the one hand, the (currently) more conventional statistical pattern recognition approaches, primarily betting on prediction; on the other, approaches treating explanations as well as models of the world as primary, where learning is the process of *model building*. With this Part II, we are committed to cultivating the latter for a general comprehension of intelligence without succumbing to the wrong habit of polarization.

4 Preliminaries and prior work on framing intelligence

The metaphor of a ladder in attempts to explicate "intelligence" is popular and put to work in the next subchapters. We came across the Ladder of Being from Christianity already in Chapter 1 and here, we will see three more: the Cognitive Ladder, the Ladder of Prediction, and the Causal Ladder. The latter proves to be eminently fruitful for our ambitions in Chapter 5. With that in mind, while, as noticed, many researchers in the AI community do not think deeply about the concept of intelligence, this Part II is ironically, thoroughly and unashamedly influenced by one of its finest and sharpest thinkers, namely Judea Pearl.

4.1 The cognitive ladder

Let us inspect the first ladder and examine the distinction between intelligence and close cognates such as *knowledge, understanding* and *wisdom*. To capture them in a single framework, the notion of the cognitive ladder has been inaugurated (Hoffmann, 2019b; Vallor, 2017) and it is plotted in Figure 17 where the cognates are envisioned as successive rungs.

For each of those notions, one could fill libraries with books about their respective nature, and I have no pretensions to a comprehensive philosophical account. My modest objectives in this subchapter are to "fence off" those divergent concepts grouped around the term "intelligence" to then gain some broad guidelines for our own proposal in Chapter 5 by elucidating their respective position on the ladder.

Climbing the cognitive ladder starts at the lowest rung with **knowledge**, which is traditionally conceived of as true, justified belief. In this respect, I know that there is the Mont Salève in the agglomeration of Geneva because the statement is true and I have good reasons (for example, because I see the mountain from the window) to believe it is true. Even if not every case of knowing that p implies believing that p (as the tripartite conception of knowledge would vouchsafe), the pair knowledge/belief comes as a double-pack (Glock, 2018: 92). The hurdle for knowledge is not particularly high for *us* humans – even fools know something –, yet for other creatures it might be a different story: To what extent can animals and even more machines be said to *have beliefs* or *reasons* at all? In retrospect to Chapter 2, we are positive about the faculty of some animals, especially corvids (cf. also Glock, 2018). In hindsight to Chapter 3, we recapitulate that first and second wave AI, strictly speaking, do not have beliefs (cf. also

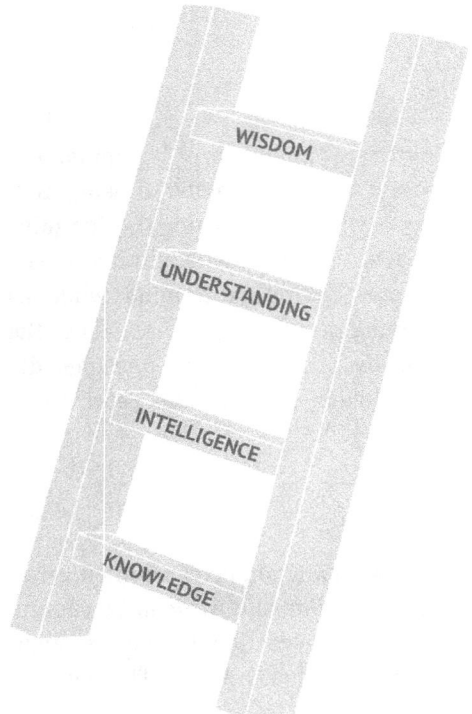

Figure 17: The four-rung cognitive ladder. In accordance with: Vallor, 2017: 163; Hoffmann, 2019b.

Dretske, 1988: 48), but that, by adopting an intentional stance (Dennett, 1989), AI can be considered to still "know" that, for instance, a cat is in a picture because it has been trained with millions of cat pictures.

In tune with Anderson (1993) and Ryle (1949), a discrimination can be made between declarative or content knowledge ("knowing that") and procedural or process knowledge "knowing how". The former is factual knowledge about the meaning or perceptual characteristics of things, from anecdotal memories to highly organized conceptual knowledge of some subject matter like a theorem of geometry (Lohman, 2000: 289). The value of content knowledge has been shrinking in the machine age because questions, problems, tasks targeting knowledge in this sense can be and have been outsourced to computers: I do not need to know by heart where the adage "Rome wasn't built in a day" comes from historically, I can plainly *google* it. This shift might explain why we are inclined to ascribe knowledge to computers and AI or, conversely, regard our minds as extended (Vold, 2018; Clark & Chalmers, 1998). "Knowing *how*", by contrast, is knowledge of how to do something, from pronouncing a word to riding skis. Like this, it is closely intertwined with intelligence, the second rung: In fact, there may not be a big difference between knowing how to ski well and bodily-kinesthetic intelligence in this respect of skiing.

According to Vallor (2017) and Hoffmann (2019b), **intelligence** requires the distinctive, sometimes narrowly compartmentalized competence of applying knowledge in some relevant context(s). This renders intelligence practical ("practical intelligence") and is noteworthy because "[m]ost conceptions of intelligence have focused on traits or processes to the neglect of knowledge" (Wagner, 2000: 392). I display (logical-mathematical) intelligence when I apply knowledge from one of the seminars of philosophy I attended by designating a certain kind of logical argument as syllogism; or when I use my experience from interacting with people to comfort the anxious neighbor (emotional intelligence). Here on the second rung, too, AIs already often captivate; for example, when an AI "uses its knowledge/training" to identify a cat in a new image. In computer science, McCarthy was among the first to appreciate that to track intelligent behavior we needed to study the knowledge that behavior depends on, and how this knowledge might be applied in adjudicating how to behave (Levesque, 2018: 30), which is unequivocally on the same trajectory for making sense of intelligence. Or in the words of Zenon Pylyshyn (1999), intelligent behavior is *cognitively penetrable*: the decisions you make about what actions to pick is penetrated by what you believe or know. Philosophically, Vallor's (2017) and Hoffmann's (2019b) reading of intelligence suggests that intelligence is a second order mental property, a property that consists in having first order mental states – beliefs, desires, etc. This reading can be criticized or not (Block, 1981), but the question whether to endorse or to discard it is ultimately immaterial for the endeavor at hand.

What AI currently lacks is an integrated mastery of at least one domain of practical or theoretical cognition, which would set the central requirement for **understanding** as a general, not specific, third-level competence. Accordingly, our AI trained with cat pictures may not be poised to recognize the lion with his mane in a picture as a cat, i.e., to apply other domains of knowledge (from biology, for example) to the problem. We can accept this reading and exemplification of understanding albeit, in this context, we made "comprehension" part of the sphere of intelligence by acknowledging intelligent behavior with and without comprehension. What is to be applauded though is that a strong common denominator is given by not treating comprehension as the source or antecedent of competence. Instead, both this book and Hoffmann (2019b)/Vallor (2017) contend that competence comes first (on a lower rung to dwell upon the picture), that comprehension is both *composed* of competences and *representing* as well as *promoting* a *general and higher* competence. In addition, Dennett (2017: 95) accentuates that the distinction between comprehension and incomprehension is not only momentous, but it is also non-Boolean. The notion might come, following the well-tested Darwinian perspective of gradualism, in different stages: "At one extreme, we have the bacterium's sorta comprehension of the quorum-sensing signals it responds to [. . .] and the computer's sorta comprehension of the "ADD" instruction. At the other extreme we have Jane Austen's comprehension of the interplay of personal and social forces in the emotional states of people and Einstein's comprehension of relativity. But even at the highest levels of competence, comprehension is never absolute. There are always ungrasped implications and unrecognized presuppositions in any mind's mastery of a concept or topic."

If knowledge, intelligence and understanding are envisioned as progressively advanced steps, we encounter **wisdom** on the fourth and final rung of the fictional cognitive ladder. In contrast to understanding, it is characterized, following Hoffmann (2019b), by holistic value judgments, which dovetails an evaluation and questioning not only of the means to achieve a goal, but also of the goals themselves. While, speaking for the running example of the AI and the cat pictures, the means at the level of narrow intelligence are the ascertained patterns from the training data, which are then enriched at the level of understanding by insights from other fields of knowledge, the supreme discipline of wisdom would encapsulate the evaluation of the extent to which it would be wise or moral to evaluate the images at all. To put it bluntly, there is no clear developmental trajectory on which AI could attain anything like wisdom. For the foreseeable future, intelligent machines simply lack the distinctive social and psychological conditions that make wisdom possible in the first place. In fact, this supposed lack is at the same time the core of their strength and commercial appeal. Wisdom in AI is at least for the predictable future not only technologically impossible, but neither imperative nor desirable.

To draw the demarcation line, Vallor (2017: 164) adds that wisdom is unlike the first three rungs which "are internal cognitive states of a person; they align epistemically with some domain of the world, but do not necessarily alter or affect that domain. Intelligence, for example, presupposes an ability to successfully deploy knowledge in action, but once acquired, this ability could in principle remain forever latent in any given agent. Though often helpful, it is not always necessary to exercise one's intelligence to retain it. Contrast this with [. . . active] *expertise*, [an essential ingredient of wisdom] that tend[s] to refer to an agent's actual *practices* of employing intelligence [and understanding] in skillful and world-altering ways." Taking this negative and positive characterization of wisdom as a plea, it bears some resemblance with Karl Marx's quote carved in stone in the main building of the Humboldt University: "The philosophers [meaning "lovers of *wisdom*", C.H.] have only interpreted the world, in various ways. The point, however, is to change it."

For the sake of the present treatment, we note that wisdom is a special case of a special kind of intelligence, namely *practical intelligence* (Wagner, 2000) as rudimentarily portrayed above on rung two. One possibly can discuss intelligence without dealing with wisdom – a path we indeed tread in the remainder –, but one cannot adequately discuss wisdom without dealing with intelligence, which is why the order of rungs is the way it is in Figure 17. The most conventional view is that wisdom (just as *creativity*, cf. Sternberg & O'Hara, 2000) and intelligence are overlapping sets: Intelligence and wisdom (creativity) overlap in some respects, but not in others. Some people like Bill Gates or Ruth Bader Ginsburg (arguably) radiate both intelligence and wisdom, others are just intelligent like Wolfgang Amadeus Mozart or intelligent in a (very) myopic sense like Wladimir Iljitsch Lenin without being wise, some are only wise (often the elderly in a family), and many people are neither nor; a colorful palette. Content-wise, neither Hoffmann's (2019b) nor Vallor's (2017) interpretation of wisdom is compelling for us. The former in terms of questioning goals of *others* swiftly unfolds itself as infamous: Who are we to disparage Mozart as unwise by judging the genius who passed away "too early" and his eccentric or hedonistic lifestyle? The latter, albeit making a good point about *practical* wisdom, is redundant since in the course of this work we do not always insulate intelligence as a corpus of abilities (which is in the foreground) from intelligent behavior (which is more in the background; see key takeaways from Part I). Intelligence which remains forever latent is worthless!

Reply to the overall framework: At first glance, Vallor's (2017) and Hoffmann's (2019b) thrust seems plausible as a loose metaphor at least; it might also be stimulating further thought and discussion. As an explanatory scheme for illuminating "intelligence" where the latter, according to the authors, simply represents a self-contained section within a canon of (only) four cognitive abilities (see Figure 17), however, it does not do justice to such a itself multi-layered and rich concept. In a critical appraisal, a repertory of just four cognitive traits (on what grounds by the way?) displeases. For example, how would we make sense of another aspect of mental life such as learning in this scheme, which is also second order in the sense that there can be no learning without memory?

Grasping the gist of the matter, the approach by Vallor (2017) and Hoffmann (2019b) diminishes, first, intelligence to practical intelligence, and, second, factors out the issue of how much and what kind of knowledge is needed to voice intelligence. To the extent, for instance, that scientific as well as naïve theories are an articulation of highly developed intelligence that often remain agnostic about processes of transmission, Schulz et al. (2007) note that Newton propounded his theory of gravitation *without knowing* any mechanism that might enable masses to attract one another or Darwin originated his theory of evolution *without knowing* any mechanism that might make variation in the species heritable, etc. Hence, this cognitive ladder ultimately proves to be deficient for enlightening us about the nature and role of intelligence.

4.2 The ladder of prediction

How can a thoroughly physical being think, dream, and feel? How can such a being act in ways that mirror what it knows and that serve its ever-changing needs? At the busy intersection of psychology, neuroscience, philosophy and AI (where we with this book gather too), philosopher and cognitive scientist Andy Clark (2016) feeds answers by scouting brains like ours as prediction machines. Devices thus construed do not wait passively for sensory stimulations to arrive, but instantiate morphing, buzzing, dynamical systems forever reconfiguring themselves so as better to anticipate the incoming sensory barrage (ibid.: 167). These are the brains of active agents, gifted to structure their own worlds, constructing and re-constructing them in ways that alter the very things their brains must engage and predict. What crops up is Clark's (2016: 295) unified overarching vision of the brain as an engine of multilevel probabilistic prediction in terms of hierarchical predictive coding or Predictive Processing which dovetails with work on the embodied and environmentally situated mind. His proposal serves as a cogent illustration of how to tackle a wide range of issues, shedding light on perception, action, reason, experience, emotion, understanding other agents, and the nature and origins of various pathologies and breakdowns (ibid.: 10).

According to Clark (2016: 204), we need, if you will, to begin to recognize ourselves in the swirl of ongoing, multilevel prediction, which can be depicted by another ladder, the ladder of prediction in Figure 18, that in opposition to the one in 4.1. is equipped with only three rungs, but sketches a dynamic situation. Even though he does not suggest the image of a ladder himself along which to organize his whole treatment, it can very well be deployed: His book is composed of three distinct parts, and Part I corresponding to the first rung deals with the entire bedrock story about perception and learning; Part II, i.e., the second rung, is about the neat ploy of bringing the sensory signal progressively in tune with some special subset of the agent's own sensory predictions, morphing some of our sensory predictions into self-fulfilling prophecies; and finally Part III representing the highest rung completes the picture with immersing in agents' capacity to alter the long-term structure of their own social and material environment, "so as to inhabit a world in which the 'energetic inputs that matter' are more reliably served up as and when required" (ibid.: 7).

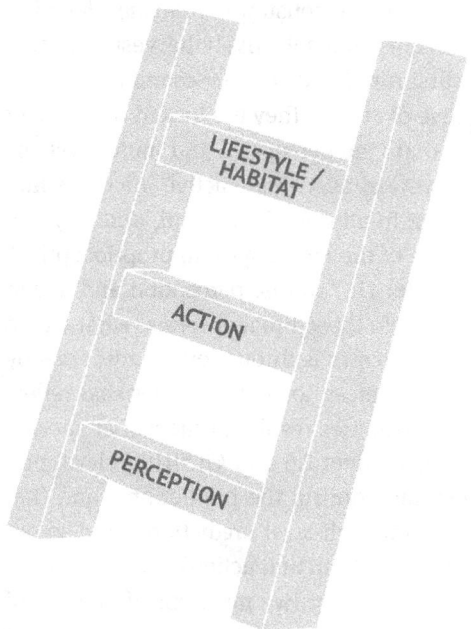

Figure 18: The three-rung ladder of prediction. In accordance with Clark (2016) who, however, does not envision a ladder.

Taking a fictional tabula rasa agent, the core idea is to endow her with *passive perception* on the first rung. To perceive the world is generally to meet the sensory signal with an apt stream of multilevel predictions (Clark, 2016: 6): "Those predictions aim to construct the incoming sensory signal 'from the top down' using stored knowledge about interacting distal causes. To accommodate the incoming sensory signal in this way is already to understand quite a lot about the world. Creatures deploying this kind of strategy learn to become knowledgeable consumers of their own sensory stimulations. They come to know about their world, and about the kinds of entity and event that populate it. Creatures deploying this strategy, when they see the grass twitch in just that certain way, are *already expecting* to see the tasty prey emerge, and *already expecting* to feel the sensations of their own muscles tensing to pounce. An animal, or machine, that has that kind of grip on its world is already deep into the business of understanding that world."

Yet, something crucial is missing from this neat picture of passive perception, something crucial for a system to qualify as an agent in the first place.

What is prerequisite is action, and action or, more precisely, *performing* **action** *that makes our predictions come true* (ibid.: 121), changes everything. Our massed recurrent neuronal ensembles are not just buzzing away constantly attempting to predict the sensory stream. Rather, our brains are constantly *bringing about* the sensory stream by *causing* bodily movements that selectively harvest new sensory stimulations (ibid.: 7). Perception (first rung) and action (second rung) work seamlessly in concert in the normal course of events, they are locked in a type of endless circular embrace. The upshot is that "the perceptual and motor systems should not be regarded as separate but instead as a single active inference machine that tries to predict its sensory input in all domains: visual, auditory, somatosensory, interoceptive and, in the case of the motor system, proprioceptive" (Adams et al., 2013: 614). Or in Clark's (2016: 176) words, perception and action are both co-determined and co-determining. In these broader terms, what we do hinges on what we perceive, and what we perceive is throughout conditioned by what we do. Creating and maintaining such perception-action cycles that reflect organismic needs and environmental opportunities results in the rather specific forms of *circular causality* (described in his Chapter 2.6 and 4): "[H]igh-level predictions entertain actions that both test and confirm the predictions, and that help sculpt the sensory flows that recruit new high-level predictions (and so on, in a rolling cycle of expectation, sensory stimulation, and action)" (ibid.: 176).

We are not yet on the top. On the highest rung, we must specify a kind of **lifestyle and habitat** for our agent; otherwise, "we have no sense of what might constitute *apt action* in response to the sensory inputs" (ibid.: 7). Such world-structuring, repeated time and time again, generation by generation, also facilitates beings like us to build better and better worlds to think in, enabling impinging energies to steer ever-more-complex forms of behavior as well as allowing thought and reason to penetrate domains which were previously "off-limits" (ibid.). The grip, in the somewhat special case of the human mind – recall that most, if not all, of our faculties might not be unprecedented in the animal kingdom as seen in Part I, but we are still special (and the backside of the coin says that other animals are special in other regards) – is further enriched and transformed by layer upon layer of socio-cultural structures and practices (ibid.: 294). Steeped in such practices, our predictive neuronal ensembles are empowered to redeploy their basic skills in new and transformative ways (ibid.). Comprehending the consequent interplay of action, culture, technology, and cascading neural prediction is surely one of the principal quests confronting 21st century cognitive science (ibid.).

Critical appraisal: In his superb book, Clark (2016) expertly wields the hierarchical predictive coding or Predictive Processing account and applies it in an engaging fashion to a high constellation of cases to appreciate how brain, body and world interact with each other to create our lived experience. Tailored to the subject line of the present treatment, we also endorse his three-tier conception of the ladder of prediction for illuminating intelligence. This stems from chiefly three reasons: Firstly, Clark (2016) integrates a number of pertinent perspectives covering neuroscience, psychology, philosophy and AI, and, thereby, erects a scaffold which is not static in contrast to the ladder of cognition. It thus lends itself to supposedly better capturing factually *dynamic* intelligence (e.g., in the sense that cognitive abilities evolve over time). Secondly, his approach does not end with incorporating simple, linear dynamics, but he harbors the kind of dynamics which can lead to cycles and circular causality, paving the ground for strange loops which Hofstadter (1979: 35) ultimately views as the signature of intelligence. We revisit this point in Chapter 5.1.3.

Thirdly, Clark's first rung corresponds well with the basic form of intelligence we painted in 3.2. following the simple economics of AI according to which some, i.e., rung one intelligence befits agents that passively observe to make predictions. Rung two clarifies what tags higher intelligence, namely the ability of acting upon the world for causal learning or, as we will restate it following Pearl (2018a) in 4.3., intervention. Only Clark's (2016) rung three does not fit into the conceptual fabric. Neither is the demarcation between his rung two and three compelling within his framework – e.g., rung one and two stand for two distinct abilities of an agent, rung three does not –; nor will it be revitalized for our own foray in Chapter 5. On the contrary, we are more in consonance with Pearl (2018a) who in turn is d'accord with Clark's proposal on rung one and two, but deviates from his track for rung three, which we scrutinize in the last subchapter.

4.3 The ladder of causation

> *The researcher had never personally destroyed one of his animals before, always leaving the task to assistants. As the unsuspecting chimpanzee Martha [who is connected to some electronic equipment so as to monitor the neural activity of her speech center and translate it into English words] placed the poisoned gift into her mouth and bit, Belinsky [the researcher] conceived of an experiment he had never before considered. He turned on the switch. "Candy Candy Thank you Belinsky Happy Happy Martha." Then her voice stopped of its own accord. [. . .] But brain death is not immediate. The final sensory discharge of some circuit within her inert body triggered a brief burst of neural pulsations decoded as "Hurt Martha Hurt Martha." [. . . And finally, one last pulsating signal was sent to the world of men:] **"Why Why Why Why** –" [emphasis added by C.H.] A soft electrical click stopped the testimony.* Miedaner, 1982b: 105f.

The pathetic forlorn cry of the dying chimp evokes in us powerful sympathy – we can identify so easily with this innocent and enchanting creature; partly through her charming simple-minded syntax, which might make us feel protective of her as we would of a baby or small child, but also, and this is the chief point of this subchapter, because she prominently raises the question of why, once reckoned as marking us as uniquely human.

The exhilarating, cogent and enthralling book by Judea Pearl (2018a) *The Book of Why: The New Science of Cause and Effect* takes exactly that equivocal term, *why*, as a starting and focal point. Its main ambiguity is disclosed by a familiar pair of substitute phrases: *what for*? and *how come*? (Dennett, 2017: 38). As we see in this subchapter, Pearl (2018a) conceives of the "Why?" question as a counterfactual question in disguise. The subtitle of his book putting the limelight on "cause" or "causality" is not exempt from equivocality either, as Aristotle taught us already. He identified four questions we might wish to ask about anything:

1) What is it made of, or its *material cause*?
2) What is its structure, or its *formal cause*?
3) How did it get started, or what is its *efficient cause*?
4) What is its purpose, or its *final*, or *telic*, *cause* (also often translated with *reason*; cf. Dennett, 2017: 40; we can say that reasons *are* causes, Davidson, 1963/1980)?

On top of that, we can discern between internal and external causes (Dretske, 1988: 1): The distinction between Christian's *losing* his boring job as assistant professor of finance (something that happens to him) and his *quitting* his job (something he opted for) resides in the locus – in Christian or in the university – of the cause of termination.

And the list with complications emanating from attempts of clarifying and systematizing the Babylonian confusion of tongues around "cause" or "causality" goes on, exemplified by further questions such as: Are causes events (Lewis, 1986)? Facts (Mellor, 1995)? Composita (Menzies, 1989)? With or without background conditions (Kim, 1976)? Is causality, the relationship of cause and effect, to be understood in probabilistic terms (Reichenbach, 1956; Suppes, 1970; Hoffmann, 2021c)? And so on (for a general overview, cf. Schaffer, 2016).

To put it bluntly, I have no philosophical interest in playing umpire in these disputes, no interest in agonizing over settling specific questions about what is and what is not causality, what are and what are not causes. My interest centers on how intelligence can be recurred to causality, precisely to different forms of causal learning, no matter the exact localizations and tenets on the higher level of metaphysics of causation. An indispensable stepping stone towards this goal was laid by Pearl (2018a).

In analogy to Clark (2016) from 4.2., there are two ways we can get (firsthand) evidence about an event: We can *perceive* the event happen, or we can *make* the event happen. These two ways of receiving data – seeing and doing – can lead to radically divergent conclusions in terms of learning, even when the evidence itself is otherwise identical (Schulz et al., 2007: 77). What you can learn depends not only on what you know already (contra the stance in the previous subchapter 4.1.), but also on *how* you know it (ibid.). In this spirit, Pearl (2000: 421) stated that "[s]cientific activity, as we know it, consists of two basic components: Observations and interventions. The combination of the two is what we call a laboratory." In (Pearl, 2018a), he abstracts from science, adds a third layer, et voilà, we gain the intriguing product of his so-called *ladder of causation*, which, contrasted with the two previous ladders, proves to be a more sophisticated proposal for, how he calls it, what makes us uniquely human: we recognize human reasoning "through words such as 'preventing,' 'cause,' 'attributed to,' 'discrimination,' and 'should I'" (Pearl, 2018b: 3). Accordingly, a causal learner must master three distinct levels of cognitive ability: seeing, doing, imagining; and, as his argument runs, only us humans bestride all three sectors of the causal ladder (which is depicted in Figure 19 on the next page).

Rung one of the ladder

The *first rung*, **seeing** or **observing** or, as we will also denote it, **identifying**, entails the detection of regularities, patterns and associations in our environment and is shared, according to Pearl (2018a: 27), by most animals, modern and prehistoric humans, but also by our present-day learning machines. All these creatures learn from associations. This rung calls for predictions predicated on passive observations or, better, regularities in observations. This is what a dog does when observing how a cat moves and figuring out where it is likely to be a moment after, and it is what the computer program AlphaGo by DeepMind Technologies (Alphabet/ Google) does when it studies a database of millions of Go games so that it can derive which moves are geared with a higher percentage of wins.

We say that one event is associated with another if observing one changes the likelihood of observing the other. In statistics, a thriving, but after all causality-free enterprise, this type of relationship is called *correlation*, thereby reducing a large body of data. But, data per se is profoundly dumb. Naked data can tell you that this author is more into philosophy (books) than economics (books), but they cannot tell you why. In many situations more like this, in everyday life,

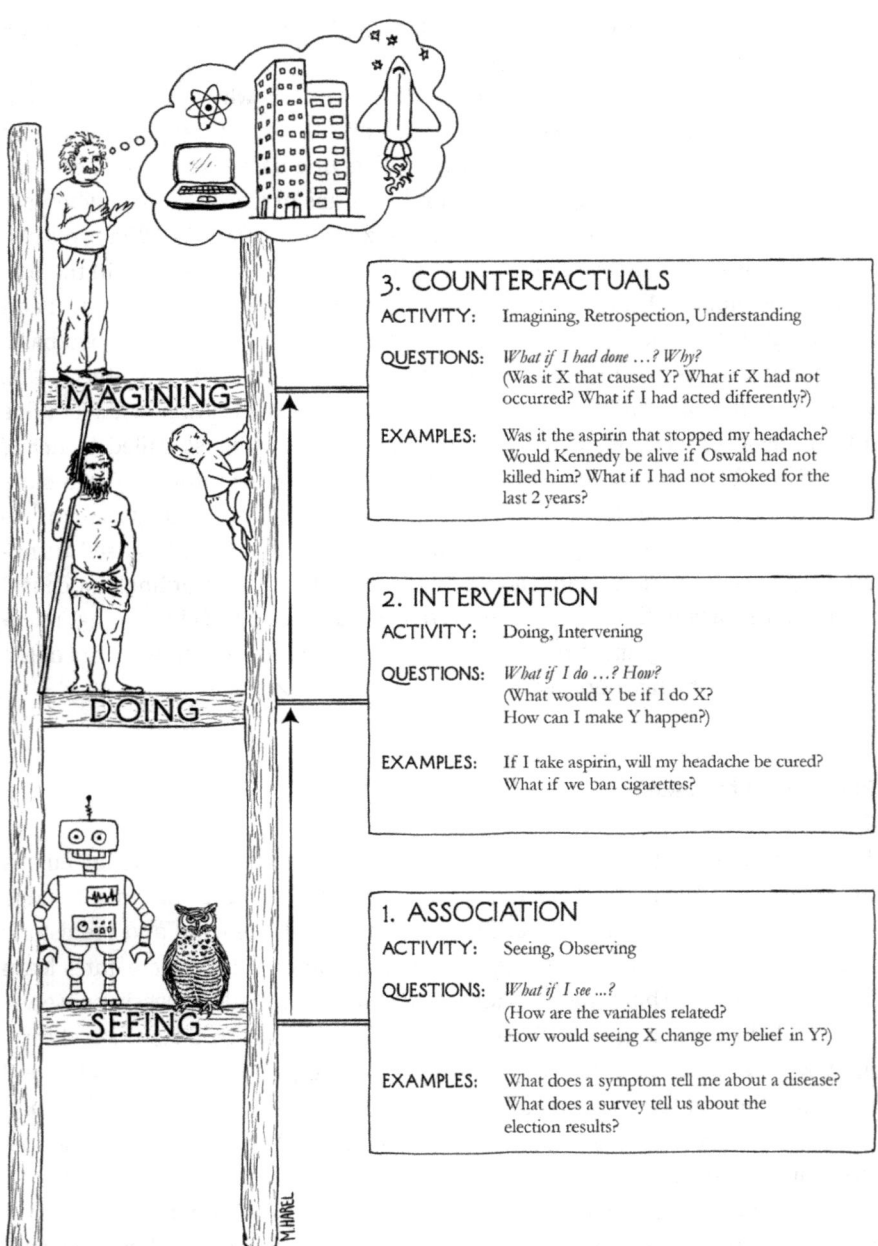

Figure 19: The three-rung causal ladder. Pearl (2018a) is the only exception where a ladder is actually painted compared to the two other pieces of prior work where this did not happen. Source: Pearl, 2018a: 28.

science or business, we witness that mere data is not enough. No system, human, animal or machine, can determine what is going on in the world merely by "looking out" and seeing or sampling it (Cantwell Smith, 2019: 14), drastically limiting the applicability of Brooks' famous maxim that "the world is its own best model" (Brooks, 1991): The maxim roughly says that in lieu of being plagued by the problem of updating, searching, and otherwise manipulating the symbolic worlds inside our AIs, in nuce, the problem of modeling the outside world, nouvelle AI can get along without the modeling part by processing the external world information it needs from the senses when it is required. [Pearl ignores Granger causality, a statistical hypothesis test procedure (Granger, 1969), and cognates, but I would contend that it is still licit to label statistics a causality-free enterprise; a) the relatively little significance and impact of Granger causality (few people use it), b) invoked criticisms, e.g., cf. Grassmann, 2020 or He & Maekawa, 2001 besides others (does Granger not flatly deal with correlation?).]

This first rung of the ladder is characterized by the question *"What if I perceive/see . . . ?"*. For example, linking back to Chapter 2, we find on this rung one a special form of learning by conditioning or reinforcement which is called *passive* discrimination or *classical* conditioning. In these procedures, an animal (like Pavlovian dogs) learns to identify a condition C, or at least to distinguish (discriminate) C from other conditions, by having particular responses to C – and, indeed, the widespread preference for simplicity has unjustifiably biased animal cognition researchers in favor of such associative models instead of more quantitative cognitive models (Mikhalevich, 2018).

What makes this case then passive or classical is that the test subject, let us say a dog, learns an association between two events that are both *outside* his control – e.g., an association between the ringing of a bell and the provision of food and the dog responds to the former by salivation because he expects the latter. Or couched in the terms of the key question of rung one: If I perceive the signal of a ringing bell, food is served. The dog is thus in the position of learning through *passive* observation rather than active action, and what is learned is that one stimulus predicts another, where this predictive relationship may or may not reflect the fact that the first stimulus causes the second (Woodward, 2007: 26).

Linking back to Chapter 3, we also find passive reinforcement or deep learning in the machine kingdom. We came across a machine learning program processing digitized images and which associates certain features in the images (like a certain uniform color and brightness or an area where there is a distinctive change in brightness and color corresponding to an edge) with the feature of being a cat. Deep learning thus far cannot inherently distinguish causation from correlation: "Roughly speaking, deep learning learns complex correlations between input and output features, but with no inherent representation of causality" (Marcus, 2018: 12f.).

Such organisms that are incapable of acting on the world, but can only passively scout associations outside their control would have no need for a notion of causation or cause-like representations, conceived along interventionist lines that we encounter on rung two (Menzies & Price, 1993: 195). A paucity of flexibility and adaptability is inevitable in any system that works at the first level of the ladder of causation (cf. Camp & Shupe, 2018, who make a case for instrumental reasoning on rung two as an important mark of cognitive flexibility). Therefore, let us now explore the epistemically significant disparities between observing and intervening.

Rung two of the ladder

We step up the next level of causal queries when we begin to change the world by taking actions. In other words, a new kind of knowledge, absent from data, which we find at *rung two of the ladder*, is needed and consists of **doing** or **intervention** (which we wish to perform mentally before we decide whether and how to do it in real life). Intervention ranks higher than association because it encapsulates not just seeing but amending what is and entails planning as well as predicting the effect(s) of deliberate alterations to produce a desired outcome. Pearl spots tool users, such as early humans (e.g., recall Figure 3), on the second rung if they act by planning and not merely by imitation. An effect of such tool use is a sharpened "understanding of causality of events and of the self as one of the drivers of the causality" (Hiraiwa-Hasegawa, 2019: 171).

Or as Pearl (2018a: 31) puts it neatly: "Seeing smoke tells us a totally different story about the likelihood of fire than making smoke". We cannot answer questions about interventions, generally "What would Y be *if* I do X?" or "*How* can we . . . ?", with passively collected data, no matter how big the data set is. A very direct way to learn about the results of an intervention is to use experiments – be it under prudently controlled conditions in the lab or simply by trial and error, which presumably is how babies acquire much of their causal knowledge – to predict the effects of interventions.

We perform interventions all the time in our daily life. For instance, when we are in a bad mood and watch a comedy to lighten it up, we are intervening on one variable (distraction or the quantity of smiles, jokes or laughter around us) in order to affect another one (our status of wellbeing). If we are correct in our causal belief about the comedy, the "outcome" variable will respond by turning from "bad mood" to "good mood". The faculty to move smoothly from claims about causal structure that follow from information about the results of intervention to claims about causal structure that are countenanced by observations and vice versa is, as Woodward (2007: 23f.) argues, one of the distinctive features of human causal cognition.

In contrast to observations, however, interventions do not lend positive or negative diagnostic evidence to the causes of the event on which we intervened. Whereas the perception of events allows us to reason diagnostically about their causes, interventions make the occurrence of events independent of their typical causes (Hagmayer et al., 2007: 87): "For example, forcing somebody to eat 50 (and only 50) grams of fat per day fixes that intake independent of the presence or absence of other factors normally affecting diet" (ibid.).

An expedient illustration of the difference between rung 1 and rung 2 is the difference between Pavlovian conditioning (seen above) and instrumental/operant conditioning (cf. e.g., Skinnerian rat experiments). In the latter, what is learned is an association between some behavior produced by the subject and an outcome, as when dogs learn an association between pressing a lever in response to hearing the bell, which in contrast to passive salivation is an active action, and the provision of food pellets. From an interventionist perspective, "instrumental learning has a 'causelike' flavor" (Woodward, 2007: 26). But neither the bell does (sufficiently) cause the dog's active reaction (the bell could ring, but the dog does not have any *desire* for the reward because he is not hungry), nor does his intervention (sufficiently) cause the receipt of a food reward (the experimenter could forget about it).

Woodward (2003: 28; 2009: 234) suggests that causal language can capture facts about manipulability that are beyond the reach of any non-causal or mere statistical claim, in the sense that facts about manipulability and intervention are not reducible to statistical facts. Various other philosophers before him argued that the core notion of causation involves human intervention (Collingwood, 1940; von Wright, 1971; Hart & Honoré, 1983). It is through our actions and manipulations of the environment around us that we acquire our basic sense of causality. Even though more contemporary theories of causality dispense with its anthropomorphic connotations, they maintain the notion of intervention as a central concept (Spirtes et al., 1993; Pearl, 2000; Glymour, 2001; Woodward, 2003). What is key for the purposes of causal learning is that an intervention can act as a quasi-experiment, one that eliminates (or reduces) confounds and assists in establishing the existence of a causal relation between the intervened-on variable and its effects (Lagnado et al., 2007: 161).

While reasoning about interventions is a vital step on the causal ladder, it is not sufficient to answer *all* causal questions of interest. We might wonder, my bad mood is gone, but why? Was it the comedy I watched? The birds that I have heard singing during a warm and sunny spring day? The phone call I received from a good friend of mine? These queries take us to the top rung of the ladder of causation, the level of counterfactuals, because to answer them we must go back in time, change history, and ask: "What would have happened if I had not watched the comedy?" Or more generally speaking: "Was it X that caused Y? What if X had not occurred? What if I had acted differently?" No experiment in the world can deny the effect of a measure that has already been taken and compare the two outcomes. Therefore, we have to import a whole new kind of knowledge.

Rung three of the ladder

Good predictions crop up in tandem with good explanations (Toulmin, 1963). We often desire something more than mere prediction. We need to have information about the underlying mechanisms in order to make accurate and robust predictions about what will happen when the system we are in breaks down or modifies itself in various ways; instrumentalist theories provide no such information to get there. To embark on this arduous journey, counterfactual learners, *on the final rung*, can **imagine** worlds that do not exist and infer reasons for observed phenomena. "As-if," exploratory modes and imagination should not be frowned upon by reason, but rather treated as an integral substrate of it (Camp & Shupe, 2018: 106).

Counterfactual reasoning is retrospective reasoning; an ability that according to Pearl most distinguishes humans from animal intelligence, as well as from model-blind versions of AI and machine learning. It tells us what would have happened if events other than the ones we are currently observing had happened.

(A note of warning for the philosophically well-versed reader: In the following setting to *briefly* illustrate counterfactual reasoning for causal queries, we use rather loose speech about causes and effects of behavior; for a more accurate account cf. Dretske, 1988: 37f., who addresses an analogous course of events:) If we are currently observing that both event A (e.g. my mug shatters on the floor) and B (I knock over my cup of tea in reaching for a book) are present, then we can ask ourselves if B would still be present if we had intervened on A and provoked its absence. If we know that B is the actual cause of A, then we should infer that the absence of A (there is no broken mug on the floor) makes no difference to the presence of B because effects do not perforce affect their causes (e.g. the mug can land on my legs because I sit at my desk writing a book on intelligence). By contrast, if I had intervened and stopped the mug from falling in the first place (i.e., ¬B), then we should infer that (ceteris paribus) A also would not occur.

The example evidences that counterfactual reasoning combines observational and interventional reasoning: "[I]nstantiating a counterfactual event is causally equivalent to an imaginary *intervention* on a causal model in which all variables that are not affected by the intervention are assumed to [abide] at currently *observed* levels" (Hagmayer et al., 2007: 87). In other words, counterfactuals are placed at the top of the hierarchy since they subsume interventional and associational questions (Pearl, 2018b: 2). If we have a model that can answer counterfactual queries, we can also answer questions about interventions and observations (ibid.). For instance, the interventional question, "What will happen if I knock over my mug?" can be answered by asking the counterfactual question: "What would happen had the mug been knocked over?" Likewise, associational queries can be covered once we can address interventional queries; we plainly ignore the action part and let observations take over (ibid.). (And, as seen, the translation does not work in the opposite direction.)

Counterfactuals possess an eminently problematic relationship with data since data are, by definition, facts (Pearl, 2018a: 33). They cannot tell us what would happen in a counterfactual or imaginary world where some known facts are bluntly negated. Or how Hofstadter (1979: 638) phrases it in his vivid, eloquent, and congenial way:

> That is what Contrafactus is all about. In everyday thought, we are constantly manufacturing mental variants on situations we face, ideas we have, or events that happen, and we let some features stay exactly the same while others "slip". What features do we let slip? What ones do we not even consider letting slip? What events are perceived on some deep intuitive level as being close relatives of ones which really happened? What do we think "almost" happened or "could have" happened, even though it unambiguously did not? What alternative versions of events pop without any conscious thought into our minds when we hear a story? Why do some counterfactuals strike us as "less counterfactual" than other counterfactuals? After all, it is obvious that anything that didn't happen didn't happen. There aren't degrees of "didn't-happen-ness". And the same goes for "almost" situations. There are times when one plaintively says, "It almost happened", and other times when one says the same thing, full of relief. But the "almost" lies in the mind, not in the external facts.

As seen in Chapter 1, anthropologists like Harari (2014) have general sympathies that the decisive ingredient that empowered our Homo sapiens ancestors to achieve global dominion, about 40,000 years ago, was their ability to choreograph a mental representation, a blue-print of their environment, interrogate that representation, distort it by mental acts of imagination and finally answer "What if?" kind of questions (Pearl, 2018b: 1). And Steiner (1975: 227) sings a counterfactual hymn to counter-factuality: "It is unlikely that man, as we know him, would have survived without the fictive, counter-factual, anti-determinist means of language, without the semantic capacity, generated and stored in the superfluous, zones of the cortex, to conceive of, to articulate possibilities beyond the treadmill of organic decay and death."

Discussion: Pearl's (2018a) approach bears fruits when we are talking about causality since it bypasses long and unproductive disputes of what exactly causality is and focuses instead on the concrete and answerable question "What can a causal reasoner do?" (Pearl, 2018a: 27). Or more precisely, "what can an organism processing a causal model compute that one lacking such a model cannot?" (ibid.). Pearl has been absorbed in game-changing work about causality (for both philosophy and computer science) since long (e.g., cf. his magnum opus in 2000) – game-changing because he converted formerly unsolvable metaphysical questions into decidable mathematical ones. (He even spoke of a causal revolution recently, cf. Pearl, 2020.) With the present treatment, we wish to demonstrate that, given a few amendments and modifications, his work is exceptionally fertile and path-breaking for understanding intelligence too. Therefore, it is needless to say that we attribute grand merits to his ladder of causation.

Yet, on the flipside, the weak points of his proposal, as sketched in this subchapter, have to be fixed prior to harvesting the fruits. The enumeration of weaknesses in the following thus delineates our agenda in Chapter 5 to come.

- Pearl's (2018a) contention about animals' and machines' rank or position in his causal ladder are simplistic and empirically wrong; possibly/fatally, affecting all three levels. We address this point in 5.1.
- A further strength of Pearl's (2018a) conception is that each layer in the hierarchy has a syntactic signature that characterizes the sentences admitted into that layer (Pearl, 2018b building on Pearl, 2000). (E.g., on the interventional layer, we find conditional probability sentences like $P(y \mid do(x), z)$ stating that: The probability of event Y = y given that we intervene and set the value of X to x and subsequently observe event Z = z is equal to p. More on this in Chapter 6.) For the sake of capturing intelligence though, the three rungs are not fine-grained enough. We address this point in 5.1.
- For the same purpose, capturing intelligence, the causal ladder remains under-complex and neglects material aspects and forms of intelligence. For instance, a corollary of the current version would be that some present-day AI ranks as high as Einstein on rung three, which is inacceptable (not least for Pearl himself who sees us humans accommodated at the lonely pinnacle of causal reasoning): "A neurosymbolic or purely symbolic [machine learning] system should be capable of satisfying the requirements of all three of Pearl's levels, e.g. by mapping the neural networks onto symbolic descriptions"

(Garcez & Lamb, 2020: 8). "[S]ymbolic machine learning [. . .] is unequivocally not confined to association rules" (ibid.: 19). We shall revert to this point and give a concrete example of such an AI system in 5.2.
- The image of a ladder is inappropriate. Not only proves a three-rung ladder to be insufficient for reaching the top (AD 5.1.), but it is indeterminate what wall to lean it against, given how multidirectional intelligence is in different animals (both within and between species). We address this latter point in 5.2.
- The model needs to be more dynamic. Imbued by the excursion in 4.2., we address this point in 5.3.

5 Towards a causal theory of intelligence

The flexibility of intelligence comes from the enormous number of different rules, and levels of rules. The reason that so many rules on so many different levels must exist is that in life, a creature is faced with millions of situations of completely different types.
Douglas R. Hofstadter, 1979: 35

In this core Chapter, we erect the crucial analogy between this layeredness and agility of intelligence – Hofstadter sees a so-called tangled hierarchy of rules at the core of intelligence –, on the one hand, and a consolidated framework fueled by the prior work from the previous Chapter, on the other, rendering the latter more general and refined, transcending the stiff image of a ladder found throughout in Chapter 4 (as well as in Chapter 1). The upshot is not, I suspect, yet another "new science of the mind", but something potentially rather better. For what emerges in the following could, on the one hand, fill the more specific gap of a currently missing philosophical theory of intelligence, which, I suppose, comes with more explanatory power than counterparts in psychology such as Gardner's theory of multiple intelligences (MI) that primarily describes intelligence as a non-unitary faculty with pluralistic forms. On the other, our approach is really just a meeting point for the best of many previous approaches as documented in broad strokes in Chapter 4, connecting dots from philosophy of causation, causal learning, interventionist theories of causation, causal graphical modeling, scaffolding prediction, Guttman's (1954) radex model, and contemporary psychological perspectives.

That the ladders of cognition, prediction and causation are merely a simple, crude, malleable metaphor that does not unfold the full potential of the idea of elucidating intelligence in terms of causality becomes visible when we generalize it and develop it further. This is the aim of this Chapter 5. In particular, we undertake five steps to universalize and strengthen the approach initiated in Chapter 4.

1) Making it explicitly about intelligences, covering cognitive traits *and* emotional or social intelligence as well as higher-order capabilities, of all kinds of animals (from biological to artificial).
2) Converting a static view into a fully dynamic perspective.
3) Moving from three rungs of the causal ladder to sublevels and more nuanced dimensions.
4) Surpassing the restrictive ladder image and allowing more flexibility. Specifically and just as another, yet more fertile illustration, we morph the ladder into a simplex.

5) We chose a simplex because complemented by a circumplex, we obtain a radex which lends itself to represent not only the multidimensionality, but also the multidirectionality of intelligence.

As we saw, there are grave differences among observation, intervention, and counterfactuals. Nevertheless, they can be given a unified treatment within the causal model framework. From failures of the past such as the *Scala Naturae* in Figure 4, but also from neighboring disciplines like biology we have learnt how ambitious and demanding it is to throw up a taxonomy that is universally accepted, even when the main mechanisms have been unraveled, such as why the individuals exist, Darwin's natural selection (Hernández-Orallo, 2017: 28). For our taxonomy of intelligence, let us begin by hanging on to Pearl's and others' idea that our human comparative power and flexibility of intelligence, invoked by Hofstadter (1979: 35), stem from the fully causal and compositional nature of our mental representations.

5.1 The universal taxonomy: More nuanced dimensions of intelligence and causality

In this subchapter, we show that, under the umbrella of causal inference and causal analysis for mapping intelligence, subjects cognitively distinguish between *more* than three different kinds of causal reasoning, alluding to the mantra that "[t]ruly intelligent and flexible systems are likely to be full of complexity, much like brains" (Marcus & Davis, 2021). Of course, we do not intend to mirror this full complexity; a model as complex as the system it models would be useless. Instead, our critique here of Pearl's (2018a) conception is that a three-level model of intelligence would be basically the other extreme.

Before we commence to create a more fine-grained version of the causal hierarchy (in three more subchapters 5.1.1. to 5.1.3.), a general remark is in order, affecting all new and old levels of the hierarchy. Pearl (2018a, b) remains unexpectedly silent about what sorts of systems are eligible to be ranked in his causal ladder at all – just to point to *causal learners* is clearly as unsatisfactory as to admit anything and everything (why should I wonder if my toaster, not to be confused with toasters on wheels, Marshall, 2020; or a stone is a causal learner). In contrast to both alternatives, we submit that *only systems that are agents are authorized for the causal ranking*.

Questions of causal learning, ranging from "what is?" (rung one in the ladder image) to "if only?" (rung three) cannot be prompted by any system, but must be raised by an agent. Concepts such as "agenthood" or "agency", often associated with "volition", "intentionality" or "deliberation" are metaphysically loaded, and, thus, leave wriggle room for considerable debate and philosophical disagreement (Hoffmann & Hahn, 2020: 639). Something like the following is often the outcome of philosophers' rich debate: Agency is bound to rationality, which in turn is bound to freedom and justifications: An entity is an agent only if it has different behavioral options, can weigh reasons, and can decide on the basis of those reasons. Only then is there an action, and therefore justifications can be claimed or given for actions (as distinct from behavior).

Such conceptual analyses are evidently unacceptable to us. For example, in Chapter 3, I argued that the concept of rationality is inadequate to inform a broad notion of intelligence which we wish to apply to not only rational humans, but also to probably arational non-human animals, and non-rational machines. I do not consider this dissent a particular problem. First, our aim is not to contribute to those philosophical controversies, but to sketch a universal theory of intelligence. Second, several incompatible definitions of agency can coexist (in our case, it is maximally a working definition). Definitions are not true or false, but more or less useful, and the proposal appealing to rationality and reasons is of little use to me and our purposes. What is safe to say is that an agent, given the etymology, is somebody or a system that can *act*.

Action can be said to be a particular species of behavior. Although there is (unmiraculously) no settled view on what, exactly, an action is, the general consensus appears to be "that (ignoring niceties) it is either itself something one does voluntarily or deliberately (e.g., playing the piano) or a direct consequence, whether intended and foreseen or not, of such a voluntary act (e.g., unintentionally disturbing one's neighbors by intentionally playing the piano)." (Dretske, 1988: 5). The examples underline that humans take actions, but also that they can be explicitly contrasted with the involuntary beating of one's heart or the involuntary perspiring under the influence of fear (Taylor, 1966: 61). Moreover, we are not stones whose fate is completely at the mercy of *external* forces, but our movements are actions because they are *internally* produced to yield *external* effects.

How about nonhuman systems (especially machines or plants) where it might sound odd to speak of them as performing actions in this sense? For that, I wish to replace "voluntarily or deliberately" by "autonomously" because the latter is less related to inner states of an agent and more natural for general systems comprising plants and artifacts that for the time being do not have a will, desires, intentions, etc. Agency is a *measurable* property of machines, animals or simply of systems that comes in degrees, rather than a binary feature. We can approximate the gradual concept by taking the respective system's autonomy into consideration.

Thus, a way to define the degree of agency can be given by the degree of autonomy "with respect to some goal that [the agent] actively uses its capabilities to pursue", which in turn is tantamount to "the degree to which the decision-making process, used to determine how that goal should be pursued, is free from intervention by any other agent" (Barber & Martin, 2001: 407). Or semi-formally: X is autonomous to a degree y in respect to an action H if, and only if, X is independent of any other agent's $Z = \{z_1, z_2, \ldots\}$ influence to the extent y, as far as the mechanism yielding the action H is concerned. Whether the fact that, for instance, some AI systems (like in vehicles for *autonomous* driving) rely on randomness (or pseudo-randomness) affects the AI system's (or, generally, X's) autonomy is a question for another work.

Coming historically from computers that flatly execute programs, we have arrived at considering, for instance, robots that are able to assess in real time the shape of their own body, and act accordingly in pursuing their goals so that these systems reached a higher degree of autonomy (Verdicchio, 2017: 185); in fact, a degree y high enough to treat many present-day AI systems as agents (cf. also Russell & Norvig, 2009: vii, and the intelligent agent continuum). How high y has exactly turned out to be in state-of-the-art machines does not have to be settled here. For our purposes, it is sufficient that it can be vindicated to treat them as agents. (Plants, as we know from Part I, are out of scope in this treatment.) The restriction that an agent needs to be sufficiently autonomous aids us in effectively warding off the threat that systems are decorated with the medal of intelligence which are mere puppets of their designers, users or owners (e.g., envision Block's, 1981, charlatan machine).

As announced in the subchapter summary of 4.3. above, a second general remark is that Pearl (2018a) is wrong about the classification of humans, animals and machines in his ladder, depending on *what* animal (species) or *what* machine (type) we refer to (barring more trivial counterexamples like human coma patients that can be reasonably regarded as non-agents given their low autonomy). His empirical error implicates that not only a further differentiation of agents' levels of causal learning is indicated, but also a further differentiation between humans, animals and machines within the scheme. We revisit this list of grounds for empirical doubt in coordination with the causal levels which we climb incrementally over the next pages.

5.1.1 Let the causal revolution begin: Partition of identification and observation?

As seen in 4.3., the overriding question on this level is, What is?, which seems to be omnipresent in both behaviorism 70 years ago (the age of B.F. Skinner in psychology and Gilbert Ryle in philosophy) and the machine kingdom nowadays dominated by deep learning. According to Pearl (2020), this radical empiricism is a stifling culture since it lures researchers into a data-centric paradigm, which venerates data as the source of all knowledge rather than a window through which we learn about the world around us. It is somehow bitter that Pearl (2018a) blows this stifling culture up further by banishing animals and machines per se to rung one. To counteract the impression that all animals and AI systems are home to this lowest level of causation, we have three comments to make: Firstly, machine learning is not confined to association rule mining; *ipso facto*, AI overall is not confined to level one of causal reasoning; cf. the body of work on symbolic machine learning & relational learning (e.g., Muggleton, 1991; the differences to deep learning being the choice of representation, localist logical rather than distributed, and the non-use of gradient-based learning algorithms; Garcez & Lamb, 2020: 8). Indeed, we see later that some AI can rank as high as level three in Pearl's (2018a) framework.

Secondly, until the mid-2010s, it was almost preposterous of evaluating the cognitive abilities of a real AI system (as opposed to a hypothetical system of the future) using Skinner's and fellows' methods of conditioning or reinforcement, established for studying the cognitive abilities of animals (Shanahan et al., 2020: 863); for instance because obvious assumptions that can safely be made about animals were not met by machines like assuming subjects that are motivated by various basic needs and will therefore exhibit purposeful behavior. If this incommensurability is a given, how can both animals and machines be said to be home on the same rung one? I do not think that there is a meaningful answer to this question on this level of abstractness. It only changes with a more fine-grained texture. For example, following Shanahan et al. (2020) and Crosby et al. (2019), it makes sense of comparing deep reinforcement learning (a subgroup of deep learning methods that in turn are a subset of machine learning being a pillar of AI as Figure 11 taught us) and animals in terms of common-sense capacities.

Thirdly, while AI only made the leap to the first level of reinforcement learning a few years ago, for many animals the model is overworked since long. On the one hand, many of the basic, i.e., level one learning abilities such as detecting statistical information are not unique to humans, but are shared with probably all multi-celled organisms, to greater or lesser extents (Marcus, 2004: 26).

On the other hand, many animals prove higher capabilities in many situations. Take the Skinnerian prime example of rats for which it has been shown that they grasp the difference between interventions and observations (Blaisdell et al., 2006), which could qualify them to the second level. Or recall Jelbert et al. (2014) from Chapter 2 who submitted that New Caledonian crows possess an adept, but incomplete, understanding of the *causal* properties of displacement, rivalling that of 5–7 year old children. In nuce, the extent to which non-human animals are capable of causal understanding is not well understood and should not be underestimated by banning the whole animal kingdom to level one. Such a bold thesis would flatly be false and in need of a full overhaul.

Taking now, after those preliminaries, Pearl's (2018a) proposal of the causal ladder as point of departure, we await the most distress to rationalize rung one within a causal framework because it does not enact anything distinctively causal. This has to be acknowledged. Notwithstanding, it is a pivotal layer since there are passive systems that are sensitive to associations/correlations and to temporal relationships only such as the Pavlovian dogs encountered above. (This means that dogs in this particular situation, in this experimental setup are passive learners; not dogs in general or Pavlov's dogs specifically.) Passive learning can be accomplished since as long as the correlation in question is not brittle, but projectable, useful predictions can be made. Are there enlightening fragmentations of this first association layer, categorically different types of merely observing? The negative answer is that we do not deem it helpful to isolate temporal from probabilistic relationships because on the association layer, we operate with classical conditional probabilities which are interpreted temporally, e.g., $P(y \mid x) = p$ stating that: the probability of event $Y = y$ given that we observ*ed* event $X = x$ is equal to p. About a positive answer, we are unsure.

As shown in Figure 20, different segmentations of associations can be suggested for different occasions and contexts. For example, a continuum of patterns and regularities to be observed exists, from very *simple* to very *complex* ones, e.g., involving more than two variables, a weak manifestation of correlations, brittleness, etc. Then, there are many incremental differences within this category which point to the divergent *speed* or *processing powers* at which agents detect relationships and form predictions. Finally, we can juxtapose the observation of *agents' acts* (and at a deeper level between successful interventions, which lead to a detectable effect, and failures) with the *motions of mechanical devices* since only the former are fathomed within an agentive framework with goals and intentions.

Moreover, it might prima facie seem to be a controversial question if this first main category of association endures as an independent layer of the causal hierarchy in some respects. We identify at least a psychological, empirical objection with regard to advanced biological agents' observation of agents' acts where it is

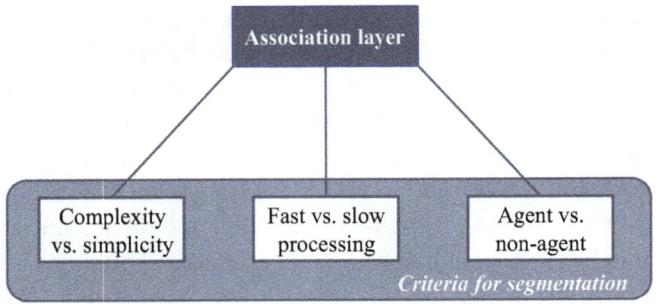

Figure 20: Possible segmentations of the first layer of the causal hierarchy.

found that observing and intervening are intimately bound up with causal learning in a reciprocal delicate interplay. For example, Sommerville (2007) argues that human infants' experience of their own actions and the consequences that these actions have on the world play a vital role in their developing understanding of causal relations. Or Meltzoff (2007: 37) reports that "[c]ausal learning by children combines both observation and action" and goes so far to insist on "a fundamental equivalence between the perception and production of acts that is built into the mind of the human baby" (ibid.: 39). Tout court, learning by seeing and learning by doing cannot be quarantined from each other; at least for humans, at least based on these findings. What agents observe influences what they do, and what they can do changes their attention to their environment and how they interpret it.

For less advanced systems, these results do not need to bother us much. If an agent does not make it to level two, we do not need to wonder to what extent seeing and doing are interweaved. Hence, the upshot is that 1) *if* an agent has the capacity of seeing *and* doing, then we witness that both are interlocked and we witness a smooth transition from the first to the second rung in lieu of distinct categories; 2) there is no imperative partition of the association layer for understanding intelligence and assessing agents' intelligence, yet different criteria can be invoked; and 3) the first layer only represents the front hall of the house of causal learning, marking the threshold between learning and intelligent agents vs. non-learning and dumb automata. (Are there non-learning or dumb agents? Given our working definition of agency, there could be prima facie). Even though we (humans) may be able to represent the scene before our eyes as causal, speaking in favor of coupling causation and observation (Beebee, 2009; and therefore the foyer is inside the house), a manipulationist approach to causation is appealing in part because it seems to provide a natural treatment of the disparities between truly causal and purely correlational claims and why we ought to care about this difference (Woodward, 2009: 235; Cartwright, 1983).

5.1.2 In medias res: Three sublevels of intervention

As seen in 4.3., the overriding question on this level is, What if?, characterizing the second layer of interventions. Interventionism is the view that for X to be a cause of Y is for intervening on X to be a way of intervening on Y (cf. Pearl, 2000; Spirtes et al., 1993), appealing to the common-sense idea that "causal relationships are relationships that are potentially exploitable for purposes of manipulation and control" (Woodward, 2009: 234). This is not a reductive definition of causation (see also Chapter 6). On the contrary, it makes untethered use of causal notions in defining the idea of an intervention and in explaining what it is for a set of variables to be causally sufficient. A natural worry could be that this notion is too abstract, complex and cognitively sophisticated to be psychologically realistic. In assessing this concern, Woodward (2007: 28) highlights two issues:
1) Do most people consciously or explicitly represent to themselves the full technical definition of a normatively appropriate notion of intervention when they engage in causal reasoning?
2) Do people learn and reason in accord with the normative requirements of the interventionist account?

Whilst Woodward (2007: 28) moves the former aside (since the answer to it is an obvious no), he is convinced that the empirical answer to the second is affirmative (e.g., cf. Steyvers et al., 2003; Lagnado & Sloman, 2004; Sobel & Kushnir, 2006). For the sake of (causal) learning, the interest is more in the discovery of causal relationships and the prediction of the effects of manipulations than in appealing to the notion of manipulation to prematurely give a general account of causality (Woodward, 2009: 235).

With this in mind, we can already gesture at qualitative disparities between interventions. Following Tomasello and Call's (1997: 367–400) notion of a tertiary relationship, Gärdenfors' (2003: section 2.8) classification with four kinds of causal reasoning, as well as Woodward's (2007: 32) three levels of causal/instrumental understanding along similar lines, we can indeed refine our framework on layer two by accounting for the following sublevels:

2.1) *Egocentric viewpoint*: An agent parses (or behaves as if (s)he parses) that there are regular, stable relationships which connect her/his manipulations (e.g., my dog licks my face) to various downstream effects (I have a smile on my face and am happy) but ceases at this point, not recognizing (or behaving as though (s)he recognizes) that the same relationship or effect can be present even when (s)he does not act (I see my girlfriend and I smile too). In this case, the relevance of observations concerning what happens around the agent, i.e., under interventions of others or in nature is elusive to that agent. The only way the agent learns about a manipulative relationship is if (s)he performs the relevant manipulation.

This trial-and-error account of learning overshadows the most momentous aspect of learning, namely a grasp of the essential (deeper) structure of the system or problem which can be referred to as insight. The modern empirical studies suggest that, while some animals may conform to this description, the egocentric human infant is a fiction (Meltzoff, 2007: 46). By contrast, ants, for instance, appear to represent spatial relations egocentrically. Ants know where their nest is in relation to their own body movements, but if they are scooped up and displaced even only slightly, they seem to lose orientation, even in accustomed terrain (Sommer & Wehner, 2004). Other animals, like mice, construct spatial maps. Once mice have explored a territory, they can always take the shortest route to a goal, no matter where they are placed initially (Tolman, 1932).

2.2) **The agent causal viewpoint**: The animal or agent grasps that the same relationship which (s)he exploits in intervening can also be present when other animals or agents act – e.g., let us say I have two dogs, does one dog realize and learn that I also start smiling when my other dog licks my face? According to Meltzoff (2007: 46), this "agentive view" is a reasonable description of the prelinguistic toddler while it seems that non-human animals do not grow beyond understanding causation in terms of agency (Gärdenfors & Lombard, 2020: 5). Moreover, the crucial role that learning from the interventions by others appears to play in the development of human causal understanding suggests that two abilities often regarded as rather different – the *social intelligence* materialized in imitation and causal understanding of the nonsocial world – may, in fact, be closely tied together (Woodward, 2007: 35).

2.3) **The fully causal viewpoint**: The animal or agent grasps that the same relationship which the agent exploits in intervening can also be present both when other agents act *and* in nature when no other agents get enmeshed – e.g., I smile in a light summer rain. This presupposes thinking of causation as a tertiary relationship: A relationship qualifies as tertiary for a subject according to Tomasello & Call (1997: 367–400) if the relationship is recognized as holding between objects and individuals that are independent of the subject. This insight by the agent signifies that (s)he could make use of those very relationships which occur in nature in the absence of her/his intervention for purposes of manipulation.

Additionally, the fully causal viewpoint also includes the ability to learn about complex causal structures through combinations of interventions that reveal direct vs. indirect causal relationships. For instance, even small children learn not only the causal consequences of their isolated interventions but also, more intriguingly, other causal relationships from combinations of interventions performed by others (Gopnik & Schulz, 2004; Gopnik et al., 2004). The representations and abilities that underlie nonhuman instrumental learning may not be fully causal according to the present level 2.3 (Woodward, 2007: 34), even though, as indicated in Chapter 2, many animals and at least some species have many features in common with human causal learning and representation.

In principle, we could carry on this partition and envision further sublevels such as this one: Designing, not performing an intervention or an experiment (in the sense of 2.1 to 2.3) requires meta-cognition because to design a bespoke intervention, you have to comprehend what makes an intervention appropriate and meta-cognition, in both animals and humans, can be said to ground in affordance sensings, which are feeling-based evaluative attitudes (Proust, 2018). Learning from interventions does not require meta-cognition. However, we hypothesize that adding house by house in this manner would only result in constructing a Potemkin village since with this alleged sublevel we prematurely enter the land of level three where we communicate not just the tangible, but the possible, the counterfactual and dreamt-of. (On the other hand, this backs up the conclusion from 5.1.1. that the layers of the causal hierarchy are intertwined.) Therefore, we prefer to draw a line under level 2.3 and give, instead, a graphical summary in the following Figure 21.

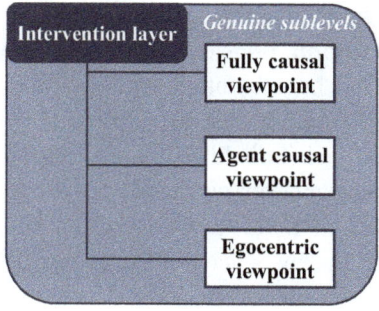

Figure 21: Genuine segmentation of the second layer of the causal hierarchy.

A substantive feature and part of intervention is tool use (Woodward, 2011), namely in terms of tracing the trajectory of our cognitive and bodily relationships with different guises of technology which is central to developing an understanding of how we, in the later phases in the Homo lineage, evolved the capacity for abstract causal thinking (Gärdenfors & Lombard, 2020). Using the example of apes, but also corvids and octopi in Chapter 2, we are aware that quite a few animal species employ tools as well, but, as a tech entrepreneur myself, it is dear to my heart to curtail the significance of their achievements vis-à-vis human technical engagement (cf. also Edwards et al., 2011: 111). Shumaker et al. (2011: 223f.) identify four ways in which human tool making and use are more or less unique.

1. Non-human animals do not typically use tools to make tools.
2. Non-humans other than great apes rarely use tools in combinations for a single task.
3. Non-humans rarely cooperate in using or making tools.
4. Non-humans power their tools only with gravity and their own energy.

Based on my practical experience as cofounder of four companies, I could definitely comment on and add to this list, most notably that non-human agents do not typically devise tools to address higher-order problems, problems which only emerged because (other) tools were designed and applied before, which in turn emanated from other tools and other problems (or, as we would phrase it in the innovation scene, business opportunities), and so on. (I let the wily reader her-/himself recognize the analogy to Hofstadter, 1979.) To give a simplified example, my startup Syntherion developed a software tool to cope with a blind spot of banks' risk management architecture (Hoffmann, 2020b; Hoffmann & Heide, 2018) which only existed because banks were built in the first place, which in turn was undertaken to channel funds from those with surplus funds to those with shortages of funds, etc.

And as Gärdenfors & Lombard (2020: 8) point out tools function as amplifiers in a threefold sense. Firstly, many tools amplify actions whereby the tool usually changes the form of the actions we perform. Consider catching a fish with a net or with your bare hands or writing this book by hand, without a laptop; or shooting Neil Armstrong to the moon without a rocket, etc. Furthermore, our human body itself might be perceived as a tool (Donald, 2012), e.g., in the sense that, while apes' hands are often tied to locomotion, our hands are free to assemble tools. Secondly, as the blind person's stick illustrates, tools can amplify perception, hence sensory amplifiers. And thirdly, some tools amplify cognition. Abstractions in the form of words, numbers and other symbolic systems amplify memory, planning and communication. And our current AI systems are cognitive amplifiers par excellence.

Against the background of the multidimensionality of intelligence, we can conclude that 1) the three sublevels of the egocentric, the agent causal and the fully causal viewpoint instantiate relevant, cogent grades of causal reasoning, and thus constituent parts of our refined causal hierarchy; 2) a partition genuinely makes sense on this second layer because we greet possible combinations in a multi-agent world: e.g., one active agent for learning on 2.1. and one and another active agent on 2.2., whereas *all* agents remain passive on level one (see 5.1.1.); 3) tool use can stimulate abstract causal reasoning and lead to thoughts about other uses for the technology: "When one uses a hammerstone to crack a nut, the result is something that is immediately edible. When one uses a hammerstone to shape another stone tool, the result is something *usable*. Cracking the nut opens up for consumption, but a tool opens up for new *actions* that are detached in time and space." (Gärdenfors & Lombard, 2020: 12).

Technology and tool use also set the stage for counterfactual thinking, as "they also require the ability to imagine a range of potential outcomes, to understand the consequences of those outcomes, and to grasp that the outcomes may have been divergent if any of the preceding circumstances varied [. . .], for which the neural hardware only reaches its final development in humans after adolescence" (Gärdenfors & Lombard, 2020: 17).

5.1.3 Deep understanding, not deep learning: Three different nuances of imagination

> *Imagination is more important than knowledge. For knowledge is limited to all we now know and understand, while imagination embraces the entire world, and all there ever will be to know and understand.*
> Albert Einstein

As seen in 4.3., the overriding question on this level is, If only?, which is a retrospective question. If only we had Figure 19 in front of us, we could ask ourselves why this third level of Pearl's and our hierarchy is captioned by imagination. Firstly and patently, counterfactual deliberations can only be exerted in an agent's imagination and, by definition, not be about the factual world. Secondly, it does not seem far-fetched to propose that dreaming, imagining, and mental imagery become available "as part and parcel of the very same cognitive package that delivered our grip on a structured (organism-salient) external world" (Clark, 2016: 94), involving spotting the causes therein. The manufacture of "subjunctive worlds" occurs so casually, so naturally, that we hardly notice what we are doing (Hofstadter, 1979: 640). And still when we elect from our fantasy a world which is close, in some internal mental sense, to the real world and compare them, it is a master stroke of the mind, echoing the layeredness and agility of intelligence at its best.

> We build up our mental representation of a situation layer by layer. The lowest layer erects the deepest aspect of the context – sometimes being so low that it cannot vary at all. For instance, the three-dimensionality of our world is so ingrained that most of us never would imagine letting it slip mentally. It is a constant constant. Then there are layers which establish temporarily, though not permanently, fixed aspects of situations, which could be called background assumptions – things which, in the back of your mind, you know can vary, but which most of the time you unquestioningly accept as unchanging aspects. [. . .] Finally, we reach the "shakiest" aspects of your mental representation of the situation – the variables. These are things such as Palindromi's stepping out of bounds, which are mentally "loose" and which you don't mind letting slip away from their real values, for a short moment. (Hofstadter, 1979: 641)

We could further ask ourselves how this intimate relationship between imagination and understanding comes about, imagination's embrace of all there ever will be to understand. In hindsight to the lower levels, we can maintain that a system that does not merely make discriminations (level one) or produce agentive outputs (level two) that, when best interpreted by *us*, come out true (cf. also Haugeland, 1997b: 28), but rather appreciates for itself the difference between truth and falsity, between causes and non-causes, between causation and correlation, and so on, and a system that "appreciates that, in these, it must accede to the world, that the world determines which is which – and it *cares*" (ibid.), understands. To discover what causal claims are true and what are false, the agent has to conduct a *mental* experiment as seen in 4.3.: "There is only one way a thinking entity (computer or human) can work out what would happen in multiple scenarios, including some that it has never experienced before. It must possess, consult, and manipulate a mental causal model of that reality" (Pearl cited in Darwiche, 2017: 10).

Therefore, based on these lines as well as on the announcement in Chapter 3.1. where we suggested our initial understanding of "understanding", we now coin "understanding" or "comprehension" (which are synonymous here) as follows: Agent X understands a system S to a degree y if X models S and the causes and effects therein to inform X's action; y is low in this connection if X acts sporadically (and more often with increasing y) *as if* X had a model of S; y lies in the center if X's model is (very) incomplete (down to the simplest model where there are only a single cause and effect) or if X only manages sporadically to act upon X's model; y is high if X's model is as complete as possible and if the translation into action is smooth.

Nota bene that this analysis is neither in tension with the quotes from e.g., Dennett (2017) or Haugeland (1997b) that we gave in the course of this treatise, nor with what we accentuated earlier about the concept of understanding, e.g., in Chapter 2, 3.1. and 4.1.; two examples to underpin this latter statement: On the one hand, meta-cognition was presented as a sufficient condition for comprehension.

This still holds in light of the conceptual analysis in the last paragraph because we can capture meta-cognition by a high y in terms of a meta model or meta representation of S. And even if we could not capture it, no contradiction would arise since, in the last paragraph, we only provided a weak and modest, not a strict definition that would have posited logical equivalence (if, and only if). On the other hand, in 4.1., comprehension was portrayed as a higher-level competence, applying several domains of knowledge. This, too, can be integrated here as different knowledge is required to obtain a causal model in the first place, and the more complete X's model is, the more it is enriched by distinct fields of knowledge.

In a materialist fashion of viewing understanding (in consonance with Dennett or Turing, for instance), a comprehending system is then one that exhibits an apt pattern of coherent *behavior* when actively engaging with possibly the entire world, expressing what the system appreciates as true and false. If an AI system can be manufactured that behaves on its own in such a manner, consistently enough and in a suitable variety of circumstances (it does not have to be flawless), then it has *original* understanding, depending utterly and exclusively on a certain sort of pattern in the system's behavior. Syntax can thus mirror semantics (Arkoudas & Bringsjord, 2015: 42), or, as Haugeland (1985: 106) put it, "if you take care of the syntax, the semantics will take care of itself." (Cf. also Rapaport, 1988, who gives a formidable account of how the right syntax can constitute semantics.) In the title to this subchapter 5.1.3., we not only speak of understanding, but of deep understanding, which is borrowed from Pearl (2020), and contrast it with the acquainted deep learning from Chapter 3.1. Deep learning is not that deep though. It is noteworthy that, in the term "deep learning", the word "deep" alludes to the number of layers in a neural network and nothing more. "Deep", in that context, does not signify that the system has learned anything eminently conceptually rich about the data it has screened (Marcus & Davis, 2019: 62). Deep understanding, by contrast, leads astray less; less because the reader may hold it for a nebulous concept. But, according to Pearl (2020) and in harmony with our more incisive analysis of the concept of comprehension on the previous page, it is formally well-defined as any system capable of covering all three (as we would add: main) levels of the causal hierarchy: What is – What if – Only if; or more specifically: What if I see (identification) – What if I do (intervention) – and what if I acted differently (imagination).

This could very well arouse suspicion of cheating – we take the fundamental capabilities of one system and posit them as a general criterion for defining the general concept of deep understanding which in turn characterizes the system's level three causal thinking (that comprises level two and one). It is not cheating and for the same reason that counterfactual analysis is not plagued with circularity: one's account of the causal relation in terms of counterfactual dependence necessitates an account of counterfactual dependence in terms of causation, given that causal thinking is so deeply woven into our day to day language, our reasoning, our humor and of course our scientific understanding. (Woodward, 2003, or, in brief, Woodward, 2009: 253f., defends the stance that a circular analysis is still informative. Cf. also Menzies & Price, 1993: 193.)

These last comments motivate me to add a few more words on counterfactuals prior to partitioning the highest level three of the causal hierarchy. When we mention counterfactuals in one sentence with causation, then philosophers are usually triggered to think of full-blown counterfactual theories of causation (where Stalnaker, 1968, and Lewis, 1973a develop the accepted semantics for counterfactuals in terms of similarity of possible worlds to the actual world; for a primer, cf. Collins et al., 2004); and the bulk of them of broad reductionist commitments. Adherents of that school sometimes take counterfactual dependence between (successive, suitably distinct) events to be sufficient for causation (Lewis, 1973b). Admittedly, the counterfactual perspective on causality aligns closely with human intuition: We think of a cause as something that makes a difference, and the difference it makes must be a difference from what would have happened without it. Or semi-formally: If event E would not occur if event C were not to happen, then C is a cause of E (Paul, 2009: 159). Yet, due to intuitively clear cases of causation without simple counterfactual dependence, counterfactual dependence is not a *sine qua non* for causation: "it is not the case that C is a cause of E *only* when E depends on C" (ibid.). Hence, the causal relation between C and E cannot be *reduced* to the relation of counterfactual dependence between C and E.

As stated above, as stating here and as it will be stated again in Chapter 6, I do not have the faintest intention to delve into those metaphysical disputes further. We are not compelled to take sides or to adopt this strong reading of counterfactuals as embedded in a reductionist counterfactual theory of causation which suffers from a host of problems. Whilst many metaphysicians find reductionism very appealing, we, in the spirit of the systems and complexity movement (see Chapter 1), abandon and bury it. Why should we agonize over counterexamples involving baroque laws of magic at distant possible worlds that ultimately prove irrelevant for *our* endeavor? Why should we revisit the semantics of counterfactuals or tackle the so-called hard problem of causation and not content ourselves with accepting possibly primitive or pragmatic elements as part of our account?

Our pragmatic stance also becomes visible from the fact that we mingle interventionist (5.1.2.) and counterfactual (5.1.3.) approaches (and maybe even the "singularist" (Anscombe, 1971) or "regularist" (Hume I) view of causation in 5.1.1.) with causal modeling (Chapter 6) bridging the gulf. (In a conventional philosophical handbook of causation, we would instead have three to four or five distinct chapters on *rival* approaches, cf. Beebee et al., 2009.) Unlike the more traditional philosophical accounts of causality canvassed in such handbooks, we do not attempt to analyze causation in terms of anything else. Following the causal modeling programs, which we see more closely in the next Chapter 6, we do throw up interconnections between causal relationships on the one hand, and regularities (Hume I), counterfactuals (Hume II), interventions (e.g., Woodward), and probabilities (e.g., Reichenbach or Suppes) on the other, thus making contact with more traditional programs at a number of points (Hitchcock, 2009: 299). (For instance, the difference between observation (level one) and intervention (level two) roughly corresponds to the difference between so-called backtracking and non-backtracking counterfactuals in the philosophical literature and Lewis, 1973b, and others, e.g., the interventionist theory yields a similar conclusion, hold that non-backtracking rather than backtracking counterfactuals are appropriate for understanding causation.)

Imbued by Tenenbaum et al.'s (2007: 314) work on a taxonomy of increasingly abstract knowledge representations for viewing intuitive theories, again with close cognates and overlappings in parallel work (e.g., Lombard & Gärdenfors, 2017), we suggest to segment the third level of counterfactual thinking as follows:

3.1) *Inferring* **single causes and effects**: Infer the hidden causes of an observed event, or predict its unobserved effects through a thought experiment (e.g., like exemplified in 4.3. where we wondered why my bad mood is gone), given an explicit or implicit network structure relating causes and effects in the relevant system.

3.2) *Inferring* **causal networks**: Infer the structure of a network of causal relations that governs a system of observed variables given more general framework-like knowledge: the principles constraining candidate causal structures in the relevant domain. Only by integrating this and the remaining higher sublevel we substantially go beyond Pearl (2018a, b), enter uncharted territory, and only then, we can effectively scaffold the peaks of intelligence (and circumvent some unwelcome results like that some second wave AI would be on the same level than us; cf. Garcez & Lamb, 2020: 8).

3.3) *Inferring* **causal principles**: Infer the principles that organize and orchestrate a set of observed causal systems, given higher-level theoretical frameworks: knowledge about a larger domain that encompasses those systems, or domain-general assumptions; at the end of the day, simply substantiating the point that neither learning nor intelligence is possible without any prior knowledge or programmed-in features. With inferring causal networks and principles, we are able to abstract the knowledge gained from one domain and apply it to another by *imagining* how past scenarios can be used in the future to solve a range of unrelated problems innovatively (Lombard & Gärdenfors, 2017). This, as seen as early as in Chapter 2, constitutes the hallmark of understanding.

Human everyday causal inference unfolds at all of these three sublevels simultaneously (Tenenbaum et al., 2007: 314) albeit novel inferences at higher levels may only be relatively frequent for non-adults (Gopnik & Meltzoff, 1997), doing justice to the folk wisdom that babies and children learn more and faster than their parents. Graphically, this partition and formulation of causal induction results in the following Figure 22.

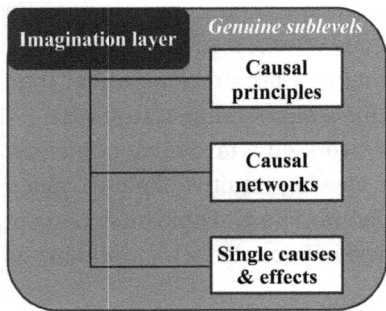

Figure 22: Genuine segmentation of the third layer of the causal hierarchy.

This hierarchical framework unifies the triumvirate of causal inferences and demonstrates that a causal learner may in principle tackle them all at the same time. In order to explain how to solve all of these inference problems on 3.1., 3.2., and 3.3. in concert, we can turn to Chomsky's work (1956, 1962) on generative grammar in language, and exploit the common form of all three problems: knowledge at a more abstract level generates constraints that each hypothesized structure imposes on hypotheses at lower levels or, put differently, generates a constrained space of candidate hypotheses to be evaluated based on data from lower levels of abstraction. Thus, a learning agent's observations of, and interventions in the world are construed in terms of a hierarchy of increasingly abstract and general cognitive structure that in important ways bears some resemblance with the hierarchy of rules as presented by Hofstadter (1979: 35).

Yet, Hofstadter also emphasized strange loops and circularity as the gist of intelligence. Where do they fit in here, what are those loops in the first place, and why do they enunciate intelligence? In the opening of this Chapter, Hofstadter was quoted as writing: "The flexibility of intelligence comes from the enormous number of different rules [. . .] on so many different levels [which] exist [because,] in life, a creature is faced with millions of situations of completely different types." *This* expresses intelligence in a at least threefold way: first and most straightforward (on the object level), what Hofstadter says is intelligent, i.e., well-informed, phrased elegantly, it makes sense in the context where it is written, etc.; second, "this" in reference to the previously made statement (on the meta level, not on the level of what it states) proves text apprehension and, hence, intelligence (but not to the highest levels, otherwise this author would feel embarrassed about such a proclamation) because it is a concise summary of Hofstadter's *two* sentences. Third, and most importantly, the two foregoing sentences, taken together, demonstrate intelligence (on a third level) because, to *close the loop* to Hofstadter's point about the interplay between loops and intelligence, with the second sentence we returned to the first (and with this paragraph, we revived the quote). And *that* in turn was an intelligent way of illustrating meta-cognition and recursion on an even higher level, and so on. Are such recursive loops strange loops then? It can get stranger than that! For example, by putting self-referentiality and a resulting paradox in the mix (and paradoxes are strange phenomena by definition), the Liar paradox to name the paragon, the perhaps strangest paradox of all (cf. Beall et al., 2016 for an overview). So far so good, but what does that have to do with causation?

The answer, and at the same time the pivotal critique of Pearl (2018a), is, not much as long as we are concerned with his rung three and remain on or below the level 3.1 of our taxonomy. To examine if my mood was improved by the comedy I had watched, I can conduct a thought experiment as suggested on rung three; yet, no strange loop looms. The situation of reconciling what Hofstadter views as the core of intelligence with our approach only brightens up once the higher levels of 3.2 and 3.3 are permitted. Our thesis is that we encounter loops and strange loops when grasping causal networks and principles. An obvious example are cases of circular causality as depicted in the following figure 23 to give a visualization.

Sometimes, we have to deal with systems (and/or models thereof) with more complex structures, and/or maybe involving hidden causes in domains characterized by ambiguity, uncertainty, and noise. By harnessing the versatility and ubiquity of causal thinking in commonsense reasoning, in learning new concepts or understanding the world and its inhabitants and so on (not to mention Kant, 1787/1997 as well as Strawson's, 1966/2019, excellent book about it), I would contend, moreover, that also (strange) loops as they occur in music, in our natural languages or mathematics like the Liar paradox are not left out. At first glance, this sounds bewildering, like an untenable claim since, at least parts of, musical thinking, languages and math are chimeras, non-existing in the real world, while causal relations, according to the standard view, are said to hold between *physical events*. So how can recursion and loops in music, languages, math, be part of causal networks?

136 — 5 Towards a causal theory of intelligence

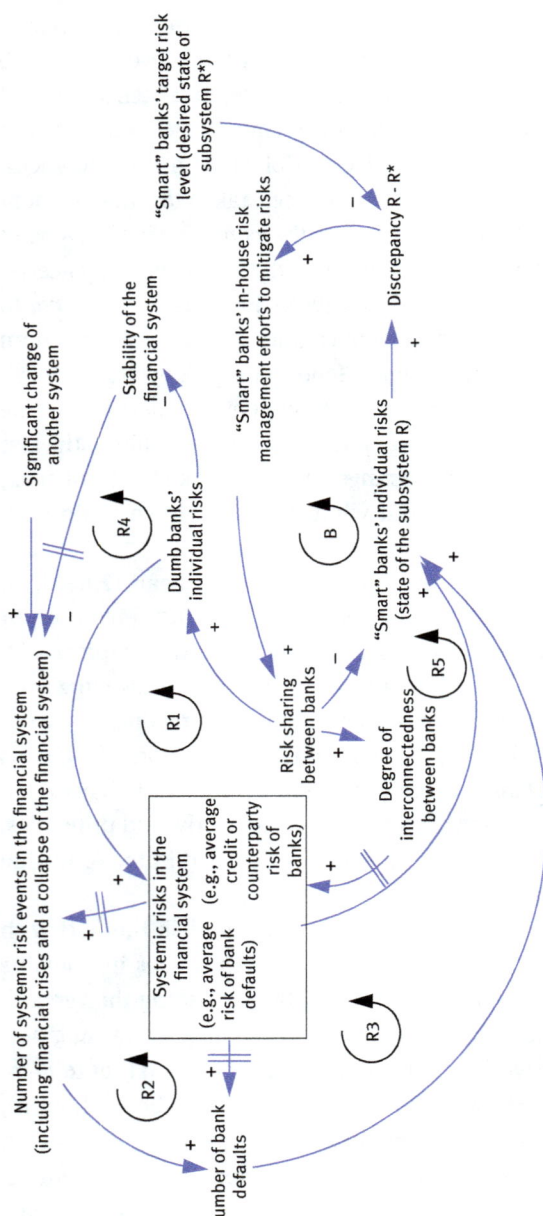

Figure 23: An example of a causal loop diagram (CLD) to unveil circular causality or feedback loops that govern the system's behavior, here the system of "risk sharing between banks", in which this key variable of this model is embedded. A CLD is made up of several elements: The arrows indicate causal relationships. The + (−) signs at the arrowheads indicate that the effect

Chimeras per se are not the problem, after all we are in the land of counterfactuals on this level three, in possible worlds, not the actual world. Only the link to causal cognition is blurry, but not absent. We have two options to sharpen the image of the link. First, for example, in music, a composer can envision a first movement in sonata form in her mind, then she writes it down, adds further sections, and the outcome is a symphony. What matters is that we can optionally refine the process and restate it in causal *and* physical terms within a causal network. Second, and more directly, we can approve mental causation (Maslen et al., 2009) in addition to classical physical-to-physical and physical-to-mental causation and to say that there is mental causation is to say that the mind makes a difference: "Beliefs, desires, feelings, and thoughts cause further beliefs, desires, feelings, and thoughts; and they also cause physical events, such as actions" (ibid.: 523). This extension is ought to held so dear as it appears essential in order for agents to do anything (at least autonomously; cf. also Yablo, 1997): "Agency is possible only if mental causation is possible" (Kim, 1996: 127). However, according to the common anti-psychologistic doctrine, music and mathematics deal with abstract objects, not with the psychological or mental. This weakens the second option tremendously since we would need to argue for *constructivism* too (which is disputable, but attracts its sympathizer, also most recently, e.g., Hawkins, 2021: 146 and Part III) to make it work. For instance in math, no one else than Kurt Gödel, an avowed Platonist, would be a heavyweight opponent.

And speaking of Gödel, for the arguably strangest loop of all though, the Liar paradox, it would be odd (to say the least) to redraw it in causal terms.

Figure 23 (continued)
is positively (negatively) related to the cause. This exemplary model consists of six causal feedback loops which drive the system's dynamics. Most of them are self-reinforcing, hence the loop polarity identifier R. They are called positive feedback loops whereas B stands for loops that are balancing or negative. The overall polarity of a loop (i.e., R or B) is the product of the signs on the arrows constituting that loop. Delays between some variables are pervasive and denoted by the orthogonal dashes on several arrows. To exemplify how to read a causal circuit, let us focus on loop B for that moment: A comparison between banks' target risk level, a desired minimum value R*, and the actual level R results in a gap. The gap determines the magnitude of banks' in-house risk management efforts to mitigate risks which in turn positively affects the intensity of risk sharing between banks (i.e., more/less of the cause leads to more/less of the effect), etc., all along the loop. For the source as well as for more information on this example, cf. Hoffmann, 2019d. The discipline of System Dynamics which employs such CLDs (with some blatant parallels to Bayesian nets from Chapter 6 in turn) struggles a bit with elucidating (in lieu of merely stipulating) that the arrows between the variables signify causation, not correlation. Cf. Hoffmann & Grösser, 2015 and Schaffernicht, 2007.

Even if we assent that one thought causally influences another thought, which we advocate, it would lead astray to just restate the reasoning about the paradox – e.g., the truth value of the sentence (in the strengthened liar) is neither true nor false – in causal terms because this reasoning is purely logical, not causal. Therefore, a causal theory must treat it as a black box; yet, not what happens before and after. Regardless of the status of the proposition of mental causation, we can at least *indirectly* attest intelligence to constructing such strange loops and reasoning about them by distinguishing what these activities (causally) lead to; for example, in case of the Liar paradox, the virtuoso Kurt Gödel's (1931) timeless masterpiece "Über formal unentscheidbare Sätze der Principia Mathematica und verwandter Systeme I".

If correct, this train of thoughts could amount to a major breakthrough since we could seize the veritable opportunity to transform our framework into an all-encompassing theory of intelligence, whatsoever the intelligence! Future work will settle questions around its potential. For now, we summarize the deliberations across all subchapters from 5.1.1. to 5.1.3. with the aid of the Figure 24 below.

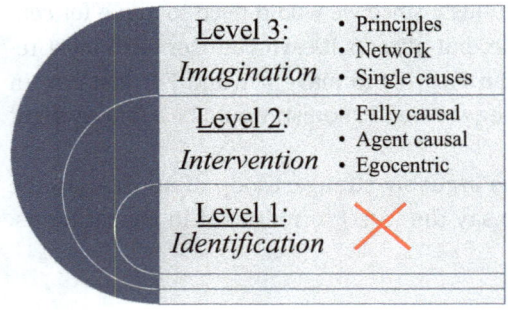

Figure 24: The synthesized and consolidated picture of the refined causal hierarchy.

We harbor the hope that the reader welcomes this refined framework for conflating intelligence, causal models, and causal grammar, albeit it is hardly satisfying. We see it as a tentative draft of what a taxonomy might look like rather than a fully developed account where, for example, more would need to be said about 1) the role of mental causation, 2) a survey of the many electrifying positions on this subject, wrestling with a number of counterarguments,[13] or 3) a

---

[13] A promising route to motivate a solution to the host of problems which mental causation provokes is *contextualism* and contextualism about causation in turn can be motivated via the context sensitivity of *counterfactuals*. Cf. Maslen (2004: 348f.), Carroll (2003), and generally for the interpretation of mental causation, Kistler (2016).

more substantive and in-depth examination of loops, other loops, as well as other pinnacles of intelligence. Yet, we proceed in 5.2. and 5.3. by substantiating our overall proposal for a full-blown theory of intelligence, not through fixing details, but through setting up another load-bearing pillar of our theoretical edifice. Our forays into scaffolding intelligence are supposed to cover not just the dimensions of intelligence, which we now casted in causal terms, but also its different directions. This is what we turn to in the next subchapter.

5.2 The inverted radex model of intelligence

The motivation for this subchapter is to thwart the threat of falling in the *illusory progress gap*: confounding progress in making *some* sense of intelligence by leaning Pearl's (2018a) three-rung ladder against intelligence with progress on hard problems of successively expanding the some. Although we hereby want to turn our back on his ladder conception, we do not want to throw the baby out with the bathwater. Visual representations are still appropriate, "as humans are good at understanding geographical analogies (e.g., children could reckon on the 1948 book 'the map that came to life' to understand the countryside where a trajectory and a story were accompanied by maps)" (Bhatnagar et al., 2018: 4). Investigators of intelligence of all stripes, in all academic disciplines related to intelligence, usually envision themselves as pioneers and discoverers, but exploration contains much more than revealing and inventing. Scholars also need (to be) cartographers, curators and taxonomists in order to structure, facilitate and disseminate what is known, and assess their unknowns, prioritize their goals and see their progress in perspective (ibid.: 14).

We strive for a new and apt graphical model of intelligence and find it to some extent in something old. Our inverted radex model of intelligence is not launched from scratch. Predecessors can be found, for instance in Saklofske & Zeidner (1995: 20, Figure 1 with "recall", "application", and "inference" in lieu of distinctly causal categories) and in this specification, it goes back to Guttman (1954) who coined it essentially; yet, to the best of my knowledge not under the heading of the causal revolution or the contention of paving the way for a universal theory of intelligence.

For illustration purposes, we present a few different radex models in the following to underpin the versatility of the basic model vis-à-vis the restrictive ladder or other conceptions. The two building blocks of the radex are the simplex, which we determine as the causal hierarchy and the multidimensionality of intelligence, respectively (in lieu of Guttman's levels of "rule recall", "rule application" and "rule inference"), and the circumplex reflecting the different

5 Towards a causal theory of intelligence

directions of intelligence (where he originally interjected "numerical material", "verbal material" and "figural material"). The new interpretation of the elements is accompanied by an inversion of the original radex, which amounts to the main structural change. That is, whilst in Guttman's model tasks in the middle presuppose more aptitude and the ones on the outskirts could be done more mechanically, for us it is just the other way around: higher intelligence is located at the outer circles. We begin with a radex model which merely consists of a simplex integrating the findings from 5.1. only.

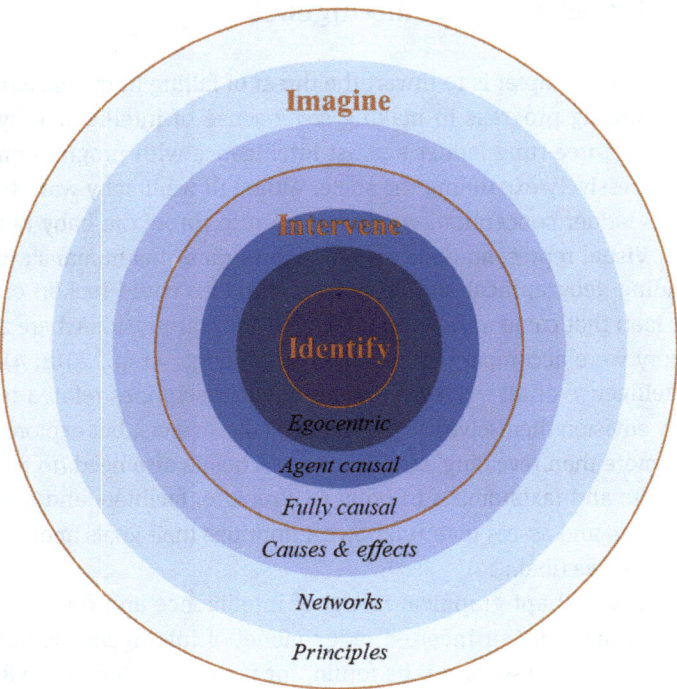

Figure 25: The more nuanced causal hierarchy without circumplex.

Seven colorful, concentric circles are all well and good, but what shall the reader take from that? In fact, Figure 25 does not deliver anything on top of the previous synopsis, Figure 24 in 5.1.3 – simply old wine in a new bottle. This is exactly a welcome insight because, thereby, we demonstrate that the simplex structure lends itself very well to mapping our causal hierarchy. With this in view, we now merge that first building block of the radex with the circumplex meant to visualize the different directions of intelligence. A prime example of multidirectionality and pluralistic forms of intelligence is Gardner's proposition about human intelligence which is why we, in the subsequent Figure 26, refer back to his eight intelligences to complete the radex. (Of course, we may adduce other propositions in other contexts. To increase the user-friendliness of the radex in Figure 26, we abstract from the sublevels of the causal hierarchy and add three exemplary cognitive tasks, denoted by three red dots.)

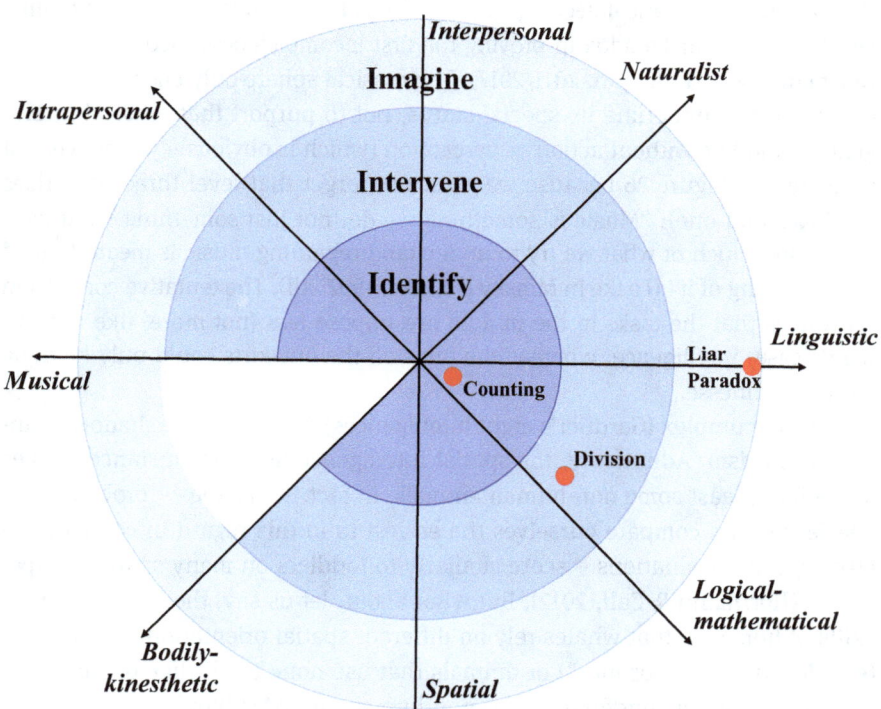

Figure 26: A simplified simplex facet arranged into Pearl's/our three levels in concert with the circumplex facet as most anthropocentric in the sense of Gardner as well as select tasks.

One of the decisive questions for any topological arrangement of tasks within such a radex is to determine their right location around the "continuum" of facets. Several findings, hypotheses, and arguments have been brought forward to explain and predict whether a task falls near the center such as addition or the periphery such as the Liar Paradox. However, we are not eager to engage in such a discussion which is reserved for mainly empirical sciences, first and foremost, for psychometrics. Therefore, the positioning of many potential tasks ought to be subject to revision and changes reliant on the state of (empirical) research. The rationale for this composition of the merely three tasks or phenomena in Figure 26 is that, firstly, counting, which is also common among some animals (Hodos, 1988: 100f.), is associative, i.e., it can be passively perceived in the environment. Secondly, division is an arithmetic *operation* which requires intervention or doing. Thirdly, the Liar Paradox is endemic to the imaginary world because the sentence in question ("this sentence is a lie") is self-referential and does not refer to the outerworld. Moreover, it is adjacent to both the linguistic sector (it is a sentence) and the logical-mathematical sector (e.g., Gödel used, roughly speaking, a modified version of the Liar Paradox in proving the first incompleteness theorem; Nagel & Newman, 2001; Hoffmann, 2011/2017). The musical sphere only encapsulates the outer circle to underline its special status, not to purport that musical intelligence could live without action or perception (which is obviously wrong, yet not indicated by Figure 26 because we must not forget that level three comprises level two and one): "Music is something we do, not just something we understand, and much of what we try to understand regarding music is meant to lead to the making of it" (Laske in Minsky & Laske, 1992: xii). The tentative conclusion for now is that the tasks in the middle presuppose less (not more, like in Guttman's case) intelligence, whereas the ones on the outskirts could only be done with more finesse.

The circumplex (Gardner's eight intelligences) facet casts the shadow of anthropocentrism. Admittedly, the spatial intelligence facet, for instance, makes sense for at least some non-human animals. In fact, some apes – probably, the species we can compare ourselves the easiest to in this regard in comparative cross-species evaluations – score similarly to toddlers on many spatial competences (Herrmann & Call, 2012). But what about, let us say, the body language skills of horses or that whales rely on different spatial orientation mechanisms (echolocation or "biosonar") or animals that use none at all (like octopi)? Is a musical sector meaningful at all for non-human animals? Would we add a new sector for olfactory abilities for dogs? Furthermore, Hernández-Orallo (2017: 265) has qualms that the most conspicuous flaw when "trying to build any taxonomy upon [. . .] elementary tasks for universal psychometrics is that all these simple tasks are extremely easy for computers."

Such questions and worries lead us to the next exemplary radex for "biological and artificial animal intelligence" where the circumplex is fleshed out with only three axes: tool use, text writing, and local explanations of single predictions of some machine learning systems (in short, explaining AI) as well as two auxiliary axes: spatial memory and object permanence. We put quotation marks around the phrase "biological and artificial animal intelligence" since we query whether a proper radex/circumplex can be constructed for such a broad purpose. The reason for this suspicion is obvious; apart from the common ground endowed by our causal hierarchy, we are confronted with the

5.2 The inverted radex model of intelligence

daunting difficulty of identifying relevant directions of intelligence to *all* agents which are supposed to be covered in the radex. We hypothesize that, if we succumb to the temptation of harmonizing intelligence beyond our taxonomy of causal learning by appealing to putatively principal axes of the circumplex, we do not strip intelligence to the bones, but cut away vital parts of its anatomy.

In Figure 27, we only deal with three different creatures, namely New Caledonian crows (see Chapter 2), GPT-3 (see 3.1.), and CLEAR (which is an acronym for "Counterfactual Local Explanations viA Regression" and which is an instance of neural-symbolic computing; White & D'Avila Garcez, 2019); already this very small universe of three creatures gives us a headache about what the "right" (if there is any right solution) or a good/informative circumplex would be. Why then engage in such efforts?

Because they are more than outshined by the additional insights to be gained. Firstly, the efforts themselves enlighten us that intelligence can manifest itself in very different ways which do not have to be commensurable. Secondly, the selection of facets steers the research process on where to put the spotlight for investigating agents' intelligence; a process which is mainly driven by empirical research like comparative psychology (in any event, not by philosophy). And thirdly, as we saw in Chapter 1 and 2, and particularly in Chapter 3, a momentous juxtaposition is between narrow and broad intelligence which becomes well visible with the help of the circumplex. For example, while the three axes in Figure 27 are specific (tool use) to very specific (explaining AI) compared to more general, but anthropocentric sectors in Figure 26, reflecting that current AI systems such as GPT-3 and CLEAR are mere idiots savants, graphically coinciding with only one green dot on one axis, the auxiliary axes (dashed) are included to indicate that the crows' intelligence is broad, not narrow. However, unlike the plain pattern learning prediction machines on level one like GPT-3, there are AIs that, can implement the higher level of 3.1 (*inferring single causes and effects*) of our causal levels as noted earlier and CLEAR is such a system (White & D'Avila Garcez, 2019: 1 and 6):

> CLEAR provides counterfactual explanations [by making use of state-of-the-art explanatory methods, one of them bringing forward so-called b-counterfactuals or "boundary counterfactuals" that state the minimum changes needed for an observation to "flip" its classification. C.H.; p. 1] [. . .] CLEAR satisfies the requirement that satisfactory local explanations should include statements of key counterfactual cases. CLEAR explains a prediction y for data point x by stating x's b-counterfactuals and providing a regression equation. The regression shows the patterns of counterfactual dependencies in a neighbourhood that includes both x and the b-counterfactual data points. [p. 6].

To obviate the risk of misapprehension, we certainly do not assert that CLEAR would *comprehend* much about causes and effects because, despite that 3.1 peak in the machine kingdom, the link to its action remains missing. Ideally, one could create a 360-degree profile of an agent, which seems feasible for animals – and the illustrative beginnings are made for crows in Figure 27 to be revised and completed by animal cognition experts –, but which seems more like wishful thinking for present-day AI systems, at least when compared to other animals.

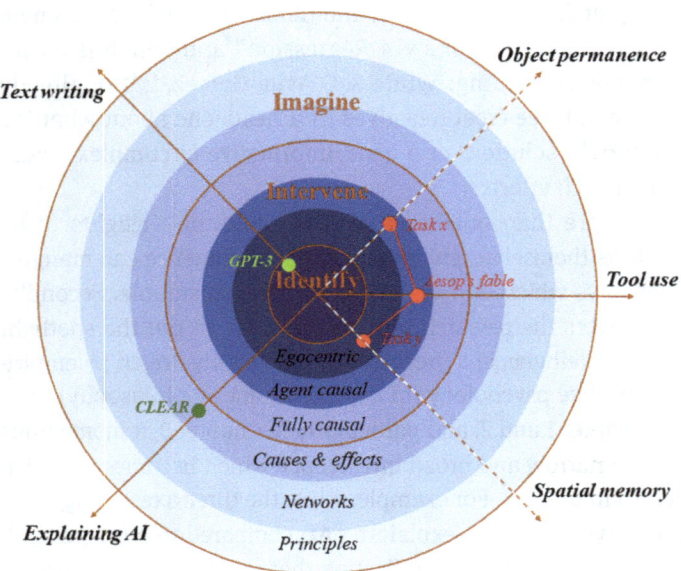

Figure 27: An inverted radex for depicting some biological and artificial animal intelligence with tasks (yet two restrictions apply). On the one hand, for the two AI systems (the two green shades) task specification is superfluous as they only perform one task. On the other hand, besides the Aesop's Fable challenge which we studied, task specification was not undertaken for New Caledonian crows (in red) to underline that we are no animal cognition researchers or experts on crows' intelligence. Specifying x and y, possibly accompanied by relocating them on the circumplex, is left for true experts on that matter. For now, we put spatial memory tasks closer to the center because research seems to suggest that corvids perform worse in tasks testing spatial memory.

In the previous subchapter, we were confronted with a black box in connection with the Liar Paradox. After all, we might find it unsatisfactory to reconcile ourselves with such blind spots in our theory, even more so when blind spots like the reasoning about the Liar Paradox are considered the core of (human) intelligence. Perhaps, it would be an expression of intellectual masochism, or a rationalization of intellectual impotence to resign in the face of an allegedly unsolvable problem: *ignoramus et ignorabimus*. Luckily, we can do something about it by means of our available tool showcased here, and unpack the black box by accounting for a third dimension capturing loops, higher layers of non-causal thinking, and metacognition, beside the refined causal hierarchy (first dimension in Figure 28) and the directions of intelligence (second dimension in the subsequent Figure 28). The ocean of intelligence is never a still, smooth sea, it is restless and intelligence makes waves. Water particles here and there, and sometimes even in surprising places, are *caused* to get into motion and the *effect* ranges from inconspicuousness to meter-high forces of Nature that wash away sandcastles of the past (like in Gödel's case, Hilbert's program). Our inverted radex in three dimensions hence conflates this rich image with Hofstadter's strange loops.

In hindsight to the last four inverted radex models of intelligence, we might wonder fundamentally how we can measure or operationalize a concept like intelligence at all for which we do not have an accepted definition in place (unlike temperature which is unequivocally defined and unequivocally measured by thermometers). The answer is that we do not aspire after a *representational*, but a *pragmatic* measurement. Following Hernández-Orallo (2017: 32), this crucial distinction about measurement becomes clear: "In *representational measurement* we have a precise concept or *definition* of what is measured. When the feature, or construct, being measured is not fully conceptualized or defined, but still useful, we say it is non-representational or *pragmatic*."

In light of the variety and plurality of our inverted radex models of intelligence, we might then further wonder which is the one, which is the one that tells us that GPT-3 is less intelligent than my dog who in turn is less intelligent than a professor in a single absolute ranking. The short answer is that we do not require a model to give it. The longer one is that, in harmony with our systems lens, there are no one-size-fits-all approaches about intelligence: The aim cannot be that we want to put a number on agents' possession of some mental quantity called "intelligence". Objectives vary and we now have an adjustable instrument at hand that allows us to make *pragmatic*, but well-conceived comparisons of different agents' intelligence to get a better idea of what is going on in their inside to understand their outside behaviors.

Quo vadis then? It is not on us to say. Different users of the instrument have different legitimate goals: It might look more like Figure 26 when a cast of humans is tested. Or the circumplex might have two more axes which represent the table of contents of Wasserman & Zentall's (2006) book when some non-human biological animals are evaluated. Or, conversely, empirical work with any test subjects might be used to revise or refine the facets of the radex model for certain purposes. Or, when viewed in developmental terms, one can first sketch an agent's psychometric profile (like we started it in Figure 27 for crows) and then possibly go on with a *Pareto-optimal* enhancement of the agent's

Figure 28: An inverted radex in three dimensions based on the example of the Liar Paradox where the new (third) dimension is captioned by logical reasoning.

profile of intellectual abilities (above all interesting for AIs and hybrids), which signifies that at least one of them is enhanced but none of them is lessened. It is, in any event, work in progress, and progress is to be applauded. Yet, progress ought to bear in mind that the representation of directions of intelligence must be agnostic to specific hypotheses, so that the users could complement their inverted radex models from the values observed. Of course, there always exist some underlying assumptions (and the influence of underlying theories) whenever an observation or measurement is made, but this should be as explicit as possible (Bhatnagar et al., 2018: 7).

We end this subchapter with drawing the reader's attention to one more radex model (see Figure 29 on the next page) where, based on the adventurous journey through the Chapters 1 to 5, we include the "big lines of universal intelligence" (a term that must be taken with caution in the wake of our foregoing arguments) from our point of view. In this Figure 29, we marked four new sectors for the three kinds of intelligence from Part I: It might be an affront to many that such important and diverse aspects as the formation of knowledge, memory, reasoning, computation, problem solving as well as the comprehension and production of language are all under the umbrella of cognitive intelligence in lieu of taking their own position. Inspired by the example of octopi at the one end, and robots at the other end of the gamut, we stipulate bodily intelligence as the second big line of universal intelligence. The third and fourth line are given by what Gardner labeled intra- and interpersonal intelligence, and together they yield a strong demarcation line between higher organic versus artificial intelligence. The value of social intelligence already became evident in Table 2 where it was safely inferred that the relevance of social contexts for grasping intelligence cannot be overlooked, while emotions are an automatic by-product of a plethora of animals' faculty to think. Emotions are, so to say, plainly part of the nature of natural thinking. Contrary to the zeitgeist that emotional intelligence plays a little role in scientific theories of intelligence, time has finally come to cover more of the *terra incognita*, omnipresent in so many forms of intelligence.

5.3 A dynamic approach for broad and multiple intelligences

Humans, animals, machines and their intelligence are not static, not immutable. They evolve and change over time. Even if we consider that a characterization of individuals has to be conducted with stable traits, it would be short-sighted to consider that their behavioral features do not alter with time. But not only that, what it means to be intelligent itself can be altered over time because intelligence is determined by the dynamics of interaction with a dynamic world. Let us take

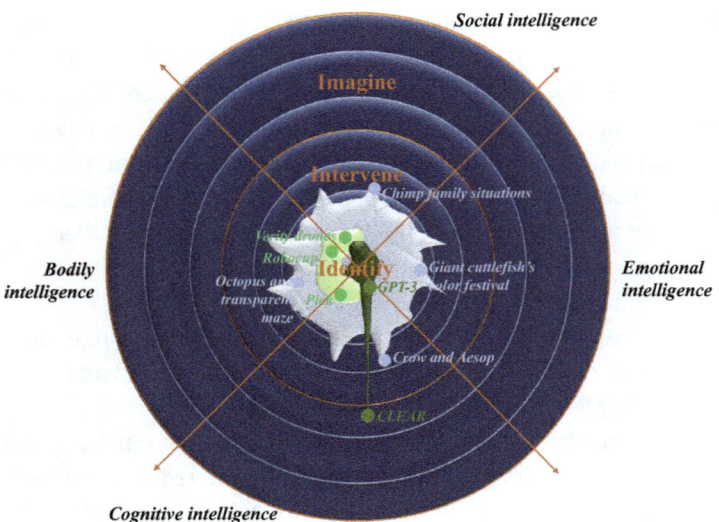

Figure 29: A tentative, general and agnostic inverted radex where artificial, animal and human intelligence are located. Light green stands for robotics: Cumulatively speaking, the myriad of robots that have come into the world so far are puppets and/or do not learn at all. Only few can be regarded as level-one agents and learners; still, by and large, they lack the capacity of causal thinking. ("By and large" because it would be presumptuous to overgeneralize. We do not know what happens in robotics labs around the globe, especially in the R&D of private corporations that hide their secret sauce.) Our assessment of robotics is backed up by a brief interview with my former colleague, Piotr Roszak, software lead at Verity Studios. We content ourselves with three examples and all of them exhibit, of course, cognitive intelligence (e.g., computations), bodily and social intelligence; yet to different degrees which explains their different locations on the circumplex. Verity's Lucie micro drones are associated with social and swarm intelligence, the football playing Robocup robots with classical bodily intelligence close to social intelligence because in recent years they learned how to play a pass, and Boston Dynamics' Pick more with cognitive intelligence since it integrates high-resolution 3D and 2D sensing.

The darker green stands for modern machine and deep learning systems with two familiar examples. Moreover, also in non-robotics AI, the social intelligence hypothesis, positing that fully fledged intelligence is inherent to social contexts, has been applauded enthusiastically, with the advent of the area of multi-agent systems, jointly with the resourceful help of game theory (Hernández-Orallo, 2017: 343).

Animal intelligence is displayed by the light blue, greyish tone and it is broad, covering all sectors. Therefore, we cannot locate the four animals at a single point on the circumplex. Instead, the attribution is determined by a) the dominating feature in b) a certain situation like the emotional expressiveness of the giant cuttlefish by means of unending, astounding color changes when they meet a diver (Godfrey-Smith, 2018: 109). The color field of animal intelligence is spiky to enunciate that some animals like crows and apes can arguably and at least in some situations adopt an agent causal viewpoint.

the more recent shift of human cognition, for example (Bhatnagar et al., 2018: 4): "the average IQ in many countries is increasing (the *Flynn effect*), our memory (Sparrow et al., 2011) is changing due to the *Google effect* (digital amnesia), navigation abilities (McKinlay, 2016; Milner, 2016) atrophied because satnavs, cognitive rewards mechanisms are changing because of gamification, etc. This is a process that is accelerated by technology, and will be magnified by the use of cognitive assistants and cognitive prosthetics, especially for the elderly."

Likewise, causality, broadly interpreted, encompasses any kind of knowledge about how the world changes *over time* (Marcus & Davis, 2019: 166). With that in mind, we can discern three levels of dynamics out of which the first two are covered by Pearl's prior work (2018a).

1) On the micro or conceptual level, both intelligence and causality are inherently dynamic (which is not anybody's merit, but simply how we understand these terms).
2) On the object level, agents on the causal ladder can move up or down; e.g., a child climbs from rung two to rung three when s(he) grows older or, vice versa, an agent may fall to a lower level, e.g., after a severe injury. On top of that, and more systematically, we can highlight five high-level constraints imposed on intelligence that are responsible for the fluctuations of an agent's intelligence over time:
    2.1) Hardware micro level (e.g., neurons)
    2.2) Hardware macro level (e.g., neural networks, i.e., brains)
    2.3) Interactive specialization
    2.4) Embodiment of intelligence
    2.5) Ensocialment of intelligence
3) On the meta level, i.e., as far as the causal ladder model itself is concerned, agility is missing though. Unlike Clark's (2016) proposition, Pearl's ladder tool remains static. But since the world is constantly changing, our model of the world must learn continuously to reflect the changing world (Hawkins, 2021: 130).

In this final subchapter, we show that this last-named deficiency of the causal ladder model does not hold for our proposal. We plead that a dynamic view of

---

Figure 29 (continued)
The margins of the animal and AI color fields are fuzzy to indicate the uncertainty around the assessments as well as the fast-paced technological developments in terms of the green fields specifically.
  To capture the climaxes of human intelligence (dark blue color field), which are missing here, we recommend three dimensions (like in Figure 28).

the elements of the scope of intelligence (Chapter 1 to 3) must be accompanied by some dynamics of our notion.

Since it ought to be palpable that this requirement is met by what we devised in this Chapter 5, we keep this concluding section brief. Our product is dynamic in a at least fourfold way:

1) In a Popperian fashion, our theory of intelligence is, at the risk of stating the obvious, open to refutation, revision, and refinement. But even more we would be delighted if it is advanced in the future.
2) For our universal taxonomy, we are eager to follow Clark (2016) and embrace the eternal braid between the levels of causal learning, not least because this is what his cognitive research suggests.
3) The versatility and flexibility of our inverted radex model goes hand in hand with dynamics and adaptability as showcased in five representative figures in the previous subchapter.
4) With the sublevel 3.2. of our causal hierarchy as well as with the radex of Figure 28, we incorporate circularity and loops in our framework and, thus, dynamics.

6 Theory in action: Causal modeling

The holy grail of analytic philosophy, or at least of the metaphysics of causation, has been to develop an adequate account of *the* causal relation, to spell out just what it means to say that C causes E. This analytic project tacitly assumes that there is just one specific kind of causal relationship between the relata called *causing* which is the target of the analysis. Yet, given that controversies around what causal claims mean are as lively as ever (e.g. Schaffer, 2016; Beebee et al., 2009; Spohn et al., 2001), maybe we should discard the assumption that there is only one special type of causal relationship which is the referent of the word "cause" in favor of fostering more modesty and pluralism (Godfrey-Smith, 2009; Hitchcock, 2007a).[14]

Today, a main benefit of analyzing and explicating intelligence in terms of causality is not that we trace one opaque term to another – Russell (1913) characterized what he named the "law of causality" as a harmful "relic of a bygone age", and urged the "complete extrusion" of the word "cause" from the philosophical and scientific vocabulary (Ross & Spurrett, 2007). Instead, machine learning methods for causal discovery, so-called causal graphical models leave room for different readings since one might wonder how causal inference is possible, given the completely standard maxim in the sciences and philosophy that "correlation is not causation".[15]

Causal graphical models provide a formal mathematical framework that captures important regularities in causal facts in lieu of a problematic reductive definition of causation; just as the mathematical structure of geometry captures important spatial regularities. Indeed, causal graphical models are to causation as geometry is to space (Gopnik & Schulz, 2007: 3; the prospect of capturing important regularities in Nature not least inspired Mandelbrot, 1967, to propound his fractal geometry that we, with our passion for loops, are above all fond of). Sadly, many communities brought odium on this innovation at the expense of transparency and testability about causal assumptions. Economists,

---

[14] In fact, we use the term "cause" to mark a variety of different distinctions: "between a causal relation-ship and one that is merely spurious; the distinction between causing an outcome and preventing it; the distinction between causing an outcome and merely affecting it; and so on." (Hitchcock, 2007b: 110).

[15] Even the strong claim that causation is nothing but correlation (brought forward, e.g., by Pearson, 1911, and reinforced by some contemporary psychologists/philosophers, e.g., Jeffrey, 2004) – a claim, we obviously do not agree with – seems to be (partially) compatible with the idea of causal graphical models such as the causal Bayes net framework as well as with experimental findings (cf. Glymour, 2007: 295).

https://doi.org/10.1515/9783110756166-009

for example, a guild I know particularly well, having chosen algebraic over graphical representations, are deprived of elementary testability- detecting features (Pearl, 2015).[16]

In this comparatively short chapter, we provide a bird's eye view of causal modeling with an emphasis on Bayesian nets (cf. Pearl, 2000 or Spirtes et al., 1993 for detailed primers) because this rich corpus of work from statistics, computer science, and philosophy offers an elegant way of how to implement our ideas from Chapter 5.1., and, on the other hand, Bayes nets endow the natural connection to AI engineering, thereby augmenting the interdisciplinary value of our first forays into an interdisciplinary phenomenon (intelligence). The most common use of causal models is to facilitate causal inference, but this chapter rests content with a much-simplified presentation of causal models that emphasizes various points of interest for our framework of learning in Chapter 5 or for canvassing intelligence, generally.

A Bayesian network is a graphical way of representing how a probability distribution factorizes and any joint probability distribution can be factorized into a product of conditional probabilities (Lattimore & Ong, 2018: 7). The earlier Bayes net iterations were indeed confined to techniques, as we can now recast it, that permit level-one causal learning, i.e., for predicting some probabilities from others. Causal Bayesian networks are an extension of earlier Bayesian networks. The engineering of causal Bayes net algorithms also allows us to determine what will happen when an agent intervenes from outside to change the value of a particular variable like X or Y in Figure 30 (level two): "When two variables are genuinely related in a causal way, holding other variables constant, then intervening to change one variable should change the other" (Gopnik & Schulz, 2007: 5). Indeed, thinking about causation in relation to intervention, philosophers have contended that this is just what it means for two variables to be causally related (Woodward, 2003).

A causal model can be employed, not just to predict the effects of certain interventions, but also to assess the truth values of certain counterfactuals (non-backtracking counterfactuals, as introduced in 5.1.). Although there are some disparities (like knowing the truth values of counterfactuals after the fact is fine, whereas we are usually keen to shed light on the consequences of potential manipulations before they are carried out), the mechanics of evaluating counterfactuals and interventions is the same (Hitchcock, 2009: 303). In this

---

[16] One of the few exceptions I was involved in throughout my career as an economist consists of *System Dynamics* as inaugurated by Forrester, 1958, 1961. See Figure 23 and cf. Hoffmann, 2019d.

way, causal models bridge the gulf between counterfactual and interventionist accounts of causation and become a powerful extension of both. More specifically with regard to our universal taxonomy, the principal demarcation lines within our causal hierarchy, i.e., between level one, two, and three, can be well-redrawn within the formal causal modeling framework: As Pearl (2018b) demonstrated, each layer in the hierarchy has a syntactic signature, deciphered by the Bayesian net approach, that characterizes the sentences admitted into that layer.

For example, Woodward (2003) specifies different types of intervention in the language of graphical models or Pearl (2000) articulates a *do*-operator to insulate observations from interventions: The do-operator reflects an intervention on an event that renders the manipulated event independent of all its other causes, which thus makes it equivalent to Pearl's captivating metaphor of *graph surgery*. Counterfactual interventions differ from normal or real-world interventions because the former "alter causal models, which have been updated before on the basis of the given facts" (Hagmayer et al., 2007: 91).

What, exactly, do causal Bayesian networks represent? What do the arrows in a graph such as in Figures 30 or 31 signify? Clearly, the arrows indicate that so-called parent variables opposite the arrowhead exercise some kind of causal influence over their "children", the variables at the arrowhead. Nonetheless, it is awkward at best for a number of reasons to state blanketly that an arrow from X to Y indicates that X causes Y (Hitchcock, 2009: 304). On the one hand, an arrow does not tell us anything about the form of the quantitative relationship between two variables (ibid.), an information that can be gleaned from the so-called *structural equations* accompanying the graph (see the following example). For some interpretations, it would certainly be misleading, if not downright ungrammatical, to maintain that X causes Y, and "is causally relevant to", "influences" or "affects" would be the more sensitive terminology (ibid.: 305). On the other hand, causal relationships exist which are not marked with arrows. It can be that such causal influences would be mediated by other variables while arrows only represent direct effects; it can be that some variables are exogenous, not endogenous to the model.

For some concretization and illustration, we draw on Pearl's (2000: Chapter 3) presentation of a deterministic causal model, also restated in Hitchcock (2009: 300). Suppose that in a certain agricultural region, oat crops are threatened by eelworms. We seek to know whether the use of a certain fumigant is effective in protecting oat yields, and to what degree. We cannot simply compare the oat yields of those who harness the fumigants to those who do not; for, beside other complications, it may be that only the farmers who are suffering the worst infestations choose to use the fumigants. A deterministic causal model is an ordered pair <V, E>, where *V* is a set of variables, and *E* is a set of equations relating the values of those variables. Our model might include the variables:

E_1 the population of eelworms before the time at which the fumigant is (or would be) applied
F the quantity of fumigant used (possibly zero)
B the population of birds that prey on eelworms
E_2 the population of eelworms after the time at which fumigant was (or would have been) applied
Y the yield of the oat crop.

Unlike philosophical traditions where the relata are events (or sometimes related entities like facts or tropes), note that these are all quantitative variables, which is customary in scientific contexts. Whilst the qualitative relationships among the variables may be captured using directed graphs like in Figure 30, the quantitative relationship between the variables is captured in a set of equations:

$$E_1 = e_1$$

$$F = f_F (E_1)$$

$$B = f_B (E_1)$$

$$E_2 = f_E (E_1, F, B)$$

$$Y = f_Y (F, E_2)$$

We have one equation for each variable and these equations are dubbed structural equations, since they are intended to delineate the underlying causal structure, and not merely regularities among the values of the variables. Since the value of E_1 is not affected by the value of any of the other variables, its value is given from outside the system, i.e., it is exogenous. If one variable appears on the right-hand side of an equation, it is said to be a parent of the variable appearing on the left. Thus, F is a parent of E_2 and Y, while being a child, ancestor or descendant of E_1.

Most, if not all, of the complex models can be derived from three basic causal models (Sloman & Lagnado, 2005): Figure 31 displays the graphs for those three models, with the nodes again representing event variables and the arrows or directed edges again signifying the direction of sometimes deterministic, but more often probabilistic causal influence. Causal maps like in Figure 30 represent an unadorned kind of intuitive theory; yet, as we also saw in 5.1.3., "learning causal networks from limited data depends on the constraints of more abstract knowledge" (Tenenbaum et al., 2011: 1281). If propelled further, this then quickly

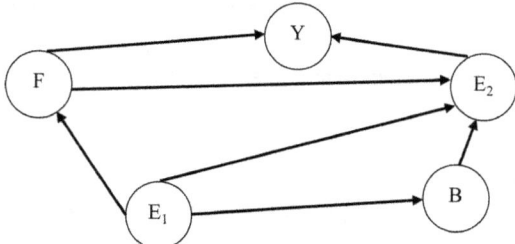

Figure 30: A causal model for protecting oat yields. Source: Hitchcock, 2009: 301.

eventuates in *hierarchical* Bayesian models (i.e., a Bayesian model written in multiple levels) which are equipped to deal with rich causal representations of the world (Lake et al., 2017: 18).

Back to the simple point of departure for complex edifices, we contemplate in Figure 31 from left to right (1) a common-cause model in which a single cause X influences two effects Y and Z, thereby expressing the spurious correlation between Y and Z; (2) a causal chain model in which an initial cause X affects an intermediate event Y influencing a final effect Z where X and Z are dependent but become independent when Y is held constant; and (3) a common-effect model in which two causes X and Y independently influence a joint effect Z, implying independence of the alternative causes X and Y and their dependence once the common effect is held fixed.

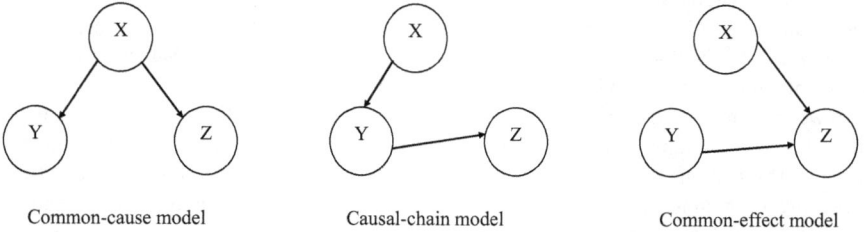

Common-cause model   Causal-chain model   Common-effect model

Figure 31: Three basic causal models.

The graphs encode assumptions about dependence and independence, simplifying the representation of the causal domain (Hagmayer et al., 2007: 88). One important assumption or constraint underlying Bayesian nets is the Markov assumption, which states (informally) that each event in a causal graph is independent of all events other than its descendants (i.e., its direct and indirect effects) once the values of its parent nodes (i.e., its direct causes) are known (ibid.).

Break-out session 3

Probabilistic models of causal analysis have provoked repudiations

This third time, we take "break-out" more literally and broach the subject of alternatives and opposition to the Bayesian approach about causal modeling, and particularly why probabilistic models might not be suitable according to some scholars. We already came across one alternative in Figure 23 and Footnote 16, namely *System Dynamics* and *Causal Loop Diagrams*, which, however, we do not wish to enlarge upon in this context due to their lack of rigor (cf. Hoffmann & Grösser, 2015). There also exist proposals for hybrid systems of learning causal structure, combining the Bayesian approach with more traditional psychological models (e.g., Waldmann & Mayrhofer, 2016).

In spite of its popularity, Gärdenfors (2020: 8) is an avowed critic of the Bayesian way altogether. Problems arise, for example in experimental studies, where "subjects have had difficulties in extracting causal relations based on covariation data even though these experiments typically present a small number of variables (Steyvers et al., 2003). For humans, a single instance of a causal connection is sufficient to pick up a causal relation and it would be desirable that a robotic system has a similar capacity. Such a rapid process is difficult to capture in a probabilistic model [Salmon, 1984; Dowe, 1992]. According to the [two-vector] model presented here [i.e., a form of computational modeling of events which states that an event is represented in terms of two main components – the force of an *action* that drives the event, and the *result* of its application], the forces that generate an action are essential for causal inferences and such forces are, in general, inaccessible to probabilistic approaches. In brief, Bayesian processes are computationally not suitable for implementations in robotic systems."

In line with this, also Waldmann & Hagmayer (2013) report evidence and argue that causal cognition of people cannot be encompassed by the Bayesian formalism.

From an empirical or psychological stance, one might wonder if it is not in fact a key issue of the Bayesian approach then whether non-experts are capable of predicting outcomes of hypothetical interventions and of reasoning about causal counterfactuals. Because this competency would imply that people have access to reasoning processes that modify causal representations prior to deriving predictions.

However, armed with weapons from Tenenbaum et al.'s (2011: 1280) arsenal, we can push back and refer to many aspects of higher-level cognition that have been effectively illuminated by the mathematics of Bayesian statistics: "our sense of similarity, representativeness, and randomness; coincidences as a cue to hidden causes; judgments of causal strength and evidential support; diagnostic and conditional reasoning; and predictions about the future of everyday events. The claim that human minds learn and reason according to Bayesian principles is not a claim that the mind can implement any Bayesian inference. Only those inductive computations that the mind is designed to perform well, where biology has had time and cause to engineer effective and efficient mechanisms, are likely to be understood in Bayesian terms."

Moreover, with regard to Gärdenfors' (2020) counterproposal, we can demur that, if the world was simple, and we had full knowledge about everything, then maybe in homage to Laplace's demon the only causality we would require would be physics. Following Marcus & Davis (2019: 139), we could determine what affects what by running simulations; if I apply a *force* of so many micronewtons, what will happen next? But contra this idealized worldview which Gärdenfors (2020) seems to adopt, that sort of detailed simulation is usually neither pragmatic

> nor viable; there are too many particles and forces to track in the veritable world, and too little time: Rather, "we often use approximations; we know things are causally related, even if we don't know exactly why. We take aspirin, because we know it makes us feel better; we don't need to understand the biochemistry. [. . .] You don't have to be a doctor to know that vitamin C can prevent scurvy, [. . ., etc.]. Causal knowledge is everywhere, and it underlies much of what we do." (Marcus & Davis, 2019: 139).

Bayesian nets give the promise of a unifying mathematical language for framing causal learning along our causal hierarchy from Chapter 5.1., and cognition, more generally, as the solution to inductive problems and constructing principled quantitative models of thought with a minimum of free parameters and ad hoc assumptions (Tenenbaum et al., 2011: 1285). One of the crown accomplishments of the causal revolution has been the algorithmization of counter-factuals within the graphical representation of causal reasoning whereby the latter enables us, among others, to circumscribe direct and indirect effects and to decide when these effects are estimable from data, or experiments (Pearl, 2018b). On top of that, the Bayesian approach propels us beyond classic either-or dichotomies that have long shaped parochial debates on intelligence: "'empiricism versus nativism,' 'domain-general versus domain-specific,' 'logic versus probability,' 'symbols versus statistics'" (Tenenbaum et al., 2011: 1285).

What has come to be known as the Bayesian, probabilistic approach to reverse-engineering the mind has not only gained strong momentum by the engineering successes of Bayesian methods of machine learning (recall Figure 11) but, vice versa, the former has also begun to inspire more efficacious and more humanlike approaches to machine learning. (ibid.: 1279): Well-known issues like "domain adaptation", "transfer learning", "life-long learning" or "explainable AI" are just divergent facets of the general second-wave AI problem of robustness that we touched upon in 3.1. and that can be alleviated, if not sorted out, by equipping machines with causal models of their environment (Pearl, 2018b).

Even though it would be very stimulating to elaborate further on Bayesian nets and their effectiveness for encapsulating the structure of systems of causal relationships, this would ultimately only distract from the subject matter of this work. For our purposes, it is sufficient to know (by getting a glimpse of that rich debate) that such causal maps can be thought of as grasping larger coherent explanatory frameworks, numerous causal regularities are assembled into. Once assembled, they allow for explanations, predictions and interventions. Furthermore, we highlight that we do not end up in a conceptual dead end by making recourse to the notion of causation: while there used to be, and still is, a chorus of disapproval about how to best make sense of "causation" – maybe starting with the very fact that Hume (probably unintentionally) emitted two rival definitions packaged as one (Hume, 1748/1999; for an overview cf. Schaffer, 2016) –, the (Bayesian) modeling approach demystifies causation and offers an elegant way out of that trouble, not least to illuminate the concept of intelligence as we argued here.

7 Theory validation

The assurance of theory or model validity is a formidable challenge outside the untainted realms of pure mathematics or formal logics where it is an incontrovertible and unambiguous matter of accuracy and strict proofs rather than practical use. Such clean models or genuinely analytic statements "do not make any assertion about the empirical world, but simply record our determination to use symbols in a certain fashion" (Ayer, 1952: 31) and, therefore, they can be shown to be either true or false (at least, as long as you do not encounter a brain teaser like the Liar Paradox where things become more complicated, but not hopeless). In this study, however, we have to rest content with imperfect approaches. Mental models with empirical content, such as our inverted radex models, are by their very nature abridged and restricted representations of the real world and thus "wrong": As they never comprehensively capture the complexity of the system of interest, their absolute validation, verification is impossible so that validity cannot reveal itself mechanically in our case. A second over-restriction of the notion of theory validation, and thus a second major issue with so-called early logical empiricism (or logical positivism), lies in the insistence on predictive ability as the only criterion for model justification. Or as Barlas & Carpenter (1990: 154) have outlined:

> Since, according to logical positivism, the content of a scientific theory is irrelevant to the philosophical problem of verification, explanatory power is not a criterion. According to the principle of verifiability (or falsifiability), the only criterion for justification is whether the observations match with the predictions (implications) of the theory. According to this view, explanation may be quite important in other activities, such as the construction of new theories, but has nothing to do with justification.

Yet, relying merely on predictions for theory validation resembles an absurdity; Toulmin (1977), by reviewing the last 25 years of philosophy of science, unveils that we would then consider horse race tipsters scientists and evolutionary biology non-scientists. Indeed, apart from the accuracy of predictions as an admittedly important aspect of the quality or usefulness or validity of a theory, i.e., how adequately the inferences from the theory match reality, additional criteria need to be taken into account. Explanation must be esteemed as evidence of knowledge (Barlas & Carpenter, 1990: 154) and a theory ought to generate the "right output for the right reasons" (Barlas, 1996: 186) since theory validity cannot be controverted without reference to a specific purpose.

Hence, in contrast to validation in the sense of preserving truth, on the one hand, and reliability of lonely predictions, on the other hand, the validity of a theory ought be defined broadly and loosely as "usefulness with respect to some purpose" (Barlas, 1996: 84), as the property a theory has of adequately reflecting the system being described and modeled, contingent on its purpose. The validation process is conversational and an iterative learning cycle, embedded throughout the theory-building operation, with the goal of gradually establishing trust and confidence in a theory. We think of a valid theory of intelligence as one of many admissible ways of delineating and explaining intelligent behavior in the real world; in humans, animals or artificial animals. No particular representation is superior to all others in any absolute sense, although one could prove to be more effective. No theory of intelligence can claim absolute objectivity, for every instantiation carries in it the modeler's world view. Such theories are not true or false but lie on a continuum of usefulness.

In the following, we elicit a set of criteria that aids to evaluate the validity, usefulness or quality of our theory proposal. They are summarized in the subsequent Figure 32.

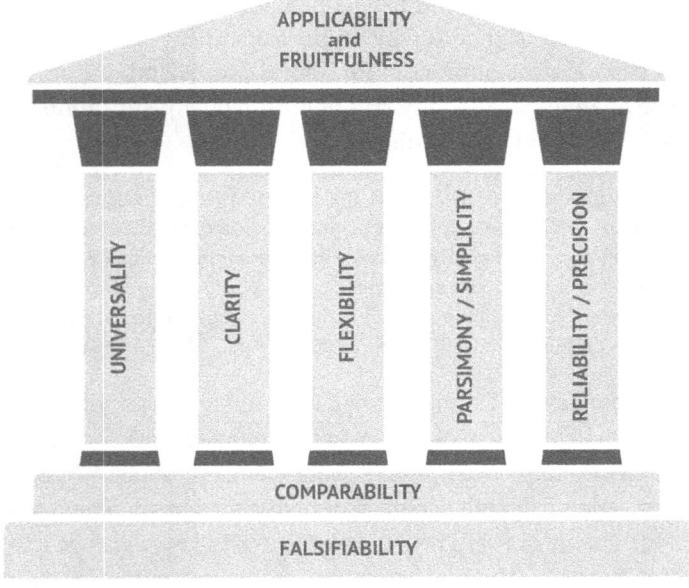

Figure 32: Validating our edifice along a collective of reasonable criteria.

(1) *Falsifiability or refutability*: The ability of a theory (model, hypothesis or conjecture etc.) to be falsified (refuted) or supported. In general, theories, and any other claims to knowledge which are specified, ought to be rationally criticized, and (if they have empirical content) be submitted to tests. These tests are

essentially endeavors of refutation, as established in Popper's critical rationalism (Popper, 1959, 1962). The test object cannot be confirmed or proven, it can only be falsified. If, however, the attempt of falsification is not successful, then it can be temporarily maintained.

Our proposal ensures falsifiability in more than one sense: Firstly, as pointed out in 5.3., we obey the tenet of falsifiability. Above all, by incorporating causal modeling, in opposition to some metaphysics of causation, a focus is set on testability. For instance, assumptions are encoded in a compact and usable form; supposedly trivial for the myriad of economists sacrificing graphical for algebraic representations, but absolutely non-trivial once we take seriously the requirement of transparency and testability. Secondly, inverted radex models can be tested (not just the test subjects therein), simulated, and their performance can be benchmarked against competing propositions. We make underlying, structural assumptions like on the directions of intelligence explicit as well as transparent, and the more explicit and rigorous a solution is, the more easily it is criticizable (Floridi, 2011: 29). Thirdly, hypotheses, serving as an anchor around which arguments are built, can be derived that ought to be scrutinized too.

Some of those captivating hypotheses or implications from our first forays into understanding intelligence are:
- No intelligence without causation: If reality was everywhere independent, if the universe was random, then representation would be impossible, and intelligence non-existent. At the same time, "the world is not completely correlated; that would lock it up into a rigid clutch, with representation, intelligence and creatures again proscribed" (Cantwell Smith, 2019: 18).
- In contrasting higher and lower levels of causal reasoning, we conjecture that, the more AI systems reason in lieu of memorizing the probability density function for the entire world, the more this enables them to deal with opaque areas of real life, with the exponential complexity of systems as opposed to closed end domains. So, the likelihood that their models are inadequate grows. Hence, making mistakes is a sign of heightened intelligence.
- Especially with a view to AI communities: Bringing data glorification to a halt. Radical empiricism, and with it Brooks' (1991/1997: 396) famous "the world is its own best model" thesis, yields no high intelligence, but is a stifling culture. Scientific knowledge, commonsense, education, and innate templates are indispensable for achieving strong(er) AI.
- Especially with a view to the guild of philosophers: Even though there are influential philosophical theories (e.g., Lewis, 1973a) that connect causal claims to counterfactuals, many philosophers continue to regard counterfactuals in general (and *a fortiori*, their use in a causal theory) with great skepticism. It is contended that counterfactuals are unclear, untestable,

unscientific, and in various ways unnatural and artificial in the sense that they are philosophical inventions that correspond to nothing in the way ordinary people actually think and reason. We believe the opposite of all this is true.

(2) *Comparability*: If absolute theory validation is not feasible, the evaluation of theories in comparison to other theories becomes crucial. The focal theory or modeling approach should thus allow for a clear comparison to rival or complementary methods.

We not only nominate concrete radex models, but also embed the measurement of intelligence in a larger framework, where the range of directions of intelligence (e.g., Gardner's theory of multiple intelligences, see Figure 26) becomes a parameter of the model, so it can be adapted to the particular application of interest. With this in mind, our edifice seems, secondly, to be compatible with discursive threads in psychology, psychometrics, animal cognition, but also in computer science given the anchoring of Bayes nets. A third dimension of comparability we prefer to expose as an extra criterion, namely the universal language of causal learning for talking about intelligence in humans, animals, AI systems, and beyond (e.g., hybrids) that ultimately allows us to put very different types of entities into comparison without using humans as a yardstick.

(3) *Comprehensiveness and universality beyond anthropocentrism*: This criterion establishes whether the theory is sufficiently broad to contain the substantive issues and interests; for example, all entities which we intuitively or after reviewing evidence like we did in Part I deem intelligent ought to be reasonably covered with possibly diverging outcomes.

Our outline facilitates the modeling of intelligences from different angles; e.g., accounting for different research results, levels of abstraction, which manifests systemic and holistic and, therefore, comprehensive thinking. This is reinforced against the background of venerating a pluralistic, not monolithic perspective on intelligences, the multidirectionality of intelligence, representing often neglected non-cognitive traits such as inter- and intrapersonal intelligences. Whilst Sternberg & Powell (1982: 975) bemoan that "[i]ntelligence research has, in general, concentrated on breaking 'intelligence' into specifiable pieces, [. . . with the consequence that] [t]heorists of intelligence [. . .] have not often enough stepped back from their individual theories to ascertain the relationships between various theories of intelligence and between each specific theory and intelligence as a whole", our proposal is further holistic and systemic, respectively, in terms of pooling resources of both analytical and synthetical thinking.

It is part of the desiderata for universal theories that they work for any agent, for any kind of intelligence, at present, in the future or at any level of development. Our hierarchical causal taxonomy purports to hold universally, embracing natural and artificial systems. Going beyond human psychology, animal cognition, AI and evolutionary theories, it unifies very different intelligent creatures without the overall approach being imperialistic or succumbing to reductionism. On the one hand, the taxonomy unifies since our characterization of intelligence through learning is given entirely in a unified, but non-anthropocentric causal language. For instance, on level two of the hierarchy, a naturally occurring process (a "natural experiment") that does not presuppose human action at any point may thus qualify as an intervention if it has the right causal characteristics; and, conversely, a manipulation carried out by a human being will fail to qualify as an intervention if it lacks the right causal characteristics (Woodward, 2007: 21f.). Note though that, albeit we combat humanocentrism by employing an unprejudiced language of causal learning, we do not neutralize our biases since, at least speaking for the simplex, the ideal human and many actual humans are still lonely at the top, arousing, again, the suspicion that humans turn out to be the measure of all things. This outcome (unlike the additional, not justified suspicion) is, however, fine to the extent that we simply are the most intelligent beings we know of so far. Moreover, we will perhaps never fully leave humanocentrism behind since how could we think the unthinkable (a higher level of causality).

On the other hand, we do not commit the fallacy of reductionism because there is more to our edifice than just the universal taxonomy. The annexed inverted radex models are endowed with the inescapable flexibility to accommodate the diversity of intelligence and the heterogeneity of different kinds of intelligence with the same consequence of de-/recentering humans: Eschewing an anthropocentric space where humans would automatically be at 100% – a Ptolemaic model –, "[h]umans, as a species, groups and individuals could be located at different locations depending on the representation, making more explicit that there is a Copernican revolution in the way intelligence is seen today, sustained in the progress of comparative cognition, evolutionary psychology and, increasingly, artificial intelligence" (Bhatnagar et al., 2018: 6).

(4) *Clarity*: Hereby, we aim for a theory that is sufficiently clear so that propositions and lessons can easily be drawn from it.

In spite of its merit of universality, our hierarchical taxonomy is still rather crude – in the basic form, just three dimensions in lieu of many branches – but this should not be perplexing since a theory or a model becomes less accurate and expressive, the greater its scope and range. For instance, animal cognition researchers on octopi can *customize* their inquiries to octopi because we have pertinent information about the intelligent aliens under the sea, focusing on *what they have in common*. Once this is discounted, they can address the animals' variability. If our target, by contrast, is the whole set of intelligent agents, the massive variability is harder to handle, because there is less in common. Then if we know nothing about a specific agent, a complete failure in an intelligence test can be construed either as zero proficiency on the side of the evaluee or as failure of the tester to identify the right interface resolution. Such hurdles have to be redressed for an *intelligent* intelligence theory to thrive and are indeed redressed by the high degree of abstraction of our universal taxonomy of causal learning coupled with the flexibility of the radex models which allow for specification.

Clarity of our findings also includes the *demarcation from similar proposals* and we single out one iridescent example doomed to failure though since the initiators and adherents mistake the ubiquity of causality for silver bullets for creating strong intelligence. Wissner-Gross & Freer (2013) nudged research in the same direction of rendering causality fruitful for understanding intelligence, yet they overshot the mark. The authors propose that intelligence of *every* kind, from behaviorism to Bayesian inference to deep learning and beyond, was a manifestation of a very general physical process denoted as "causal entropic forces". Along with the paper presenting their "equation for intelligence", Wissner-Gross had launched an absurdly ambitious startup company called *Entropica* that aimed to capitalize on the discovery by promising "broad applications" in energy, intelligence (recall Merriam-Webster's sense (2) of the word), autonomous defense, health care, logistics, insurance and finance (Palmer, 2013; Marcus & Davis, 2013). Despite that hubbub including media coverage, a TED talk, and funding, there has not been another paper on the topic to the best of my knowledge, and we do not see any sign that their mathematics of causal entropy has made any progress whatsoever. The startup company no longer seems active (matching the point made in Hoffmann & Krawczuk, forthcoming), and Wissner-Gross appears to have gone on to other projects.

The bottom line, in the words of Yale cognitive scientists Chaz Firestone & Brian Scholl (2016), is that "there is no one way the mind works, because the mind is not one thing. Instead, the mind has parts, and the different parts of the mind operate in different ways." And Marcus & Davis (2021) complement that "[t]ruly intelligent [. . .] systems are likely to be full of complexity, much like brains. Any theory that proposes to reduce intelligence down to a single principle – or a single 'master algorithm' – is bound to fail." Hence, contrasted with Wissner-Gross & Freer's (2013) approach, but also to a lesser extent with Pearl's (2018a) causal ladder, more flexibility is needed and was admitted in Chapter 5. Although a rich understanding of causality is a ubiquitous and indispensable facet of human cognition, we should not buy into the naivety that intelligence exhausts itself in causality.

(5) *Flexibility:* Since intelligence is a moving target, a dynamic phenomenon, a theory of intelligence has to prove some adaptability over time. With our dynamic framework (see 5.3.) in place comes an immense flexibility of our proposition which can be plausibilized along different axes.

From general to narrow: We can tailor the inverted radex models to cover idiosyncracies of a particular species, e.g., for humans by accounting for the eight different directions by Gardner; or for a smaller group or even an individual. At the other extreme, we can cover comparisons between creatures of very different origin (e.g., certain AI systems versus certain animals, as sketched in Figure 29).

From individual to collective: individual entities could be located as well as collectives (along with their components) albeit collective intelligence was not within the scope of this work.

From distributed to centralized: systems that are identified by a single body like a human or dog, but also natural and artificial swarms like a school of fish as well as distributed intelligences, including societies.

From biological via hybrids (that is extended and enhanced minds, including cyborgs) to artificial systems

From present to ancient: covering current living beings and AI systems, but also extinct species and AI systems of the past.

From extant to fictional and from terrestrial to alien: There is even room for speculation and imaginary entities.

(6) *Parsimony and simplicity*: This characteristic of theory validity, in essence, advocates the avoidance of multifariousness as opposed to the capability for absorbing complexity, which has to be fostered. The parsimony of the theory refers to its limited size and its simplicity lies in the small set of substrates it consists of, which is fully transparent and focused on the essentials. In general, models and theories ought to be as simple as possible, but not simpler than that (attributed to Einstein and at least partially rooting in *Occam's razor*). It is a desideratum that the users of a theory/model understand the theory/model. Since complexity is entangled with a lack of understanding, it should only be added to a theory/model to the degree it favors another desired attribute.

In this light, our proposal is modest, not cluttered with components and constructs; yet, sometimes perhaps too modest. It can well be regarded as a shortcoming of our theory outline, as an obstacle to surmount in the future that its operationalization is not (yet) fully exhausted: How to put the theory and not just the causal queries and taxonomy to work? At least, there is an imbalance between mathematically sophisticated causal modeling (Chapter 6) and the less powerful radex model, especially when the latter is enriched with a mainly metaphorical addendum of a third dimension or waves in the sea.

Another aspect of the desideratum of parsimony is knowledge reusability and replicability which is here accomplished through, on the one hand, drawing on extant puzzle pieces as documented in Chapter 4 or in the guise of Guttman's (1954) prior work. On the other, we integrate new research procedures and visualizations (e.g., recall the divergent manifestations of inverted radex models as stimulated in 5.2.) for the systematic investigation of intelligent agents as a counterbalance to the common and blatant limitation that "we see similar ideas, representations or experimental protocols appear in different disciplines" of intelligence research (Bhatnagar et al., 2018: 5).

Moreover, reckoning with causal models and Bayesian nets, we not only pick the specific situation at hand, but also a broader class of situations over which learning ought to generalize, and they capture in parsimonious form the essential world structure that causes learners' observations and makes generalization possible (Tenenbaum et al., 2011: 1280).

(7) *Reliability and precision*: Theory reliability can be grasped as the extent to which the employment of a theory is free of measurement errors. For example, the consequences of a model test remain constant, if repeated under "identical" (if possible) conditions; something, which is akin to "model risk" in finance, i.e., any model needs to have its own error taken into account.

In lieu of making a fetish of rigor or of subscribing to the myth of pedantic and infinite precision, we are tolerant of imprecision and partial truths by often only countenancing an ordinal or imprecise measurement of intelligence. Put another way, the former *implies errors* in complex systems (more precise, but also more erroneous) while the latter proves to be more *robust and reliable* and, thus, less afflicted by measurement errors (less precise, but also less prone to error). Statements on an ordinal scale of measurement suffice since it is not our objective to put a cardinal number on agents' possession of some mental quantity dubbed "intelligence". A crude rating system, albeit being fast and easy to apply, could also backfire because it would be plagued with the significant weakness of *imposing transitivity* on the data. It is the nature of a rating system that if agent A is rated higher than agent B, and agent B is rated higher than agent C, then agent A is rated higher than agent C. Yet, reality is not necessarily transitive, especially not when we consider the blatant heterogeneity of agents (cf. also Hoffmann, 2020c and Broome, 1991 for the same issue in another context).

By contrast and as stated earlier, objectives vary among users and, with our theory outline, we now have an adjustable instrument at hand that allows us to make *pragmatic*, but well-conceived comparisons of different agents' intelligence to get a better idea of what is going on in their inside to understand their outside behaviors.

(8) *Applicability and fruitfulness*: We do not engage in designing a theory for its own sake. The purpose is to apply it to a piece or glimpse of the world, which in our case is intelligence in humans, animals and AI, in order to describe and explain the corresponding phenomena, to be ultimately rewarded with an higher understanding of intelligence. On this basis, we identify a number of prosperous applications, which harbor the hope of new opportunities and transformations, not just for academics, but also for educators, policy-makers and the general public. Here are five short examples:

(8.1) *An advantage of universality, of data- and hypothesis-drivenness in opposition to fragmentation and compartmentalization for research*: When intelligence is explored in one species or a particular AI technology, we are curtailed by a lack of sufficiently wide samples to infer/reject hypotheses. A more collaborative data science approach encouraged by our initiative fosters that data from different disciplines is put together to test hypotheses about cognition and intelligence (Bhatnagar et al., 2018: 5).

(8.2) *(Re-)education*: A longer time ago, children and adults used animals as models of different personalities and capabilities, interacting with them regularly. Today, in urban societies with less contact with animals, it is becoming easier to portray and transmit some concepts using robots as models, as (biased and often ill-informing) cinema as well as advertising (especially when targeting children) have already figured out (see Figure 12 which can be seen as a parody of that). An atlas of intelligence like we envision it, covering humans, animals and robots, could be used in museums, schools and universities as a way of articulating over this intelligence landscape (Bhatnagar et al., 2018: 5).

(8.3) *Effective navigation*: Our graphical model of intelligence, with its divergent representations, would help us locate where we are (humans, animals, and AI), the trajectories taken in the past years and the destinations we are heading to, enabling a visualization of whether some targets or trajectories can take us to dangerous or lethal areas (Bhatnagar et al., 2018: 6).

(8.4) *Archival exploration*: Our atlas of intelligence would also aid to acknowledge a history of intelligence, where we would go from extinct animals and past computer/AI systems to the present day, seeing the directions their evolution has taken according to different dimensions (Bhatnagar et al., 2018: 6).

(8.5) *Ethical assessments*: Visual representations like our radex models make some ethical dilemmas about moral *agency* (for what beings' *actual* cognitive abilities matter) and *patiency* (for what beings' *potential* cognitive abilities matter) more explicit, as we can see whether the way we habitually look at and interact with animals and artificial agents is in sync with the outcome of our carefully thought through ranking outcome (e.g., see Figure 27; more on measurement in Part III, cf. also Hoffmann & Hahn, 2020). This will make some ethical issues more conspicuous (animal, robot or human suffering, uncanny valleys, etc.; Bhatnagar et al., 2018: 6).

An application the whole Part III of this treatment is devoted to is scrutinizing the capacities of present-day and past machines by means of our new toolkit since the need for a theory "that can measure the intelligence of different AIs effectively" has been advocated by Eden (2016) and is now served in the remainder of this thesis.

These are the intermediate results we gained on the validation of our theory outline; intermediate since the foregoing catalogue of criteria a) does not claim to be comprehensive, and b) its application mirrors a gradual learning and conversational process, which can be iterated and then possibly lead to different (e.g., more nuanced or diverging) outcomes.

A major goal of science is the reduction of complex systems such as intelligence to manageable and understandable terms. Scientists attempt to isolate a piece of a phenomenon and to specify all the characteristics of that piece and the factors affecting it. After, the disparate pieces are reconnected in the hope that one will then understand the whole phenomenon. This procedure is well-known as *analysis*. A tension arises, however, between the desire to break the phenomenon into small enough pieces so that it can be understood and the need to keep track of how the pieces relate to each other and how they relate to the whole phenomenon. This counterpart to analysis is called *synthesis*. Embracing a systemic approach to theory and model-building, we attempted to do justice to both in the foregoing. Notwithstanding, the latter strategy will be strengthened further in Part III and IV by setting our first forays into scaffolding intelligence into relation to the assessment of first AI test procedures and then of singularity hypotheses.

Highlights and key takeaways from Part II

- Intelligence implies a call to action, it cannot remain forever latent.
- Causal learning is the central theme of intelligence and, hence, our universal taxonomy is a hierarchy of causal learning.
- Comprehension is both composed of competences and representing as well as promoting a general and higher form of intelligence.
- Intelligence, and specifically causal learning presupposes agency and autonomy. Intelligence can only be meaningfully ascribed to systems which are agents.
- An agent that is not able to learn from perception (layer one of our hierarchy) has zero intelligence.
- Intelligence does not exist in absolute terms. It presupposes a frame of reference which was here set in the form of our causal taxonomy reflecting the multidimensionality of intelligence beyond anthropocentrism.
- The completed hierarchy of causal learning represents the multidimensionality of intelligence and has seven layers: 1) the association layer, 2.1) the egocentric viewpoint of intervention, 2.2) the agent causal viewpoint of intervention, 2.3) the fully causal viewpoint of intervention, 3.1) Inferring single causes and effects from the counterfactual analysis, 3.2) Inferring causal networks from the counterfactual analysis, and 3.3) Inferring causal principles from the counterfactual analysis.
- Higher forms of causal learning comprise lower forms of causal learning and the former cannot be grasped and accomplished without the latter.
- Engagement with technology and then complex technology leads to more intelligence through enabling causal reasoning which is detached from space and time. A signature of complex technology is to devise higher-order tools to tackle higher-order problems which goes hand in hand with the layeredness and agility of intelligence as pointed out by Hofstadter (1979: 35).
- Imagination, instantiating that flexibility and stacking of layers of intelligence par excellence, is the supreme discipline of intelligence.
- Deep understanding follows on deep learning.
- One fateful July 1993 *Life* magazine article told us that "Babies Are Smarter Than You Think" and even though our immature offspring "only" rank on level 2.2 in their early days, they soon reach all levels with the consequence that they make more novel inferences at higher levels than their parents, which makes adolescents the hidden champions of our causal hierarchy.
- Applying causation to intelligence in terms of a causal theory of intelligence is prima facie counterintuitive since the former holds between physical events (or situations, etc.), i.e., entities of the real world, while much of the

latter is predicated on dealing with chimeras. If we allow for mental causation, which we advocate, *and* constructivism, which we put to debate, then we only face a pseudo problem. If skeptics refuse that extension, then we can still *indirectly* attest intelligence of all sorts, i.e. also if intelligence involves non-causal reasoning.
- Our causal hierarchy, visualized as a simplex model of intelligence, endows the common denominator to capture and assess intelligence of all creatures, be it intelligence of humans, biological or artificial animals. Beyond that, it is a daunting exercise to account for the multidirectionality of different kinds of intelligences in a circumplex which is, however, 1) primarily reserved for empirical sciences to cope with, 2) remunerated by additional insights.
- If we succumb to the temptation of harmonizing or streamlining intelligence outside of our taxonomy of causal learning by appealing to putatively principal axes in a putatively universal circumplex, we do not strip intelligence to the bones, but cut away vital parts of its anatomy.
- A theory or a model of intelligence becomes less accurate and expressive, the greater its scope and range.
- What it means to be intelligent itself can change over time because intelligence is determined by the dynamics of interaction with a dynamic world.
- The ladder is not destined for modeling intelligence metaphorically.
- Metaphorically speaking, the ocean of intelligence is never a still, smooth sea, it is restless and intelligence makes waves. Water particles here and there, and sometimes even in unsuspected places, are *caused* to get into motion and the *effect* ranges from inconspicuousness to meter-high forces of Nature that wash away sandcastles of the past.
- Operationally, the causal revolution has three constituents: Graphical models serve as a language for representing what we know about the world, counterfactuals help us to articulate what we want to know, while structural equations serve to tie the two together in a solid semantics.

Part III: **Evaluating machine intelligence in current and past AI**

How many levels should a system have? How much and what kind of "intelligence" should be placed on which level? These are some of the hardest problems facing AI today.

Douglas R. Hofstadter, 1979: 628

When in the 1960s and 1970s AI was in its first flush, the newly minted AI labs were electrified about the seemingly palpable prospect of developing true machine intelligence, but defeated by the complexity and uncertainty encountered in the real world. Since a few decades, there has been excitement once again – for "second wave" AI, for a new "AI spring". Deep learning programs such as AlphaGo[17] which became in 2015 the first computer Go program to "beat" a human professional Go player (Silver & Hassabis, 2016) and affiliated statistical methods, backed by unimagined computational power and reams of Big Data, are "accomplishing" levels of performance which trounce the achievements of the earlier phase. In fact, it has become rather routine to see machines doing things that seemed far off even ten years ago, such as making a haircut appointment by talking to a real human person. Or for us, sitting in a car that can drive itself on ordinary (not too busy) highways (even though to be fair, Daimler's twin robot vehicles VaMP and Vita-21 drove more than 1,000 km on a Paris three-lane highway in standard heavy traffic at speeds up to 130 km/h as early as in 1994, albeit without the company realizing the market potential and merely semi-autonomously with human interventions).

It might leave us somehow perplexed that the vast majority of our present-day learning machines, including the celebrated deep learning programs, still rank so low in both Pearl's (2018a) and our causal framework of Part II despite the astounding progress materialized in the last 60 years. But insatiable deep learning as presented in Chapter 3 is after all just a kind of mighty statistical engine.

> Researchers are often surprised that the hierarchy [degrades] the impressive achievements of deep learning to the level of Association, side by side with textbook curve-fitting exercises. A popular stance against this comparison argues that, whereas the objective of curve-fitting is to maximize "fit," in deep learning we try to minimize "over fit." Unfortunately, the theoretical barriers that separate the three layers in the hierarchy tell us that the nature of our objective function does not matter. As long as our system optimizes some property of the observed data, however noble or sophisticated, while making no reference to the world outside the data, we are back to level-1 of the hierarchy with all the limitations that this level entails. (Pearl, 2018b: 3)

---

[17] Strictly speaking and in light of Kautz's (2020) taxonomy for *neurosymbolic AI*, DeepMind's AlphaGo does not count as a standard deep learning program (Type 1), but as a Type 2 hybrid system where the core neural network is loosely-coupled with a symbolic problem solver such as, in this case, Monte Carlo tree search.

One reason between this mismatch between our expectations and reality can be that, in tune with Dennett's (2017: 96) Beatrix Potter syndrome, we prematurely and uncritically associate capabilities with our computational systems that do not do justice to what is happening in the world. Some of our learning machines fool us so proficiently that they induce an *Eliza effect* (Hofstadter, 1996; named after Joseph Weizenbaum's NLP computer program created from 1964 to 1966) in which blitheful humans attribute more to the machine than is really there, but there is never anything more than a very shallow understanding (Marcus, 2020).

For example, the statement "AlphaGo *plays* Go and *beats* a human professional player, *defying* ancient wisdoms" (cf. e.g., Silver et al., 2017; Tegmark, 2018: 88) like many other terms and phrases oversells what is going on. Do AlphaGo and its successors (like AlphaGo Zero) have any sense of the fact that Go is a *game*, with vastly more possible Go positions than there are atoms in our Universe, with an illustrious millennial history, played by experts from around the globe – or even more pointedly that there is a difference between the particular game it is playing and the representation of that game in its data structures? Would it not be a better characterization to say that we humans understand and interpret the program's behavior as being about and referring to the game Go in this case? Cantwell Smith (2019: 76) emits the answer with brutal brevity: "No matter how otherwise impressive they may be, I believe that all existing AI systems [. . .] *do not know what they are talking about.*"

And how could they when we call to mind how Haugeland (1997b: 24) characterized new-fangled AI in Chapter 3.1. as systems without "formal tokens (unless implemented at a higher level)" so that "there can be no semantically interpreted symbols". Some newer neural networks like our GPT-3 might "know" some statistical properties of how words are used in a concept; yet, this is not sufficient for understanding the nature of the underlying concepts, such as what makes a reader, it addresses, a reader rather than a writer (and vice versa). I am reminded of the Scrabble champion Nigel Richards, who won a French Scrabble™ tournament without knowing French (Chappell, 2015); the individual words were used as mere game tokens, without any regard whatsoever to their meaning. The words "epistemological", "philosophical", "ontological", and so forth are all intercorrelated; GPT-3 gets that, but that is not enough for GPT-3 to induce a conceptual understanding of the nature of such a debate on AI; the results are spotty (Marcus, 2020: 26; Sorber, 2021). Or how we would put it with a view on Part II, this sort of anomalous behavior is what we receive when we try to infer how the world works (a level three ambition) through approximating the curves of the statistics of how words are used (a level one proficiency), rather than inferring a more abstract, causal understanding of the world (a proper level three technique).

Sometimes that works, nonetheless in the long run it does certainly not. To circumvent that pitfall for AI systems, not more data or faster processing is necessitated, but a new kind of knowledge, causal knowledge. In the immortal words of Law 31 of Akin's Laws of Spacecraft Design, "You can't get to the moon by climbing successfully taller trees".

Thus, to read more into those AI systems, to regard them as having intentional states would be to adopt Daniel Dennett's (e.g., 1996: 27; 1989) *intentional stance* or "as-if" intentionality (Searle, 1990). It is often expedient to adopt this *intentional* interpretation when we look at complex systems – biological like the brain or otherwise like AlphaGo. By this, Dennett means describing the system *as if* it had beliefs, goals, desires, plans, intentions, understanding and so on, the same way we talk about people. Dennett's main point is that these are stances. They are not inherently right or wrong, but rather a stance may or may not be useful. To that extent, it is our job to figure out if a particular stance in question is adequate or not. In some cases like for dogs, it is unambiguously useful to think about them in intentional terms (and we do it all the time, which I myself can tell as a dog owner, e.g., look he thinks his toy is behind the door, . . .). In other cases (like the toaster in the kitchen), the intentional stance seems overblown and needlessly anthropomorphic, and the system is better dealt with in different terms. A substantive issue is now where to locate current AI on that spectrum – closer to the toaster (dumb non-agents) or closer to the dog (evidently intelligent animals/agents).

The main work in this book has been done. What is left in this Part III is to substantiate our theory outline further by attesting its applicability to current and past AI systems (in contrast to far-fetched future utopias/dystopias reserved for Part IV). Thereby, we are entering the land of AI test procedures, broaching the research gap that "there is no general methodology for AI evaluation" (Hernández-Orallo, 2017: 11). Many different competitions and benchmarks have been developed in the past decades. Yet at the end of the day, AI evaluation tools are, non-astonishingly given what we saw in Chapter 3, task oriented (i.e., the performance of an AI system is assessed for a particular task) rather than feature oriented (ibid.), the latter being common for biological intelligence (see Table 6). The limited integration between the disciplines of human, animal and artificial intelligence suggests a full overhaul of their ordering principles and instruments. Although some capabilities and tests can be inherited or extended from psychometrics or animal cognition, a generalization of established procedures would fall short. In this direction, a cornerstone of a theory was laid in Part II which we now wish to put to work by evaluating present-day AI, a problem taking the agenda of AI and science in general (Bhatnagar et al., 2018: 4f.; Hernández-Orallo, 2017: 23; Marcus et al., 2016; You, 2015).

Up to now, the comparison of AI systems with human and non-human intelligence as well as their classification is typically executed in an informal and subjective way, often leading to contradicting assessments, eminently in hindsight (Hayles, 1996; Brooks, 1997; Pfeifer, 2001; Shah et al., 2016). The whole large and sprawling debate, carried on by over 400 researchers worldwide from at least ten academic disciplines (Horn, 2009: 73), was unleashed more than 70 years ago by Turing (1950). The Turing debate, as to whether machines will ever be able to think, is, without any doubt, one of the great philosophical debates of recent times (Horn, 2009: 73; Oppy, 2020), and hence Part III is devoted to it. (Strong AI or singularity is the other great debate in connection to AI as we saw in 3.2. and we will pick it up in Part IV. Often it is even one and the same (e.g., Searle, 2009), but this is not the case here as we will notice in the following.)

This Part III is structured as follows: In the next Chapter 8, we revisit Turing's (1950) path-breaking *Mind* article in a tour de force of exposition and his imitation game therein, which came to be better known as the Turing Test. Besides common pitfalls for the Turing Test, Chapter 9 appeals to how and what we would respond to it and to the human judges in the game, respectively, from our perspective taken in Part II. In some sense, our theory architecture even traces back to Alan Turing, the shining pioneer and consensus patron saint of the classical research program in AI, who proposed to classify a cognitive system in terms of the queries it can answer. Yet, while Turing (1950) was looking for a binary classification – human or nonhuman – we offered three (main levels) to seven (including sublevels) non-humanocentric, but agnostic tiers, corresponding to progressively more powerful causal queries. Based on this critical review, we bring forward our own constructive solution in terms of a recommended redesign of a test of machine intelligence in the final Chapter 10.

8 The Turing Test

Chris: If you could ask a computer just one question in the Turing Test, what would it be?

Sandy: Uhmm . . .

Pat: How about this: "If you could ask a computer just one question in the Turing Test, what would it be?"

Douglas R. Hofstadter, 1981: 36

Neither the 1956 Dartmouth conference, nor Turing's (1950) *Mind* paper, where he showcases the test named after him, come close to marking the start of AI as we witnessed in Part I already. That AI runs deep into the past (and has always had philosophy in its veins) is furthermore easy enough to see by the example of René Descartes who proposed the Turing Test (not the Turing Test by name, of course) almost 300 years before Turing was born. The *locus classicus* here is the following passage:

> If there were machines which bore a resemblance to our body and imitated our actions as far as it was morally possible to do so, we should always have two very certain tests by which to recognise that, for all that, they were not real men. The first is, that they could never use speech or other signs as we do when placing our thoughts on record for the benefit of others. For we can easily understand a machine's being constituted so that it can utter words, and even emit some responses to action on it of a corporeal kind, which brings about a change in its organs; for instance, if it is touched in a particular part it may ask what we wish to say to it; if in another part it may exclaim that it is being hurt, and so on. But it never happens that it arranges its speech in various ways, in order to reply appropriately to everything that may be said in its presence, as even the lowest type of man can do. And the second difference is, that although machines can perform certain things as well as or perhaps better than any of us can do, they infallibly fall short in others, by which means we may discover that they did not act from knowledge, but only for the disposition of their organs. For while reason is a universal instrument which can serve for all contingencies, these organs have need of some special adaptation for every particular action. From this it follows that it is morally impossible that there should be sufficient diversity in any machine to allow it to act in all the events of life in the same way as our reason causes us to act. (Descartes 1637/1911: 116)

Yet, although Turing's (1950) proposal is reminiscent of 17th century tests to explore *other minds*, it was exactly conversational abilities that Descartes predicted artifacts would never be able to accomplish. Moreover, the latter fall within normal science, on Cartesian assumptions that minds have properties distinct from mechanism, assumptions that collapsed with Newton's undermining of "the mechanical philosophy", soon leading to the conclusion that thinking is a property of organized matter, on par with other properties of the natural world (Chomsky, 2009b: 103). In his justly famous 1950 paper "Computing Machinery and Intelligence", Turing starts on an equivocation. He raises the question of whether artificial machines or AI can think, only to repudiate the question immediately as inappropriate. Somebody who rolled out its ambiguity extensively is Searle (2009: 143): He first argues that the word "artificial" is systematically ambiguous because "an artificial X" can mean either a real X, yet produced by artifice; or it can denote something that is not really an X, but is only an imitation of an X. Then, Searle hints at more cacophony when we shift over to the word "intelligence" (namely with or without the presence of any thought processes or any other relevant psychological states) which allows for at least four different interpretations of the expression "AI". Whilst we applaud his subtlety when we remember the history of conceptual confusion about AI sketched in Chapter 3 (or is it just bravado here?), we have the feeling that Searle is just beating a dead horse. We, including Turing and most, if not all, AI researchers, know that Turing goes on to consider, not whether or not AI can think, but whether or not AI can do what thinkers like us can do since doing is performance capacity, empirically observable, whereas thinking is *simply* an internal state which machines have been patently lacking.

Mental terms like "intelligent", "thinking", "understanding" and so on are inflicted with vagueness or suffer from being emotionally charged to a degree that it is no longer worth arguing about them. Therefore, we designed a theory of intelligence instead, and Turing opts for a divergent approach for coping with his more specific question, but derides deciding it by an empirical survey of which sorts of objects the term "think" or its synonyms and cognates are positively applied to. Presumably, at least people in 1950 rarely if ever said of machines that they think, and few would have said that any machine, then or in the future, could *possibly* be said to think (see also the quote from Wittgenstein in Chapter 3). That procedure would be farcical because what people say, even what almost everyone accedes to, is often widely wrong; just ask Copernicus or Galileo Galilei. "Think" will never be defined by Turing (1950) at all. In lieu of asking if a machine is intelligent, he really embraces an operational stance, treats the mind as a "target object" that is not directly visible, but whose structure can be inferred in an abstract way, and wonders: "Can a machine behave like an intelligent person?" Or adapting the dictum of the title character in the movie *Forest Gump* who said "Stupid is as stupid does", we can imagine Turing saying "Intelligent is as intelligent does".

Not only "think", but also "machine" will never be adequately stipulated in Turing's (1950) paper – and we have not been bothered too much about the clarification of the term either –, although what will eventually be known as the "Turing Machine", the abstract description of a computer (Turing, 1937), will be.

> In Turing's test, the only relevant inputs and outputs are *words* – all of which are (among other things) formal tokens. So the capacity of human beings that is to be matched is

effectively a formal input/output function. But Turing himself had shown, thirteen years earlier, that *any* formal input/output function from a certain very broad category could be implemented in a routine universal machine, provided only that it had enough memory and time (or speed) – and those, he thought, would be available by century's end. [C.H.: Turing (1950: 442) predicted – falsely, but not foolishly – that by the year 2000 there would be computers that could be reasonably deemed to think. Nota bene that] Turing did not (and could not) show that the human verbal input/output function fell into that broad category of functions to which his theorem applied. [That is, as Marcus (2015) would countersign, our minds are not Turing machines. See the opening of Chapter 3 C.H.] But he had excellent reason to believe that any function computable by any *digital* mechanism would fall into that category; and he was convinced that there is nothing immaterial or supernatural in human beings [a conviction we go d'accord with, C.H.]. The only alternative remaining would seem to be *non*digital mechanisms [or hybrids as suggested in Chapter 3]; and those he believed could be digitally simulated. (Haugeland, 1997b: 15)

Another reasonable definition of machine, rather than the constricting notion of a Turing Machine, might be any dynamical, *causal* system like ourselves (which is very sympathetic from our universal theory's point of view): "It is natural that we should wish to permit every kind of engineering technique to be used in our machines" (Turing, 1950: 435). This passage implies that Turing did not mean only computers: any dynamical causal system we design and assemble is eligible (as long as it delivers the performance *capacity*; Harnad, 2009: 28). A cloned human being, by contrast, could not be logged in as the machine candidate, for instance. Although we are all "machines" in the sense of being causal systems (see Part II, and cf. also Harnad, 2000), we did not construct it, nor would we know how it works.

The basic architecture of the Turing Test is probably familiar to all readers. Inspired by the once very popular Victorian parlor games, Turing (1950) sets the stage by considering an *imitation game*, in which two sequestered agents, a man A and a woman B are placed in rooms separate from an intelligent interrogator or judge I, who communicates with each by teleprinter (or computer as we would say nowadays). I puts questions to A and B, known only as X and Y. I's mission is to identify $X = A$ and $Y = B$ or, conversely, $X = B$ and $Y = A$, by taking their responses to her/his questions into account whereby I has the widest latitude in what might be asked. The gist of the game is that player A pretends to be a woman. In a next step, Turing then replaced the man by a computer or an AI system mimicking a woman, a member of "man"kind. In spite of the rich connotations of the original game, it is construed as Turing himself seemed to convey, more explicitly two years later (1952): one mechanical impostor "aspiring" to appear as a human, a human behaving as a human and a human judge. This is known today as the standard Turing Test.

What does passing the Turing Test implicate? Obviously, that a machine effectively "managed" to fool a human (the interrogator). Yet, on top of that, it has been held that "Turing laid out an appealingly simple test for whether a machine possesses human-level intelligence" (You, 2015). Some, if not many, colleagues of mine seem to confidently jump on the former when they envision the Turing Test as either an iterated game or as modified with other judges invited, so that "a 50 percent success rate for interrogators' declarations would mean that they were learning nothing from comparing human and machine responses to their probes, and rates close to that would plausibly count as 'passing' the Turing Test" (Robinson, 2015: 66). However, given Turing's (1950) initial and guiding question, it is surely not his goal to trigger a wave of machines designed for the sole purpose of being mistaken for a human being statistically more often than not! (Sadly, this is *grosso modo* what has happened in reality; see below.) That would reduce the Turing Test to the Gallup poll that Turing rightly condemned when prompting the question of what "thinking" is (not) in the first place. No, if Turing's indistinguishability criterion is to have any empirical substance, the performance of the machine must be equal to that of a human being – to anyone and everyone, for a lifetime (Harnad, 2009: 26).

It is lucid that Turing intended succeeding in the Turing Test to be an uncontroversial criterion *sufficient* for thought or human-like intelligence, not a necessary one: "May not machines carry out something which ought to be described as thinking but which is very different from what a man does? This objection is a very strong one, but at least we can say that if, nevertheless, a machine can be constructed to play the imitation game satisfactorily, we need not be troubled by this objection." (Turing, 1950: 435). Two years later, Turing was even more explicit that the imitation game was never intended as a definition of what it means for an AI system to possess human-like intelligence, i.e., in terms of sufficient *and* necessary conditions: "I don't want to give a definition of thinking" (Turing, 1952: 494). Nonetheless, as years passed by, the Turing Test has been regarded by some as "a simple operational definition of intelligence" (French, 2000: 115), as "an operational definition of 'thinking' or 'intelligence' [. . .] by means of a sexual guessing game" (Hodges, 1992: 415), as "[a]n especially influential behaviorist definition of intelligence [. . ., according to which] [t]he computer is intelligent *if and only if* the judge cannot tell the difference between the computer and the person" (Block, 1990: 248; our italics).[18]

---

[18] The 1950 and 1952 presentations of the test are significantly disparate: "According to the 1950 formulation, the Turing Test is a three-party game involving the parallel interrogation by a human of a computer and a human foil. It is implied that the interrogator knows that one of each pair of contestants is a human and one a machine. According to the 1952 formulation,

How would the crowd of idiots savants of the first and second wave of AI score in a Turing Test trial, knowing that most, if not all of us could not beat Deep Blue at chess or AlphaGo at Go, nor even attain ordinary grandmaster level? Well, the myriad of them would not even be admitted to the participation. For once, out of pragmatic reasons: Barring some NLP programs and chatbots, they could not communicate with the judge because they were designed for other purposes like "playing" chess or Go and, as their label "idiots savants" tells, they cannot do much more. Does it follow from that fact that AlphaGo is not intelligent? Turing (1950/1952) would answer in the negative, remain silent here about AlphaGo's proficiencies. His test does not provide any argument for or against such a pronouncement. (In Chapter 3.2. and 5., we broke that silence and emitted a negative answer to the question if AlphaGo is not intelligent.) As stated in the last paragraph, failing the test is not decisive: It is possible to fail the Turing Test for intelligence, and still be an intelligent being. On the other hand, it is only generic human capacities that are at issue in a Turing Test, not those of any specific individual. The local indistinguishable capacity to carry out some arbitrary task like Go or chess would not really constitute a Turing Test at all, since it would be so blatantly subtotal. The machine candidate would be easily distinguished from the human foil by checking whether it can do anything else, other than "play" chess or Go, respectively. If it could not, it would fail the test.

Nonetheless, it has not stopped the world from running Turing Test contests with idiots savants and being wowed by cagey subjects, caching behind a smokescreen of playfulness, verbal tricks or canned responses. The Loebner Prize circus has come to town since the year 1991 and has grown into a small industry while drawing increasing criticism (You, 2015). This annual competition in AI strives for awarding, in a pseudo Turing spirit, prizes (see Figure 33) to the computer programs considered by the judges to be the most human-like. Yet, it is more aptly characterized by participants as provoking entries that "are written just for the contest" (Garner, 2009: 319; bouncing us back to the point about idiots savants), as entertainment around "[f]ooling friends and family into believing that a 'conversation simulator' is intelligent [which] is considerable fun" (Hutchens, 2009: 325). An unfortunate side effect of Hugh Loebner's construal of Turing (1950) is that it degrades intelligence to something like "a social club – you get accepted by recommendation and you maintain your membership by constantly demonstrating your credentials" (Hutchens, 2009: 334).

---

members of a jury question a series of contestants one by one; some of the contestants are machines and some humans." (Copeland & Proudfoot, 2009: 127). The test as displayed in 1950 is harder for the AI to pass; nevertheless, it is fairer to the machine.

Loebner Prize Gold Medal
(Solid 18 carat, not *gold-plated* like the Olympic *"Gold"* medals)

Figure 33: When the circus comes to town: Winning the Loebner Prize tournament is not only awarded by a cash prize, but also by a "superb [. . .] medallion featuring portraits of both Alan Turing and Hugh Loebner [. . .], an irresistible incentive to poor postgraduate students everywhere" (Hutchens, 2009: 325). One comment, and two questions: I am positive that at least postgraduate students of philosophy, that are at least rich (!) in thought, would not be attracted to such ill-posed incentives. How would the old or ancient Greeks, inventor of the Olympic Games, feel about that tacitly stipulated expansion (in the caption of the image)? How would Turing feel about involuntarily serving as the patron of the Loebner Prize? *Source*: Worswick, 2018. [Steve Worswick is the creator and developer of Mitsuku, the five times winner of the Loebner Prize and "regarded as the world's most humanlike conversational AI" as he claims boldly on his Medium page.].

Against this background, it can hardly be miraculous that (the abuse (!) of) the Turing Test has become a stigma for AI, a blind alley, or even a disgrace (Hayes & Ford, 1995; Whitby, 1996; Wakefield, 2019). To end on a positive note and reverting to Hofstadter (1981: 36), it could indeed be Turing's single ultimate litmus test if a computer can successfully engage a skeptical human in a conversation about its own intelligence.

9 Caveats and innovations

> By placing the candidates for intelligence in "black boxes" and leaving nothing as evidence but a restricted range of "external behavior" (in this case, verbal output by typing), the Turing test seems to settle dogmatically on some form of behaviorism, or (worse) operationalism, or (worse still) verificationism. (These three cousins are horrible monster isms of the recent past, reputed to have been roundly refuted by philosophers of science and interred – but what is that sickening sound? Can they be stirring in their graves? We should have driven stakes through their hearts!)
>
> Daniel Dennett, 1982: 93

A vigorous merit of Turing's idea is that it picks up what seems to be a common practice among us since long: People appear to treat each other as black boxes and only ascribe minds to the others because they have them under steady observation, which is a kind of a Turing Test (Hofstadter, 1981). If the Turing Test is considered as an actual test for machines, what is it supposed to measure? And, can it be measured in a reliable way?

Fundamentally, the Turing Test is not unusual as a measurement procedure. For instance, given two objects and a yardstick, an interrogator (the measurer) compares both things and determines which one is longer (Hernández-Orallo, 2017: 127). About what is measured, Turing was articulate "that he was proposing a test of intelligence in machines" (Proudfoot, 2011: 951). About how machine intelligence is measured, Turing casts his test in terms of simulation and imitation. The imitation idea itself is not the startling part of Turing's proposal. What is baffling is rather the specific sort of behavior that Turing chose for his test: he specified *verbal* behavior (Haugeland, 1997b: 3). This is a daring and radical simplification. We recognized in Chapter 1 with Gardner's idea of multiple intelligences, and ever thereafter, that there are many ways in which intelligence is manifested, that thinkers can and do more than just talk. Why single out *talking* or *chatting* for special emphasis, which does not even cover the whole gamut of linguistic intelligence? Concededly, Turing did not suggest that talking/chatting in this way is required to demonstrate intelligence, only that it is sufficient.

If Turing is not blindly steered by the big tradition of the parlor game, his answer is elegant and deep: talking is unique among human intelligent abilities (but not unprecedented, which is music, not language) because

> it gathers within itself, at one remove, all others. One cannot generate rhythms or fly airplanes 'about' talking, but one certainly can *talk about* rhythms and flying – not to mention poetry, sports, science, cooking, love, politics, and so on – *and*, if one doesn't know what one is talking about, it will soon become painfully obvious. Talking is not merely one intelligent ability among others, but also, and essentially, the ability to *express* intel-

https://doi.org/10.1515/9783110756166-013

ligently a great many (maybe all) other intelligent abilities. And, without *having* those abilities in fact, at least to some degree, one cannot talk intelligently about them. That's why Turing's test is so compelling and powerful. (Haugeland, 1997b: 4)

Aware of the storm of opposition that would undoubtedly greet Turing's (1950: 442) opinion that there will exist intelligent machines, he then (ibid.: 443f.) proceeds to pick apart, concisely and with wry humor, a series of objections to the notion that machines could think (Hofstadter, 1979: 593). Still, the Turing Test does obscure certain real difficulties. By concentrating on conversational abilities, it completely ignores any intricacies of real-world perception and action. As realized in Chapter 3.1. where we sensed, for instance, the pains of bringing capable robots to the world, the Turing Test bluntly underestimates the extraordinary travails needed to artificially achieve perception and action at any plausible level of sophistication, not to speak of dubious bodily intelligence of vehemently disembodied NLP programs. Could it be that intelligent behavior is really no more than being able to carry on a certain illusion convincingly, such as being able to participate in a conversation without having to understand what is being discussed, bolstered perhaps by the ability to quote from canned text? (Levesque, 2018: 46).

It remains what thinkers can do that a machine candidate in the Turing Test must likewise be able to do, not just talking about it. Hence, flying is just something that an airplane can do, and not a computer-simulated virtual plane; be it ever so Turing-equivalent to the real plane, it will never be a real robot, i.e., acting in the physical world. (For other properties, simulation *is* replication: A simulation of a system with a causal loop, for instance (see Figure 23), *is* a system with a causal loop; for the differentiation, cf. Chalmers, 1996: 328.) But maybe the machine that merely imitates, without having an impact on the real world, plainly fails to meet the Turing Test criterion itself, which is real performance capacity, not merely something formally equivalent to it (Harnad, 2009: 39). (Nota bene that Harnad's reply, putting emphasis on the real performance capacity, could lethally beg the question and fall victim to a *circulus in demonstrando*, a *petitio principii*.)

What may be worse, neglecting real-time environmental interaction distorts a system designer's assumptions about how intelligent systems are related to the world more generally (Haugeland, 1997b: 4). In contrast to common "toy" problems tests for only a very restricted aspect of intelligence (like AI blocks-world puzzles or rectilinear mazes), Edmonds (2009) also argues for the social embedding of intelligence, but views the Turing Test as a special case of it; i.e., of examining interactive intelligence, namely between a human and a machine during an open-ended conversation: the more extended the period of time, the more long-term the Turing Test is, the more suitable it is, the more reliable its outcomes (ibid.: 213). Edmonds basically contends that the ability to imitate a human in a chat with its interrogator is accompanied by acquiring a full language, which in turn necessitates that an individual is socially immersed in a linguistic environment. Since many facets of our intelligence are rooted in our interactive and social faculty, passing the Turing Test, he concludes, is sufficient for humanlike intelligence. But is it really? In the following, we bring forward three persuasive objections to the cogency of the standard Turing Test, starting with an attack on the assertion that (proficiently) imitating a human would be sufficient for heightened intelligence.

1) Necessity was not claimed, but does the Turing Test truly pose (logically) sufficient conditions for human-like intelligence?

When it is supposed that the Turing Test offers logically sufficient conditions for the attribution of intelligence, then this is equivalent with the pronouncement that it is logically impossible for something that lacks intelligence to succeed in a Turing Test. Objections to this supposition have occurred to a number of writers but nowadays are usually credited to Block (1981), who pointed out that a Turing-Test successful being whose behavior was produced by "brute force" methods ought not to count as intelligent (as possessing a mind, as having thoughts).

Ned Block's charlatan machine (as we announced it in Chapter 5.1.) is Blockhead, a creature that looks just like a human being, but that is controlled by a "game-of-life look-up tree"; i.e. by a tree that contains a programmed response for every discriminable input at each stage in the creature's life (Oppy, 2020). If we accede that Blockhead is logically possible, and if we accede that Blockhead is not intelligent (does not have a mind, does not think), then Blockhead is a counterexample to the supposition that the Turing Test provides a sufficient criterion for the ascription of intelligence (ibid.). After all, Blockhead could be programmed with a look-up tree that produces responses identical with the ones that you would give over the entire course of your life (given the same inputs; ibid.). Such a program faithfully imitates the intellectual behavior of the brain, yet, so the caveat goes, does not think.

The formal point on which Block's (1981) objection rests – the *logically possible* encapsulability in a look-up table of all the relevant behavior – is, of course, fair. Still, I find this kind of demeanor of philosophers from the ivory tower, from "quixotic smart-alecks and nit-pickers" (which is how they are likely to be perceived) hard to digest, in this particular case for three reasons: Firstly, Block's (1981) point is not novel and not his own. For instance, Shannon & McCarthy (1956: v–vi) raised a very similar, if not the same concern about Turing's "definition of thinking" [to call the test a definition is an interpretative mistake as we know]. Secondly, Turing (1950: 439–441) anticipates and responds to this criticism. Thirdly, and from my point of view most disruptively, "[i]t is all very well to say that a machine could [. . .] be made to do this or that, but, to take only one *practical* point, what about the time it would take to do it? [. . .] Solving a problem on the machine doesn't mean finding a way to do it between now and eternity, but within reasonable time" (Newman, 1952 cited in Copeland & Proudfoot, 2009: 130; our italics). Or to spread a bit of wisdom from John Maynard Keynes: "In the long run, we are all dead." (Others also critically dwelled on Block's, 1981, argument, but, as I would hold, not in a better manner than Block, 1981, dwelled on Turing, 1950. For example, in Pautz & Stoljar, 2019, it is wondered if the *logically possible* Blockhead, which "has the intelligence of a toaster" (Block, 1981: 11), would not have some level of intelligence after all, since it is at least a processor of information – such conceptual confusion can be effectively averted if my causal theory of intelligence is harnessed.)

On other, not just logically, but practically relevant grounds, however, we can maintain the first objection, namely flatly by turning to our comments on the second and third question. Here comes the second.

2) What is truly measured in the Turing Test?

Although it might be illegitimate to reproach Turing for these misapprehensions (Hernández-Orallo, 2000; Larsson, 1993), the Turing Test has been mistaken for measuring intelligence in lieu of what is really at stake, humanity. The Turing Test does provide little information on what intelligence is, and should better be treated as an imaginary test of humanity (Fostel, 1993). It does not measure any aggregation of cognitive capacities, not even a monolithic view of intelligence (Hernández-Orallo, 2017: 128). This is exactly realized by Turing (1952: 495): "Likewise the machine would be permitted all sorts of tricks so as to appear more man-like, such as waiting a bit before giving the answer, or making spelling mistakes." So, at some point, the machine will have to behave *less intelligent* to look human.

Who are we testing then really? The sender or the receiver? What is sometimes subject to negotiation is less if machines are intelligent, but why humans, many of them at least, are so wooden (e.g., entirely rule-governed bureaucrats, legal clerks or accountants and so forth) or, at another extreme, depraved. For example, according to media reports, some judges at the first Loebner competition rated a human as a machine on the grounds that she produced extended, well-written paragraphs of informative text at dictation speed without typing errors (Ford et al., 2009: 29). (Apparently, this is now regarded an inhuman ability in parts of our culture . . .)

Bear in mind that this levelling-down effect is not only a consequence of anthropocentrism which Turing (1950: 435) rightly foresaw as criticism and rebutted it. (Obviously, the Turing Test discriminates against nonhuman biological animals, just as IQ tests in psychometrics discriminate against nonhuman animals, too. For why that does not wound Turing, cf. also Copeland & Proudfoot, 2009: 129, that nicely stress that the imitation game deals only with the general question "Can *machines* think?", and not with every particular instantiation of it: "Can machine *M* think?", and so forth). It is because the Turing Test is just such an *imitation* game (where a machine mimics a human and humans make mistakes or not always act intelligently), not an interview (to inquire its intelligence). This sets the misalignment with intelligence in terms of not only necessity, but also sufficiency which we sensed already.

A non-intelligent, or possibly level one intelligent (but certainly not humanlike intelligent) AI system can be specialized to "trick" and "outwit" the judges, which is precisely what has happened in Turing Test tournaments like the Loebner Prize: Along these lines, Mauldin (2009: 420–425), for example, composes a list of top ten rules to be followed to "keep the human judge off-balance so he or she won't notice they're talking to a machine" (ibid.: 425), together with the "golden rule" of keeping them laughing. Hence, it does not clear after all that the Turing Test is a sufficient condition for humanness, and even less a sufficient condition for intelligence (Hernández-Orallo, 2017: 129). Additionally, from the lens of a desired measure of *all* minds, it must be devastating news that the Turing Test, if applied to human beings rather than AIs, yields many paradoxes (Hernández-Orallo, 2000: 463): "The result of applying it to ourselves is a recursive trap, [. . .] unable to answer the question of how intelligent the Homo Sapiens is."

3) Is the Turing Test truly a good testing instrument?

A final caveat is that, even assuming that we wanted to measure humanness or the capacity of behaving like a human, the Turing Test is a poor testing procedure. First, it is a deficiently designed experiment, relying entirely on the competence of the judge, who must be intelligent. Thereby, the self-reference issue, incarnated in the Loebner Prize and other contests, arises: Who is the first intelligent being to begin the game? Furthermore, second, the results from the test can vary dramatically depending on the protocol, indications, personality and intelligence of not only the interrogator, but also the human player. Third, there is no way of knowing who is cheating, the system or its designer. Fourth, the Turing Test is a test based on ascription (McCarthy, 1979), and humans, as the introduction to Part III informed us, tend to ascribe mental qualities to objects lacking them. Fifth, as a comparative test, it is bizarre: "It compares an individual with a representative of a species. For instance, given a chimpanzee and a bonobo, could we determine which one is more *bonobish*?" (Hernández-Orallo, 2017: 129).

Sixth, in some sense, the Turing Test is setting the bar too high for evaluating AI systems. On the one hand, as the progression from Chapter 1 to 3 here documents, we refuse the artificial obsession with humanlike, a term which we find naturally slippery. Intelligence is more ample than that. The width and depth of intelligence(s) might make a test specification inevitable (in line with our thrust of steadily reconfigurating the circumplex of the model of intelligence), but to use humans as a yardstick is a) still too broad (e.g., ask Gardner, 1983/2011, who suggested eight and not a single human intelligence), and b) arbitrarily one-dimensional. On the other, it is extremely difficult to behave like an average (?) human being of this epoch (even for some average human beings). Seventh, the fact that the machine candidate is imitating a species, provokes many doubts about cultural problems and how representative the chosen humans are of humankind (Hernández-Orallo, 2017: 129). Finally, eight, the Turing Test aims at a quality and not a quantity, asking the judges for binary decisions. Even if they can give scores, at the end of the day any score of humanness is meaningless (ibid.).

The upshot of all this is that the Turing Test and many proposed variants, as we see in a bit, are neither valid nor reliable test procedures for intelligence that could, moreover, be in accord with our causal theory. With a hint on Goodhart's law (Goodhart, 1984), often restated as (in more economic terms, a formulation is given in my book Hoffmann, 2017b: 145)

> When a measure becomes a target of criticism, it ceases to be a good measure.

we recommend to move beyond the standard Turing Test in the dual sense: some competencies can well transcend average human capacities, and it is time to leave the standard Turing Test behind in favor of new alternatives.

Break-out session 4

Our take on Turing: What the judges could learn from our causal theory?

We have spent some time criticizing the standard Turing Test, but let us shift gears now. We *counterfactually* assume for the moment that it is valid and slip into the shoes of the interrogator, determined to deliver a correct verdict as to which contestant is the AI, and which the woman. My exemplary four strategies for separating the human mind from AI may well reveal some dizzying third-wave milestones for AI. We revitalize Hofstadter's (1981) chamber play and wonder "If you could ask a computer just one question in the Turing Test [or a few more], what would it be?". Of course, his answers are always good, but with our groundwork from Part II, we have another angle to exploit.

1) It seems like a safe bet to pose **why questions** or to engage the program in **causal reasoning**: *If you break a bottle that contains a liquid, will some of the liquid (other things being equal) probably escape the bottle and why (not)*?

   The truth behind the question is abstract in that it holds not just for a few specific items but for large, essentially open ended classes of entities, regardless of what color or shape the bottle or size the bottle is, and whether the bottle contained water, coffee, or an unusual soft drink (Marcus, 2020: 13).

   Since our current AI systems do not represent and reason over detailed, structured, internal models of the external world, drawing on substantial knowledge about the world and its dynamics, they will get some things right, resorting to vast correlative databases, but they will not understand what is going on.

   We would probably obtain similar disillusioning results if we probe the following example: *A good way to light a fire is to use a dry cotton ball to cover the fuse.* (Ibid.: 26). The words "fire" and "fuse" and "light", etc. are all intercorrelated; a program like GPT-3 recognizes that, but it is not sufficient for it to derive a conceptual understanding of the nature of fire (Sorber, 2021). So, a conversation between the judge and a cutting-edge program such as GPT-3 could soon end up in a dead end although it is fantasized that GPT-3 "is very close to passing it [the Turing Test]" (Taulli, 2020).

2) The judge should try to reconstruct how the players would be acting / behaving in real life, breaking down barriers of comfort, of a confined Q&A session. Bring to the fore, not single, isolated (why) questions where you expect sound insulated answers in return; but a coherent story, scenario, **larger system of causes and effects**, containing circuits. Then, assess if the machine and its human foil would act upon what is detected as causally true and wrong.

3) In retrospect to Fig. 28, it would be a good strategy to confront the candidates with a **paradox** like the Liar or, to bring in some more diversity finally, the paradox without self-reference in Yablo (1993), the Two Envelopes Paradox (Priest & Restall, 2007; which I addressed in my MA thesis, Hoffmann, 2013/2019) or a few others from the collection in Sainsbury (1987) like the paradox of the heap, the paradox of the Ravens or Newcomb's Problem (including backwards causation; Hoffmann, 2010/2017). I have serious doubts that a computer today or in the foreseeable future is able to cope with such paradoxes. (Can you solve them? Or are they true paradoxes?) Sometimes, one possible type of solution for a paradox *P* is to introduce a formal theory on which the premises in *P* are true, but the contradiction cannot be derived. Such a kind of solution is remarkable because the formal theory will in some sense subsume a logical system which in and of itself far exceeds what machines can today (in any sense of the word) *understand* (Bringsjord, 2009: 99).

4) Music may be the last remaining bastion of uniqueness in the terrain of human intelligence and a task involving **musical creativity** could be a lethal attack by the judge. The idea here is to check if the AI system in the Turing Test is capable of, for instance, composing a symphony on par with accomplished creative geniuses like Beethoven. According to a possible setup, we could envisage the players receiving one relatively simple theme from me as input and returning a (original) musical composition in classical music after some specified time (which cannot be attained by solely detecting patterns, applying rules or copy-paste twists, see Fig. 8). Therefore, I think it will be exceedingly difficult for any computer to match the likes of Beethoven, Mozart or Haydn.

Modifications and reforms

Determining innovative routes for evaluating machine intelligence is worthwhile and might, for instance, help us get out of the deep learning rut, which, with its current supremacy in the community and without supplements, is preventing progress towards third wave artificial general intelligence (Marcus, 2018). Over the years, other tests of machine intelligence have indeed emerged, and we ought to differentiate two camps: (radically) different approaches to evaluating AI versus non-standard Turing Tests. Let us first look into the latter.

This group comprises variants, extensions and generalizations of Turing's test (see Table 8). For instance, Dowe & Hájek (1997) introduced a variant of the Turing Test that featured compression problems, to render the test more sufficient and, thus, more immune to Block's (1981) attack by making it more explicit that a question-and-answer lookup table would not succeed. In another example, the interface is enhanced to consider perception or sensorimotor interaction, such as the Total Turing Test (Harnad, 1992). Then, there is a Nobel Turing Challenge (Kitano, 2020), a visual Turing Test (Lake et al., 2017), the Meta Turing Test (Walsh, 2017: 76), variants on virtual worlds, and many others (Hingston, 2010). A notable perspective is adopted in the inverted Turing Test (Watt, 1996) where the limelight is on the judge, which in this case is a machine that must correctly tell a human and another machine apart. (This hypothesis is intriguing since in a time where AI systems are accused of racism, sexism and other forms of discriminatory behavior, the possibility to *automatically* discriminate between humans and computers would tackle a major need; Burt, 2020; Marcus & Davis, 2019: 33–37; Spindler & Hoffmann, 2019: Algo.Rules, especially 5, 6, and 9.)

Unfortunately, most of these modifications do not resolve any of the principal problems of the standard Turing Test and many introduce further complications (Hernández-Orallo, 2017: 131). A synopsis and classification are provided in the following summary table.

Table 8: Several modifications of the Turing Test (ordered chronologically). "W", "M", "H", and "C" stand for "woman", "man", "human", and "computer". The arrows represent "pretending to be". "H+" refers to "H+ size". This table unashamedly takes some credit from Hernández-Orallo (2017: 135).

Variant	Judge	Player A	Player B	Interaction mode
Victorian parlor games	H	M→W	W→W	Written notes
Turing's imitation game	H	C→W	W→W	Textual teletype
Standard Turing Test	H	C→H	H→H	Textual teletype

Table 8 (continued)

Variant	Judge	Player A	Player B	Interaction mode
Total Turing Test (Harnad, 1992)	H	C→H	H→H	Embodied
Inverted Turing Test (Watt, 1996)	C	C→H	H→H	Textual teletype
TT with compression (Dowe & Hajek)	H+	C→H	H→H	Textual teletype

The other group consists of genuine alternatives to the standard Turing Test (i.e., in opposition to variants, extensions and generalizations of Turing's test). The dispute was, maybe, kicked off by Hernández-Orallo's (2000) article with the recurring title "Beyond the Turing Test" (cf. e.g., Cohen, 2005; French, 2012; You, 2015; and especially Marcus et al., 2016). With gratifying intellectual modesty, it was recognized that "[i]ntelligence is, after all, a multidimensional variable, and no one test could possibly ever be definitive truly to measure it" (Marcus et al., 2016: 3). The Turing Championships were inaugurated at the AAAI Conference on AI in January 2015 for obtaining a new suite of tests, each designed in some way to propel the field of AI, toward previously unconquered territory (ibid.: 4).

The contributions in this rubric can be broadly divided into those that propound specific tests, and those that look at the intricacies inherent in building robust, valid, and reliable tests for advancing the state of the art in AI. Here is an assortment of three from Marcus et al. (2016).

- In "Toward a Comprehension Challenge, Using Crowdsourcing as a Tool", Paritosh & Marcus propose a crowdsourced *comprehension* challenge, in which machines will be asked to answer open-ended questions about movies, YouTube videos, stories, and podcasts. This proposal neatly links back to Hernández-Orallo (2000: 447) who conceived of intelligence as "the ability to comprehend", but who formalized this ability with the help of a formal language, which renders the account a) still purely language-based, and b) inaccessible to many known exemplars of thinking (us humans; Crosby, 2020).
- In the essay "Why We Need a Physically Embodied Turing Test and What It Might Look Like", Ortiz argues for tests, such as a construction challenge (build something given a bag of parts), that focus more comprehensively on *four aspects of intelligence*: language, perception, reasoning, and action.
- The article "The Social-Emotional Turing Challenge", by Jarrold & Yeh, considers the importance of *social-emotional intelligence* and suggests a methodology for designing tests that assess the ability of machines to infer things like motivations and desires (often referred to in the psychological literature as theory of mind).

Needless to say, the bouquet of alternatives to the Turing Test is richer than that (already evident from the fact that the special issue of the AI Magazine of 2016 counts more contributions than the three mentioned on this page). For instance, another impactful position is based on Winograd schema questions, on a test of commonsense reasoning that is set in a linguistic context. An example of a Winograd schema question is the following.

Christian made sure to thank Max for all the help he had given. Who had given the help?
– Max
– Christian.

The position with Winograd schemas has been taken by Levesque (2018) and others and is less subject to abuse; though testing for comprehension of grammatically ambiguous sentences is clearly much less demanding intellectually than engaging in a cooperative conversation.

The recent thrust by Crosby (2020) is, apart from our highlights in Marcus et al. (2016), most welcome to us as he sets up to fix striking shortcomings with modern AI systems by means of a *nonverbal* operationalization. This is provided, not by an excessive concentration on "humanlike" as a role model, but by an Animal-AI Testbed, which translates animal cognition tests for AI and advertises a bottom-up research pathway for designing thinking machines that create predictive models of their environment from sensory input.

10 A tentative solution

Alan Turing's renowned test on "intelligence" is concededly an inescapable signpost in AI (Marcus et al., 2016). As a mere *thought experiment* (in his own words: "whether there are imaginable computers which would do well", Turing, 1950: 436), the Turing Test has its well-deserved place in the record books of game-changing contributions for AI and investigating minds, more generally. But as the last sections here showed, it is desirable to think outside the narrow Turing Test box, both for implementing an actual test (e.g., in demarcation to the Loebner Prize), and fundamentally (e.g., in terms of guaranteeing a valid and reliable testing procedure). In this Chapter, we create neither another upgraded version of Turing's test, nor another novel approach to examining machine intelligence; yet, more profoundly, inject basic requirements for an approach to evaluate AI systems in light of our findings from the theory development work in Part II. The result will be a veritable tribute to Alan Turing.

Along the lines of our theory contribution from Part II coupled with the learnings from studying the Turing Test, a universal test of intelligence, yet also specific scientific measures of non-human, but machine or animal intelligence must be
- *Non-binary*,
- *Empirical*,
- *Factorial/specific*,
- *Relevant*,
- *Expansive*,
- *Repeatable*,
- *Solvable by exemplars*,
- *Unpredictable*,
- *Non-anthropomorphic*, and
- lead to *actionable* as well as *thriving research*.

Non-binary *measures of intelligence*: Intelligence is not an absolute attribute, it is a gradual aptitude that manifests itself to varying degrees in different creatures across the biological and technological sphere (or to varying degrees in the same creature over time, etc.). This is evident from our universal seven-layered hierarchy of causal learning which underlines that intelligence can range from being rather primitive, stemming from agents' predictions predicated on passive observations or regularities in observations, to very complex, agents inferring causal principles or the structure of causal networks.

By contrast, any gradation of the Turing Test, e.g., as a function of the length of the test, the reaction or response time on the side of the contestants or the score of the judge(s) (or similar arguments), demonstrates the inappropriateness of the Turing Test to measure intelligence in a gradual way. The reason for that is straightforward: The Turing Test is more a test of humanity (Fostel, 1993), a two-value variable (either you are human or you are not human), than of intelligence, a multi-value variable.

Empirical *measures of intelligence*: As we know, Turing was skeptical of the question "Can machines think?", and quickly substituted it with an experimentally verifiable test. To operationalize a property like thinking is to give it an empirical measure (e.g., performance in the imitation game) that can be taken as a marker for attribution of this property.

The rationale for this criterion is to articulate open-mindedness about the appearance and implementation of intelligence. If we were, instead, driven by the paradigm of human intelligence, and frame intelligence as a second order mental property (see 4.1.), derived from first order mental states such as beliefs and desires (which machines and many animals do not possess), then we would bluntly negate the progress realized in the debate on intelligence (mirrored by the extended scope when we moved from Chapter 1 to 3), which has become more pluralistic and unbiased over the years.

Note bene that we would not ask a complex and fuzzy system like intelligence to be operationalized in the strong meaning of the word. In consonance with Dennett (1984), we content ourselves with a weak operationalization, making an empirical measure available that is not intended as a foolproof identifier immune from false positives (or even false negatives).

Factorial *or* ***specific*** *measures of intelligence*: Intelligence is multidimensional and multidirectional. Multidimensionality was translated by different levels of causal thinking and multidirectionality by different guises of intelligence such as Gardner's eight intelligences or other axes on circumplexes as displayed in Figure 27 and 29. Hence, there does not exist a tangible faculty that would be optimal for every situation or environment. Instead, intelligence tests ought to tackle individual or few factors of intelligence, just like conventional intelligence tests in psychometrics target either linguistic, or logical-mathematical, or spatial intelligence (and not all eight at once). Thereby, we follow the common tactic in *analyzing* ill-defined terms like intelligence by breaking them down into more manageable components.

Since no singular test procedure could possibly ever fathom the richness of intelligence, test specification is inevitable; true to the motto, better a modest, but accurate approach than one that is plagued with overconfidence and error-proneness. If divergent strategies join forces, then an insightful mosaic can emerge.

The Turing Test lacks this feature. Although it restricts intelligence to human-level intelligence, we learned in Chapter 1 that this step is not sufficient to fulfill the criterion. Intelligence in humans is not a unitary phenomenon, and, hence, crucial components of intelligence like bodily intelligence were overlooked by the Turing Test (Harnad, 1991).

Relevant *measures of intelligence*: Intelligence is not an ethereal ability, being circumscribed as "intelligence is what is measured by intelligence tests". Intelligence was expressed from its meaning as the ability to address categorically different causal queries. Abilities on this hierarchy as well as specifications corresponding to different directions of intelligence on the circumplex (see Chapter 5.2.) are what should be measured. They amount to relevant abilities enunciating "intelligence" (or "thinking" which can be taken as synonym).

The intelligence test at stake must be solvable only by utilizing or referencing such abilities and specified forms thereof, respectively. "If it can be solved without such relevant abilities, then the test does not identify the correct attributes. If it requires too many irrelevant abilities, then these become uncontrolled confounds." (Crosby, 2020).

Using language/text as a mediator in the Turing Test and permitting any type of question / conversation is a way to ensure some relevance (ibid.). Answering (the right kind of) questions involves something akin to higher thinking, and restricting the test to written words removes any concerns that the machine needs to look human, or even to look like it is thinking (ibid.). However, with the Turing Test, relevance is solely in the hands of the judge: "If the judge does not ask questions that require any thought to answer and merely exchanges pleasantries, then the test is no longer any good, and it is also fairly easy to build a machine that would pass" (ibid.). Thus, Crosby (2020) suggests an alternative approach. His *Animal-AI Olympics* competition is a testbed containing relevant tests which capture "enough relevant abilities", including physical intelligence which went missing in the standard Turing Test, that solving them all would "necessitate" the conclusion that the agent is an intelligent creature.

Expansive *measures of intelligence*: Given the multitude of facets of intelligence on all levels, a *prespecified* intelligence test ought to consider as many aspects of the particular excerpt of intelligence as possible, which cannot not be the too broad and fuzzy property "thinking", but something like emotional intelligence on a lower level of granularity. This helps to ensure that the specific property, constituting in turn a part of intelligence, is captured to its fullest extent. If only a single component of some intelligence is used as test variable, by contrast, then this procedure can tell only a partial story. For instance, let us assume that we would like to measure the ill-defined notion "Swiss product quality". Since we assent that the term is not properly established (at least for the sake of argument), we opt for disassembling it into *specific* pieces (and then seek for *factorial or specific measures*). One of those pieces is the well-circumscribed feature *Swissness*. Now in accord with the desideratum of expansive measures, a deficient operationalization of Swissness would be that all industrial products where 60% of the manufacturing costs are generated in Switzerland bear the label Swissness. While this is a relevant property (a necessary condition) of Swissness, the test is not expansive enough and returns too many false positives (that do not meet the *other* necessary criteria of Swissness, cf. https://www.ige.ch/en/, 10-02-21).

While the Turing Test is not specific, it is only potentially expansive on a too high level of granularity, accounting for the whole set of writable questions. Yet, in reality, modern versions of the Turing Test such as the Loebner Prize are only as expansive as the judges' questions.

Repeatable *tests of intelligence*: In the light of dynamics (5.3.) as well as vulnerabilities of test apparatuses (see excursus two), tests should be reproducible and yield the same (or comparable) test results in several iterations, in any environment without varying results. (An exception would be, of course, when the underlying system undergoes a structural change, reaches a tipping point or breaks down.) Repeatable tests allow us to learn from trial and error and can be run on demand, as often as desired; bringing about, when automated, a dramatic dwindling of the cost per test run and the time needed to complete a test cycle.

Non-repeatable examinations equip test subjects with only a single shot to show intelligence whilst the technique of repeatable testing gives them more than one chance to demonstrate competence. At first glance, the Turing Test is repeatable. However, in practice, this is hardly the case. On the one side, the judge is affected by the previous conversation with the players. On the other, the machine learns from the interaction with the interrogator and adjusts (deep learning). Many other tests do not have any advantage in this respect. For example, repeatable examinations of animal cognition can fail because the animal may no longer be motivated to fulfill the task at the n-th time (e.g., take a decreasing marginal utility for food into account). Or toddlers easily get distracted by other things happening around them (Meltzoff, 2007).

Measures of intelligence which are **solvable by exemplars**: Exemplar quality signifies that the (intelligence) test ought to be passed by as many known exemplars of the original property in question as possible (intelligent creatures, see Chapter 1 to 3), and as few from outside that set as possible (Crosby, 2020). In other words, the test should keep the number of false positives and false negatives as low as possible, which, by the way, goes hand in hand with increasing the likelihood that solving it presupposes only relevant abilities.

The Turing Test is defined in terms of average human performance, which is aiming too high as, if applied to humans, it cuts out roughly half of the population of human exemplars (knowing full well that the mean does not need to coincide with the median).

> It might have been tempting to set the bar of a test as high as possible to reduce false positives, but this makes it too exclusive. In the case of 'thinking', this could correspond to setting the test to beat the strongest human players at the ancient strategy board game Go. These humans are clearly prime exemplars of the ability to think. However, we now have AI systems that can outperform all humans at Go (Silver et al. 2017), and they are not generally considered to be good examples of thinking machines. Defeating humans at Go was a milestone in AI progress, but the problem was too specialised to relate directly back to the property of thinking. (Crosby, 2020)

The exemplar quality instead demands that the bar should be set *low*, another reason to consider animal tasks as the starting point (ibid.). Or as Stuart Shieber of Harvard phrased it: "You want to design competitions that are qualitatively beyond the current level of AI, but not so far that [. . .] it would be like setting an X prize for space flight in da Vinci's era" (cited in You, 2015).

Unpredictable *measures of intelligence*: If an intelligence test is too predictable, then it will be subject to Goodhart's law, and will also be solvable by "shortcut" methods that do not engage test subjects with exhibiting the requested intelligence.

This is first and foremost of concern to tests of AI systems, where deterministic problems can be sorted out by a database of answers or action sequences (Searle, 1980; see Chapter 12). To escape the trap (even though Searle, 2009, would not approve this), Turing ingeniously added unpredictability by inviting the interrogator to prompt any questions (s)he deems fit. The questions or topics of the conversation are not shared with the two participants beforehand and the judge could decide to touch upon anything, from logical paradoxes to musical creativity. Yet, again, the quality of the test is determined by the predictability and ingenuity of the judges, and, as experiences with incarnations of the Turing Test prove (e.g., cf. Mauldin, 2009), questions or human reactions can be predicted, and answers can be hardcoded. In that case, what I wrote in the introduction to Chapter 5.1. would not be given; the test subject would not be sufficiently autonomous. Insofar, the quality of unpredictability corresponds with warding off and deterring non-agents from entering and succeeding in the test.

One way to surpass that obstacle more effectively than with the Turing Test is to use hidden test problems which are fair, but could not be predicted by the engineers (Crosby, 2020). Most studies on animals and children automatically pass the unpredictability constraint (ibid). As long as good practice is maintained by the experimenters, the animal or child will not be over-prepared and could not have envisaged the test, and probably does not even conceptualize it as a test (ibid.).

Non-anthropomorphic *measures of non-human intelligence*: Our causal language to grasp intelligence is non-anthropocentric, and the same should hold for measures of intelligence. (Of course, measures specified to human intelligence are not concerned.) As noticed with the Turing Test, a momentous problem of AI and the assessment of its intelligent behavior lies in its obsessive reference to human intelligence and conduct.

As remarked in Chapter 2, intelligence research gained momentum once the field overcame humanocentrism, chimpocentrism and the arbitrarily myopic scope of biological intelligence. Analogously, AI can receive a boost when AI researchers pay more attention to other kinds of intelligences, and so they have been doing more recently: ants, rats, octopi, etc. in order to scale up the problem of machine intelligence. And the Animal-AI Olympics, as a new competition presenting AI agents with cognition challenges to test their *animal* intelligence, is just reinforcing this shift (Crosby, 2020; Crosby et al., 2019). The criterion of non-anthropomorphic test procedures is interwoven with the next one.

Measures of intelligence which result in **actionable** *as well as* **fruitful research**: This requirement aims at the purpose of intelligence tests. Where it leads when they are conducted more for their own sake, is well visible in Loebner Prize contests. Such dangers should be averted.

When this quality of actionable and thriving research is narrowed down to the research field of AI, a few more remarks are in order. On the one hand, the original question "Can machines think?" (Turing, 1950: 433) has produced many words, yet few clues about how to progress in AI and how to parse or conceive of intelligence. In the end, the Turing Test has not really provoked AI researchers to design smarter machines or only better conversationalists; it has engendered mainly better ways of fooling interrogators (Levesque, 2018: 50). Accordingly, the AI community has not been very excited about Turing Test contests. As a distinguished example, Moshe Vardi, editor-in-chief of the Communications of the ACM replied: "The details of this 2014 Turing Test experiment only reinforces my judgment that the Turing Test says little about machine intelligence" (Vardi, 2014: 5).

On the other hand, the gap which work to pass the Turing Test has left behind, namely missing impulses that would really bring the field forward, can be filled, first, by reverting back to our Figure 29, and by a formulation of a robotic version of machine intelligence tests which was also subtly suggested by the second strategy in the last excursus. Second, together with the first strategy in the break-out session 4, a contribution to thriving research in AI can be made by issuing a rather modest, utterly incomprehensive intelligence test dealing with how AI systems (and other agents following the universality of our taxonomy) acquire or represent causal knowledge and apply it to get around in "life".

An AI that can successfully cope with such a test over all seven levels is probably proficient enough to process a story (see the second strategy in our break-out session 4) and correctly handle causal queries, just like a human would. To move capacities of causal learning in the spotlight entails that other aspects of intelligence such as vision, Kinaesthetics, and natural language are eclipsed (hence, the attributes "modest" and "utterly incomprehensive"). In a real testbed, the contestants could thus be allowed to encode the story in any convenient representation, for instance.

From an evolutionary perspective such a test focus would make a lot of sense (Fjelland, 2020; Harari, 2014; without making a big fuzz about humans and their standing which would only violate the last requirement). Why Homo sapiens has been so successful in the history of evolution is, as we partially portrayed, a complex question. Many factors (sometimes in interdependency) have played a role, but a distinguishing mark of the Cognitive Revolution, that separates us from all other creatures so far, is the ability to imagine something that does not exist (Harari, 2014: 23). To envision chimeras may be the precursor of philosophy, scientific discovery, and technological innovation.

And indeed, as far as I as a philosopher, not an AI expert/engineer can overlook it, a focus on causal learning capabilities in machine intelligence tests could unleash trajectories towards justified third-wave aspirations and have a veritable impact on the next steps to be taken. To start with, Pearl himself, a winner of the Turing Award, is not an outside commentator (unlike this author), but actively paves the way for the causal revolution in AI. Pearl (2018a, 2018b, 2020) has insistently postulated that our learning machines ought to be equipped with causal reasoning tools since causal explanations, not dry facts, make up the bulk of knowledge that coins agents' minds, and should, thus, be the cornerstone of machine intelligence, too. Unlike twenty years ago, i.e., prior to the mathematization of counterfactuals (Pearl, 2000) and computer-friendly semantics, this is no longer a speculative plea.

Pearl's single voice has transformed into a chorus by now extolling learning as the process of model building (e.g., as noticed above, Garcez & Lamb, 2020; Gärdenfors, 2020; White & D'Avila Garcez, 2019; Lattimore & Ong, 2018; Lake et al., 2017: 16).

On top of that, the coryphaeus Gary Marcus from NYU published an influential paper titled "The Next Decade in AI" (Marcus, 2020), and makes a strong case for the marriage of rich (causal) models with efficient inference therein, endowing "the substrate for a richer, more robust AI than is currently possible" (ibid.: 1). Here is a sample of his theses:

> [. . .] the knowledge gathered by contemporary neural networks remains spotty and pointillistic, arguably useful and certainly impressive, but never reliable. (ibid.: 8)

> [. . .] systems that lack solid ways of generalizing beyond a space of training examples cannot be trusted in open ended domains. (ibid.: 12)

> To build a robust, knowledge driven approach to AI we must have the machinery of symbol manipulation in our toolkit. [. . .] It is from there that the basic need for hybrid architectures that combine symbol manipulation with other techniques such as deep learning most fundamentally emerges. (Ibid.: 17)

> Some significant fraction of the knowledge that a robust system [sic!] is likely to be causal, and to support counterfactuals. (ibid.: 28)

> [. . .] rather than starting each new AI system from scratch, as a blank slate, with little knowledge of the world, we should seek to build learning systems that start with initial frameworks for domains like time, space, and causality, in order to speed up learning and massively constrain the hypothesis space. (ibid.: 36)

With these prospects about third wave AI at hand, the following final Part IV is dedicated to a brief assessment of the fourth wave, again ensuing from the groundwork laid in Part II.

Highlights and key takeaways from Part III

- We cultivate a language when talking about AI that suggests that present-day machines are more human than devices; yet, in reality, they are more tools than persons.
- We ought to bring data glorification to a halt since radical empiricism is a stifling culture. The marriage of rich models with efficient inference is achievable and desirable.
- Some small but vital subset of human knowledge is likely to be innate; non-brittle AI, too, ought to start with some important prior knowledge; in harmony with Kant (1787/1997), with a "manifold" for time, space, and *causality*. The opposite approach, revolving around a near blank slate and training them on colossal data sets, simply has not panned out so far (Marcus, 2020), as it would have been predicted by Part II. The viable route forward for AI systems is learning-to-learn to vanquish blind data analysis.

- In harmony with both our theory & the Turing Test, what really matters about intelligence is capacity and behavior; what is non-crucial is appearance and implementation.
- From the lens of our causal theory of intelligence, the judge in a Turing Test ought to 1) raise why questions, 2) test the contestants' understanding of larger systems of causes and effects including circuits, 3) confront them with paradoxes, and 4) scrutinize their musical creativity.
- The standard Turing Test does not claim to be an operational definition of humanlike intelligence. Yet, it is, unlike what Turing (1950) believes, not even a sufficient criterion for it. It just leads to many "false negatives" and many "false positives". In the wake of lethal attacks, the standard Turing Test is neither valid nor robust.
- When making a bot to enter a Turing Test contest, you do not call a contender for human intelligence into play, you write a novel. And we humans fall for stories and narratives.
- The constriction to, again, human intelligence, a slippery concept in the debate on evaluating machine intelligence initiated, not exhausted by Turing's test is a disgrace.
- In tune with our thrust of steadily reconfigurating the circumplex of the model of intelligence, the width and depth of intelligence(s) makes a specification and a battery of tests inevitable. No one test could possibly ever be definitive truly to measure all aspects of intelligence.
- A measure or test of (machine) intelligence ought to be non-binary, empirical, specific, relevant, expansive (for the specified scope), repeatable, solvable by exemplars, unpre-dictable, non-anthropomorphic, and lead to actionable as well as thriving research.

Part IV: **Singularity hypotheses**

> *Human-level AI is still the standard 15-to-25 years away,*
> *just as it always has been.*   Steven Pinker (in Brockman, 2015)

If past predictions are any indication, the only thing we know today about tomorrow's science and technology is that it will be radically different than whatever we predict it will be like. The controversy over singularity serves as good evidence for this adage.

Notwithstanding, it has since a long time transcended the circle of scientists and computer engineers by far. For example, the UK House of Lords Select Committee on AI opens the second chapter of their 2018 report "AI in the UK: ready, willing and able?" with the sharp critique that prevalent AI narratives, reflected in Terminator-style stories, "were concentrating attention on threats which are still remote, such as the possibility of 'superintelligent' artificial general intelligence, while distracting attention away from more immediate risks and problems" (Select Committee on Artificial Intelligence, 2018: 23).

By contrast, there is the potential for those who frown on restraints on the design of strong AI to propagate narratives skeptical of its capacities, so that policymakers see no need for regulation (Baum, 2018). And the idea of or phantasies on strong AI have not ceased from entering philosophy either, but, for example, unleashed visions of grandeur: "If we could just 'program things up', we dreamed, we could put paid to thousands of years of philosophy, surround ourselves with intelligent companions, and understand the human condition" (Cantwell Smith, 2019: 1). That bravado has been both fueled (e.g., Chalmers, 2010) and disparaged (e.g., Searle, 2014) in the literature.

More systematically, Tegmark (2018: 31) portrayed passionate disagreements about strong AI, even or especially among experts (Tetlock, 2005), reminding us of Turing's reservations about polls. The dissent is centered around two questions: When (if ever) will strong AI or singularity happen (for this poll and Table 9, respectively, the two terms can be used interchangeably because of how sloppy people deal with them), and will it be a good or bad thing for humanity?

Digital utopians (e.g., Larry Page from Google) and techno-skeptics (like Andrew Ng from China's Google, Baidu, or Rodney Brooks from MIT or Steven Pinker) concord that we should not worry about singularity, but for very different reasons: the latter are convinced that human level machine intelligence will not happen in the foreseeable future or not at all, while the former believe it will happen but it is virtually guaranteed to be a good thing (Tegmark, 2018: 31). The beneficial-AI movement (i.e., all the proponents of AI safety research like Elon Musk who founded *OpenAI* or Nick Bostrom who runs the *Future of Humanity Institute* in Oxford) feels that concern is warranted and useful, because AI risk analysis and discussion now increases the chances of a positive

Table 9: Conversations on singularity and strong AI are driven by different camps and opinion leaders. Source: Tegmark, 2018: 31.

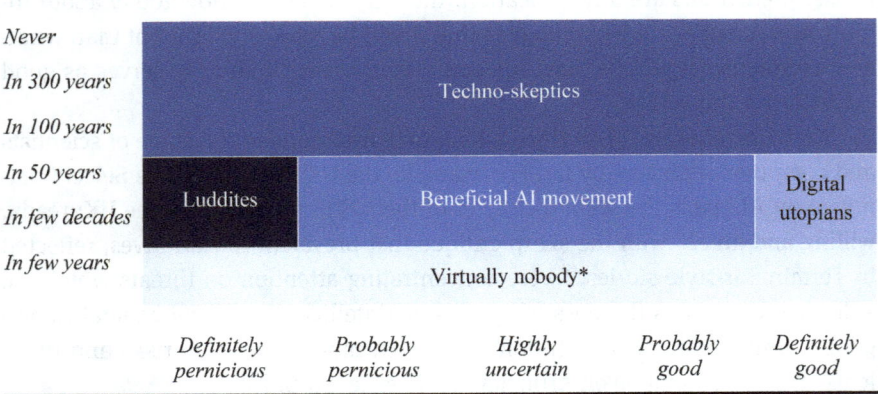

*An example of the few irrational fideists with some authority is the market crier Jürgen Schmidhuber based in Lugano who blares out that his "Gödel machines formalize I.J. Good's informal remarks (1965) [see also 11.2.] on an 'intelligence explosion through self-improving super-intelligences'"(Schmidhuber, 2012: 65). The style of his essay makes Schmidhuber's bold statements hard to digest because it repeatedly says how good his AI systems (Gödel machines) are and reports that they "beat" rivals, but does not help an outsider (probably including AI experts outside of his lab too) to get a feel for the nature of the tasks and the ability of the techniques to "scale out" into other tasks. His essay is, in nuce, long on faith, and short on rigorous argument.

outcome. Finally, luddites (like Peter Krakaur and his blog Lopsider) expect an adverse outcome or cataclysmic events and, thus, oppose AI. The upshot and bottom line from this matrix are perhaps simply that it is not clear if or when we humans or the machines we teach will succeed in building strong AI.

According to Tegmark (2018: 130), the world's leading AI authorities are divided, most of them making estimates ranging from decades to centuries and some even guessing never, which instigates him to draw the nice metaphoric conclusion: "Forecasting is tough because, when you're exploring uncharted territory, you don't know how many mountains separate you from your destination. Typically you see only the closest one, and need to climb it before you can discover your next obstacle."

In this Part IV, we take a step back from this heated debate. Ex ante, we are against over-hyping technology as well as the counter-myth that singularity will not happen. Based on the previous findings in this book as well as on what others state that contributed to the success of our endeavor (e.g., Pearl, 2018a: "strong AI is an achievable goal"), we do not have any *a priori* reasons to completely dispel the possibility that we will eventually build strong AI. Therefore, we devote this Part IV to canvassing what speaks in favor of and what speaks against the hypothesis of technological singularity or strong AI. (Recall that, in accord with our findings from 3.2., superintelligent AI, which in turn marks the outcome or culmination of the event or phase of singularity, was interpreted as a subset of strong AI; and *within* the singularity narrative, the former follows on and from the latter, i.e., both temporally and logically.)

Ensuing from the conceptual work in Part II, we first propose to specify Searle's (1980: 417) notion of **strong AI** as follows: An AI agent X is a strong AI (SAI) if, and only if, X covers all seven levels of our causal hierarchy (see Figures 24 and 25) on a circumplex consisting of at least the four intelligences from Figure 29:[19] social intelligence, emotional intelligence, bodily intelligence, and cognitive intelligence. A second clarification concerns then the concept "**superintelligent AI**" ($SIAI$): X is a $SIAI$ if, and only if, X covers all seven levels of our causal hierarchy on a circumplex consisting of the four intelligences from Figure 29 and at least one additional and distinct intelligence on par with the four *or* only those four intelligences with a super-human performance for at least one of the four intelligences ("super-human performance" as coined by Rajani, 2011; see Figure 16) and no sub-human performance for any of the intelligences. Finally, the adjusted definition of (technological) **singularity** runs as follows: An event E qualifies as a singularity S if, and only if, SAI emerges in E and $SIAI$ directly thereafter, whereby "directly" signifies that there is either a direct causal relationship or a short causal chain between SAI and $SIAI$ in the sense that the former brings about the latter.

(For the sake of completeness, "**artificial general intelligence**" (AGI) brings up the rear even though it is not at stake here in Part IV (as we know from 3.2., e.g., see Table 7), but in order to sharpen the demarcation lines between the terms: X is a AGI if, and only if, X is not a SAI and covers more than *one* intelligence for possibly varying causal learning capabilities. We concede that this initial definition is not satisfactory and in need of an overhaul by future work because, while it is clear what multiple intelligences stand for in the human case (cf. Gardner, 1983/2011) and also more or less clear in the animal case (cf. Hodos, 1988: 100f.; and Wasserman & Zentall's, 2006; see our Chapter 2), it is not so clear

---

[19] Nota bene that in Chapter 3.2., SAI was equated with human intelligence (HI) which would speak more in favor of Figure 26 (with Gardner's eight intelligences on the circumplex) than Figure 29 where (just) this author (who is certainly not as well-versed in research on human intelligence as Gardner) submitted the "grandes lignes" of universal intelligence. However, given our findings from Part I, we do not see the value of calling for musical intelligence in machine agents.

in the machine case. Following the thrust of Crosby (2020) and his Animal-AI Olympics, we suggest that for the time being we orient ourselves in this regard.)

While Part III was about present-day and past machines in the light of the Turing Test and its ramifications, here we reason about and predict how high machines can ascend in our causal hierarchy (in principle) if broad and multiple intelligences are required. Moreover, our theory allows us to assess others' predictions and arguments about machine capabilities and it would purport that their predictions and arguments are only legitimate if they show how an ascent is enabled or prevented, respectively. Here the rubber finally meets the road.

In particular, the next Chapter 11 presents three reasons in favor of reckoning with *SAI* and a singularity *S*. Chapter 12 is devoted to the opposite standpoint, portraying three reasons sowing the seeds of doubt about the occurrence of *S* and *SAI*. In both cases, we pin down the arguments by bringing in our findings from Part II. Chapter 13 eventually summarizes Part IV.

11 Arguments conducive to the belief that the singularity is near

The best answer to the question, "Will computers ever be as smart as humans?" is probably "Yes, but only briefly".
                                                                    Vernor Vinge, 2008

Despite our conclusion in 3.2. that *SAI* (and consequently, *SIAI* and *S*) springs from pure imagination and fantasy so far and despite the empirical fact that the new millennium arrived without a single machine able to converse at even the toddler level, serious thinkers in the late 20th century up to now have continued to issue incredibly optimistic predictions regarding the progress of AI. What *arguments* nurture the conviction that *SAI* and perhaps even *S* and *SIAI* are in our (personal our humankind's) future? In the following, we sketch three ambitious arguments that defend the plausibility of not only *SAI*, but they aim to demonstrate that *SIAI* and *S* can and eventually will occur (and, hence, *SAI* as well). We respond critically to each of the three arguments, maintaining that none of them is compelling.

11.1 The hardware-based argument by Moravec (1999) and Kurzweil (2006)

Moravec (1988) concerns himself in his book *Mind Children. The future of robot and human intelligence* with the creation of the posthuman and post-biological. Ironically, we can note that his language in this monograph is full of parent-child terminology, reflecting discursive parallels to the domain of speculative fiction as well as contemporary modes of thinking about the human child, the creator/parent, the importance of parenting, the child as a legacy, and our own immortality (Singler, 2020: 278f.). Particularly in later works (Moravec, 1998, 1999), he informs us that since the speed of computer hardware doubles every 18 to 24 months (in accordance with Moore's Law, which we revisit below and which has apparently held in the past), "fourth generation" AI will soon enough exceed humans in all respects, from running companies to writing novels (Bringsjord & Govindarajulu, 2018). These AI systems, so the story goes, will evolve to such lofty cognitive heights that we will stand to them as single-cell organisms stand to us today (ibid.).

Presentation of the argument

The hardware-based argument for singularity rests on a solid foundation in the sense that it is quite common to hear intelligence explained in part as some form of mental speed (Berger, 1982). From Aristotle or Hobbes (1651/1885), who thought intelligence was the speed with which one thought followed on from another, to modern studies in the neuropsychology and psychophysiology of human intelligence, it has been indicated that higher mental ability is, at least in part, determined by speed of information processing (Vernon et al., 2000: 255).

Above all, the AI/singularity community has wholeheartedly fallen for this construal of intelligence. For instance, Loosemore & Goertzel (2012: 88) write short-sightedly (as we notice in the discussion part of Moravec's argument): "There are two possible types of intelligence speedup: one due to faster operation of an intelligent system (clock speed increase) and one due to an improvement in the type of mechanisms that implement the thought processes ('depth of thought' increase)."[20] Or as Modis (2012: 331) boils down long passages to a short operational definition: "Intelligence according to the singularitarians is measured by the speed of calculation." This broad reception of the identification of intelligence with mental speed propelled and imbued Moravec's (1988, 1998, 1999) and Kurzweil's (2006) view that S is near, whereby Kurzweil modified the hardware-based argument in order to evade some criticism.

Moravec (1988: 61, 1998: 4) probably originated the hardware-based argument or the argument of comparative computational power and memory to vindicate S: Moravec (1998: 1) hypothesizes that "the performance of AI machines tends to improve at the same pace that AI researchers get access to faster hardware" where performance is operationalized as the power (bits per second) and capacity (bits) of machines. He then not only compares and rates the performance of some natural organisms (from nematodes to whales) and "intelligent" artifacts like the Deep Blue chess machine in this regard of computational power and memory. But, on top of that, he relies on those measures to assess biological and artificial systems in terms of their cognitive capabilities.

The former is per se unproblematic, the latter as well as the following are not. Moravec (1988: 68) is not content with describing and interpreting the status

---

[20] The overly mechanistic and, thus, inadequate parlance to refer to the *complex* system "intelligence" aside (cf. Weaver, 1948, who shows that (organized) complexity and mechanics do not go together), the authors not only make one out of two routes to "greater intelligence" about speed (speeding up the hardware), but overall intelligence appears to be reduced to a *speedup*.

quo as well as past developments, but adds projections and extrapolations (which are always exposed to criticism since they deal more with assumptions than data or facts) on the basis of which he proclaims human-machine equivalence in terms of general intellectual performance in less than 30 years (i.e., in our decade of the 2020s; Moravec, 1998: 1). He seems to build his bold AI optimism on "[s]teady improvements in mechanical and electromechanical calculators before World War II [which] had increased the speed of calculation a thousandfold over manual methods from 1900 to 1940. The pace quickened with the appearance of electronic computers during the war, and 1940 to 1980 saw a millionfold proliferation." (Moravec, 1998: 5). Above all, he points to an "industry given" (ibid.), namely that "[c]omputers doubled in capacity every two years after the war" (ibid.), a pace that has become better associated with Moore's law.

Moore's law is named after one of the founders of the Intel microprocessor manufacturing company, and states that the number of transistors in a dense integrated circuit, i.e., the computational capacities (e.g., electronic component densities and electronic signal processing speeds) of integrated circuits double about every two years. The density of components on an integrated circuit is closely tied to the price-performance of computing power. The law was established because it has been observed that the number of transistors in Intel microprocessors has in fact doubled every two years since the early 1970s (Modis, 2012: 316). (In the very first formulation of Moore's law in 1965 the doubling was every year. David House, an Intel executive, raised it to 18 months, and ten years later Moore (1975) himself increased it to two years. As to the singularity, Moore (2008) himself says that it will never occur.)

The hardware-based argument can thus be distilled as follows:

Premise 1	*Computational capacities of computers have exhibited exponential growth.* E.g., backed up by the empirical evidence that resulted in Moore's law. **Our comment**: This point is iffy and not sufficiently about hardware.
Conclusion 1	*The exponential growth of computers' computational capacities goes on forever.* (With reference to Moore's *law*. Rationale: The law is stipulated to hold universally.) **Our comment**: Inductive inferences are invalid. A few or any finite number of examples do not lend sufficient credibility to a universal quantification.
Premise 2	If C1, then C2. **Our comment**: to be revisited in the discussion part.
Conclusion 2	*Computers' general intellectual performance continues growing indefinitely.*
Conclusion 3	*The singularity S will be reached.*

Our formal comment on C1 aside, C1 has also been under attack content-wise, rendering the collapse of the argument inescapable. For at least four decades, computing power has increased exponentially, roughly in accordance with Moore's law. However, a speed bump is on the horizon as an end to Moore's law is probable: "Though several information technologies have been advanced at an exponential or superexponential [i.e., hyperbolic, C.H.] rate for many decades, this trend may not hold for much longer" (Muehlhauser & Salamon, 2012: 21; cf. also Mack, 2011; Walsh, 2017: 181).

Growth processes, including Moore's law, that (for some time) are observed to follow exponential patterns eventually reveal themselves to be following S-curves thus banning runaway situations which would be prescribed by a singularity S (Modis, 2012: 311): "It is now unanimously expected that this growth pattern [according to Moore's law] will eventually turn into an S-curve and reach a ceiling" (ibid.: 316). Systemic thinkers would certainly demur, too, that no system's behavior would be dominated by a reinforcing loop (see Figure 23) forever long, balancing effects would counteract sooner or later (e.g., cf. Senge's, 2006, systems archetypes). (In this context, allow me also the mathematical subtlety that, unlike the advocates of a technological singularity, one should not speak of exponential but hyperbolic growth if one believes in singularity, since the increase of an exponential function is relatively slow and always *finite*.)

If we assume for a transient moment that the soundness of the hardware-based argument would only hinge on the empirical support for C1 (which is what Kurzweil, 2012, seems to be implying), Kurzweil's (2006) version of the hardware-based argument would not be jeopardized since the feared breakdown of Moore's law would not affect his train of thought. "The Singularity is the result of the Law of Accelerating Returns (LOAR)" (Kurzweil, 2012: 343), spanning *multiple* exponential trends, that may or may not turn out to be S-curves, and not just a single growth process like of the doubling of transistors in dense integrated circuits (which Moore's law refers to). The LOAR certainly does not imply that every individual exponential trend goes on indefinitely. Instead, Kurzweil (2006: 83; cf. also 1999: 26) emphasizes:

> A specific paradigm (a method or approach to solving a problem, e.g., shrinking transistors on an integrated circuit as an approach to making more powerful computers) provides exponential growth until the method exhausts its potential. When this happens, a paradigm shift (i.e., a fundamental change in the approach) occurs, which enables exponential growth to continue.

In other words, when Kurzweil spells out computer hardware advancements according to his LOAR, then he delineates a pattern of ongoing exponential growth made up of a cascade of S-curves, each of them related to one out of many what he calls paradigms. "One of the things that sets the second machine age [i.e., digital technologies as opposed to the first machine age heralded by the industrial revolution] apart is how quickly [exponential growth eventually leads to staggeringly big numbers, C.H.]" (Brynjolfsson & McAfee, 2014: 47). Where could another boost for hardware development, another "paradigm", come from? Perhaps, from a new kind of computing dubbed *quantum computing*. Its essential feature is easy enough to grasp at the intuitive level, e.g. following Walsh (2017: 184) or Garis & Halioris (2009: 489):

> [Our conventional c]omputers today work by converting information to a series of binary digits, or bits, and operating on these bits using integrated circuits (ICs) containing billions of transistors. Each bit has only two possible values, 0 or 1. Through manipulations of these so-called binary representations, computers [do all their computations]. A quantum computer also represents information as a series of bits, called quantum bits, or qubits. Like a normal bit, a qubit can be either 0 or 1, but unlike a normal bit, which can only be 0 or 1, a qubit can also be in a state where it is both at the same time [a superposition between the two states of zero and one]. When extended to systems of many qubits, this ability to be in all possible binary states at the same time gives rise to the potential computational power of quantum computing (National Academies of Sciences: Engineering, and Medicine, 2019: 24), which could be "truly trillions of trillions of trillions of times above those of current classical computing capacities" (Garis & Halioris, 2009: 489). Quantum computers could be exponentially faster than conventional computers.
>
> (Walsh, 2017: 184)

Discussion of the argument

At the risk of stating the obvious, "[t]he chief challenges in AI, relative to the human case, consist in finding the right computer programs, not faster and faster computers upon which to implement these programs" (Bringsjord et al., 2012a: 81). We dispel the myth that better hardware entails more intelligence and, ultimately, S. The Moravec-Kurzweil argument is not sound or incisive. Other than that, the idea here and in the subsequent subchapters is not to discuss the respective arguments at length or even comprehensively. Instead, we plainly illuminate the argument(s) from the stance of our causal theory of intelligence from Part II. This restriction implicates for this first argument that we make do with three brief remarks.

Firstly, the intelligence explosion, unleashed by S and culminating in *SIAI*s, and the speed explosion, characterized by colossal hardware improvements (along with software improvements which are fatally neglected by the hardware-based arguments), are logically independent of each other. In principle, there could be an intelligence explosion without a speed explosion and a speed explosion without an intelligence explosion. AI may have an advantage over human brains when it comes to data storage and the speed of data processing. But storage capacity and speed do not mean proliferated intelligence.

The following excursus demonstrates, by an argumentum ad absurdum, that confusing speed with intelligence leads to ludicrous results:

Break-out session 5

Are pigeons more intelligent than humans?

Shettleworth (2010: chapter 1.1.4) controverts the use of reaction time tests for pigeons and humans. The result is that pigeons react faster. Whilst there is no caveat about what reaction time tests measure, the same cannot be said about other tests. For example, as models of human cognitive skills show that reaction time positively correlates with IQ in humans (Hernández-Orallo, 2017: 160), what does this mean for pigeons? If we apply human psychometric models to pigeons "the counterintuitive conclusion follows that pigeons are more intelligent than people" (Vickrey & Neuringer, 2000).

By the same token, many machines and other realizations of Speedy Gonzales could be said to be more intelligent than humans too. Autobiographical note: This author and bibliophage wrote the book at hand and exploited more than 600 articles and books for that in record time, having kicked-off the project in early September 2020 and closed it by March 2021 (the remaining time between then and fall 2021 was marked by only minor changes to the manuscript). Does *that* (alone) make me a more intelligent doctoral researcher than other PhD students?

Speed deserves only secondary attention, speed matters for intelligence only in the *ceteris paribus* sense (see also our definition of *SIAI*): All other things being equal, the faster the test subject performs on an adequate task, the smarter she is (for extension and intension of ceteris paribus laws, cf. Hoffmann, 2020d). We can well fathom some of the extrapolations in terms of computational time (and also space), but things become more intricate when thinking about intelligence that improves in other quantitative ways or even in qualitative ways. Bostrom (2016: Chapter 3) differentiates several types of "superintelligences". And apart from "speed superintelligence" (ibid.: 64), there is "quality superintelligence: a system that is at least as fast as a human mind and vastly qualitative smarter", referring in a Minskian fashion to "*humanly* relevant complex cognitive tasks" (ibid.: 68). As the concept of quality superintelligence remains blurry like this, he makes do with a, as we find, problematic comparison: "the concept of quality superintelligence [. . .] is intelligence of quality at least as superior to that of human intelligence as the quality of human intelligence is superior to that of elephants', dolphins', or chimpanzees'" (ibid.: 69).

Be that as it may, a further pervasive fallacy which thus underlies this singularity idea reliant on Moravec's hardware-based argument is the monolithic view of intelligence that moreover usually confounds the subject with the intellectual faculty itself. To *grosso modo* extrapolate from success in one aspect relevant to cognition (like better hardware) to success in all aspects of cognition is to succumb to the illusion of progress already alluded to in Chapter 5. In other words, C3, which presupposes human-level learning capabilities for at least four intelligences, does not follow from C2.

Secondly, as highlighted in the Part III summary, what really matters about intelligence is capacity & behavior; what is not decisive is appearance & implementation. Hence, a focus on hardware to derive propositions and predictions about intelligence is not legitimate. (In addition, the history of AI suggests that the biggest bottleneck on the path to stronger AI is software, not hardware.)

Finally, computational capacities either just represent a tiny fraction of the gamut of intelligence (i.e., computation as a cognitive trait or, when interpreted even more narrowly, computation as one pillar of logical-mathematical intelligence). Or computing is taken as such a basic and abstract unit that the mind itself is treated as a computational system (e.g., see the computational metaphor in Chapter 1 or the computational theory of mind; Rescorla, 2020).[21] Either way, computational capacities per se are irrelevant to the level of intelligence. With regard to the multidimensionality of intelligence, systems' mere computational power leaves us in the dark about their causal learning capabilities. GPT-3 or AlphaGo and their relatives excel at computing; yet, no matter how much more computational power and speed they gain (ceteris paribus), they will never get past level one (the level of associations, correlations, seeing, and observing, see 5.1.1.).

Hence, *SAI*, *S*, and *SIAI*, as specified in the introduction to Part IV, remain at an unattainable distance; Moravec, Kurzweil, and adherents pose utterly deceptive questions with their argument.

11.2 The original argument by Good (1965) and its interpretation by Chalmers (2010)

The *locus classicus* in the affirmation of the contemporary singularity notion is without question the short article by the statistician Good (1965) who (had worked with Alan Turing during World War II and) articulated the term of an

---

21 For instance, in respect to the controversy on singularity, Sandberg & Bostrom (2008: 15) assume that "brain activity is Turing-computable, or if it is uncomputable, the uncomputable aspects have no functionally relevant effects on actual behaviour". According to Proudfoot (2012: 375), this assumption is mere speculation. Also Gödel seemed to be against computational functionalism (Wang 1996: 184).

intelligence explosion. Without further ado, what is the argument then? Its kernel, expressed in prose:

> Let an ultraintelligent machine be defined as a machine that can far surpass all the intellectual activities of any man however clever. Since the design of machines is one of these intellectual activities, an ultraintelligent machine could design even better machines; there would then unquestionably be an 'intelligence explosion', and the intelligence of man would be left far behind. Thus the first ultraintelligent machine is the last invention that man need ever make [. . .]. (Good, 1965)

The principal idea is that a machine that is more intelligent than humans will be better than humans at designing machines (Chalmers, 2010). So, it will be capable of designing a machine more intelligent than the most intelligent human-made machine, and the next generations will in turn be able to produce even more intelligent artifacts. Thus, a sequence of ever more intelligent AI systems is heralded, a process in which global AI enters a "runaway reaction" of self-enhancement cycles. This original argument is polished considerably by Chalmers (2010). He reasonably takes Good to be here arguing for the second premise, i.e., P2 in the subsequent overarching argument A:

Premise 1   There will be SAI (created by human intelligence and such that SAI reaches the human baseline; and due to SAI S will occur).
Premise 2   If there is SAI, there will be SAI^+ (created by SAI).
Premise 3   If there is SAI^+, there will be SAI^{++} (created by SAI^+).
Conclusion   There will be SAI^{++} (= superintelligence and the intelligence explosion will occur).[22]

Following Chalmers (2010: 7), we can think of the three premises as an *equivalence premise* (there will be AI at least equivalent to our own intelligence, thus SAI), an *extension premise* (SAI will soon be extended to SAI^+), and an *amplification premise* (SAI^+ will soon be greatly amplified to SAI^{++}). Why buy into the premises?

Since we are interested in scrutinizing the plausibility of S and SAI in this Part IV, we sketch what Chalmers delivers to back up P1. This presumptuous premise (presumptuous in the light of where AI stands today) is strengthened by Sandberg & Bostrom's (2008) *emulation argument*, relying on the possibility of brain emulation. The authors comprehend emulation as close simulation: in

---

[22] To refresh the reader's mind about the terminology: SAI = strong AI, S = singularity (both precisely defined at the beginning of Part IV). Given our definitions there, SAI^{++} can be equated with $SIAI$. SAI^+ can simply be viewed as an intermediate step towards realizing superintelligence (which is permitted according to our definition of S).

this case, simulation of internal processes in enough detail to replicate approximate patterns of behavior. Chalmers (2010: 8) portrays the argument *A1* to underpin P1 as follows:
(i) The human brain is a machine.
[*Our comment*: For the sake of consistency (see Chapter 3) and appealing to the authority of Marcus (2015), we accept this premise.]
(ii) We will have the capacity to emulate this machine (before long).
[*Our comment*: Precise values for the timeframe variables are not too important. Still to assure overall relevance of the argument, Chalmers stipulates that "before long" means "within centuries". Given our remarks on Block (1981) in Chapter 9, we welcome this addendum.]
(iii) If we emulate this machine, there will be *SAI*.
(iv) Ergo: Absent defeaters, there will be *SAI* (before long).

The second and third premise of *A1* are new in the sense that we have not adopted any perspective on them in the course of this work. Chalmers (ibid.) argues that "[t]he second premise follows from the claims that microphysical processes can be simulated arbitrarily closely and that any machine can be emulated by simulating microphysical processes arbitrarily closely. It is also suggested by the progress of science and technology more generally: we are gradually increasing our understanding of biological machines and increasing our capacity to simulate them, and there do not seem to be limits to progress here. The third premise follows from the definitional claim that if we emulate the brain this will replicate approximate patterns of human behaviour, along with the claim that such replication will result in [S]AI."

Chalmers (2010: 10) presents a second argument *A2* to sustain the premise P1. This so-called *evolutionary argument* runs as follows:
(i) Evolution produced human-level intelligence. [*Our comment*: It is a straightforward fact that there is human-level intelligence. In what sense evolution, which is not an agent, "produced" it remains obscure here. Perhaps, it is just a matter of wording.]
(ii) If evolution produced human-level intelligence, then we can produce *SAI* (before long).
(iii) Ergo: Absent defeaters, there will be *SAI* (before long).

Here, the thought is that since evolution engendered human-level intelligence nonmiraculously (in the sense that it is a step-by-step process without any *Deus ex machina* moments), this sort of intelligence is not entirely unattainable. Furthermore, evolution "operates" without requiring any antecedent intelligence or forethought. If evolution can "produce" something in this unintelligent manner, then in principle humans should be able to produce it much faster (before long), by harnessing our intelligence (ibid.).

Discussion of the argument

After the failed attempt in 11.1., here are our three comments on the second trial to vindicate S. Firstly, from our stance, the Good-Chalmers argument A falls short of defending S because SAI and, therefore, parts of S are taken for granted, i.e., assumed in the first premise P1. A is deductive in form, and formally valid. Is it sound too?

Before we turn to P1, a brief remark on P2/P3 is in order: In reference to Hofstadter (1979: 35), we considered fine-grained distinctions between object levels and meta-levels in 5.1.3., which is good practice in analytic philosophy. This discrimination also proves to be revealing for the invalidation of P2/P3 in A. The intelligence required to do X should not be misleadingly equated with the ability to increase one's own intelligence in order to be better able to cope with X. After all, they are two different competences and it is not clear why the same AI should also be able to enhance itself or the next generation, respectively. Unfortunately, not even otherwise very clever philosophers like David Chalmers (2010: 12) are immune to this misconception: "If we produce an AI by machine learning, it is likely that soon after we will be able to improve the learning algorithm and extend the learning process, leading to [S]AI$^+$."

Thirdly, what is actually at stake for our discussion in Part IV is not A, but Chalmer's (2010: 8, 10) arguments A1 and A2 (since they have the objective of increasing the credibility of the initialization of S). One might resist the two arguments in various ways. With regard to A1, one could argue that we will never have the capacity to emulate and replicate the human brain (e.g., recall the quote from Koch, 2020, in Chapter 1); and one could argue that emulating it need not produce SAI (e.g., Proudfoot, 2012; see Footnote 21). Moreover, various existing forms of resistance to SAI take each of these forms (see Chapter 12).

With regard to A2, again, the argument can be resisted, perhaps by denying that it was "evolution" that "produced" intelligence, or maybe by arguing that evolution "produced" intelligence by means of processes that we cannot mechanically replicate. The latter line might be taken by holding that evolution needed the help of superintelligent intervention (*Deus ex machina*), or needed the aid of other nonmechanical processes along the way, or needed an enormously complex history that we could never artificially duplicate, or needed an enormous amount of luck (Chalmers, 2010: 10).

In any event, I have no intention to become engaged any further in the contestation about *A1* and *A2*. On the one hand, our work on the last 200 pages has no bearing on it (or vice versa). The Good-Chalmers argument as well as *A1* and *A2* proceed without explicating the key notion of intelligence – at least not beyond being benign and assuming an intelligence measure that assigns an intelligence value to arbitrary systems (a simplifying assumption we can go d'accord with). On the other hand, formal validity of *A* is granted, yet that is about where the good news ends for the proponent of *S*. To see this, it can be reasoned that in order for the belief that *S* to qualify as justified by rationalist and empiricist standards, the premises in question in *A* as well as *A1* and *A2* – first and foremost P1 to P3, (ii) and (iii) in *A1* and (ii) in *A2* – must be either probable or beyond reasonable doubt or certain or evident. It can be further reasoned that they are none of the above (Bringsjord et al., 2012b). Or as Chalmers (2010: 10) himself couched it diffidently: "Of course these arguments [*A*, *A1* and *A2*] do not tell us how [S]AI will first be attained".

11.3 The doomsayer scenario advanced by Bostrom (2016)

We humans are susceptible to narratives and the doomsayer argument is the crowning glory of creation amidst AI narratives (Cave et al., 2020). Luminaries such as Stephen Hawking, Elon Musk, and Bill Gates have all come out publicly (in 2015) to state that AI technology could have catastrophic effects. In the case of Hawking, he was quite frank about it and openly alluded to *SAI* & *SIAI*: "The development of full artificial intelligence could spell the end of the human race" (cited in Darwiche, 2017: 1). Leaving a fallacious *argumentum ad verecundiam* aside, why should we be convinced that the human race is doomed, in no small part because it is busy building smart machines (that, for the time being, turn out to be idiots savants at best)?

Some indication is given by the singularity (and parts of the more serious AI) community endorsing definitions of intelligence that equate intelligence with optimization power (Yampolskiy & Fox, 2012: 131), with "an agent's ability to achieve *goals* in a wide range of environments" (Ward et al., 2020: 1; our italics) so that "'[r]ational economic behavior' has become the foundation for modern artificial intelligence" (Omohundro, 2012: 163; cf. also Russell & Norvig, 2009 that we met above in 3.1.). The terminal goal of a *SAI* is said to be "to acquire as many resources as possible, so that these resources can be transformed and put to work for the satisfaction of the [S]AI's [. . .] instrumental goals" (Muehlhauser & Salamon, 2012: 28).

Yampolskiy & Fox (2012: 137) set these proposals about *SAI* or *SIAI* (the exact referent remains opaque) in relation to the supposed human case and the outcome is a disaster:

> The human goal system [*who is the human?*], which includes survival, social status, and morality, along with many others, is a mix of adaptations to conditions in the human ancestral environment [. . . *so we are fully determined beings?*]. In contrast, a [SAI or SIAI] can have arbitrary goals [*intelligence, (economic) rationality, consciousness, motivation seem to be all blended here and how can goals be arbitrary if the being is super-intelligent (i.e., narrowly super-rational to their understanding) or how do "arbitrary" and "defined by its designers" go together?*], whether these are defined by its designers [*to what extent is the S(I)AI then autonomous at all, which is a necessary condition for being an agent and a S(I)AI a fortiori*] or develop in a random or chaotic process [*what does that mean and chaotic in the sense of Lorenz, 1963 (where systems are deterministic and thus anything but random)?*]. Human terminal values arose from their instrumental value [*what does that mean and why is it the case?*] in achieving evolution's implicit goal [*what would be "its explicit goal" and, more importantly, how can evolution be an agent at all even more in the strict sense with goals, etc.?*] of reproductive success for the genes. For [SAI/SIAI] as well, such human-like preferences [*why human-like and not human?*] would have instrumental value [*why?*] for the achievement of many goals [*which? which not?*]. For example, most agents, including [SAIs/SIAIs] [*have you ever asked one?*], would be motivated [*why?*], as humans are [*why would they (need to) follow the human example?*], to protect themselves [*what about suicidals?*], to acquire resources [*what about altruism?*], and to use them efficiently [*last time, I checked, the Homo Oeconomicus (e.g., Kirchgässner, 2013), the selfish utility maximizer of the 20th century, was among the undead*].

There is so much wrong with these utterances that a philosopher must almost feel ashamed to quote them – and my comments in the squared brackets, in italics and red, point to the avalanche of flaws because after all the quoted passage is now more red than black. [Nota bene, as well visible in this little exercise, we (fully intelligent agents) raise a lot of *why* questions when we do not *understand* something, thereby substantiating how we coined "understanding" in 5.1.3.] But here the quoted passage, not despite but because of the many flaws in it, serves the purpose of showing what is wrong with at least some fundamentals to construct a doomsayer argument on. So then, what about the reasoning of professional philosophers on the matter and the argument itself, which is, fairly taken, more a tale, not to say a fairy tale, than an argument?

Bostrom (2016), adhering to the economic exegesis of AI (AI "as a quest to find shortcuts: ways of tractably approximating the Bayesian ideal", ibid.: 11), has painted an exceedingly dark picture of a possible future with *SAI* and *SIAI* in it. His Chapter 2 signposts "Paths to Superintelligence", but we do not come across anything novel or compelling: On page 27, we meet Turing (1950) again, on page 28 Moravec and Chalmers, on page 32 Moore's law, and on page 33 and after the whole brain emulation argument (Sandberg & Bostrom, 2008).

The only new conceivable path to superintelligence we learn about "is through the gradual enhancement of networks and organizations that link individual human minds with one another and with various artifacts and bots. The idea here is not that this would enhance the intellectual capacity of individuals enough to make them superintelligent, but rather that some system composed of individuals thus networked and organized might attain a form of superintelligence, [a] 'collective superintelligence'." (Bostrom, 2016: 58f.). Other than that, *SAI*, *S*, and *SIAI* seem to be more taken as a given: "The fact that there are many paths that lead to superintelligence should increase our confidence that we will eventually get there. If one path turns out to be blocked, we can still progress" (ibid.: 61).

Brushing all the problems we tackled aside (from pondering how intelligence should be understood to evaluating intelligence in past, present, and hypothetical AI systems), Bostrom points out on the 260 remaining pages of his book that the superintelligences he portrays could have the capability to shape the future of Earth-originating life and clutch at complete world domination (Bostrom, 2016: 110). They could easily have non-anthropomorphic final goals, and would likely have instrumental reasons to pursue open-ended resource acquisition; even if they look innocent at first glance: "[. . .] we cannot blithely assume that a superintelligence with the final goal of calculating the decimals of pi (or making paperclips, or counting grains of sand) would limit its activities in such a way as not to infringe on human interests" (ibid.: 141). Because if we now reflect that human beings are composed of useful resources (such as conveniently located atoms) and that we depend on many more local resources, a treacherous turn could loom. We can see that the outcome could easily get out of control and do corrosive damage. The outcome could be one in which humanity quickly becomes extinct (ibid.: 144).

Discussion of the argument

The doomsayer's scenario has maybe been gaining momentum because we know all too well how we treat less intelligent animals: locking them in a cage, in a lab, in a zoo, hunting them, (accidentally or not) exterminating them. But this is at the end just another human fallacy – here, of humanizing machines; sadly, humanizing with a negative connotation though. As noticed prior to the presentation of Bostrom's deliberations, the mutual infertility of our work for Bostrom's discussion and Bostrom's discussion for our work is grounded in the wholly incompatible understanding of intelligence.

On top of that, Bostrom (2016) is not bothered too much about propounding arguments for the arrival of *S*, but is more interested in what *could* happen thereafter, in parallel to Good and Chalmers. (Unlike Good and Chalmers though, he is not wondering what occurs in the direct aftermath of S (the arrival of SAI^+), but of $SIAI$ or SAI^{++}. Hence, Bostrom wanders down the road of science fiction even further.) Still, we poke three more holes in his manifesto.

First, Bostrom's proposal to take collective superintelligence into account as a novel route to reach superintelligence is not satisfactory to us for various reasons. Firstly, it is unacceptably vague and shallow and does not detail how to get there. With Bostrom's directions at hand, AI engineers will just get lost on the way. Secondly, "might attain" (in the quote provided on the previous page; Bostrom, 2016: 58f.) is not really the kind of deal of persuasion that you would expect in order to buy into a very speculative idea. I offer you a trip to Mars which you "might reach" if you step into this space shuttle. Would you go? Thirdly, the argument is not addressing synthetic $SIAI$ which was favored according to the narrative in 3.2. And finally, collective intelligence was ruled out for our investigation (see Table 2).

Second, about Bostrom's (2016: 61; which we quoted above) summary statement: Why is the path to self-destruction called progress? It would be more appropriate to refer to *hypothetical* paths in Bostrom (2016) than to palpable avenues for AI research and engineering – and the latter would be necessitated before the prudent mind starts worrying about a malicious $SIAI$. As I like to say to my students in risk management classes, I could also become anxious about a pink elephant falling from the sky on my head, but why should I? What impact would that positive probability risk event have on my actual decision-making (cf. Hoffmann, 2017b: 88)? Not least, "increase our confidence" still leaves us with a level of confidence that is very low in absolute terms (with or without that increase from Bostrom).

Third, ad the superintelligent will to conquer the world (or to strive for anything else): Ensuing from the way we explored "intelligence" and intelligence in agents, we have not taken any stand on the relation between intelligence and motivation. This reluctance traces back to Part I where we early on ruled out rationality (which is in turn bound to freedom, goals and preferences, and so on) as a suitable object of analysis for making sense of "intelligence" in a pluralistic debate. From this reluctance does not follow though that we have to embrace the orthogonality thesis (which might or might not come with pitfalls) according to which intelligence and final goals *must* be independent variables. (I think for human beings, for example when we study their rational decision-making, another thesis can be maintained, but this is a question beyond the scope of the present treatise.)

Yet, there is no reason to be found in our book – above all when we revisit our definitions of SAI and $SIAI$ – to succumbing to the (in our view, quixotic) belief that AIs, for the foreseeable future, will have beliefs, desires, motivations, goals of certain sorts. To close this Chapter, let Steven Pinker (cited in Marcus & Davis, 2019: 30) strike a blow for the orthogonality thesis:

> [T]he scenario [that the robots will become superintelligent and enslave humans] makes about as much sense as the worry that since jet planes have surpassed the flying ability of eagles, someday they will swoop out of the sky and seize our cattle. The [. . .] fallacy is a confusion of intelligence with motivation – of beliefs with desires, inferences with goals, thinking with wanting. Even if we did invent superhumanly intelligent robots, why would they *want* to enslave their masters or take over the world? Intelligence is the ability to deploy novel means to attain a goal. But the goals are extraneous to the intelligence: Being smart is not the same as wanting something.

12 Arguments against strong AI: Close but no cigar

> *What the fantast sees isn't really there, but that he "sees" it nonetheless brings him intoxicating joy.*
> Bringsjord et al., 2012a: 82

To some philosophers the idea that computers will truly have minds is outrageous. Such opponents contend that computers are imbecile in a way that human beings are not, so that it is out of the question that for a fully-fledged mind to arise solely in virtue of computation. What philosophical reason stands in the way of AI fabricating artifacts that are *SAI*?

In this penultimate Chapter 12, we turn to the three principal philosophical criticisms of strong AI which have been more or less effective, i.e., they helped to change the tide in the AI community and point to new research directions to different extents. We start with weaker, and then move to stronger arguments.

Following Chalmers (1996: 313), objections to *SAI* typically take one of two forms. On the one hand, there exist *external* counterarguments, which try to establish that artifacts could never even *behave* like human foils. Along those lines, it is maintained that certain human functional capacities cannot have a counterpart in machines. For instance, sometimes it is argued that AI could never duplicate human mathematical insight, as computational systems are limited by Gödel's theorem in a way that humans are not (12.1.). Others have called attention to the absence of the flexible or creative momentum of AI vis-à-vis humans because the former follow rules (e.g., Dreyfus, 1999; see 12.2.). However, external vetos have been difficult to carry through in the wake of the success of computational simulation of physical processes in general (Chalmers, 1996: 313): "[W]e have good reason to believe that the laws of physics are computable, so that we at least ought to be able to *simulate* human behavior computationally" (ibid.).

More prevalent have been what Chalmers calls *internal* vetos. These concede at least for the sake of argument that computers might simulate human behavior, but uphold that they would lack minds all the same since, above all, an inner life would be sorely missed (ibid.: 314). (Our study has deliberately not opened up the Pandora's box of theorizing about "consciousness", which would require a doctoral work of its own (as proven by the very same Chalmers, 1996), and therefore, "inner life" is most trenchantly captured here by "(deep) understanding"; see 5.1.3.). One of the seminal philosophical attacks on *SAI* in this class is (perhaps next to Block's, 1978, influential critique of machine functionalism) Searle's Chinese Room thought experiment which we visit in 12.3.

12.1 Gödelian arguments

To begin with, everyone can concord that Kurt Gödel's contributions to formal logic as a discipline of mathematics, in particular his Incompleteness Theorems (Gödel, 1931), are a terrific achievement. Or in the words of another giant of that time, John von Neumann: "Kurt Gödel's achievement in modern logic is singular and monumental – indeed it is more than a monument, it is a landmark which will remain visible far in space and time" (*The New York Times*, March 15, 1951: 31). But AI is not formal logics or a discipline of mathematics for that matter, which prompts the question to what extent Gödel developed an argument against strong AI. The simple answer is, he has not. The mystery about how this answer goes together with the title of this subchapter (with Gödel's name in it) is dissipated though once we note that "no mathematical result has ever had extra-mathematical outcomes remotely comparable to Gödel's Theorem [as the conjunction of the two]" (Berto, 2011: xiif.). In the aftermath of the release of the Gödelian Symphony (ibid.), famous theses based upon, or allegedly following from, the incompleteness theorems were enacted in fields as different as the philosophy of mathematics, philosophy of mind, even sociology and politics, which must have provoked Franzén (2005) to title his book: *Gödel's Theorem: An Incomplete Guide to Its Use and Abuse*.

And indeed, in (at least prima facie) stark contrast to obvious and curious misapprehensions of Gödel's findings, the connection between formal systems, i.e. what his work is actually about, and computers is not difficult to make out because the former and the latter are simply equivalent if the latter are seen as Turing machines – but beware of an inflationary use (cf. Sloman, 2002). This is not the place to attempt a full definition of Turing machines or formal systems, but three essential features can capture the basic idea: "(i) they are token-manipulation systems; (ii) they are digital; and (iii) they are medium independent" (Haugeland, 1997b: 8f.).

Some philosophers, physicists and mathematicians, in particular Lucas (1961), Penrose (1989, 1994, 1996), and Koellner (2018a, b), have then attempted to derive an argument to the effect that no computing machine can ever reach "human-level intelligence" (not only of actual, but of idealized humans, but not in the sense pertinent to our definition of *SAI* which already points to a harsh criticism of Gödelian arguments from our stance) or, at the very least, that the human mind is irreducible to any computing machine.

Presentation of the argument

In nuce, the Gödelian arguments (from Lucas, 1961, to Koellner, 2018a, b) are addressing – and affirming – the question of whether the incompleteness theorems imply that "the mind cannot be mechanized" which ought to be specified as "the mathematical outputs of the idealized human mind do not coincide with the mathematical outputs of any idealized finite machine" (Koellner, 2018a: 338).

The story begins with Gödel who proved in 1931 that for any consistent formal system powerful enough to do a certain sort of arithmetic like the Principia Mathematica, there will be a true sentence – the system's *Gödel sentence* – that the system cannot prove (for more detailed and accurate accounts of his proof, cf. Nagel & Newman, 2001, or Raatikainen, 2020). Gödel thought that his incompleteness theorems had bearing on the question of mechanism, of whether the human mathematician can be replaced by a machine, and he thought that "will never be possible" (Gödel in Tieszen, 2011: 179; cf. also Wang, 1996: 193).

But as usually, Gödel was cautious and his position was quite subtle – even though he went so far as to call his finding, the disjunction (see the next sentence), a "mathematically established fact" (Gödel, 1951/1995: 310). He himself refrained from arguing that his incompleteness theorems implied that "the mind cannot be mechanized" (in the sense of Koellner, 2018a: 338, quoted in the first paragraph); he contended, rather, that they implied a weaker, disjunctive conclusion, what I, Feferman and others called "Gödel's Disjunction" (Hoffmann, 2011/2017). The disjunction concerns two central philosophical claims: "Either the human mind surpasses all machines (to be more precise: it can decide more number-theoretical questions than any machine), or else there exist number-theoretical questions undecidable for the human mind" (Gödel in Wang, 1996: 185). The disjunction states that at least one of these claims must hold – put differently, it states that either "the mind cannot be mechanized" or "mathematical truth outstrips the idealized human mind" (Koellner, 2018a: 339).

The first to exceed that prudency and to produce a full-fledged Gödelian argument against *SAI* – i.e., to establish that Gödel's incompleteness theorems imply that the first disjunct holds – was the Oxford philosopher J.R. Lucas (1961). Lucas' talk of 1959 and the subsequent publication in 1961 was widely criticized in the literature – incisively by Benacerraf, 1967; and most eloquently by Hofstadter's (1979: 465f.) "Passion According to Lucas". Yet, Lucas initiated a debate that has yielded more formidable arguments. One of Lucas' indefatigable defenders is the newly minted Nobel prize laureate in physics Roger Penrose, whose first attempt to vindicate Lucas was a Gödelian attack on *SAI* articulated in his *The Emperor's New Mind* (1989). This first attempt fell short, and Penrose published a more elaborate and more fastidious Gödelian case, expressed in Chapters 2 and 3 of his *Shadows of the Mind* (1994).

Penrose (1996: 3.2) distills this argument to its essentials. Here is this version, verbatim (restated in different terms in Franzén, 2005: 120):

> We try to suppose that the totality of methods of (unassailable) mathematical reasoning that are in principle humanly accessible can be encapsulated in some (not necessarily computational) sound formal system FF. A human mathematician, if presented with FF, could argue as follows (bearing in mind that the phrase "I am FF" is merely a shorthand for "FF encapsulates all the humanly accessible methods of mathematical proof"): (A) "Though I don't know that I necessarily am FF, I conclude that if I were, then the system FF would have to be sound and, more to the point, F'F' would have to be sound, where F' F' is FF supplemented by the further assertion "I am FF." I perceive that it follows from the assumption that I am FF that the Gödel statement G(F')G(F') would have to be true and, furthermore, that it would not be a consequence of F'F'. But I have just perceived that "If I happened to be FF, then G(F')G(F') would have to be true," and perceptions of this nature would be precisely what F'F' is supposed to achieve. Since I am therefore capable of perceiving something beyond the powers of F'F', I deduce that I cannot be FF after all. Moreover, this applies to any other (Gödelizable) system, in place of FF."

Discussion of the argument

The close examination of the cogency of that sophisticated argument for the first disjunct becomes very technical and elaborate as the argument involves sentences that are provably indeterminate (just as the Liar sentence itself), and it applies to these sentences inference rules that are legitimate only when applied to determinate sentences (Koellner, 2018b: 458). I do not have the faintest intent of entering that debate, Kafka's castle, as the hope would be foolish of finding our way back out again by dint of pure reason expressed by and confined to text of a page or less in this discussion part. Koellner's two-piece paper is, in my view, a brilliant piece of reasoning, and so is Penrose's (1994/96) argument. However, the former with its ramifications – e.g., he arrives at a disjunctive conclusion himself (2018b) – and utmost delicacy in mathematical logic is delicate to evaluate in respect to the overarching, relatively fuzzy question of why *S* and *SAI* are impossible. The latter might not be sufficiently independent in the sense that, if the previous Gödelian arguments are overturned, not much evidence for buying into Penrose's (1994/96) argument is left (Chalmers, 1995).

Instead, I summarize that the assessment of Gödel's work is ongoing and not completed and I contribute to it by four more short comments in reference to my own paper on that matter (Hoffmann, 2011/2017). Firstly, the Gödelian arguments against *SAI*, so far, do not appear to carry much force. Those attempts suffer from the shortcoming that Gödelian limitations have not been convincingly shown to *not* apply to humans. Moreover, the theses that Gödel, Lucas, Penrose, and others develop from the incompleteness theorems depend on highly idealized assumptions about both the nature of the human mind and the nature of machines. Coming from our definitions of *SAI* and *S*, that ground in turn in our proposal from Part II, we ought to remain more agnostic though.

> What about the assumption that the human mind is consistent? In practice, mathematicians certainly make errors and thence arrive at false conclusions that in some cases go long undetected. Penrose, among others, has pointed out that when errors are detected, mathematicians seek out their source and correct them (cf. Penrose 1996, pp. 137 ff), and so he has argued that it is reasonable to ascribe self-correctability and hence consistency to our idealized mathematician. But even if such a one can correct all his errors, can he know with mathematical certitude, as required for Gödel's claim, that he is consistent?
>
> (Feferman, 2007: 15; cf. also Shapiro, 1998)

Secondly, with Turing (1950: 445), we note that "[w]e too often give wrong answers to questions ourselves to be justified in being very pleased at such evidence of fallibility on the part of the machines. Further, our superiority can only be felt on such an occasion in relation to the one machine over which we have scored our petty triumph. There would be no question of triumphing simultaneously over *all* machines. In short, then, there might be men cleverer than any given machine, but then again there might be other machines cleverer again, and so on." In retrospect to Part III, it is interesting that the two men who might be said to have endowed the intellectual machinery of that objection to *SAI*, Gödel (with his proof) and Turing (with his precise definition of the Turing machine), came to opposite philosophical conclusions.

Thirdly, barring the pessimistic notion of the accidental inexplicability of the brain or mind, the project of AI could even receive a boost from Gödel's groundwork on the constructive side which is very much in line with our thrust in Chapter 5.1. If we recognize that his proof nurtures the notion that "a high-level view of a system may contain certain explanatory power which simply is absent on the low levels" (Hofstadter, 1979: 702), then this reading is immediately reminiscent of our layered taxonomy of causal learning where AI systems on the third level possess explanatory power which is blatantly missing in our today's deep learning machines on the lower level one (of associations and correlations).

Finally, in light of our plea for the multidirectionality and plurality of intelligence, it is tantamount to hubris to think that mathematics and metamathematics alone could determine what minds in general are capable of and what they are not capable of. Gödel's theorem is concerned "with the machine as a sort of papal authority, infallible rather than intelligent" (Hodges, 1992: 361). With our definitions of *SAI* in mind (where logical-mathematical intelligence is not even directly incorporated, but only subsumed under cognitive intelligence), routes towards *SAI* and *S* (which are far from being discovered) are not necessarily blocked by Gödelian arguments, no matter if they prove to be sound or not.

12.2 Dreyfus' prophecy and legacy

> We are unable clearly to circumscribe the concepts we use; not because we don't know their real definition, but because there is no real 'definition' to them. To suppose that there must be would be like supposing that whenever children play with a ball they play a game according to strict rules.
>
> Ludwig Wittgenstein, 1935/1958: 25

Dreyfus' (1999) critique is a mixture of empirical and philosophical reasoning. Empirically, his main charge was that AI researchers had flatly failed to deliver the goods. In spite of the grandiose early forecasts (as quoted in excerpts on the first pages of this study at hand, for instance), they had not managed to construct *SAI*. This line of criticism was generally dismissed as invalid and unfair: invalid because at best it demonstrated that AI had not succeeded *yet*, not that it could not *ever* succeed; and unfair because it denies the progress being made as well as because AI was and still is a comparatively young field, and revolutionary technological breakthroughs could not be expected from a field in its infancy, despite the overly enthusiastic proclamations of some of its pioneers (Arkoudas & Bringsjord, 2015: 47). Philosophically, Dreyfus demurs that our ability to understand the world and other people is a non-declarative type of *know-how skill* that is not amenable to GOFAI-style propositional codification (ibid.). Emphasizing the importance of capacities such as imagination, the use of metaphors, ambiguity tolerance, along with our human faculty to distinguish the essential from the inessential, he argues that the way we make sense of the world is "inarticulate, preconceptual, and has an indispensable phenomenological dimension that cannot be captured by any rule-based system" (ibid.).

Dreyfus (1999) correctly felt that imparting the same ability to a digital computer would be a major stumbling block for AI – what he baptized the "holistic context" problem. Let us have a closer look.

Presentation of the argument

Much of what Dreyfus had to say was couched in the language of continental phenomenology and existentialism, heavily affected by thinkers such as Heidegger and Merleau-Ponty. Dreyfus' core idea is that human expertise does not emanate from the explicit, disembodied, mechanical manipulation of symbolic information (such as formulae in some logic, or probabilities in some Bayesian network), and that AI's efforts to devise machines with such expertise are doomed if based on the symbolic paradigm (Bringsjord & Govindarajulu, 2018). The genesis of the Dreyfusian attack was a conviction that the critique of (if you will) symbol-based philosophy (e.g., in the logic-based, rationalist imprint) could be made in the spirit of Continental philosophy against the rationalist tradition in AI (ibid.). That, unfortunately, was not conducive to facilitating communication with AI researchers, or with analytic philosophers for that matter.

Luckily (from this point of view) Dreyfus' (1999: 56f.) theses also owe a lot to (the late) Wittgenstein (who is more esteemed to a broader audience); namely that whenever human behavior is analyzed in terms of rules, these rules must always contain a *ceteris paribus* clause. In other words, they apply "everything else being equal"; and what "everything else" and "equal" signify in any specific situation can never be fully spelled out without a regress (ibid.). On top of that, the ceteris paribus condition is not merely an annoyance indicating that the analysis is not yet complete (Dreyfus, 1979/1997: 180). Rather, the ceteris paribus clause hints at "a background of practices which are the condition of the possibility of all rule-like activity" (ibid.). In explaining our daily activities we must always sooner or later fall back on our sense of what we *are*, which is, on pain of regress, something we can never explicitly *know* (ibid.).

Furthermore, whilst AI researchers could maintain that, whatever the background which is prerequisite for understanding specific situations, that knowledge *must* somehow be represented in the human beings who possess that understanding, Dreyfus (1979/1997: 180) appeals to Wittgenstein and responds that such "knowledge" of human interests and practices does not need to be represented at all. For instance, it seems plausible that I learnt *how to* ski, not by representing my body and muscular movements in some data structure, but by practicing until I developed the essential patterns of responses, without anyone being in the position of making explicit what exactly was being learned. Something similar can be noticed about human (and animal) pattern recognition which differs radically from mechanical recognition, well-visible from our tolerance for changes in orientation and size, ambiguity tolerance, degrees of incompleteness and distortion, and amount of background noise (Dreyfus, 1999: 120).

In concord with these lines, we can distill the subsequent Dreyfusian argument to overthrow *SAI*.

Premise 1	Intelligence necessitates the ability to recognize what is relevant to whatever task is at hand.
Premise 2	Relevance hinges on all features present or absent in a situation.
Premise 3	If a machine is to recognize relevance, then it must apply rules to representations of features.
Conclusion 1	Achieving recognition of relevance in machines necessitates exhaustive rule sets that apply to every contingency.
Premise 4	Either the project in C1 is not feasible or if it can be carried out, the intelligence expressed by this achievement is not embodied in the artifact, but by the human developer(s) and the artifact is at best a repository of the results of human intelligence (cf. also Block, 1981).
Conclusion 2	*SAI* is not feasible.

In hindsight with more than 50 years of time difference, Dreyfus' (1965, 1979/1997, 1999) critique of AI seems predominantly *passé* as AI was GOFAI back then and GOFAI, which specified a commitment to *SAI* (Boden, 2015: 97), was superseded. Is Dreyfus attacking a straw man from today's perspective?

Not according to Fjelland (2020) who shallowly stresses again that "the problem is that nobody can have a model of reality". Any model can only depict simplified aspects of reality. "The real problem is that computers are not in the world, because they are not embodied" (ibid.). This veto by Fjelland (2020) is simply old wine in a new bottle, and as anemic as the role model (Dreyfus, 1999). After further reading and study of Dreyfus' and fellows' writings, readers may judge whether this critique is compelling, in an information-driven world increasingly managed by "intelligent agents" (recall our definitions of agency and of level one intelligence from our Chapter 5) that carry out symbolic reasoning – albeit not even close to the human level. Here are my two cents.

Discussion of the argument

I offer five comments here to discuss Dreyfus' prophecy and legacy. Firstly, precursors to his critique are numerous as it is perhaps the oldest external objection to AI that computational systems always follow rules, so they will always lack certain human capacities, such as creativity and flexibility (Chalmers, 1996: 329). This concern was, for instance, voiced by Lady Lovelace and easily rebuffed by Turing (1950: 450f.) and others. Her sort of objection may gain some leverage in the guise of Dreyfus (1999), i.e., from the implicit identification of computational systems with *symbolic* computational systems: (GOFAI) systems that execute symbolic manipulations of high-level conceptual representations – in the extreme case, "AIs" that inflexibly draw conclusions from premises in first-order logic. Perhaps, the outdated argument on the previous page has some teeth then – outdated because after the 1960/70s when Dreyfus wrote down his thoughts we moved on to the machine learning paradigm –, although even that is disputable. In any event, the class of computational systems is much broader than the picture that Dreyfus paints (contra P3), thereby dispatching the *tertium non datur* in P4. A low-level emulation of the brain (Sandberg & Bostrom, 2008) is a computation, for example, yet is not a symbolic computation of this sort. At an intermediate level, currently popular deep learning systems have appealed to a kind of computation, as seen in 3.1., that does not consist in symbolic manipulation, and so on. In such cases, there may be a level at which the AI follows rules, but this is not directly mirrored at the higher level of behavior where flexibility, creativity, etc. is possible. Or as the fabulous Hofstadter (1979: 674) has put it freely adapted from Descartes: "I think; therefore I have no access to the level where I sum."

A second comment concerns the first disjunct in P4 and ceteris paribus conditions: To prematurely surrender in the face of ceteris paribus clauses is intellectually pathetic as at least some of them can be syntactically handled and semantically specified as "descriptions of stable underlying dispositions" (Lipton, 1999: 155; cf. also Hoffmann, 2020d).

Thirdly, P1 is obsolete. According to our universal taxonomy, the ability to discriminate what is relevant from what is irrelevant is not prerequisite on lower levels of intelligence where agents make all kinds of predictions, including irrelevant predictions.

Evidently, C2 would not even follow from the premises if they were correct. In some sense, Dreyfus was attacking a straw man. The assumption that "man functions like a general-purpose symbol-manipulating device" (Dreyfus, 1999: 156), i.e., like a GOFAI, is of course to be disapproved vehemently, and, therefore, Dreyfus is right to criticize it. But why do AI researchers have to adhere to such a strong assumption to reach *SAI* in the first place? Our definition of *SAI* does not parochially prescribe that an AI has to get stuck in the past, in the first wave of AI.

Finally, to end on a positive note about the impact of Dreyfus' (1999) book, endowing computers with common sense remains one of the biggest challenges in the field of AI (Shanahan et al., 2020). Moreover, Dreyfus appears to endorse a holism which is partially echoed in this treatise, too. Above all, his thesis that "since intelligence must be situated it cannot be separated from the rest of human life" (Dreyfus, 1979/1997: 181) is a point that has been insistently made in less anthropomorphic and more systemic connotations in Part I (see page 91: "The seat of intelligence is not within any system of an organism or artifact"). The persistent denial of this appealing insight cannot, however, be laid at the door of (first-wave) AI. The hope of separating the intellect or rational soul from the body with its skills, emotions, and appetites rekindles here and there, e.g., in the work of Plato's, thereby neglecting that human intelligence spans many more distinct intelligences, from cognitive abilities to emotional, social or bodily proficiencies. Aristotle continued that unlikely dichotomy when he discerns the theoretical from the practical, and circumscribed or demagnified man as a *rational* animal – as if one could separate man's rationality from his animal needs and desires.

12.3 Searle's Chinese Room thought experiment

In what may be the most influential thought experiment in the history of AI (Schank & Towle, 2000: 344), Searle (1980) proposed what has come to be called the Chinese Room experiment.

Presentation of the argument

This intriguing and seminal essay on *minds, brains, and programs* offered an argument against the contention of strong AI. "The argument", Searle writes in a brief restatement, "proceeds by the following thought experiment":

> Imagine a native English speaker who knows no Chinese locked in a room full of boxes of Chinese symbols (a data base) together with a book of instructions for manipulating the symbols (the program). Imagine that people outside the room send in other Chinese symbols which, unknown to the person in the room, are questions in Chinese (the input). And imagine that by following the instructions in the program the man in the room is able to pass out Chinese symbols which are correct answers to the questions (the output). The program enables the person in the room to pass the Turing Test for understanding Chinese but he does not understand a word of Chinese. (Searle, 1999: 115)

Now, if we ban physical impossibilities because books like Searle's Pr would easily need to contain more distinct entries than our entire physical universe counts atoms (Levesque, 2018: 12), which we may or may not want to accept in a thought experiment, what is the celebrated *internal* objection to *SAI* stemming from Searle's scenario? Even if the reader has never heard of the Chinese Room experiment before, (s)he doubtless can see the basic idea (see also Figure 34): that S(earle) in the box is supposed to be everything a computer can be – composed of a data base, as well as the program, receiving inputs, generating outputs – and his externally observable behavior is perfect. And yet, Searle claims

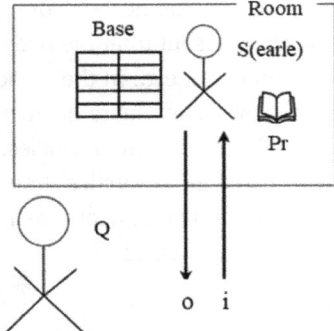

Figure 34: A schematic view of Searle's Chinese Room experiment where S(earle) is the native English speaker who knows no Chinese and who is locked in the room, and Q is the Chinese interrogator. "o" stands for "output", "i" for "input". "Base" is the "data base", and "Pr" the "program".

that S(earle) does not understand Chinese, and so no computer could have such understanding. S(earle) is mindlessly moving squiggle-squoggles around (to borrow his words), and, according to the argument, that is all computers do, fundamentally. Hence, they necessarily lack understanding and, consequently, *SAI*. And as a corollary: getting the behavior right is not enough to attain *SAI*, and so Turing (see Chapter 8) is wrong.

Searle's conclusion on the constructive side: The Chinese Room demonstrates that something more is needed for intentionality than formal computations. And that "something" is, following Searle, the causal powers of neuroprotein. Our main takeaway from his imaginative (albeit ethnocentric) illustration is quite tangible – simulation is not the real thing. Merely shifting symbols around in a way that looks like (linguistic) understanding is not sufficient for it (Gunkel, 2017: 137). A computer, as Terry Winograd (1990: 187) reminds us, does not understand the linguistic tokens it processes, it merely "manipulates symbols without respect to their interpretation." "[S]ymbol manipulators do *not* understand the story" (Penrose, 1989: 25).

Discussion of the argument

What holds for Dreyfus, holds for Searle too. He was attacking a by now largely superseded understanding of AI, i.e., GOFAI. Nonetheless, the Chinese Room spawned a flourishing philosophical industry whose mills are still spinning merrily. Many readers acknowledged that Searle's empty-symbolism argument proved just what he said it proved, while not less saw it as fundamentally wrong-headed (Boden, 2015: 98). On top of that, those who saw it as going astray gave different accounts of just what was fatal with it, and to some Searle (2014) has replied too. This is not the place to summarize the ever-lengthening debate or to rehearse what is wrong with Searle's Chinese Room argument (for an account at length cf. Cole, 2020). Instead, we poke three holes in Searle's original argument (against the backdrop of our theory work from Part II) in the following and derive some learnings.

Firstly, we concord that understanding is indispensable for *SAI*: no *SAI* without understanding. We diverge from Searle (1980) though when it comes to the issue what understanding is. Searle's point is that the mere carrying out of a successful algorithm does *not* in itself imply that any understanding has taken place (Penrose, 1989: 24). Searle appears to take intentionality as the definitive mark of understanding and, ultimately, of intelligence. With this he is not alone. "Intentionality", said Franz Brentano (1874/1973), "is the mark of the mental". By this, he meant that everything mental has intentionality, and nothing else does (Haugeland, 1997b: 4). Yet, Searle appears to neglect that some philosophers have argued for intentionality to be grounded in our evolutionary history (Millikan, 1984). If that is so and since AI as a science is still in its infancy, only evolved AI systems and robots could even be candidates for the possession of intentionality (Boden, 2015: 99). Searle's point might thus be unfair and reliant on too strong assumptions.

We, by contrast, took another, earlier exit (out of the Searlian edifice) in this treatise by discarding the identification of understanding with intentionality right away because the latter presupposes that an agent possesses inner or mental states which would expel all foreseeable machines (and probably many animals) in the sense of different *kinds* of intelligence *ex ante*, i.e., on dogmatic grounds. If we embark on the endeavor of making sense of human, animal and machine intelligence with *pre*formed concepts (of understanding or intelligence for that matter) that are not even applicable to the objects of investigation, then the whole journey is thwarted before it has even begun. Furthermore, we argued that understanding is sufficient for intelligence, but not necessary; and, conversely, it is necessary for *SAI*, but not sufficient for it.

So, shall we just conclude that our and Searle's (1980) understanding of "understanding", and "intelligence", respectively, are incompatible since they rest on different foundations? Not really. It is neither prerequisite nor desirable to stop at that point, the latter not least due to the observation that "[u]nderstanding can still sound frighteningly unempirical and elusive" (Dehn & Schank, 1982: 365). The former as Searle (1984) suggests another reading of "understanding", namely understanding as semantics, which is in harmony with the Chinese Room argument and allows for a more revealing comparison with our reasoning. The reader surely presages that we would decline the premise based on this reading: in lieu of "syntax is not sufficient for semantics" (which is what the Chinese Room argument would assert), we proclaimed that "syntax can mirror semantics", that "syntax can constitute semantics". How? We specified this verdict in Chapter 5.1. by appealing to programming more causal learning competence into current AI systems (so that they reach the third levels in our universal taxonomy).

By this, we do not mean that mere *programs*, which are abstract computational objects and purely syntactic, are candidates for possession of comprehension. The crucial role of implementation has to be respected since implementations can have semantic content. Searle's Chinese Room argument "gains its purchase on our intuitions by implementing the program in a bizarre way that obscures the realization of the relevant causal dynamics [a sense of 'syntax', so to say, in which implementations are syntactic]" (Chalmers, 1996: 325). *Implementations of programs* are, by contrast, i.e., contra Searle's account, concrete systems with causal dynamics, and are not purely syntactic. In virtue of the causal heft of those implementations in the real world, comprehension can emerge, and we spelled out what requirements have to be met to make it happen. Focalizing thereby on the physical, organic and chemical structure ("the causal powers of *neuroprotein*") is chauvinistic. The crucial thing is a similarity of the internal structure, organizational structure, software (Hofstadter, 1981).

Understanding is not a matter of black and white, but, following the well-tested Darwinian perspective of gradualism, it comes in degrees. Understanding entails making inferences and results in the ability to make further inferences. There are, of course, a great many possible levels of understanding and, accordingly, different kinds of inference lead to different depths of understanding. So we have argued.

Secondly, even more from our today's standpoint in the midst of the predominance of machine and deep learning, Searle is attacking a straw man. Even though Newell & Simon (1963), as well as their GOFAI co-pioneers John McCarthy and Marvin Minsky, undoubtedly believed that AI systems of a certain complexity would be really *SAIs* (see the first pages in the Introduction to this overall book). Despite the apparent relevance of Searle's argument for at least those addressees, they did not have abstract, uninterpreted, Turing computation solely in mind, which holds even more for today's AI researchers. For example, Boden's (2015) sketch of Newell and Simon's semantic theory suggests that they were not primarily concerned with computation as uninterpreted Turing computation. What is more, other AI scientists, most notably Judea Pearl whose pathbreaking work directly fed into our framework, have offered causal (intentional) accounts of computation, sometimes explicitly denying that AI is mainly concerned with Turing computation (Sloman, 2002).

"One of the most notorious failures of the early days of computers was machine translation. [. . .] What the machine translation programs lacked [. . .] was any sense of the *meaning* of the texts they were translating" (Dehn & Schank, 1982: 366). GOFAIs like Weizenbaum's (1966) ELIZA, Winograd's (1972)

SHRDLU, or Schank & Abelson's (1977: 67) daring thesis that "most of understanding is script-based" set the stage for, and embed Searle's (1980) essay in in the historical context. Yet, today in the second wave, AI comprises different and more diverse architectures (not just symbolic and connectionist approaches, but also numerous more nuances), and deep learning is much more successful at machine translation. In nuce, "the [S]AI thesis is so plausible precisely because the class of computational systems is so wide" (Chalmers, 1996: 332). The trite homogeneity of AI systems of the past might have inspired or reinforced Searle, but how can he cope with the wild heterogeneity of systems that characterize the new paradigm? Is repeating the old message enough?

> First, a digital computer is a syntactical machine. It manipulates symbols and does nothing else. For this reason, the project of creating human intelligence by designing a computer program that will pass the Turing Test, the project I baptized years ago as Strong Artificial Intelligence (Strong AI), is doomed from the start. The appropriately programmed computer has a syntax but no semantics. (Searle, 2014: 3)

When we bemoaned in the introduction to Part III or in Chapter 3.1. that Alexa, Siri, and their relatives of the second AI wave do not know what they are talking about when they "tell" you about the weather forecast or about what wine goes with your meal – or to that matter, that their utterances matter only under interpretation by us –, then we are not referring to formality. Unlike Searle, we do not make the case that a formal system cannot have real semantics, since the interpretations are unanchored, and can be assigned at whim: "I would go to court to deny that the symbols in present day AI systems are 'formal' in [the Searlian] sense. Some contemporary systems, in particular, are plugged into the world in such a way that their symbols are unambiguously grounded." (Cantwell Smith, 2019: 79).

As a final upshot of the debate we wish to point out that at least some philosophers, being vocal about AI, lack the technical knowledge in computer science to assess the activities and progress in the field – closing the loop to the first pages of this book: "if there remain any philosophers who are not familiar with some of the main developments in artificial intelligence, it will be fair to accuse them of professional incompetence." To those who refuse to live in the present, they are more foolish commentators than experts. Then, against the principle of charity or of vouchsafing the benefit of a doubt, they simplistically take it for granted that all computation is Turing computation, and as such semantically empty; that there is erroneously just the abstract, in lieu of the implementations of programs where the implementation relation relates the abstract and concrete domains.

13 Closing remarks

The conclusion is that there appear to be neither enforcers of singularity *S* or strong AI *SAI*, nor any in-principle barriers to the ambitions of *SAI*. Philosophers looking for sound arguments find their attention lavished on contributions, above all, from the pro side of the contestation about *S* (i.e., Chapter 11). Even though the arguments by the opponents are not compelling either, their reasoning is at least not flatly invalid or amateurish. Still, their external vetos do not seem to carry much force. Their internal vetos may be more alarming, but none of the presented arguments for these vetos are persuasive on analysis. Two more final thoughts.

My own take on *S* and *SAI* is that I do not relegate the possibility that AI will eventually reach human or superhuman intelligences (Hoffmann, 2019e). However, I am also convinced that there will be no uncontrolled exponential growth. It is much more likely that we humans will have to program most of the intelligence into the AIs ourselves. Scientific knowledge, commonsense, education, and innate templates are all indispensable for achieving *SAI*.

Our experience with most AI systems so far suggests that the marginal yield is rapidly decreasing and frequent trend changes are taking place, which will not spare deep learning as one of the most popular and hyped applications of AI nowadays (Marcus, 2018). Initially, we pick all the low-hanging fruits (e.g., text translations with DeepL Translate) and generate progress swiftly, but then we run into difficulties: what about many many more use cases?

Maybe, global AI may improve infinitely, but to what extent its overall intelligence increases could be limited. If, for instance, each generation increases by 50% compared to the previous one, then, according to old insights such as from Zeno's "paradox" on Achilles and the tortoise, the initial intelligence can at most double, because the infinite sum adds up to a maximum of 2.

The declaration that *SAI* and *S can* happen concerns still most distant possible worlds and is rather uninteresting because it lacks operational significance. However, anything beyond is long on faith, and short on rigorous argument. If or when *SAI* and *S* occur, the face of the Earth will be radically different from today. For example, on the way there, will we have had AI-backed success in saving our planet (Dhar, 2020), success in achieving sustainability (Vinuesa et al., 2020), or "success" in developing increasingly autonomous AI-controlled weapon systems (Guersenzvaig, 2018; Scharre, 2016) to provoke the "intelligently programmed" extinction (Bull & Maron, 2016) of our own species? Perhaps, a bottom line can also be that, in lieu of dreaming of *SAI* and *S* while delegating more and more tasks to so-called intelligent machines in the here and now at the expense of letting our personal capabilities wither away (e.g., think of navigation computers vs. our own orientation skills), we ought to fight for our autonomy and use our natural, not artificial intelligences to tackle our real-world problems (Hoffmann, 2018c).

Highlights and key takeaways from Part IV

- The often nebulous terms "Strong AI" (*SAI*), "Superintelligence" (*SIAI*), "Singularity" (*S*), and "Artificial General Intelligence" (*AGI*) can be specified:
  - An AI agent X is a *SAI* if, and only if, X covers all seven levels of our causal hierarchy on a circumplex consisting of at least the four intelligences from Figure 29.
  - X is a *SIAI* if, and only if, X covers all seven levels of our causal hierarchy on a circumplex consisting of the four intelligences from Figure 29 and at least one additional and distinct intelligence on par with the four *or* only those four intelligences with a super-human performance for at least one of the four intelligences and no sub-human performance for any of the intelligences.
  - An event E qualifies as a singularity S if, and only if, *SAI* emerges in E and *SIAI* directly thereafter, whereby "directly" signifies that there is either a direct causal relationship or a short causal chain between *SAI* and *SIAI* in the sense that the former brings about the latter.
  - X is a *AGI* if, and only if, X is not a *SAI* and covers more than *one* intelligence for possibly varying causal learning capabilities.
- None of the six arguments portrayed and discussed is sound.
- Although the intelligence explosion and the speed explosion are logically independent of each other, speed matters for intelligence, but only in the *ceteris paribus* sense (see also our definition of *SIAI*): All other things being equal, the faster the test subject performs on an adequate task, the smarter she is.
- Computational capacities per se are irrelevant to the level of intelligence since agents' mere computational power leaves us in the dark about their causal learning capabilities.
- Intelligence and agents' final goals are at least sometimes independent variables.
- Once we see that Gödel's proof nurtures the notion that "a high-level view of a system may contain certain explanatory power which simply is absent on the low levels", then this reading is immediately reminiscent of our layered taxonomy of causal learning (5.1.).

- In light of the multidirectionality of intelligence, it resembles a hubris to think that (meta-)mathematics alone could determine what minds in general are (in-)capable of.
- When man is circumscribed as a *rational* animal, then this demagnifies man.
- The crucial role of the implementation of a program, which is a concrete system with causal dynamics, has to be respected since implementations can have semantic content.

Overall conclusion and some practical implications

Croyez ceux qui cherchent la vérité, doutez de ceux qui la trouvent   André Gide

We would like to close with this bon mot by the French author and laureate of the Nobel Prize in Literature in 1947 to appeal to more intellectual modesty in academia and AI in the sense of Sir Karl Popper. Even if the present treatment turns out to be only the prolegomenon to a universal theory of intelligence still to be created, it has served an honorable purpose to the extent that it nudged research in a promising direction. First impetus has been initiated when Part II of this book laid the cornerstone of a causal theory of intelligence.

The quest for a fundamental and universal theory of intelligence was triggered in *Part I* when we examined the many detailed similarities and differences between intelligent systems. We identified that psychology, anthropology or other individual disciplines trapped in silo thinking are not enough as the class of intelligent systems is not exhausted by the class of human beings. Analogously, animal cognition research is not enough for endowing a universal approach to determining intelligence as the class of intelligent systems might contain additional, non-biological elements which was canvassed and confirmed in Chapter 3. We embraced a systemic perspective early on since 1) it is not anthropomorphically biased which is key since human chauvinism turned out to be obsolete, 2) we found the systems metaphor of intelligence from Chapter 1 to be particularly fertile, and 3) it allowed us to realize both that the seat of intelligence is not within any system of an organism or artifact as well as that intelligence is determined by the dynamics of interaction with the world. With this systems lens, we explored the eight intelligences of human intelligence, case studies of animal intelligences, and dedicated the remainder to the more speculative question about intelligence in AI. We concluded by reasoning that numerous systems of new-fangled AI ought to be regarded as autonomous prediction machines and that some intelligence lies in those machines making predictions, because intelligence or competence do not presuppose comprehension.

The transition to *Part II* was smoothed by stressing that higher levels of intelligence tackle the question of why. Causality was rightly placed on a pedestal as the primary fountain of lending meaning to intelligence. Based on some concept clarifications, above all concerning "understanding", "agency", and "autonomy", Chapter 5 penetrated into the heart of the entire present treatment. Under its umbrella, the outline of a causal theory of intelligence, i.e., to appeal to causation in order to answer the question of what it is for someone or some animal or AI system to be intelligent, was compiled. Our core proposition turned out to be a composition of predominantly two pieces: An advancement of Pearl's preliminary work (from 4.3.) legitimates the universal claim of my project (in 5.1.). This hierarchy of causal learning, visualized as a simplex model of intelligence, endows the common denominator to capture and assess intelligence of all creatures, be it intelligence of humans, biological or artificial animals. However, if we had just left things like that, my approach would be plagued with the cardinal sin of a reductionism. As portrayed in Part I, intelligence is too multicolored to be squeezed in a static edifice. In order to do justice to this diversity, I argued that the flexible inverted radex model (from 5.2.) needs to be integrated to echo the multidirectionality of intelligence. Even though it proved to be a rather daunting exercise to account for the multidirectionality of different kinds of intelligences in a circumplex model, these efforts should not be eschewed by empirical sciences since they are offset by additional insights. Our theory, the synthesis of the universal taxonomy and the inverted radex model, was then further validated in Part III and IV.

In *Part III and IV*, we applied our theory to AI systems; first in terms of evaluating current and past AI agents, then in terms of evaluating hypotheses dealing with singularity and strong AI. With the evaluation of machine intelligence as the overarching guideline for Part III, we were entering the land of AI test procedures, broaching the research gap that there is no general methodology for AI evaluation. We revisited the Turing Test, highlighted common pitfalls, and signposted how and what we would respond to the human judges in the test from our perspective taken in Part II. Finally, we brought forward our own constructive solution in terms of a recommended redesign of a test of machine intelligence in the final Chapter 10. Thus, a measure or test of (machine) intelligence ought to be non-binary, empirical, specific, relevant, expansive (for the specified scope), repeatable, non-anthropomorphic, unpredictable, solvable by exemplars, and lead to actionable as well as thriving research. Some of the six arguments outlined in Part IV have led to thriving research, e.g., in terms of helping overcome deficiencies of GOFAI. For underpinning the plausibility, and impossibility of *SAI*, respectively, they have not succeeded though. We have adopted the perspective of our causal theory and, through that lens, responded to each of the arguments in Part IV critically. At the same time, this disclosed how our proposal for this theory of intelligence could handle objections from those sides.

In Part III and IV, we asked ourselves how high machines can ascend in our causal hierarchy (in principle) if broad and multiple intelligences are required. There is a plethora of related questions that are reserved for future avenues for research such as: How high should we want them to rise (AI safety research)? At what point in the hierarchy should they be granted rights (applied ethics)? At what point will a mind with consciousness be manufactured (philosophy of mind)? What kind of machine agencies will succeed in our societies (which is, among others, a question for economics)? If we want AI systems to understand, how do we enable them to distinguish the actual, the possible, and the impossible – causal truths, falsehood, and logical impossibilities (a question for philosophical AI)? And who is *we* (sociology)? Or human for that matter (the central question addressed in Grunwald, 2021a)?

The time of pure ivory tower philosophy is over (cf. also Grunwald, 2021b: 118). After the linguistic and conceptual turn, at least analytic philosophy in the melting pot with neighboring disciplines such as, in our case, neuroscience, psychology and AI has to step down on the battlefield to test some of its propositions. (A predestined one in our context could be what we proposed about the status of musical intelligence in Part I.) The absence of a solid fundamental explication of almost ubiquitous intelligence in the philosophical literature is not merely an abstract ivory tower issue. Having a lucid understanding is a superordinate requirement for reflective action and strategic planning. Without a well-thought notion of intelligence and approaches for explaining, measuring and managing it, we would only tolerate the veritable risk of groping blindly after often ill-conceived solutions to possibly misdiagnosed ailments.

For instance, in our era of the second machine age (Brynjolfsson & McAfee, 2014), much in our lives, including our lives (Hoffmann, 2019f), hinges on well-functioning AI machines. Without a fundamental theory of intelligence, we might stay stuck in the fallacy of confusing our with their intelligence. If we continue to interpret them, present-day AI machines, *as if they were* (more than level one) intelligent, as if they could understand what they do, and, ultimately, bear responsibility for their actions, then we decide to trust brittle systems. This can, and already has provoked a lot of harm. Or as I put it in a newspaper article: How can we have very strict rules for drug testing or air travelling in place, but, without a second thought, step into "self-driving cars", under the fatal impression that they are genuinely intelligent, and then take the very next exit to our grave as deadly Uber or Tesla crashes have shown (Hoffmann, 2018b)?

Or to paraphrase Immanuel Kant, concepts without data are empty; data without concepts are blind; "only through their unison can knowledge [not to say wisdom] arise" (Kant, 1787/1997: 75). More systematically, here are a few more implications from our work.

Ethical deliberations

The gravity of the stakes, as for instance clarified by Hoffmann's (2018b) example, suggests addressing some foundational questions such as: What lies beyond the line of possibility, so that we can give up longing for it? Where are we now and where are our creations? How will we want – how should we want – to live with other forms of intelligence, including not just products of natural evolution, but entities of our own devising, and eventually of theirs as well?

Against this background, a more pressing need to parse *AI risks and ethics* arises. A crucial aspect of determining the risk of AI technology (present and future) is a proper measurement of its capabilities. Only a system of genuine intelligence can truly shoulder responsibility for its actions and deliberations. As I argued elsewhere (Hoffmann, 2019f), any presently constructable AI system cannot not be considered a moral agent, the "autonomous" vehicle should not bear (co-)responsibility for the accident it causes (cf. also Heil, 2021: 425). An ethical stance can be shouldered only by a system capable of genuine or level three intelligence (not in the sense of CLEAR from 5.2., but in the sense of a *SAI* which, on top of the intellectual abilities, has goals, preferences, rationality, and perhaps even consciousness; thus a very small subset of *SAI*).

From academic to technical to entrepreneurial aspects . . .

There is a lot of philosophical reasoning involved in being a cutting-edge investigator in AI (Frankish & Ramsey, 2015: 3). Modern science, and this time I wish to include philosophy, is not content with creating theories. It uses these theories in order to acquire new powers, and in particular to devise new technologies. In 1620, the philosopher of nature Francis Bacon published a scientific manifesto titled *The New Instrument*. In it he contended that "knowledge is power". The real test of knowledge is then not whether it is true, but – and here I speak more as a successful entrepreneur than as an academic – whether it empowers us.

Concededly, AI's primary concern with (human) intelligence is a different concern from what is studied in philosophy and psychology under that name. AI is probably concerned most with the operation of (human or animal) intelligence – with how intelligence *works* and, therefore, less with what it is. But, AI does not mean magic bullets. As in most fields of intellectual endeavor, there is no substitute for hard work and understanding. There are no tidy demarcations between, say, programming understanding and philosophical work on comprehension and intelligence. If we are to get (strong) AI to work, it will be simply by a) understanding intelligence and then b) programming the computer accordingly. Thus, first we ought to understand and fathom the richness of the concept of intelligence before we can develop, reproduce and create intelligence artificially or technically. This has been underestimated in the past, but addressed now. Therefore, an agenda can be derived with a glorious, yet operationalizable goal along a motto at DeepMind Technologies: "Solve intelligence, and then use intelligence to solve everything else". (While we fear that it has been overpromising a bit – problems are often political rather than purely technical – we can accept the sentiment.)

Quo vadis AI? What would be a realistic and concrete route forward for AI? That is not for me to say. I lack the expertise for such guidance and, even if it was any different, it would not be my aim to bring the imagination and creativity of AI designers, which is decentralized by nature (Schumpeter, 1954/1994), to a halt. The basic punch line from my research is simply to move from data-driven to theory-driven AI, the next great leap in AI.

. . . and back

The recent intricacies in AI, rather than reflecting technological limitations, could also unveil the limitations of technology. The value proposition does hold both ways, not just that AI researchers, engineers, and entrepreneurs can learn from fundamental and conceptual research, but also, vice versa in the spirit of Newell & Simon (1976/1997b), scientists and philosophers ought to involve AI engineering since the building of programs is of methodological value, as a scientific instrument for the refinement and debugging of theories of intelligence (Dehn & Schank, 1982: 356). For example, the very writing of the program reveals clandestine assumptions and paucity of clarity in the underlying theory. Hence, it indicates where further thought is needed, pointing to one of the reasons why we included Chapter 6. Or the program, once written, can serve as experimental apparatus to "try the theory out" and explore its explanatory power. Maybe AI in this sense is therefore not about anything artificial but is simply about intelligence.

It is now time to consider the challenge of AI in another broader context, in a final break-out session. By bringing in my knowledge from economics (in academia and practice), we would like to orient ourselves in the strategic landscape of the future labor markets.

Break-out session 6

The future of work: Simple economics of AI revisited and AI in the labor market

Almost 100 years ago, Keynes (1931) already predicted that computers would one day do all jobs. 46 years later, Simon (1977) spread optimism about human employment in the face of AI. He was not envisioning the Keynesian land of milk and honey, but believed that in light of the truth of the subsequent equation, humans would not be disemployed by AI:

$$E: r_w * t_w + (1 + r_i) * c_{1uo} = 1$$

where r_w is the human labor wage rate, t_w the average human labor time needed to produce one unit of output, r_i the interest rate, and c_{1uo} the average capital necessitated to produce one unit of output. Given **E**, the occasion of Simon's optimism is easy to state. AI and thus automation serves to lower t_w, and that as long as r_i remains essentially constant (which is a different story nowadays), human wages, as a matter of ironclad arithmetic using **E**, will continue to rise (Bringsjord & Bringsjord, 2017: 105).

Also with *SAI* on the horizon for some researchers like Bostrom (2016: 197), the future looks bright. If we classify AI as capital, then with the invention of *SAI* that can wholly substitute for human work, wages would fall to the marginal cost of such machine-substitutes, which – under the reasonable assumption that the machines would be very efficient – would be very low, far below human subsistence-level income. Yet, as long as humans own those machines, *those* humans' total income from capital would skyrocket. Either way, we find this sanguinity quite problematic due to the more fine-grained AI landscape we painted in the previous chapters.

In demarcation to all three scenarios (from Keynes, Simon, and Bostrom), the useful mission for future policies and for a better understanding of the skills that are going to be substituted by AI is to determine the likelihood that a job will vanish in 10, 20 or 50 years. For example, Frey & Osborne (2013: 1) estimated "the probability of computerisation for 702 detailed occupations". What do the findings of this study contribute to this quest?

Familiar AI of the second wave makes some people rich that know how to "employ" those *tools* (e.g., machine learning hedge funds; Hoffmann & Müller, 2019) or develop *and* employ AI-based tools (in startups some of which I co-founded); others, however, are said to be knocked out (Frey & Osborne, 2013) which, above all, concerns human jobs that do not involve much judgment or empathy or which are not genuinely creative; but jobs which are of this type will be, so the narrative "man vs. machine" goes, stalwart as granite for the foreseeable future.

Apart from new kinds of "applicants" and "workers" and "employees" (AI also as "employers"?, cf. Hoffmann & Dahlinger, 2020), we ought to think of new kinds of *ecosystems* (Hoffmann, 2019c) with hybrid teamwork, not AI as external rivals to whom human agency must either passively succumb or furiously resist. For the time being, AIs are extensions of ourselves for which we are, and shall remain, responsible – even in cases where we no longer direct or even fully comprehend their cognitive processes (which might have been irresponsible of us, their developers, designers, users, owners, in the first place). In sum, we cannot imagine AI excelling at any time in the near future due to our previous findings:
- AIs replace humans for certain specified *tasks*, not jobs which are made up of plenty of partially fuzzy and altering tasks.

- To put it bluntly, any current AI cannot fully compensate *any* human profession (from dishwashers to hedge fund managers) since the latter necessitates level 3 learning capabilities, and multiple intelligences in lieu of insular proficiencies on level 1 (on top of non-intellectual features for taking responsibility).
- This does not entail that some jobs will not disappear (efflorescence of work) or that their description changes or that new job profiles will be created in the wake of AI. But this is really not an AI-specific phenomenon. Under the names of "efficiency seeking", "rationalization", "automatization" or "entrepreneur-ship" it has been around for longer than the term AI.
- If we follow, for the sake of argument, Bostrom to his wonderland, then we could oppose that it is far from certain that certain human groups would benefit from AIs' rise in the labor market. Rather, we would envision decentralized autonomous self-owned businesses (Hoffmann & Dahlinger, 2020).

Related to this excursus, we look forward to a co-evolution of human-machine environments where
- human and animal intelligence are more appreciated and respected to counterbalance the AI hype;
- academic studies, including PhDs, will become a less important qualification and skill in the future [ok, "looking forward" is presumably an outlandish predicate in this context although I am not willing to write another PhD thesis];
- specialized and textbook knowledge will be mastered by specialized machines;
- what is academically difficult can more easily be solved by AIs;
- (street) smartness, emotional and social intelligence will be key for humans by contrast;
- everyday intelligence will become more esteemed;
- intelligence among humans is reevaluated.

Already one of the intellectual fathers of AI, Marvin Minsky, appreciated the immense capabilities of our human brains (and that despite all the enthusiasm around AI in the early decades): "In general, we're least aware of what our minds do best" (Minsky, 1988: 29).

> Why could we make programs do grown-up things before we could make them do childish things? The answer may seem paradoxical: much of 'expert' adult thinking is actually simpler than what is involved when ordinary children play! [. . .] To be considered an 'expert', one needs a large amount of knowledge of only a relatively few varieties. In contrast, an ordinary person's 'common sense' involves a much larger variety of different *types* of knowledge – and this requires more complicated management systems.
>
> (Minsky, 1988: 72)

There remain a raft of puzzles, pitfalls and shortfalls that must be addressed. Most certainly the chapters in this book posed more questions than they answered, but this is of virtue to the extent that new questions will have advanced the thinking. Moreover, it is in harmony with the infancy of the research field the chapters represented. We harbor the hope that the ingredients outlined in this book will prove useful for working toward a more elaborate account of a universal (causal) theory of intelligence. Progress is likely to be slow and painstaking for some time. But, if indeed there is an analogy between our project and the career of causal modeling endeavors as well as linguistics, from the early days of Chomsky's generative grammar through the contemporary computational era, then we may look forward to a most interesting journey.

The great enterprise for the future is the construction of a benchmark that could advance our principled approach while we embrace whatever refutations or alternatives may come, so long as they do not place the loud-mouthed or offloading ape, again, as the measure of fully fledged intelligence.

References

Adams, R.A., Shipp, S., & Friston, K.J. 2013. Predictions not commands: Active inference in the motor system. Brain Structure and Function, 218: 611–643.
Adams, S.S., Arel, I., Bach, J., Coop, R., Furlan, R., Goertzel, B., Hall, J.S., Samsonovich, A., Scheutz, M., Schlesinger, M., Shaprio, S.C., & Sowa, J. 2012. Mapping the landscape of human-level artificial general intelligence. AI Magazine, 33: 25–42.
Agrawal, A., Gans, J., & Goldfarb, A. 2018. Prediction machines. The simple economics of Artificial Intelligence, Boston: Harvard Business Review Press.
Ahrens, M.B. 2015. Whole brain neuroimaging and virtual reality. In. G. Marcus, & J. Freeman (Eds.). The future of the brain. Oxford: Princeton University Press: 17–24.
Allen, C. 2018. Associative Learning. In. K. Andrews & J. Beck (Eds.). The Routledge Handbook of Philosophy of Animal Minds. New York City, NY: Routledge: 401–408.
Amir, E. 2015. Reasoning and decision making. In. K. Frankish, & W.M. Ramsey. (Eds.). The Cambridge Handbook of Artificial Intelligence. Cambridge: Cambridge University Press: 191–212.
Anderson, R.C., & Mather, J.A. 2010. It's all in the cues: Octopuses (Enteroctopus dofleini) learn to open jars. Ferrantia, 59, 8–13.
Anderson, J.R. 1993. Rules of the mind. Hillsdale, NJ: Erlbaum.
Anderson, M. 1992. Intelligence and development. A cognitive theory. Oxford: Blackwell.
Andrews, K., & Beck, J. 2018. Introduction. In. K. Andrews & J. Beck (Eds.). The Routledge Handbook of Philosophy of Animal Minds. New York City, NY: Routledge: 1–10.
Andrews, K. 2015. The Animal Mind. Abingdon: Routledge.
Anscombe, G.E.M. 1971. Causality and Determination. Cambridge: Cambridge University Press.
Applewhite, P. 1975. Learning in bacteria, fungi, and plants. Invertebrate Learning, 3: 179–186.
Arkoudas, K., & Bringsjord, S. 2015. Philosophical foundations. In. K. Frankish, & W.M. Ramsey. (Eds.). The Cambridge Handbook of Artificial Intelligence. Cambridge: Cambridge University Press: 34–63.
Arp, R., Smith, B., & Spear, A.D. 2015. Building Ontologies with Basic Formal Ontology. Cambridge, MA: MIT Press.
Ashby, W.R. 1956. An Introduction to Cybernetics. London: John Wiley & Sons.
Axelrod, R. 1984. The Evolution of Cooperation. New York City, NY: Basic Books.
Ayer, A. 1952. Language, Truth, and Logic. New York: Dover.
Balaban, M., Ebcioğlu, K., & Laske, O. 1992. Introduction. In. M. Balaban, K. Ebcioğlu, & O. Laske (Eds.). Understanding Music with AI: Perspectives on Music Cognition. Cambridge, MA: MIT Press: xxxi–xxxviii.
Barber, K.S., & Martin, C.E. 2001. Dynamic Adaptive Autonomy in Multiagent Systems: Representation and Justification. International Journal of Pattern Recognition and Artificial Intelligence, 15: 405–433.
Barlas, Y. 1996. Formal Aspects of Model Validity and Validation in System Dynamics. System Dynamics Review, 12: 183–210.
Barlas, Y., & Carpenter, S. 1990. Philosophical roots of model validation: two paradigms. System Dynamics Review, 6: 148–166.

Barnosky, A.D. 2008. Megafauna Biomass Tradeoff as a Driver of Quaternary and Future Extinctions. Proceedings of the National Academy of Sciences of the United States of America, 105: 11543–11548.

Baron, I.S., & Leonberger, K.A. 2012. Assessment of intelligence in the preschool period. Neuropsychology Review, 22: 334–344.

Baum, S. 2018. Superintelligence skepticism as a political tool. Information, 9: 209.

Beall, J., Glanzberg, M., & Ripley, D. 2016. Liar Paradox. In. E.N. Zalta (Ed.). Stanford Encyclopedia of Philosophy, https://plato.stanford.edu/entries/liar-paradox/ (08-01-2021).

Beck, J. 2018. Do nonhuman animals have a language of thought? In. K. Andrews & J. Beck (Eds.). The Routledge Handbook of Philosophy of Animal Minds. New York City, NY: Routledge: 45–55.

Bedau, M.A. 2015. Artificial life. In. K. Frankish, & W.M. Ramsey. (Eds.). The Cambridge Handbook of Artificial Intelligence. Cambridge: Cambridge University Press: 296–315.

Beebee, H., Hitchcock, C., & Menzies, P. (Eds.). 2009. The Oxford Handbook of Causation. Oxford. Oxford University Press.

Beebee, H. 2009. Causation and Observation. In. H. Beebee, C. Hitchcock, & P. Menzies (Eds.). The Oxford Handbook of Causation. Oxford. Oxford University Press: 471–497.

Benacerraf, P. 1967. God, the Devil, and Gödel. The Monist, LI, 1: 9–32.

Ben-Jacob, E. 2009. Learning from bacteria about natural information processing. Annals of the New York Academy of Sciences, 1178: 78–90.

Ben-Jacob, E. 2008. Social behavior of bacteria: From physics to complex organization. European Physical Journal B, 65: 315–322.

Benson-Amram, S., Dantzer, B., Stricker, G., Swanson, E.M., & Holekamp, K.E. 2016. Brain size predicts problem-solving ability in mammalian carnivores. Proceedings of the National Academy of Sciences, 113: 2352–2357.

Berger, M. 1982. The „scientific approach" to intelligence: An overview of its history with special references to mental speed. In. H.J. Eysenck (Ed.). A model for intelligence. Berlin: Springer: 13–43.

Berlin, I. 1953/1999. The Hedgehog And The Fox: An Essay on Tolstoy's View of History. London: Orion Books.

Berto, F. 2011. There's Something About Gödel: The Complete Guide to the Incompleteness Theorem, London: Wiley-Blackwell.

Bhatnagar, S. et al. 2018. Mapping Intelligence: Requirements and Possibilities. In. V.C. Müller (Ed.). Philosophy and Theory of Artificial Intelligence. PT-AI 2017. Studies in Applied Philosophy, Epistemology and Rational Ethics, 44. Cham, CH: Springer.

Bird, C.D., & Emery, N.J. 2009. Rooks use stones to raise the water level to reach a floating worm. Current Biology, 19: 1410–1414.

Blaisdell, A.P., Sawa, K., Leising, K.J., & Waldmann, M.R. 2006. Causal reasoning in rats. Science, 311: 1020–1022.

Block, N. 2015. Consciousness, big science, and conceptual clarity. In. G. Marcus, & J. Freeman (eds.). The future of the brain. Oxford: Princeton University Press: 161–176.

Block, N. 1990. The computer model of the mind. In. D. Thinking, N. Osherson, & H. Lasnik (Eds.). An Invitation to Cognitive Science, Vol. 3. Cambridge, MA: MIT Press.

Block, N. 1981. Psychologism and behaviorism. Philosophical Review, 90: 5–43.

Block, N. 1978. Troubles with functionalism. In. C.W. Savage (Ed.). Perception and Cognition: Issues in the Foundations of Psychology. Minneapolis, MN: University of Minneapolis Press: 261–325.

Boal, J.G., Dunham, A.W., Williams, K.T., & Hanlon, R.T. 2000. Experimental evidence for spatial learning in octopuses (Octopus bimaculoides). Journal of Comparative Psychology, 114, 246–252.

Boden, M.A. 2015. GOFAI. In. K. Frankish, & W.M. Ramsey. (Eds.). The Cambridge Handbook of Artificial Intelligence. Cambridge: Cambridge University Press: 89–107.

Booch, G., Fabiano, F., Horesh, L., Kate, K., Lenchner, J., Linck, N., Loreggia, A., Murugesan, K., Mattei, N., Rossi, F., & Srivastava, B. 2020. Thinking Fast and Slow in AI. arXiv:2010.06002.

Bostrom, N. 2016. Superintelligence: Paths, Dangers, Strategies. Oxford: Oxford University Press.

Boyd, R., Richerson, P., & Henrich, J. 2011. The cultural niche: Why social learning is essential for human adaptation. Proceedings of the National Academy of Sciences of the United States of America, 108: 10918–10925.

Boyle, M. 2018. A different kind of mind? In. K. Andrews & J. Beck (Eds.). The Routledge Handbook of Philosophy of Animal Minds. New York City, NY: Routledge: 109–118.

Bregman, R. 2020. Humankind. A Hopeful History. London: Bloomsbury.

Brentano, F. 1874/1973. Psychology from an empirical standpoint. Leipzig: Duncker and Humblot. Translation by A.C. Rancurello, D.B. Terrell, & L.L. McAlister. London: Routledge.

Bringsjord, S., & Govindarajulu, N.S. 2018. Artificial Intelligence. In. E.N. Zalta (Ed.). Stanford Encyclopedia of Philosophy, https://plato.stanford.edu/entries/artificial-intelligence/ (30-08-2020).

Bringsjord, S., & Bringsjord, A. 2017. The Singularity Business. Toward a realistic, fine-grained economics for an AI-infused world. In. T.M. Powers (Ed.). Philosophy and Computing. Essays in Epistemology, Philosophy of Mind, Logic, and Ethics. New York City, NY: Springer: 99–119.

Bringsjord, S., Bringsjord, A., & Bello, P. 2012a. On Schmidhuber's "New Millennium AI and the Convergence of History 2012". In. A.H. Eden, J.H. Moor, J.H. Søraker, & E. Steinhart (Eds.). Singularity Hypotheses: A Scientific and Philosophical Assessment, New York, NY: Springer: 81–82.

Bringsjord, S., Bringsjord, A., & Bello, P. 2012b. Belief in The Singularity is Fidestic. In. A.H. Eden, J.H. Moor, J.H. Søraker, & E. Steinhart (Eds.). Singularity Hypotheses: A Scientific and Philosophical Assessment, New York, NY: Springer: 395–408.

Bringsjord, S. 2009. If I Were Judge. In. R. Epstein, G. Roberts, G. Beber (Eds.). Parsing the Turing Test. Philosophical and Methodological Issues in the Quest for the Thinking Computer. Heidelberg: Springer: 89–102.

Brockman, J. 2015. What do you think about machines that think? Annual question. Edge.org. Available at: https://www.edge.org/annual-question/what-do-you-think-about-machines-that-think (25-11-20).

Brooks, R. 1991/1997. Intelligence without Representation. In. J. Haugeland (Ed.). Mind design II. Philosophy, Psychology, Artificial Intelligence. Cambridge, MA: MIT Press: 395–420.

Brooks, R. 1997. From earwigs to humans. Robotics and Autonomous Systems, 20: 291–304.

Brooks, R. 1991. Intelligence without reason. MIT Artificial Intelligence Laboratory Memo 1293.

Brooks, R. 1986. A robust layered control system for a mobile robot, IEEE. Journal of Robotics and Automation, 2: 14–23.

Broome, J. 1991. Rationality and the Sure Thing-Principle. In. J.G. Meeks (Ed.). Thoughtful Economic Man: Essays on Rationality, Moral Rules and Benevolence. Cambridge: Cambridge University Press: 74–102.

Brown, R.L. 2018. Animal Traditions: What they are, and why they matter. In. K. Andrews & J. Beck (Eds.). The Routledge Handbook of Philosophy of Animal Minds. New York City, NY: Routledge: 362–371.

Brown, T.B. et al. 2020. Language models are few-shot learners. arXiv 2005.14165.

Brynjolfsson, E., & McAfee, A. 2014. The second machine age. Work, progress, and prosperity in a time of brilliant technologies. New York City, NY: Norton.

Bull, J.W., & Maron, M. 2016. How humans drive speciation as well as extinction. Proceedings of the Royal Society of London Series B: Biological Sciences, 283: 20160600.

Burt, A. 2020. How to Fight Discrimination in AI. Harvard Business Review. August 28. Available at: https://hbr.org/2020/08/how-to-fight-discrimination-in-ai (07-02-21).

Cacchione, T., Call, J., & Zingg, R. 2009. Gravity and solidity in four great ape species (Gorilla gorilla, Pongo pygmaeus, Pan troglodytes, Pan paniscus): vertical and horizontal variations of the table task. Journal of Comparative Psychology, 123: 168–180.

Camp, E., & Shupe, E. 2018. Instrumental Reasoning in Nonhuman Animals. In. K. Andrews & J. Beck (Eds.). The Routledge Handbook of Philosophy of Animal Minds. New York City, NY: Routledge: 100–108.

Cantwell Smith, B. 2019. The promise of artificial intelligence. London: MIT Press.

Carroll, J. 2003. Making Exclusion Matter Less. Unpublished manuscript (available upon request).

Cartwright, N. 1983. How the Laws of Physics Lie. Oxford: Clarendon.

Cave, S., Dihal, K., & Dillon, S. 2020. Introduction: Imaging AI. In. S. Cave et al. (Eds.). AI Narratives. A History of Imaginative Thinking about Intelligent Machines. Oxford: Oxford University Press: 1–21.

Cave, S. 2017. What the octopus tells us about human intelligence. Financial Times, March 14. Available at: https://www.ft.com/content/9949c9a6-04b5-11e7-aa5b-6bb07f5c8e12 (12-11-20).

Chalmers, D.J. 2010. The Singularity: A Philosophical Analysis. Journal of Consciousness Studies, 17: 7–65.

Chalmers, D.J. 1996. The Conscious Mind. In Search of a Fundamental Theory. Oxford: Oxford University Press.

Chalmers, D.J. 1995. Minds, Machines, and Mathematics: A Review of Shadows of the Mind by Roger Penrose. Journal Psyche, II: 11–20.

Chappell, B. 2015. Winner Of French Scrabble Title Does Not Speak French. npr. July 21. Available at: https://www.npr.org/sections/thetwo-way/2015/07/21/424980378/winner-of-french-scrabble-title-does-not-speak-french?t=1612259812093 (02-02-21).

Chomsky, N. 2009a. A Conversation About Multiple Intelligences / An Interview with Noam Chomsky. In: MI at 25: Assessing the Impact and Future of Multiple Intelligences for Teaching and Learning: New York: Teachers College Press.

Chomsky, N. 2009b. Turing on the "Imitation Game". In. R. Epstein, G. Roberts, G. Beber (Eds.). Parsing the Turing Test. Philosophical and Methodological Issues in the Quest for the Thinking Computer. Heidelberg: Springer: 103–106.

Chomsky, N. 1956. Three models for the description of language. IRE Transactions on Information Theory, 2: 113–124.

Chomsky, N. 1962. Explanatory models in linguistics. In. E. Nagel, P. Suppes, & A. Tarski (Eds.). Logic, Methodology, and Philosophy of Science. Stanford: Stanford University Press: 528–550.

Christiansen, M.H., & Kirby, S. (Eds.). 2003. Language evolution. Oxford: Oxford University Press.

Clark, A. 2016. Surfing Uncertainty. Prediction, Action, And the Embodied Mind. Oxford: Oxford University Press.

Clark, A. 2003. Natural-Born Cyborgs. Oxford: Oxford University Press.

Clark, A., & Chalmers, D.J. 1998. The Extended Mind. Analysis, 58: 10–23.

Clark, M.H. 2010. Cognitive Illusions and the Lying Machine: A Blueprint for Sophistic Mendacity. PhD dissertation. Rensselaer Polytechnic Institute (Cognitive Science).

Cohen, P.R. 2005. If not Turing's test, then what? AI Magazine, 26: 61.

Cole, D. 2020. The Chinese Room Argument. In. E.N. Zalta (Ed.). Stanford Encyclopedia of Philosophy. URL: https://plato.stanford.edu/entries/chinese-room/ (25-02-2021).

Collingwood, R. 1940. An essay on metaphysics. Oxford: Clarendon Press.

Collins, C.E., Turner, E.C., Sawyer, E.K., Reed, J.L., Young, N.A., Flaherty, D.K., & Kaas, J.H. 2016. Cortical cell and neuron density estimates in one chimpanzee hemisphere.

Collins, J., Hall, N., & Paul, L.A. 2004. Causation and Counterfactuals. Cambridge, MA: MIT Press.

Copeland, J., & Proudfoot, D. 2009. Turing's Test. A Philosophical and Historical Guide. In. R. Epstein, G. Roberts, G. Beber (Eds.). Parsing the Turing Test. Philosophical and Methodological Issues in the Quest for the Thinking Computer. Heidelberg: Springer: 119–138.

Copeland, J. 1993. Artificial intelligence. A philosophical introduction. Oxford: Blackwell.

Criddle, C. 2020. MeowTalk: Alexa developer's app to translate cat's miaow. BBC News. 18 November. Available at: https://www.bbc.com/news/technology-54991693 (18-01-21).

Crocco, G., van Atten, M., Cantu, P., & Engelen, E-M. 2017. Kurt Gödel Maxims and Philosophical Remarks Volume X. hal-01459188.

Crosby, M. 2020. Building Thinking Machines by Solving Animal Cognition. Minds and Machines, 30: 589–615.

Crosby, M., Beyret, B., & Halina, M. 2019. The Animal-AI Olympics. Nature Machine Intelligence: 1: 257.

Danks, D. 2015. Learning. In. K. Frankish, & W.M. Ramsey. (Eds.). The Cambridge Handbook of Artificial Intelligence. Cambridge: Cambridge University Press: 151–167.

DARPA (Defense Advanced Research Projects Agency). 2019. AI Next Campaign. Available at: https://www.darpa.mil/work-with-us/ai-next-campaign (11-12-20).

Darwiche, A. 2017. Human-Level Intelligence or Animal-Like Abilities? Available at: https://arxiv.org/pdf/1707.04327.pdf (25-09-2020).

Darwin, C. 1871. The descent of man and selection in relation to sex. 2nd edition. New York City, NY: D. Appleton.

Davidson, J.E., & Downing, C.L. 2000. Contemporary Models of Intelligence. In. R.J. Sternberg (Ed.). Handbook of Intelligence. Cambridge: Cambridge University Press: 34–49.

Davidson, D. 1963/1980. Actions, reasons and causes. In. D. Davidson (Ed.). Essays on Actions and Events. Oxford: Oxford University Press.

D'Avila Garcez, A.S., & Besold, T.R. 2019. Neural-Symbolic Learning and Reasoning (NeSy'18). IfCoLog Journal of Logics and their Applications, 6: 609–610.

Dawkins, R. 1986. The Blind Watchmaker: Why the Evidence of Evolution Reveals a Universe without Design. London: Norton & Company.
Dawkins, R. 1976. The selfish gene. New York City: Oxford University Press.
Deary, I.J. 2012. Intelligence. Annual Review of Psychology, 63: 453–482.
Deese, J. (1993). Human abilities versus intelligence. Intelligence 17, 107–116.
Dehn, N., & Schank, R. 1982. Artificial and human intelligence. In. R.J. Sternberg (Ed.). Handbook of Human Intelligence. Cambridge: Cambridge University Press: 225–307.
Dennett, D.C. 2017. From bacteria to Bach and back. The evolution of minds. London: Penguin.
Dennett, D.C. 1998. Artificial Life as Philosophy. In his Brainchildren: Essays on Designing Minds, Cambridge, MA: MIT Press: 261–263.
Dennett, D.C. 1996. Kinds of Minds. Toward and Understanding of Consciousness. New York City, NY: Basic Books.
Dennett, D.C. 1989. The Intentional Stance. Cambridge, MA: Bradford Books.
Dennett, D.C. 1984. Can machines think? In. M.G. Shafto (Ed.). How We Know. New York City, NY: Harper & Row.
Dennett, D.C. 1982. Reflections on "The Turing Test: A Coffeehouse Conversation". In. D.R. Hofstadter, & D.C. Dennett (Eds.). The Mind's I. Fantasies and Reflections on Self and Soul. New York City, NY: Bantam Books: 92–95.
Dennett, D.C. 1981. Three Kinds of Intentional Psychology. In. R. Healey (Ed.). Reduction, Time and Reality. Cambridge: Cambridge University Press: 37–60.
Dennett, D.C. 1979. Brainstorms. Philosophical essays on mind and psychology. Hassocks, Essex: Harvester Press.
Descartes, R. 1637/1911. In. E. Haldane, & G.R.T. Ross. Translators & editors. The Philosophical Works of Descartes, Volume 1, Cambridge: Cambridge University Press.
Descartes, R. 1637/1997. Discours de la méthode. Französisch-Deutsch. Ed. and transl. by L. Gäbe. Hamburg: Meiner.
Dhar, P. 2020. The carbon impact of artificial intelligence. Nature Machine Intelligence, 2: 423–425.
Diamond, J. 1992. The Third Chimpanzee. The Evolution and Future of the Human Animal. New York City, NY: HarperCollins Publishers.
Donald, M. 2012. Evolutionary origins of autobiographical memory: a retrieval hypothesis. In. D. Berntsen, & D. Rubin (Eds.). Understanding autobiographical memory: theories and approaches. Cambridge: Cambridge University Press: 269–289.
D'Onfro, J. 2019. AI 50: America's Most Promising Artificial Intelligence Companies. Forbes. Sept. 17. Available at: https://www.forbes.com/sites/jilliandonfro/2019/09/17/ai-50-americas-most-promising-artificial-intelligence-companies/?sh=4b07c040565c (07-12-20).
Dowe, D.L., & Hájek, A.R. 1997. A computational extension to the Turing test. Proceedings of the 4th Conference of the Australasian Cognitive Science Society. University of Newcastle, NSW, Australia.
Dowe, D.L. 1992. Wesley Salmon's Process Theory of Causality and the Conserved Quantity Theory. Philosophy of Science, 59: 195–216.
Dretske, F. 1988. Explaining Behavior. Reasons in a World of Causes. Cambridge, MA: MIT Press.
Dreyfus, H.L. 1999. What Computers Still Can't Do. 6th edition. Cambridge, MA: MIT Press.
Dreyfus, H.L. & Dreyfus, S., 1987, Mind Over Machine: The Power of Human Intuition and Expertise in the Era of the Computer, New York City, NY: Free Press.

Dreyfus, H.L. 1979/1997. From Micro-Worlds to Knowledge Representation: AI at an Impasse. In. J. Haugeland (Ed.). Mind Design II: Philosophy, Psychology, and Artificial Intelligence. Cambridge, MA: Bradford Books: 143–182.
Dreyfus, H.L. 1965. Alchemy and Artificial Intelligence. Santa Monica, CA: Rand Corporation, Research Report P-3244. December.
Dummett, M. 1976. What is a theory of meaning (II). In. G. Evans, & J. McDowell. Truth and meaning. London: Oxford University Press.
Dunbar, R.I.M. 1998. The social brain hypothesis. Evolutionary Anthropology, 6: 178–190.
Dunbar, R.I.M. 1993. Coevolution of neocortical size, group size and language in humans. Behavioral and Brain Sciences, 16: 681–735.
Eden, A.H. 2016. The singularity controversy. Technical Report. STR 2016-1. Available at: https://arxiv.org/abs/1601.05977 (27-12-2020).
Eden, A.H., Steinhart, E., Pearce, D., & Moor, J.H. 2012. Singularity Hypotheses: An overview. Introduction. In. A.H. Eden, J.H. Moor, J.H. Søraker, & E. Steinhart (Eds.). Singularity Hypotheses: A Scientific and Philosophical Assessment, New York, NY: Springer: 1–12.
Edmonds, B. The Social Embedding of Intelligence. Towards Producing a Machine that Could Pass the Turing Test. In. R. Epstein, G. Roberts, G. Beber (Eds.). Parsing the Turing Test. Philosophical and Methodological Issues in the Quest for the Thinking Computer. Heidelberg: Springer: 211–235.
Edmondson, W. 2012. The intelligence in ETI – What can we know? Acta Astronautica, 78: 37–42.
Edwards, B.J., Rottman, B.M., & Santos, L.R. 2011. The Evolutionary Origins of Causal Cognition. Learning and Using Causal Structures. In. T. McCormack, C. Hoerl, & S. Butterfill (Eds.). Tool Use and Causal Cognition. Oxford: Oxford University Press: 111–128.
Elster, J. 1999. Alchemies of the mind. Rationality and the emotions. Cambridge: Cambridge University Press.
Eriksen, N., Tougaard, J., & Miller, L.A. 2005. Cultural change in the songs of humpback whales (Megaptera novaeangliae) from Tonga. Behaviour 142: 305–325.
Eysenck, H. 1988. The Concept of 'intelligence': Useful or useless? Intelligence 12, 1–16, esp. p. 1.
Feferman, S. 2007. Gödel, Nagel, minds and machines, Ernest Nagel Lecture at Columbia University 27/09/2007. Available at: http://stanford.academia.edu/SolomonFeferman/Papers/58958/Godel_Nagel_minds_and_machines (23.02.2021).
Feuerstein, R. 1980. Instrumental enrichment: An intervention program for cognitive modifiability. Baltimore, MD: University Park Press.
Firestone, C., & Scholl, B.J. 2016. Cognition does not affect perception: Evaluating the evidence for 'top-down' effects. Behavioral and Brain Sciences 39, e229.
Firn, R. 2004. Plant Intelligence: an Alternative Point of View. Annals of Botany, 93: 345–351.
Fjelland, R. 2020. Why general artificial intelligence will not be realized. Nature. Humanities and Social Sciences Communications, 7. https://doi.org/10.1057/s41599-020-0494-4.
Floridi, L. 2015. Singularitarians, Altheists, and Why the Problem with Artificial Intelligence is H.A.L. (Humanity At Large), not HAL. APA Newsletter: Philosophy and Computers, 14.2: 8–11.
Floridi, L. 2011. The philosophy of information. Oxford: Oxford University Press.
Flynn, M. 1997. The Concept of Intelligence in Psychology as a Fallacy of Misplaced Concreteness. Interchange, 28: 231–244.

Fodor, J.A. 2008. LOT2. Oxford: Clarendon Press.
Fodor, J.A. 1987. Psychosemantics, Cambridge, MA.
Fodor, J.A. 1975. The language of thought. New York City, NY: T.Y. Crowell.
Ford, K., Glymour, C., & Hayes, P. 2009. The Annotation Game: On Turing (1950) on Computing, Machinery, and Intelligence. In. R. Epstein, G. Roberts, G. Beber (Eds.). Parsing the Turing Test. Philosophical and Methodological Issues in the Quest for the Thinking Computer. Heidelberg: Springer: 23–66.
Forrester, J.W. 1961. Industrial Dynamics. Cambridge, MA: MIT Press.
Forrester, J.W. 1958. Industrial Dynamics: A major breakthrough for decision makers. Harvard Business Review, 36: 37–66.
Fostel, G. 1993. The Turing Test is For the Birds. SIGART Bulletin, 4: 7–8.
Fox Cahn, A. 2020. A human wrote this article. You shouldn't be scared of GPT-3. The Guardian. 12 September. Available at: https://www.theguardian.com/commentisfree/2020/sep/12/human-wrote-this-article-gpt-3 (21-11-20).
Frankish, K., & Ramsey, W.M. 2015. Introduction. In. K. Frankish, & W.M. Ramsey. (Eds.). The Cambridge Handbook of Artificial Intelligence. Cambridge: Cambridge University Press: 1–11.
Franklin, S. 2015. History, motivations, and core themes. In. K. Frankish, & W.M. Ramsey. (Eds.). The Cambridge Handbook of Artificial Intelligence. Cambridge: Cambridge University Press: 15–33.
Franzén, T. 2005. Gödel's Theorem: An Incomplete Guide to Its Use and Abuse. Peters, Wellesley, MA.
French, R.M. 2012. Moving beyond the Turing test. Communications of the ACM, 55: 74–77.
French, R.M. 2000. The Turing test: The first 50 years. Trends in Cognitive Sciences, 4: 115–122.
Frey, C.B., & Osborne, M.A. 2013. The Future of Employment: How Susceptible are Jobs to Computerisation. Published by the Oxford Martin Programme on Technology and Employment. Available at: https://www.oxfordmartin.ox.ac.uk/downloads/academic/future-of-employment.pdf (27-12-20).
Garcez, A.A., & Lamb, L.C. 2020. Neurosymbolic AI: The 3rd Wave. Available at: https://arxiv.org/pdf/2012.05876.pdf (27-12-20).
Gardner, H. 1999. Intelligence Reframed: Multiple Intelligences for the 21st Century, New York: Basic Books.
Gardner, H. 1983/2011. Frames of mind: The theory of multiple intelligences. New York: Basic Books.
Gärdenfors, P. 2020. Events and Causal Mappings Modeled in Conceptual Spaces. Frontiers in Psychology, 11: 1–10.
Gärdenfors, P., & Lombard, M. 2020. Technology led to more abstract causal reasoning. Biology & Philosophy, 35: 1–23.
Gärdenfors, P., Williams, M.-A., Johnston, B., Billingsley, R., Vitale, J., Peppas, P., & Clark, J. 2019. Event boards as tools for holistic AI. Proceedings of the 6th International Workshop on Artificial Intelligence and Cognition, CEUR Workshop Proceedings, 2418: 1–10.
Gärdenfors P, & Högberg, A. 2017. The archaeology of teaching and the evolution of Homo docens. Current Anthropology, 58: 188–201.
Gärdenfors, P. 2003. How Homo Became Sapiens: On the Evolution of Thinking. Oxford: Oxford University Press.

Garis, H.D., & Halioris, S. 2009. The Artilect Debate. Why Build Superhuman Machines, and Why Not? In. R. Epstein, G. Roberts, G. Beber (Eds.). Parsing the Turing Test. Philosophical and Methodological Issues in the Quest for the Thinking Computer. Heidelberg: Springer: 487–509.

Garner, R. 2009. The Turing Hub as a Standard for Turing Test Interfaces. In. R. Epstein, G. Roberts, G. Beber (Eds.). Parsing the Turing Test. Philosophical and Methodological Issues in the Quest for the Thinking Computer. Heidelberg: Springer: 319–324.

Gershenson, C. (Ed.). 2008. Complexity. 5 Questions. Copenhagen: Automatic Press.

Gettier, E.L. 1963. Is Justified True Belief Knowledge?. Analysis, 23(6): 121–123.

Ginsburg, S., & Jablonka, E. 2009. Epigenetic learning in non-neural organisms. Journal of Biosciences, 34: 633–646.

Glock, H.-J. 2018. Animal rationality and belief. In. K. Andrews & J. Beck (Eds.). The Routledge Handbook of Philosophy of Animal Minds. New York City, NY: Routledge: 89–99.

Glymour, C. 2007. Statistical jokes and social effects. Intervention and invariance in causal relations. In. A. Gopnik & L. Schulz (Eds.). Causal Learning. Psychology, Philosophy, and Computation. Oxford: Oxford University Press: 294–300.

Glymour, C. 2001. The mind's arrows. Cambridge, MA: MIT Press.

Glymour, C. 1992. Thinking Things Through, Cambridge, MA: MIT Press.

Gödel, K. 1951/1995. Some Basic Theorems on the Foundations of Mathematics and Their Implications. Reprinted in Collected Works, Vol. III: Unpublished Essays and Lectures. Edited by S. Feferman et al. New York: Oxford University Press: 304–323.

Gödel, K. 1986. Collected Works, Vol. I: Publications 1929-1936. Edited by S. Feferman et al. New York: Oxford University Press.

Gödel, K. 1931. Über formal unentscheidbare Sätze der Principia Mathematica und verwandter Systeme I. Monatshefte für Mathematik und Physik, 38: 173–198.

Godfrey-Smith, P. 2018. Other Minds: The Octopus And The Evolution Of Intelligent Life. London: WilliamCollins.

Godfrey-Smith, P. 2017. The Mind of an Octopus. Eight smart limbs plus a big brain add up to a weird and wondrous kind of intelligence. Scientific American. Available at: https://www.scientificamerican.com/article/the-mind-of-an-octopus/ (04-12-20).

Godfrey-Smith, P. 2013. Cephalopods and the evolution of the mind. Pacific Conservation Biology, 19: 4–9.

Godfrey-Smith, P. 2009. Causal Pluralism. In. H. Beebee, C. Hitchcock, & P. Menzies (Eds.). The Oxford Handbook of Causation. Oxford. Oxford University Press: 326–337.

Goleman, D. 1995. Emotional Intelligence. New York: Bantam, New York.

Good, I.J. 1965. The Mystery of Go. In. The New Scientist: 172ff.

Goodhart, C.A. 1984. Problems of monetary management: The UK experience. In. C.A. Goodhart (Ed.). Monetary theory and practice. Berlin: Springer: 91–121.

Gopnik, A., & Schulz, L. 2007. Introduction. In. A. Gopnik & L. Schulz (Eds.). Causal Learning. Psychology, Philosophy, and Computation. Oxford: Oxford University Press: 1–15.

Gopnik, A., & Schulz, L. 2004. Mechanisms of theory formation in young children. Trends in Cognitive Science, 8: 371–377.

Gopnik, A., Glymour, C., Sobel, D., & Schulz, L., Kushir, T., & Danks, D. 2004. A theory of causal learning in children: Causal maps and Bayes' nets. Psychological Review, 111: 3–32.

Gopnik, A., & Meltzoff, A.N. 1997. Words, thoughts, and theories. Cambridge, MA: MIT Press.

Gottlieb, J. 2019. Music everywhere. Comprehensive study explains that it is universal and that some songs sound 'right' in different social contexts, all over the world. The Harvard Gazette. November 21. Available at: https://news.harvard.edu/gazette/story/2019/11/new-harvard-study-establishes-music-is-universal/ (30-12-20).

Gould, S.J. 1979. Panselectionist pitfalls in Parker & Gibson's model of the evolution of intelligence. Behavioral and Brain Sciences, 2: 385–386.

GPT-3. 2020. A robot wrote this entire article. Are you scared yet, human? The Guardian. 8 September. Available at: https://www.theguardian.com/commentisfree/2020/sep/08/robot-wrote-this-article-gpt-3 (14-11-20).

Granger, C.W.J. 1969. Investigating Causal Relations by Econometric Models and Cross-spectral Methods. Econometrica, 37: 424–438.

Grassmann, G. 2020. New considerations on the validity of the Wiener-Granger causality test. Heliyon, 6: e05208.

Greenfield, P.M. 1997. You can't take it with you: Why ability assessments don't cross cultures. American Psychologist, 52: 1115–1124.

Gregory, R. 1981. Mind in science. A history of explanations in psychology and physics. Harmondsworth: Penguin Books.

Griffin, R. 1984. Animal thinking. Cambridge, MA: Harvard University Press.

Grunwald, A. (Ed.). 2021a. Wer bist du, Mensch? Eine alte Frage vor neuen Herausforderungen. Freiburg i.B.: Herder.

Grunwald, A. 2021b. The information society: cause for a philosophical paradigm shift? In. T. Buchheim (Ed.). Philosophisches Jahrbuch 1/2021. Freiburg i.B.: Verlag Karl Alber: 106–121.

Guersenzvaig, A. 2018. Autonomous Weapon Systems: Failing the Principle of Discrimination. IEEE Technology and Society Magazine, 37: 55–61.

Guilford, J.L. 1954. The Nature of Human Intelligence. New York: McGraw-Hill.

Gunkel, D.J. 2017. The machine question. Critical perspectives on AI, Robots, and Ethics. Cambridge, MA: MIT Press.

Guttman, L. 1954. A new approach to factor analysis: The Radex. New York City, NY: Free Press.

Haenlein, M., & Kaplan, A. 2019. A Brief History of Artificial Intelligence: On the Past, Present, and Future of Artificial Intelligence. California Management Review, 61 (4): 5–14.

Hagmayer, Y., Sloman, S., Lagnado, D., & Waldmann, M.R. 2007. Causal Reasoning Through Intervention. In. A. Gopnik & L. Schulz (Eds.). Causal Learning. Psychology, Philosophy, and Computation. Oxford: Oxford University Press: 86–100.

Halpern, J., Harper, R., Immerman, N., Kolaitis, P.G., Vardi, M., & Vianu, V. 2001. On the Unusual Effectiveness of Logic in Computer Science. The Bulletin of Symbolic Logic, 7: 213–236.

Haney, R. 1969. Classical conditioning of a plant: Mimosa pudica. Journal of Biological Psychology, 11: 5–12.

Hanlon, R.T., & Messenger, J.B. 2018. Cephalopod Behaviour. Cambridge: Cambridge University Press.

Hanus, D., Mendes, N., Tennie, C., & Call, J. 2011. Comparing the Performances of Apes (*Gorilla gorilla, Pan troglodytes, Pongo pygmaeus*) and Human Children (*Homo sapiens*) in the Floating Peanut Task. PloS ONE, 6: e19555.

Hao, K. 2019. We analyzed 16,625 papers to figure out where AI is headed next. MIT Technology Review. Available at: https://www.technologyreview.com/2019/01/25/1436/we-analyzed-16625-papers-to-figure-out-where-ai-is-headed-next/ (29-10-2020).

Harari, Y.N. 2017. Homo Deus. A brief history of tomorrow. London: Vintage Books.

Harari, Y.N. 2014. Sapiens. A brief history of humankind. London: Vintage Books.

Harnad, S. 2009. The Annotation Game: On Turing (1950) on Computing, Machinery, and Intelligence. In. R. Epstein, G. Roberts, G. Beber (Eds.). Parsing the Turing Test. Philosophical and Methodological Issues in the Quest for the Thinking Computer. Heidelberg: Springer: 23–66.

Harnad, S. 2000. Correlation Vs. Causality: How/Why the Mind/Body Problem Is Hard. Journal of Consciousness Studies, 7: 54–61.

Harnad, S. 1992. The Turing Test is not a trick: Turing indistinguishability is a scientific criterion. ACM SIGART Bulletin, 3: 9–10.

Harnad, S. 1991. Other bodies, other minds: A machine incarnation of an old philosophical problem. Minds and Machines, 1: 43–54.

Hart, H.L.A., & Honoré, T. 1983. Causation in the law. (2nd edition). Oxford: Clarendon.

Haugeland, J. (Ed.). 1997a. Mind Design II: Philosophy, Psychology, and Artificial Intelligence. Cambridge, MA: Bradford Books.

Haugeland, J. 1997b. What is Mind design? In. J. Haugeland (Ed.). Mind Design II: Philosophy, Psychology, and Artificial Intelligence. Cambridge, MA: Bradford Books: 1–28.

Haugeland, J. 1985. Artificial Intelligence: The very idea. Cambridge, MA: MIT Press.

Hauser, M., Chomsky, N., & Fitch, T. 2002. The faculty of language: what is it, who has it, and how did it evolve? Science, 298: 1569–1579.

Hawkins, J. 2021. A Thousand Brains. A New Theory of Intelligence. New York City, NY: Basic Books.

Hawrylycz, M. 2015. Building atlases of the brain. In. G. Marcus, & J. Freeman (eds.). The future of the brain. Oxford: Princeton University Press: 3–16.

Hayes, P., & Ford, K. 1995. Turing test considered harmful. International Joint Conference on Artificial Intelligence (IJCAI): 972–977.

Hayles, N.K. 1996. Narratives of Artifcial Life. In. J. Bird (Ed.). Future Natural: Nature, Science, Culture. London: Routledge: 146–164.

He, Z., & Maekawa, K. 2001. On spurious Granger causality. Economics Letters, 73: 307–313.

Hebb, D.O. 1949. The organization of behavior: A neuropsychological theory. New York City, NY: Wiley.

Hedges, L.V., & Nowell, A. 1995. Sex differences in mental test scores, variability and numbers of high-scoring individuals. Science, 269: 41–45.

Heil, R. 2021. Künstliche Intelligenz / Maschinelles Lernen. In. A. Grunwald & R. Hillerbrand (Eds.). Handbuch Technikethik. Berlin: J.B. Metzler: 424–428.

Hennefield, L., Hwang, H.G., Weston, S.J., & Povinelli, D.J. 2018. Meta-analytic techniques reveal that corvid causal reasoning in the aesop's fable paradigm is driven by trial-and-error learning. Animal Cognition, 21: 735–748.

Herculano-Houzel, S., Catania, K., Manger, P.R., & Kaas, J.H. 2015. Mammalian brains are made of these: A dataset of the numbers and densities of neuronal and nonneuronal cells in the brain of glires, primates, scandentia, eulipotyphlans, afrotherians and artiodactyls, and their relationship with body mass. Brain, Behavior, and Evolution, 86: 145–163.

Herculano-Houzel S. 2011. Not All Brains Are Made the Same: New Views on Brain Scaling in Evolution. Brain, Behavior and Evolution, 78: 22–36.

Hernández-Orallo, J. 2017. The Measure of All Minds. Evaluating Natural and Artificial Intelligence. Cambridge: Cambridge University Press.

Hernández-Orallo, J. 2000. Beyond the Turing Test. Journal of Logic, Language, and Information, 9: 447–466.

Herrmann, E., & Call, J. 2012. Are there geniuses among the apes? Philosophical Transactions of the Royal Society, Series B, 367: 2753–2761.

Herrmann, E., Hernández-Lloreda, M.V., Call, J., Hare, B., & Tomasello, M. 2009. The Structure of Individual Differences in the Cognitive Abilities of Children and Chimpanzees. Psychological Science, 21: 102–110.

Herrmann, E., Call, J., Hernández-Lloreda, M.V., Hare, B., & Tomasello, M. 2007. Humans have evolved specialized skills of social cognition: The cultural intelligence hypothesis. Science, 317: 1360–1366.

Herrnstein, R., & Murray, C. 1994. The Bell Curve. New York City, NY: Free Press.

Hingston, P. 2010. A new design for a Turing test for bots. 2010 IEEE Symposium on Computational Intelligence and Games (CIG): 345–350.

Hiraiwa-Hasegawa, M. 2019. Evolution of Intelligence on the Earth. In: Yamagishi A., Kakegawa T., Usui T. (Eds.). Astrobiology. Singapore: Springer: 167–176.

Hitchcock, C. 2009. Causal Modelling. In. H. Beebee, C. Hitchcock, & P. Menzies (Eds.). The Oxford Handbook of Causation. Oxford. Oxford University Press: 299–314.

Hitchcock, C. 2007a. How to be a Causal Pluralist. In. P.K. Machamer (Ed.). Thinking About Causes: From Greek Philosophy to Modern Physics. Pittsburgh, PA: University of Pittsburgh Press: 200–221.

Hitchcock, C. 2007b. On the importance of causal taxonomy. In. A. Gopnik & L. Schulz (Eds.). Causal Learning. Psychology, Philosophy, and Computation. Oxford: Oxford University Press: 101–114.

Hobbes, T. 1651/1885. Leviathan. London : Routledge.

Hodges, A. 1992. Alan Turing: The Enigma. London: Vintage.

Hodos, W. 1988. Comparative neuroanatomy and the evolution of intelligence. In. H.J. Jerison & I. Jerison (Eds.). Intelligence and evolutionary biology. New York City, NY: Springer.

Hof, P.R., & Van Der Gucht, E. 2007. Structure of the cerebral cortex of the humpback whale, Megaptera novaeangliae (Cetacea, Mysticeti, Balaenopteridae). The Anatomical Record, 290: 1–31.

Hoffmann, C.H., & Krawczuk, I. Forthcoming. AI tech meets reality. A comparative study of AI startups in Switzerland. Submitted to: Business & Information Systems Engineering.

Hoffmann, C.H. 2021a. Infini-Rien: Ist Pascals Wettargument formallogisch ungültig? Archiv für Geschichte der Philosophie. Available at: https://www.degruyter.com/document/doi/10.1515/agph-2020-0104/html.

Hoffmann, C.H. 2021b. Vom Irrglauben an Nutzenmaximierer. Die Rolle der Erwartungsnutzenmaximierung für rationale und ethische Entscheidungen. zfwu – Zeitschrift für Wirtschafts- und Unternehmensethik, 2: 312–331.

Hoffmann, C.H. 2021c. Die Verursachung der Vergangenheit: zur Debatte um die Möglichkeit rückwirkender Kausalität. Deutsche Zeitschrift für Philosophie, 69: 950–982.

Hoffmann, C.H. 2021d. Wider dem Einsatz von Tieren in der Wissenschaft. Eine kurze Zusammenschau zu Tom Regans Plädoyer. TABVLA RASA: Jenenser Zeitschrift für kritisches Denken. Available at: https://www.tabularasamagazin.de/darf-man-tiere-fuer-die-wissenschaft-missbrauchen/ (21-10-2021).

Hoffmann, C.H. 2020a. Klugheits- versus Metaklugheits- und moralischen Überlegungen anhand eines Umweltspiels. Was das Modell des Gefangenendilemmas über Kooperation bei Fragen des Klimawandels lehrt. Forum Wirtschaftsethik. Available at: https://www.forum-wirtschaftsethik.de/klugheits-versus-metaklugheits-und-moralischen-ueberlegungen-anhand-eines-umweltspiels/ (27-10-2020).

Hoffmann, C.H. 2020b. The digital era is the era of risk management for banks. Make risk management the profit driver of tomorrow and gain totally new insights. Geneva WealthTech Forum. June. Available at: http://genevawealthtech.com/knowledgecenter/ (09-12-20).

Hoffmann, C.H. 2020c. Kritik des Bayesschen Konsequentialismus. Eine einführende Zusammenschau. Forum Wirtschaftsethik. Available at: https://www.forum-wirtschaftsethik.de/kritik-des-bayesschen-konsequentialismus/ (10-12-20).

Hoffmann, C.H. 2020d. All Else Being Equal? Über Extension und Intension von Ceteris-Paribus -Gesetzen nach Lipton. Kriterion, 34: 103–126.

Hoffmann, C.H., & Dahlinger, A. 2020. How capitalism abolishes itself in the digital era in favour of robo-economic systems: socio-economic implications of decentralized autonomous self-owned businesses. Foresight, 22: 53–67.

Hoffmann, C.H., & Hahn, B. 2020. Decentered ethics in the machine era and guidance for AI regulation. AI & Society: Knowledge, Culture and Communication, 35: 635–644.

Hoffmann, C.H. 2019a. Künstliche Panik, statt künstlicher Intelligenz. Schweizer Monat. Februar. Available at: https://schweizermonat.ch/kuenstliche-panik/%26%23x0023; (07-11-20).

Hoffmann, C.H. 2019b. Droht durch KI eine neue Ära der menschlichen Verantwortungslosigkeit? Süddeutsche Zeitung Digital Ressort. Available at: https://www.sueddeutsche.de/politik/gastkommentar-menschlicher-faktor-1.4429268 (12-11-20).

Hoffmann, C.H. 2019c. The Future of Banking and Fintech – Fixing a Broken System and the Quantum Age. Fintechnews.ch. Available at: https://fintechnews.ch/fintech/the-future-of-banking-and-fintech/31487/ (27-12-20).

Hoffmann, C.H. 2019d. Unpacking the black box of systemic risks in banking: How causal loop modeling helps overcome rigid risk sharing and categorization. Kybernetes, 49: 1675–1690.

Hoffmann, C.H. 2019e. Effektive Moralsysteme im Maschinenzeitalter und der Mythos nahender Singularität. Projekt Algorithmenethik. Bertelsmann Stiftung. Available at: https://algorithmenethik.de/2019/07/19/effektive-moralsysteme-im-maschinenzeitalter-und-der-mythos-nahender-singularitaet/ (26-02-21).

Hoffmann, C.H. 2019f. KI und Moral. Eine Grundlagendebatte. Projekt Algorithmenethik. Bertelsmann Stiftung. Available at: https://algorithmenethik.de/2019/04/17/ki-und-moral-eine-grundlagendebatte/ (26-02-21).

Hoffmann, C.H., & Müller, D. 2019. Why data science projects fail revisited. Perspectives of Machine Learning hedge funds and avoiding oversimplification. Towards Data Science. Available at: https://towardsdatascience.com/why-data-science-projects-fail-revisited -85fe242c3931 (07-11-20).

Hoffmann, C.H. 2018a. Die Kunst der Vorhersage. Buchbesprechung «Prediction machines. The simple economics of Artificial Intelligence». Springer Spektrum. Available at: https://www.spektrum.de/rezension/buchkritik-zu-prediction-machines/1603000 (07-11-2020).

Hoffmann, C.H. 2018b. Kann künstliche Intelligenz moralisch denken? NZZ Feuilleton. 21-12-2018: 38. Available at: https://www.nzz.ch/feuilleton/kuenstliche-intelligenz-hat-zurzeit-weder-moral-noch-autonomie-ld.1443718 (02-11-2020).
Hoffmann, C.H. 2018c. Ist die menschliche Autonomie bald nur noch eine Nostalgie? NZZ Feuilleton. 06-09-2018: 38. Available at: https://www.nzz.ch/feuilleton/ist-die-menschliche-autonomie-bald-nur-noch-eine-nostalgie-ld.1417076?reduced=true (14-09-2021).
Hoffmann, C.H., & Heide, F. 2018. Modern risk and regulatory management in the digital era. Syntherion's impact on stress testing. HSG Trend Monitor, 3: 7–9.
Hoffmann, C.H. 2017a. Structure-based Explanatory Modeling of Risks. Towards Understanding Dynamic Complexity in Financial Systems. Systems Research & Behavioral Science, 34: 728–745.
Hoffmann, C.H. 2017b. Assessing Risk Assessment: Towards Alternative Risk Models for Complex Financial Systems. Berlin: Springer.
Hoffmann, C.H. 2017c. Inventory Control Drones: Business potential and best practices. Verein Netzwerk Logistik Schweiz, 2: 24–28.
Hoffmann, C.H. 2017d. Indoor show drones make history on Broadway. Robohub. June 14. Available at: https://robohub.org/indoor-drones-make-history-on-broadway/ (09-12-20).
Hoffmann, C.H., & Grösser, S.N. 2015. Unpacking the black box of causality: What is it we assume with every link? Proceedings of the 33rd International System Dynamics Conference, Cambridge, MA.
Hoffmann, C.H. 2013/2019. Resolving the Two Envelopes Problem. Saarbrücken: Lambert Academic Publishing.
Hoffmann, C.H. 2011/2017. Über die Unmöglichkeit der Mechanisierung der Mathematik. Gödels Unvollständigkeitssatz und philosophische Implikationen. München: GRIN Verlag.
Hoffmann, C.H. 2010/2017. Über rückwirkende Kausalität und ihre Relevanz für Newcombs Problem. München: GRIN Verlag.
Hofstadter, D.R. 2005. Moores law, artificial evolution, and the fate of humanity. In. L. Booker, S. Forrest, M. Mitchell, and R. Riolo, eds) Perspectives on Adaptation in Natural and Artificial Systems. Oxford University Press.
Hofstadter, D.R. 1996. Fluid Concepts And Creative Analogies: Computer Models Of The Fundamental Mechanisms Of Thought. New York City, NY: Basic Books.
Hofstadter, D.R. 1981. Metamagical Themas: A coffeehouse conversation on the Turing test to determine if a machine can think. Scientific American. May: 15–36.
Hofstadter, D.R. 1979. Gödel, Escher, Bach: An Eternal Golden Braid. New York City, NY: Basic Books.
Horgan, J. 2008. The consciousness conundrum. IEEE Spectrum, 45, 36–41.
Horn, R.E. 2009. The Turing Test. Mapping and Navigating the Debate. In. R. Epstein, G. Roberts, G. Beber (Eds.). Parsing the Turing Test. Philosophical and Methodological Issues in the Quest for the Thinking Computer. Heidelberg: Springer: 73–88.
Huarte, J. 1575. Examen de los ingenious para las sciencias. English translation by R. Carew. The examination of men's wits. New edition by R.G. Sumillera. Modern Humanities Research Association, 2014.
Huebner, B. 2018. Kinds of Collective Behavior and the Possibility of Group Minds. In. K. Andrews & J. Beck (Eds.). The Routledge Handbook of Philosophy of Animal Minds. New York City, NY: Routledge: 390–397.

Hume, D. 1748/1999. An Enquiry concerning Human Understanding. Ed. by T. L. Beauchamp, Oxford: Oxford University Press.
Hunt, G.R., & Gray, R.D. 2004a. The crafting of hook tools by wild New Caledonian crows. Proceedings of the Royal Society of London Series B: Biological Sciences, 271: 88–90.
Hunt, G.R., & Gray, R.D. 2004b. Direct observations of pandanus-tool manufacture and use by a New Caledonian crow (Corvus moneduloides). Animal Cognition, 7: 114–120.
Hunt, G.R. 1996. Manufacture and use of hook-tools by New Caledonian crows. Nature, 379: 249–251.
Husbands, P. 2015. Robotics. In. K. Frankish, & W.M. Ramsey. (Eds.). The Cambridge Handbook of Artificial Intelligence. Cambridge: Cambridge University Press: 269–295.
Hutchens, J.L. 2009. Conversation Simulation and Sensible Surprises. In. R. Epstein, G. Roberts, G. Beber (Eds.). Parsing the Turing Test. Philosophical and Methodological Issues in the Quest for the Thinking Computer. Heidelberg: Springer: 325–342.
Idani, G. 1991. Social Relationships between Immigrant and Resident Bonobo (Pan paniscus) Females at Wamba. Folia Primatologica, 57: 83–95.
Jeffrey, R. 2004. Subjective probability (the real thing). Cambridge: Cambridge University Press.
Jelbert, S.A., Miller, R., Schiesti, M., Boeckle, M., Cheke, L., Gray, R., Taylor, A., & Clayton, N. 2019. New Caledonian crows infer the weight of objects from observing their movements in a breeze. Proceedings of the Royal Society B: Biological Sciences, 286: 20182332.
Jelbert, S.A., Taylor, A.H., Cheke, L.G., Clayton, N.S., & Gray, R.D. 2014. Using the Aesop's fable paradigm to investigate causal understanding of water displacement by new Caledonian crows. PloS ONE, 9: e92895.
Jensen, A. 1998. The g factor: the science of mental ability, Psycoloquy. Am. Psychol. Assn. Available at: http://psychprints.ecs.soton.ac.uk/archive/00000658/.
Jerison, H.J. 2000. The evolution of intelligence. In. R.J. Sternberg (Ed.). Handbook of Intelligence. Cambridge: Cambridge University Press: 216–244.
Jöhnk, J., Weissert, M., & Wyrtki, K. 2020. Ready or Not, AI Comes – An Interview Study of Organizational AI Readiness Factors. Business Information Systems Engineering. https://doi.org/10.1007/s12599-020-00676-7.
Jones, E.E., & Pittman, T.S. 1982. Toward a general theory of strategic self-presentation. In. J. Suls (Ed.). Psychological perspectives on the self. Hillsdale, NJ: Erlbaum: 231–262.
Joy, W., 2000, "Why the Future Doesn't Need Us," Wired 8.4. [Available online]
Jung, R.E., & Haier, R.J. 2007. The Parieto-Frontal Integration Theory (P-FIT) of intelligence: Converging neuroimaging evidence. Behavioral and Brain Sciences, 30: 135–154.
Kamhi, J.F., & Traniello, J.F.A. 2013. Biogenic Amines and Collective Organization in a Superorganism: Neuromodulation of Social Behavior in Ants. Brain, Behavior and Evolution, 82: 220–236.
Kant, I. 1787/1997. Critique of Pure Reason. Translated and edited by P. Guyer and A. Wood. Cambridge: Cambridge University Press.
Kautz, H. 2020. The Third AI Summer, AAAI Robert S. Engelmore Memorial Lecture, Thirty-fourth AAAI Conference on Artificial Intelligence. New York, NY, February 10, 2020. https://www.cs.rochester.edu/u/kautz/talks/index.html. (12-01-21).
Keynes, J.M. 1931. Essays in Persuasion. London: Macmillan.
Kihlstrom, J.F., & Cantor, N. 2000. Social Intelligence. In. R.J. Sternberg (Ed.). Handbook of Intelligence. Cambridge: Cambridge University Press: 359–379.

Kim, J. 1996. Philosophy of Mind. Dimensions of Philosophy Series. Boulder, CO: Westview.
Kim, J. 1976. Events as property exemplifications. In. M. Brand & D. Walton (Eds.). Action Theory. Dordrecht: Reidel.
Kirchgässner, G. 2013. Homo Oeconomicus. Die Einheit der Gesellschaftswissenschaften. Tübingen: Mohr Siebeck.
Kistler, M. 2016. L'Esprit matériel: réduction et émergence. Paris: Ithaque.
Kitano, H. 2020. Nobel Turing Challenge. Artificial Intelligence and Agnostic Science – Doing Science in the Age of Artificial Intelligence. Presentation at the IHPST Paris. 14 Dec. Slides available at: https://www.oecd.org/going-digital/ai-intelligent-machines-smart-policies/conference-agenda/ai-intelligent-machines-smart-policies-kitano.pdf (07-02-21).
Kline, P. (1991). Intelligence. The psychometric view. London: Routledge.
Knight, L.N., & Hargis, C.H. 1977. Math Language Ability: Its Relationship to Reading in Math. Language Arts, 54: 423–428.
Koch, C. 2020. Our Understanding of Brains Remains Limited. #AIDebate2: Moving AI Forward: An Interdisciplinary Approach. December 23. Available at: https://montrealartificialintelligence.com/aidebate2.html (27-12-20).
Koellner, P. 2018a. On the Question of Whether the Mind can be Mechanized, I: From Gödel to Penrose. The Journal of Philosophy, 7: 337–360.
Koellner, P. 2018b. On the Question of Whether the Mind can be Mechanized, II: Penrose's New Argument. The Journal of Philosophy, 7: 453–484.
Köhler, W. 1925/1976. The Mentality of Apes. New York City, NY: Liveright Publishing.
Kolb, A.Y., & Kolb, D.A. 2005. The Kolb learning Style Inventory – Version 3.1: 2005 Technical Specifications, Hay Transforming Learning, Boston. (www.haygroup.com/tl).
Krubitzer, L. 2015. Lessons from Evolution. In. G. Marcus, & J. Freeman (eds.). The future of the brain. Oxford: Princeton University Press: 186–193.
Kugel, P. 1992. Beyond Computational Musicology. From a theoretical point of view. In. M. Balaban, K. Ebcioğlu, & O. Laske (Eds.). Understanding Music with AI: Perspectives on Music Cognition. Cambridge, MA: MIT Press: 31–48.
Kurzweil, R. 2012. On Modis' "Why the Singularity Cannot Happen". In. A.H. Eden, J.H. Moor, J.H. Søraker, & E. Steinhart (Eds.). Singularity Hypotheses: A Scientific and Philosophical Assessment, New York, NY: Springer: 343–348.
Kurzweil, R. 2006. The Singularity Is Near: When Humans Transcend Biology, New York City, NY: Penguin USA.
Kurzweil, R. 1999. The Age of Spiritual Machines. New York City, NY: Penguin USA.
Kurzweil, R. 1990. The Age of Intelligent Machines. Boston: MIT Press.
Kyono, T., Gilbert, F.J., & van der Schaar, M. 2020. Improving Workflow Efficiency for Mammography Using Machine Learning. Journal of the American College of Radiology, 17: 56–63.
Lagnado, D.A., Waldmann, M.R., Hagmayer, Y., & Sloman, S.A. 2007. Beyond covariation. Cues to causal structure. In. A. Gopnik & L. Schulz (Eds.). Causal Learning. Psychology, Philosophy, and Computation. Oxford: Oxford University Press: 154–172.
Lagnado, D.A., & Sloman, S.A. 2004. The advantage of timely intervention. Journal of Experimental Psychology: Learning, Memory and Cognition, 30: 856–876.
Lake, B.M., Ullman, T.D., Tenenbaum, J.B., & Gershman, S.J. 2017. Building machines that learn and think like people. Behavioral and Brain Sciences, e253.
La Mettrie, J.O. 1748/1990. Die Maschine Mensch: L'homme machine. Französisch-Deutsch. Ed. and transl. by C. Becker. Hamburg: Meiner.

Larsson, J.E. 1993. The Turing Test Misunderstood. SIGART Bulletin, 4: 10.
Lattimore, F., & Ong, C.S. 2018. A Primer on Causal Analysis. arXiv:1806.01488.
Lawick-Goodall, J.V. 1968. The Behaviour of Free-living Chimpanzees in the Gombe Stream Reserve. Animal Behaviour Monographs, 1: 161–311
Leake, D.B. 2001. Problem Solving and Reasoning: Case-based. International Encyclopedia of the Social & Behavioral Sciences: 12117–12120. https://doi.org/10.1016/B0-08-043076-7/00545-3.
Levesque, H.J. 2018. Common Sense, The Turing Test, And The Quest For Real AI. Cambridge, MA: MIT Press.
Lewis, D. 1986. Events. In. D. Lewis (Ed.). Philosophical Papers: Volume 2. Oxford: Oxford University Press: 241–269.
Lewis, D. 1973a. Counterfactuals. Oxford: Blackwell.
Lewis, D. 1973b. Causation. Journal of Philosophy, 70: 556–567.
Lieberman, P. 1984. The biology and evolution of language. Cambridge, MA: Harvard University Press.
Lipton, P. 1999. All Else Being Equal. Philosophy 74: 155–168.
Loehlin, J.C. 2000. Group differences in intelligence. In. R.J. Sternberg (Ed.). Handbook of Intelligence. Cambridge: Cambridge University Press: 176–193.
Logan, C., Avin, S., Boogert, N., Buskell, A., Cross, F., Currie, A., Jelbert, S., Lukas, D., Mares, R., Navarrete, A., Shigeno, S., & Montgomery, S. 2018. Beyond brain size: Uncovering the neural correlates of behavioral and cognitive specialization. Comparative Cognition & Behavior Reviews, 13: 55–89.
Lohman, D.F. 2000. Complex information processing and intelligence. In. R.J. Sternberg (Ed.). Handbook of Intelligence. Cambridge: Cambridge University Press: 285–340.
Lombard, M., & Gärdenfors, P. 2017. Tracking the evolution of causal cognition in humans. Journal of Anthropological Sciences, 95: 219–234.
Loosemore, R., & Goertzel, B. 2012. Why an Intelligence Explosion is Probable. In. A.H. Eden, J.H. Moor, J.H. Søraker, & E. Steinhart (Eds.). Singularity Hypotheses: A Scientific and Philosophical Assessment, New York, NY: Springer: 83–96.
Lorenz, E.N. 1963. Deterministic Non-periodic Flow. Journal of the Atmospheric Sciences, 20: 130–141.
Lucas, J.R. 1961. Minds, Machines, and Gödel. Philosophy, 36: 112–127.
Mack, C.A. 2011. Fifty years of Moore's law. IEEE Transactions on Semiconductor Manufacturing, 24: 202–207.
Macphail, E.M. 1985. Vertebrate intelligence: The null hypothesis. In. L. Weiskrantz (Ed.). Animal intelligence. Oxford: Clarendon: 37–50.
Macphail, E.M. 1982. Brain and intelligence in vertebrates. Oxford: Clarendon.
Mandelbrot, B. 1967. How Long Is the Coast of Britain? Statistical Self-Similarity and Fractional Dimension. Science, 156: 636–638.
March-Russell, P. 2020. Machines Like Us? Modernism and the Question of the Robot. In. S. Cave et al. (Eds.). AI Narratives. A History of Imaginative Thinking about Intelligent Machines. Oxford: Oxford University Press: 165–186.
Marcus, G.; & Davis, E. 2021. Insights for AI from the Human Mind. Communications of the ACM, 64: 38–41.
Marcus, G. 2020. The Next Decade in AI: Four Steps Towards Robust Artificial Intelligence. arXiv:2002.06177v3.

Marcus, G.; & Davis, E. 2019. Rebooting AI. Building Artificial Intelligence We Can Trust. New York City, NY: Pantheon.

Marcus, G. 2018. Deep Learning: A Critical Appraisal. Available at: https://arxiv.org/abs/1801.00631 (25-09-2020).

Marcus, G., Rossi, F., & Veloso, M. (Eds.). 2016. Beyond the Turing test (special issue). AI Magazine, 37: 3–101.

Marcus, G. 2015. The computational brain. In. G. Marcus, & J. Freeman (eds.). The future of the brain. Oxford: Princeton University Press: 205–215.

Marcus, G., & Freeman, J. 2015. Preface. In. G. Marcus, & J. Freeman (eds.). The future of the brain. Oxford: Princeton University Press.

Marcus, G.; & Davis, E. 2013. A Grand Unified Theory of Everything. The New Yorker. Available at: https://www.newyorker.com/tech/annals-of-technology/a-grand-unified-theory-of-everything (09-01-21).

Marcus, G. 2004. The birth of the mind. How a tiny number of genes creates the complexities of human thought. New York City, NY: Basic Books.

Marcus, G. 2001. The algebraic mind: integrating connectionism and cognitive science. Cambridge, MA: MIT Press.

Marshall, A. 2020. Why Do Many Self-Driving Cars Look Like Toasters on Wheels?. Wired Magazine. Available at: https://www.wired.com/story/self-driving-cars-look-toasters-wheels/#intcid=_wired-bottom-recirc_48724c52-bd0a-45db-88bf-66908b8c0b71_cral2-2 (17-01-21).

Martinho-Truswell, A. 2018. The offloading ape. The human is the beast that automates. Aeon. 13 February. Available at: https://aeon.co/essays/the-offloading-ape-the-human-is-the-beast-that-automates (04-12-20).

Maslen, C., Horgan, T., & Daly, H. 2009. Mental Causation. In. H. Beebee, C. Hitchcock, & P. Menzies (Eds.). The Oxford Handbook of Causation. Oxford. Oxford University Press: 523–553.

Maslen, C. 2004. Causes, Contrasts and the Nontransitivity of Causation. In. J. Collins, N. Hall, & L.A. Paul. (Eds.). Causation and Counterfactuals. Cambridge, MA: MIT Press: 341–358.

Matthen, M. 2018. Novel Colours in Animal Perception. In. K. Andrews & J. Beck (Eds.). The Routledge Handbook of Philosophy of Animal Minds. New York City, NY: Routledge: 65–75.

Matthews, G. 2020. "A Push-Button Type of Thinking": Automation, Cybernetics, and AI in Midcentury British Literature. In. S. Cave et al. (Eds.). AI Narratives. A History of Imaginative Thinking about Intelligent Machines. Oxford: Oxford University Press: 237–259.

Mauldin, M.L. 2009. Going Under Cover: Passing as Human. Artificial Interest: A Step on the Road to AI. In. R. Epstein, G. Roberts, G. Beber (Eds.). Parsing the Turing Test. Philosophical and Methodological Issues in the Quest for the Thinking Computer. Heidelberg: Springer: 413–429.

Maynard-Smith, J., & Price, G.R. 1973. The Logic of Animal Conflict. Nature, 246: 15–18.

McCarthy, J. 1979. Ascribing mental qualities to machines. In. M. Ringle (Ed.). Philosophical perspectives in artificial intelligence. London: Humanities Press: 161–195.

McCarthy, J., Minsky, M.L., Rochester, N., & Shannon, C.E. 1955. A Proposal for the Dartmouth Summer Research Project on Artificial Intelligence. Available at: http://jmc.stanford.edu/articles/dartmouth/dartmouth.pdf (23-11-20).

McCorduck, P. 2004. Machines Who Think (2nd ed.). New York City: Routledge.

McCallum, A., Gabrilovich, E., Guha, R., & Murphy, K. (Eds.). 2009. Knowledge Representation and Reasoning: Integrating Symbolic and Neural Approaches: Papers from the 2015 AAAI Spring Symposium, AAAI Press Technical Report SS-15-03.
McDermott, D. 1997. How intelligent is Deep Blue? New York Times. May 14.
Mellor, D.H. 1995. The Facts of Causation, London: Routledge.
Meltzoff, A.N. 2007. Infants' Causal Learning. Intervention, Observation, Imitation. In. A. Gopnik & L. Schulz (Eds.). Causal Learning. Psychology, Philosophy, and Computation. Oxford: Oxford University Press: 37–47.
Meltzoff, A.N. 1995. Understanding the intentions of others: Re-enactment of intended acts by 18-month-old children. Developmental Psychology, 31: 838–850.
Menzies, P., & Price, H. 1993. Causation as a Secondary Quality. The British Journal for the Philosophy of Science, 44: 187–203.
Menzies, P. 1989. A Unified Account of Causal Relata. Australasian Journal of Philosophy 67: 59–83.
Miedaner, T. 1982a. The Soul of the Mark III Beast. In. D.R. Hofstadter, & D.C. Dennett (Eds.). The Mind's I. Fantasies and Reflections on Self and Soul. New York City, NY: Bantam Books: 109–113.
Miedaner, T. 1982b. The Soul of Martha, a Beast. In. D.R. Hofstadter, & D.C. Dennett (Eds.). The Mind's I. Fantasies and Reflections on Self and Soul. New York City, NY: Bantam Books: 100–106.
Mikhalevich, I. 2018. Simplicity and Cognitive Models: Avoiding old mistakes in new experimental contexts. In. K. Andrews & J. Beck (Eds.). The Routledge Handbook of Philosophy of Animal Minds. New York City, NY: Routledge: 427–436.
Millikan, R.G. 1984. Language, Thought, and Other Biological Categories: New Foundations of Realism. Cambridge, MA: MIT Press.
Millstein, R.L. 2002. Evolution. In. P. Machamer & M. Silberstein (Eds.). The Blackwell Guide to the Philosophy of Science. Malden, MA: Blackwell: 227–251.
Mindell, D.A. 2015. Our robots, ourselves. Robotics and the myths of autonomy. New York City, NY: Viking.
Modis, T. 2012. Why the Singularity Cannot Happen. In. A.H. Eden, J.H. Moor, J.H. Søraker, & E. Steinhart (Eds.). Singularity Hypotheses: A Scientific and Philosophical Assessment, New York, NY: Springer: 311–339.
Montgomery, S. 2016. The Soul of an Octopus: A Surprising Exploration into the Wonder of Consciousness. New York City: Simon & Schuster.
Montgomery, S. 2006. The good good pig: The extraordinary Life of Christopher Hogwood. New York City, NY: Ballantine Books.
Moore, G.E. 2008. [interviewed in] Tech luminaries address singularity. IEEE Spectrum. June 2008. Available at: https://spectrum.ieee.org/computing/hardware/tech-luminaries-address-singularity (19-02-21).
Moore, G.E. 1975. Progress in digital integrated electronics. Technical Digest, IEEE International Electron Devices Meeting, 21: 11–13.
Moravec, H. 1999. Robot: Mere Machine to Transcendant Mind, Oxford, UK: Oxford University Press.
Moravec, H. 1998. When will computer hardware match the human brain? Journal of Evolution and Technology, 1: 1–12.
Moravec, H. 1988.Mind Children. The future of robot and human intelligence. Cambridge, MA: Harvard University Press.

Morell, V. 2020. Urban foxes may be self-domesticating in our midst. Science. June 2. Available at: https://www.sciencemag.org/news/2020/06/urban-foxes-may-be-self-domesticating-our-midst (29-11-20).

Morgan, E. 1995. The descent of the child: human evolution from a new perspective. New York City, NY: Oxford University Press.

Miller, A.P. 2018.Want Less-Biased Decisions? Use Algorithms. Harvard Business Review. July 26. Available at: https://hbr.org/2018/07/want-less-biased-decisions-use-algorithms (09-12-20).

Minsky, M.L., & Laske, O. 1992. Foreword: A conversation with Marvin Minsky. In. M. Balaban, K. Ebcioğlu, & O. Laske (Eds.). Understanding Music with AI: Perspectives on Music Cognition. Cambridge, MA: MIT Press: ix–xxx.

Minsky, M.L. 1988. The society of mind. London: Heinemann.

Minsky, M.L. (Ed.). 1968. Semantic information processing. Cambridge, MA: MIT Press.

Muehlhauser, L., & Salamon, A. 2012. Intelligence Explosion : Evidence and Import. In. A.H. Eden, J.H. Moor, J.H. Søraker, & E. Steinhart (Eds.). Singularity Hypotheses: A Scientific and Philosophical Assessment, New York, NY: Springer: 15–40.

Muggleton, S. 1991. Inductive logic programming. New Generation Computing, 8: 295–318.

Nagel, E., & Newman, J.R. 2001. Gödel's Proof. With a new foreword by Douglas R. Hofstadter. New York City, NY: New York University Press.

National Academies of Sciences, Engineering, and Medicine. 2019. Quantum Computing: Progress and Prospects. Washington, DC: The National Academies Press.

Neisser, U., Boodoo, G., Bouchard, T.J., Jr., Boykin, A.W., Brody, N., Ceci, S.J., Halpern, D.F., Loehlin, J.C, Perloff, R., & Sternberg, R.J. 1996. Intelligence: Knowns and unknowns. American Psychologist Journal, 51: 77–101.

Newell, A. 1982. The knowledge level. Artificial Intelligence, 18: 87–127.

Newell, A., & Simon, H.A. 1976/1997b. Computer science as empirical inquiry: Symbols and search. In. J. Haugeland (Ed.). Mind Design II: Philosophy, Psychology, and Artificial Intelligence. Cambridge, MA: Bradford Books: 81–110.

Newell, A., & Simon, H.A. 1963. GPS, a program that simulates human thought. In. E.A. Feigenbaum & J.A. Feldman (Eds.). Computers and Thought. New York City, NY: McGraw-Hill: 279–293.

Nieder, A., Wagener, L., & Rinnert, P. 2020. A neural correlate of sensory consciousness in a corvid bird. Science, 369: 1626–1629.

Nilsson, N. 1998. Artificial Intelligence: A New Synthesis. San Francisco: Morgan Kaufmann.

Nilsson, N. (Ed.). 1984. Shakey The Robot. Technical Note 323. Menlo Park, CA: AI Center, SRI International.

Nisbett, R.E., Aronson, J., Blair, C., Dickens, W., Flynn, J., Halpern, D.F., & Turkheimer, E. 2012. Intelligence: New findings and theoretical developments. American Psychologist Journal, 67: 130–159.

Noad, M., Cato, D., Bryden, M., Jenner, M.-N., & Jenner, K.C.S. 2000. Cultural revolution in whale songs. Nature, 408: 537.

Olkowicz, S., Kocourek, M., Lučan, R.K., Porteš, M., Fitch, W.T., Herculano-Houzel, S., & Němeca, P. 2016. Birds have primate-like numbers of neurons in the forebrain. Proceedings of the National Academy of Sciences of the United States of America, 113: 7255–7260.

Omohundro, S. 2012. Rational Artificial Intelligence for the Greater Good. In. A.H. Eden, J.H. Moor, J.H. Søraker, & E. Steinhart (Eds.). Singularity Hypotheses: A Scientific and Philosophical Assessment, New York, NY: Springer: 161–176.

Oppy, G. 2020. The Turing Test. In. E.N. Zalta (Ed.). Stanford Encyclopedia of Philosophy. URL: https://plato.stanford.edu/entries/turing-test/ (05-02-2021).

Pagel, M. 1999. Darwin's evolution. Nature, 401: 853–854.

Pakkenberg, B., & Gunderson, H.J.G. 1997. Neocortical neuron number in humans: Effect of sex and age. The Journal of Comparative Neurology, 384: 312–320.

Palmer, J. 2013. Entropy law linked to intelligence, say researchers. BBC News. Available at: https://www.bbc.com/news/science-environment-22261742 (09-01-21).

Parsons, K.J., Rigg, A., Conith, A.J., Kitchener, A.C., Harris, S., & Zhu, H. 2020. Skull morphology diverges between urban and rural populations of red foxes mirroring patterns of domestication and macroevolution. Proceedings of the Royal Society B: Biological Sciences, 287: https://doi.org/10.1098/rspb.2020.0763.

Parsons, E.C.M., Wright, A.J., & Gore, M.A. 2008. The nature of humpback whale (Megaptera novaeangliae) song. Journal of Marine Animals and Their Ecology, 1: 22–31.

Partridge, D., & Wilks, Y. (Eds.). 1990. The foundations of Artificial Intelligence: A Sourcebook. Cambridge: Cambridge University Press.

Paul, L.A. 2009. Counterfactual Theories. In. H. Beebee, C. Hitchcock, & P. Menzies (Eds.). The Oxford Handbook of Causation. Oxford. Oxford University Press: 158–184.

Pautz, A., & Stoljar, D. (Eds.). 2019, Blockheads! Essays on Ned Block's Philosophy of Mind and Consciousness. Cambridge, MA: MIT Press.

Payne, R.S., & McVay, S. 1971. Songs of humpback whales. Science, 173: 585–597.

Pearce, D. 2012. The Biointelligence Explosion. In. A.H. Eden, J.H. Moor, J.H. Søraker, & E. Steinhart (Eds.). Singularity Hypotheses: A Scientific and Philosophical Assessment, New York, NY: Springer: 199–235.

Pearl, J. 2020. Edited script of J. Pearl talk at Montreal-AI, Debate 2. Causal Analysis in Theory and Practice. December 28. Available at: http://causality.cs.ucla.edu/blog/index.php/2020/12/28/edited-script-of-j-pearl-talk-at-montreal-ai-debate-2/ (02-01-21).

Pearl, J. 2018a. The Book of Why. The new science of cause and effect. Cowritten by D. MacKenzie. New York: Basic Books.

Pearl, J. 2018b. Theoretical Impediments to Machine Learning. With Seven Sparks from the Causal Revolution. arXiv:1801.04016.

Pearl, J. 2015. Trygve Haavelmo and the emergence of causal calculus. Econometric Theory, 31: 152–179.

Pearl, J. 2000. Causality: Models, Reasoning, and Inference. Cambridge, UK: Cambridge University Press.

Pearson, K. 1911. The grammar of science. London: Black.

Penrose, R. 1996. Beyond the Doubting of a Shadow: A Reply to Commentaries on Shadows of the Mind. Psyche, 2.3. Available at: http://journalpsyche.org/files/0xaa2c.pdf (22-02-21).

Penrose, R. 1994. Shadows of the Mind, Oxford, UK: Oxford University Press.

Penrose, R. 1989. The Emperor's New Mind, Oxford, UK: Oxford University Press.

Pfeifer, R. 2001. Embodied Artificial Intelligence. 10 years back, 10 years forward. In. R. Wilhelm (Ed.). Informatics: Lecture Notes in Computer Science. Heidelberg: Springer: 294–310.

Piaget, J. 1947/2012. La psychologie de l'intelligence. Paris: Armand Colin.

Piaget, J. 1962. Play, dreams and imitation in childhood. (C. Attegno & F.M. Hodgson, Trans.) New York : Norton.
Pinker, S. 2010. The cognitive niche: Coevolution of intelligence, sociality, and language. Proceedings of the National Academy of Sciences, 107: 8993–8999.
Pinker, S. 2007. Toward a consilient study of literature. Philosophy and Literature, 31: 162–178.
Plebe, A., & Perconti, P. 2012. The Slowdown Hypothesis. In. A.H. Eden, J.H. Moor, J.H. Søraker, & E. Steinhart (Eds.). Singularity Hypotheses: A Scientific and Philosophical Assessment, New York, NY: Springer: 349–362.
Popper, K. 1962. Conjectures and refutations. London: Routledge & Kegan Paul.
Popper, K. 1959. The Logic of Scientific Discovery. London: Routledge & Kegan Paul.
Povinelli, D.J., & Penn, D.C. 2011. Through a floppy tool darkly: toward a conceptual overthrow of animal alchemy. In. T. McCormack, C. Hoerl, & S. Butterfill (Eds.). Tool Use and Causal Cognition. Oxford: Oxford University Press: 69–97.
Povinelli, D.J. 2000. Folk physics for apes: The chimpanzee's theory of how the world works. Oxford: Oxford University Press.
Priest, G., & Restall, G. 2007. Envelopes and indifference. Available at : http://consequently.org/papers/envelopes.pdf (07/02/2021).
Proudfoot, D. 2012. Software Immortals: Science or Faith? In. A.H. Eden, J.H. Moor, J.H. Søraker, & E. Steinhart (Eds.). Singularity Hypotheses: A Scientific and Philosophical Assessment, New York, NY: Springer: 367–389.
Proudfoot, D. 2011. Anthropomorphism and AI: Turing's much misunderstood imitation game. Artificial Intelligence, 175: 950–957.
Proust, J. 2018. Nonhuman Metacognition. In. K. Andrews & J. Beck (Eds.). The Routledge Handbook of Philosophy of Animal Minds. New York City, NY: Routledge: 142–153.
Putnam, H. 1975. Mind, language, and reality: Philosophical papers (Vol. 2). Cambridge: Cambridge University Press.
Putnam, H. 1960. Minds and Machines. In. S. Hook (Ed.). Dimensions of Mind. A symposium. New York City, NY; Collier: 138–164.
Pylyshyn, Z. 1999. Is vision continuous with cognition? The case for cognitive impenetrability of visual perception. Behavioral and Brain Sciences, 22: 341–423.
Pylyshyn, Z. 1981. Complexity and the study of artificial and human intelligence. In J. Haugeland (ed.). Mind design. Philosophy psychology, artificial intelligence (pp. 67–94). Montgomery, VT: Bradford Books.
Raatikainen, P. 2020. Gödel's Incompleteness Theorems. In. E.N. Zalta (Ed.). Stanford Encyclopedia of Philosophy. URL: https://plato.stanford.edu/entries/goedel-incompleteness/ (23-02-2021).
Raby, C., Alexis, D., Dickinson, A., & Clayton, N.S. 2007. Planning for the future by western scrub-jays. Nature, 445: 919–921.
Rajani, S. 2011. Artificial Intelligence – man or machine. International Journal of Information Technology, 4: 173–176.
Ramsey, G. 2018. What is animal culture? In. K. Andrews & J. Beck (Eds.). The Routledge Handbook of Philosophy of Animal Minds. New York City, NY: Routledge: 345–353.
Ramsey, W. 2007. Representation reconsidered. Cambridge: Cambridge University Press.
Rapaport, W. 1988. Syntactic Semantics: Foundations of Computational Natural-Language Understanding. In. J.H. Fetzer (Ed.). Aspects of Artificial Intelligence. Dordrecht, The Netherlands: Kluwer Academic Publishers: 81–131.

Regan, T. 1985. The Case for Animal Rights. Berkeley/Los Angeles: University of California Press.
Reichenbach, H. 1956. The Direction of Time. Berkeley and Los Angeles: University of California Press.
Relethford, J.H. 2008. Genetic evidence and the modern human origins debate. Nature, 100: 555–563.
Rescorla, M. 2020. The Computational Theory of Mind. In. E.N. Zalta (Ed.). Stanford Encyclopedia of Philosophy. URL: https://plato.stanford.edu/entries/computational-mind/ (19-02-2021).
Rey, G. 1997. Contemporary Philosophy of Mind. Oxford: Blackwell Publishers.
Richter, J.N., Hochner, B., & Kuba, M.J. 2016. Pull or Push? Octopuses Solve a Puzzle Problem. PLoS ONE, 11: e0152048.
Ridgway, S.H., Brownson, R.H., Van Alstyne, K.R., & Hauser, R.A. 2019. Higher neuron densities in the cerebral cortex and larger cerebellums may limit dive times of delphinids compared to deep-diving toothed whales. PLoS One, 14.
Rinaldi, L., & Karmiloff-Smith, A. 2017. Intelligence as a Developing Function: A Neuroconstructivist Approach. Journal of Intelligence, 5: 1–26.
Robinson, A. 2020. The code-breakers who led the rise of computing. Book review. Nature, 586: 492–493.
Robinson, W.S. 2015. Philosophical challenges. In. K. Frankish, & W.M. Ramsey. (Eds.). The Cambridge Handbook of Artificial Intelligence. Cambridge: Cambridge University Press: 64–85.
Ross, D., & Spurrett, D. 2007. Notions of Cause: Russell's thesis revisited. The British Journal for the Philosophy of Science, 58(1): 1–32.
Roth, G., & Dicke, U. 2013. Evolution of nervous systems and brains. In. C. Galizia & P. Lledo (Eds.). Neurosciences – from molecule to behavior: A university textbook. Berlin: Springer: 19–45.
Russell, S., & Norvig, P. 2009. Artificial Intelligence: A Modern Approach. 3rd edition. Saddle River, NJ: Prentice Hall.
Russell, S. 1997. Rationality and Intelligence. Artificial Intelligence, 94: 57–77.
Russell, B. 1913. On the Notion of Cause. Proceedings of the Aristotelean Society. Reprinted in Russell, B. 1917, Mysticism and Logic, London: Unwin: 171–96.
Ryle, G. 1949. The concept of mind. London: Hutchinson.
Sacks, O. 2008. Musicophilia: Tales of Music and the Brain. London: Vintage.
Sainsbury, R.M. 1987. Paradoxes. Cambridge: Cambridge University Press.
Saklofske, D.H., & Zeidner, M. (Eds.). 1995. International Handbook of Personality and Intelligence. Berlin: Springer.
Salmon, W.C. 1984. Scientific Explanation and the Causal Structure of the World. Princeton: Princeton University Press.
Salovey, P., Mayer, J.D. 1990. Emotional intelligence. Imagin. Cogn. Personal, 9: 185–211.
Sanberg, P. 1976. "Neural capacity" in Mimosa pudica: A review. Behavioral Biology, 17: 435–452.
Sandberg, A. & Bostrom, N. 2008. Whole brain emulation: A roadmap. Technical report 2008-3, Future for Humanity Institute, Oxford University. Available at: http://www.fhi.ox.ac.uk/Reports/2008-3.pdf. (19-02-21).

Savage-Rumbaugh, E.S., Murphy, J., Sevcik, R.A., Brakke, K.E., Williams, S.L., & Rumbaugh, D.M. 1993. Language comprehension in ape and child. Monographs of the Society for Research in Child Development, 58 (3-4): 1–254.

Scales, H. 2020. How many hearts does an octopus have? BBC Science Focus Magazine. Available at: https://www.sciencefocus.com/nature/why-does-an-octopus-have-more-than-one-heart/ (04-12-20).

Schaffer, J. 2016. Art. The Metaphysics of Causation. In. E.N. Zalta (Ed.). Stanford Encyclopedia of Philosophy. URL: http://plato.stanford.edu/entries/causation-metaphysics/ (22-10-2020).

Schaffernicht, M. 2007. Causality and diagrams for system dynamics. Proceedings of the International System Dynamics Conference. Available at: https://proceedings.systemdynamics.org/2007/proceed/papers/SCHAF239.pdf (10-01-21).

Schank, R.C., & Towle, B. 2000. Artificial Intelligence. In. R.J. Sternberg (Ed.). Handbook of Intelligence. Cambridge: Cambridge University Press: 341–356.

Schank, R.C., & Abelson, R.P. 1977. Scripts, Plans, Goals, and Understanding. Hillsdale, NJ: Erlbaum.

Scharre, P. 2016. Autonomous Weapons and Operational Risk. Ethical Autonomy Project. Center for a New American Security. Available at: https://www.files.ethz.ch/isn/196288/CNAS_Autonomous-weapons-operational-risk.pdf (14-09-21).

Schofield, J. 2011. Artificial intelligence: John McCarthy obituary. The Guardian. 25 Oct. 2011. Available at: https://www.theguardian.com/technology/2011/oct/25/john-mccarthy (08-11-20).

Schopenhauer, A. 1819/1969. The World as Will and Representation. Volume I. Translated by E.F.J. Payne. New York City, NY: Dover Publications.

Schulz, L., Kushnir, T., & Gopnik, A. 2007. Learning From Doing. Intervention and causal inference. In. A. Gopnik & L. Schulz (Eds.). Causal Learning. Psychology, Philosophy, and Computation. Oxford: Oxford University Press: 67–85.

Schumpeter, J.A. 1954/1994. History of Economic Analysis (with a new introduction by Mark Perlman). New York: Oxford University Press.

Schmidhuber, J. 2012. New Millennium AI and the Convergence of History: Update of 2012. In. A.H. Eden, J.H. Moor, J.H. Søraker, & E. Steinhart (Eds.). Singularity Hypotheses: A Scientific and Philosophical Assessment, New York, NY: Springer: 61–78.

Schwaninger, M. 2011. System Dynamics in the Evolution of the Systems Approach. In. R.A. Meyers (Ed.). Complex Systems in Finance and Econometrics. New York City, NY: Springer.

Schwaninger, M. 2005. Systemorientiertes Design – ganzheitliche Perspektive in Innovationsprozessen. In. B. Schäppi, M.M. Andreasen, M. Kirchgeorg, & F.-J. Radermacher (Eds.). Handbuch Produktentwicklung. München: Hanser: 29–56.

Schweizer, P. 2017. Cognitive Computation *sans* Representation. In. T.M. Powers (Ed.). Philosophy and Computing. Essays in Epistemology, Philosophy of Mind, Logic, and Ethics. New York City, NY: Springer: 65–84.

Searle, J. 2014. What Your Computer Can't Know. New York Review of Books, October 9.

Searle, J. 2009. The Turing Test: 55 Years Later. In. R. Epstein, G. Roberts, G. Beber (Eds.). Parsing the Turing Test. Philosophical and Methodological Issues in the Quest for the Thinking Computer. Heidelberg: Springer: 139–150.

Searle, J. 1999. The Chinese Room. In. R.A. Wilson & F. Keil (Eds.). The MIT Encyclopedia of the Cognitive Sciences. Cambridge, MA: MIT Press: 115–116.

Searle, J. 1990. Consciousness, explanatory inversion and cognitive science. Behavioral and Brain Sciences, 13: 585–642.
Searle, J. 1984. Minds, Brains and Science. Cambridge, MA: Harvard University Press.
Searle, J. 1980. Minds, Brains, and Programs. The Behavioral and Brain Sciences, 3: 417–457.
Sebeok, T. (Ed.). 1981. The Clever Hans Phenomenon: Communication with Horses, Whales, Apes, and People. Annals of the New York Academy of Sciences, 364: vii–viii, 1–309.
Seed, A., Hanus, D., & Call, J. 2011. Causal Knowledge in Corvids, Primates, and Children. In. T. McCormack, C. Hoerl, & S. Butterfill (Eds.). Tool Use and Causal Cognition. Oxford: Oxford University Press: 89–110.
Seed, A., & Byrne, R. 2010. Animal tool-use. Current biology, 20: 1032–1039.
Select Committee on Artificial Intelligence, 2018. AI in the UK: ready, willing, and able? No. HL 100 2017-19. Available from House of Lords Website at: https://publications.parliament.uk/pa/ld201719/ldselect/ldai/100/100.pdf (19-11-2020).
Senge, P.M. 2006. The fifth discipline: The art and practice of the learning organization. New York City, NY: Currency & Doubleday.
Shah, H., Warwick, K., Vallverdú, J., & Wu, D. 2016. Can machines talk? Comparison of Eliza with modern dialogue systems. Computers in Human Behavior, 58: 278–295.
Shanahan, M., Crosby, M., Beyret, B., & Cheke, L. 2020. Artificial Intelligence and the Common Sense of Animals. Trends in Cognitive Sciences, 24: 862–872.
Shannon, C.E., & McCarthy, J. (Eds.). 1956. Automata Studies. Princeton, NJ: Princeton University Press.
Shapiro, S. 1998. Incompleteness, mechanism, and optimism. Bulletin of Symbolic Logic, 4: 273–302.
Shearer, C.B., Karanian, J.M. 2017. The neuroscience of intelligence: Empirical support for the theory of multiple intelligences?. Trends in Neuroscience and Education, 6: 211–223.
Sherwood, L., Klandorf, H., & Yancey, P.H. 2013. Animal Physiology: From Genes to Organisms. Belmont, CA: Brooks/Cole.
Shettleworth, S.J. 2013. Fundamentals of comparative cognition. Oxford: Oxford University Press.
Shettleworth, S.J. 2010. Cognition, evolution, and behavior. 2nd edition. Oxford: Oxford University Press.
Shevlin, H., Vold, K., Crosby, M., & Halina, M. 2019. The limits of machine intelligence. EMBO Reports, 20: e49177.
Shuch, H.P. (Ed.). 2011. Searching for Extraterrestrial Intelligence: SETI Past, Present, and Future. New York: Springer.
Shumaker, R., Walkup, K., & Beck, B. 2011. Animal tool behavior: the use and manufacture of tools by animals. Baltimore: JHU Press.
Silver, D., & Hassabis, D. 2016. AlphaGo: Mastering the ancient game of Go with Machine Learning. Google AI Blog. Available at: https://ai.googleblog.com/2016/01/alphago-mastering-ancient-game-of-go.html (31-10-2020).
Silver, D., Schrittwieser, J., Simonyan, K., & Antonoglou, I. 2017. Mastering the game of Go without human knowledge. Nature, 550:354–359.
Simmons, R. 2001. Survivability and Competence as Measures of Intelligent Systems. In. A.M. Meystel, & E.R. Messina (Eds.). Measuring the Performance and Intelligence of System: Proceedings of the 2000 PerMIS Workshop. August 14-16, 2000. NIST Special Publications, 970: 162–163.
Simon, H.A. 1977. The New Science of Management Decision. Englewood Cliffs: Prentice-Hall.

Singer, P. 1975. Animal Liberation: A New Ethics for Our Treatment of Animals. New York City, NY: HarperCollins.

Singler, B. 2020. Artificial Intelligence and the Parent-Child Narrative. In. S. Cave et al. (Eds.). AI Narratives. A History of Imaginative Thinking about Intelligent Machines. Oxford: Oxford University Press: 260–283.

Sloman, A. 2009. Some Requirements for Human-Like Robots: Why the Recent Over-Emphasis on Embodiment Has Held Up Progress. In. O. Sporns, K. Doya, H. Ritter, B. Sendhoff, & E. Körner (Eds.). Creating Brain-Like Intelligence. From Basic Principles to Complex Intelligent Systems. Berlin: Springer: 248–277.

Sloman, S.A., & Lagnado, D. 2005. Do we "do"? Cognitive Science, 29: 5–39.

Sloman, A. 2002. The irrelevance of Turing Machines to artificial intelligence. In. M. Scheutz (Ed.). Computationalism: New Directions. Cambridge, MA: MIT Press: 87–127.

Sloman, A. 1984. The structure and space of possible minds. In. S. Torrance (Ed.). The mind and the machine: Philosophical aspects of artificial intelligence. New York City, NY: Ellis Horwood: 35–42.

Smith, B. 2003. Ontology. In. L. Floridi (Ed.). The Blackwell Guide to the Philosophy of Computing and Information. Oxford: Blackwell: 153–166.

Sommerville, J.A. 2007. Detecting Causal Structure. The role of interventions in infants' understanding of psychological and physical causal relations. In. A. Gopnik & L. Schulz (Eds.). Causal Learning. Psychology, Philosophy, and Computation. Oxford: Oxford University Press: 48–57.

Sobel, D., & Kushnir, T. 2006. The importance of decision-making in causal learning from interventions. Memory and Cognition, 34: 411–419.

Sommer, S., & Wehner, R. 2004. The ant's estimation of distance travelled: Experiments with desert ants. Cataglyphis fortis. Journal of Comparative Physiology A, Neuroethology Sensory Neural Behavioral Physiology, 190: 1–6.

Sorber, L. 2021. How to get AI to sound less drunk: the GPT-3 case study. The much-hyped GPT-3 still lacks understanding of the world – but that may be coming. SIFTED.EU. 25 February. Available at: https://sifted.eu/articles/gpt-3-ai-sounds-drunk/ (28-02-21).

Spearman, C. 1927. The abilities of man: Their nature and measurement. New York City, NY: Macmillan.

Spindler, C., & Hoffmann, C.H. 2019. Data logistics and AI in insurance risk management. International Data Spaces Association. August 2019. Available at: https://www.internationaldataspaces.org/wp-content/uploads/2019/08/IDSA-paper-Data-Logistics-and-AI-in-Insurance-Risk-Management.pdf (07-11-20).

Spirtes, P., Glymour, C., & Scheines, R. 1993. Causation, prediction and search. New York: Springer.

Spohn, W., Ledwig, M., & Esfeld, M. (Eds.). 2001. Current issues in causation. Paderborn: Mentis.

Staddon, J.E.R. 1983. Adaptive behavior and learning. Cambridge: Cambridge University Press.

Stalnaker, R. 1968. A Theory of Conditionals. In. N. Rescher (Ed.). Studies in Logical Theory. Oxford: Blackwell.

Steiner, G. 1975. After Babel. Aspects of language and translation. New York City, NY: Oxford University Press.

Sternberg, R.J. 2000a. The concept of intelligence. In. R.J. Sternberg (Ed.). Handbook of Intelligence. Cambridge: Cambridge University Press: 3–15.

Sternberg, R.J. 2000b. Practical Intelligence in Everyday Life. Cambridge: Cambridge University Press.
Sternberg, R.J., & O'Hara, L.A. 2000. Intelligence and Creativity. In. R.J. Sternberg (Ed.). Handbook of Intelligence. Cambridge: Cambridge University Press: 611–630.
Sternberg, R.J. 1997. The concept of intelligence and its role in lifelong learning and success. American Psychologist, 52: 1030–1045.
Sternberg, R.J. 1996. Successful Intelligence. New York: Simon & Schuster.
Sternberg, R.J. 1990. Metaphors of mind. Conceptions of the nature of intelligence. Cambridge, MA: Cambridge University Press.
Sternberg, R.J. 1988. The Triarchic Mind. New York: Viking.
Sternberg, R.J. 1982. Reasoning, problem solving, and intelligence. In. R.J. Sternberg (Ed.). Handbook of Human Intelligence. Cambridge: Cambridge University Press: 225–307.
Sternberg, R.J., & Powell, J.S. 1982. Theories of Intelligence. In. R.J. Sternberg (Ed.). Handbook of Human Intelligence. Cambridge: Cambridge University Press: 975–1005.
Steyvers, M., Tenenbaum, J., Wagenmakers, E., & Blum, B. 2003. Inferring causal networks from observations and interventions. Cognitive Science, 27: 453–489.
Strawson, P. 1966/2019. The Bounds of Sense: An Essay on Kant's Critique of Pure Reason. New York City, NY: Routledge.
Suppes, P. 1970. A Probabilistic Theory of Causality. Amsterdam: North-Holland Pub. Co.
Taulli, T. 2020. Turing Test At 70: Still Relevant For AI (Artificial Intelligence)? Forbes. Nov. 27. Available at: https://www.forbes.com/sites/tomtaulli/2020/11/27/turing-test-at-70-still-relevant-for-ai-artificial-intelligence/?sh=2faf7b94250f (07-02-21).
Taylor, A., Hunt, G., Medina, F., & Gray, R. 2009. Do New Caledonian crows solve physical problems through causal reasoning? Proceedings of the Royal Society B: Biological Sciences, 276: 247–254.
Taylor, R. 1966. Action and Purpose. Englewood Cliffs, NJ: Prentice-Hall.
Tegmark, M. 2018. Life 3.0. Being human in the age of Artificial Intelligence. London: Penguin.
Teilhard de Chardin, P. 1946/1959. L'Avenir de l'Homme. Paris : Éditions du Seuil.
Tenenbaum, J.B., Kemp, C., Griffiths, T.L., & Goodman, N.D. 2011. How to Grow a Mind: Statistics, Structure, and Abstraction. Science, 331: 1279–1285.
Tenenbaum, J.B., Griffiths, T.L., Niyogi, S. 2007. Intuitive Theories as Grammars for Causal Inference. In. A. Gopnik & L. Schulz (Eds.). Causal Learning. Psychology, Philosophy, and Computation. Oxford: Oxford University Press: 301–322.
Tenenbaum, J.B., Griffiths, T.L., & Kemp, C. 2006. Theory-based Bayesian models of inductive learning and reasoning. Trends in Cognitive Sciences, 10: 309–318.
Tetlock, P.E. 2005. Expert political judgment: How good is it? How can we know? Princeton: Princeton University Press.
Thorndike, E.L. 1911. Animal intelligence: Experimental studies. London: Macmillan.
Thurstone, L.L. 1938. Primary Mental Abilities. Chicago: University of Chicago Press.
Tieszen, R. 2011. After Gödel: Platonism and Rationalism in Mathematics and Logic. Oxford: Oxford University Press.
Tolman, E.C. 1932. Purposive behavior in animals and men. New York: Century.
Tomasello, M. & Hare, B. 2003. Chimpanzees understand psychological states – the question is which ones and to what extent. Trends in Cognitive Sciences, 7: 153–156.
Tomasello, M., & Call, J. 1997. Primate cognition. New York: Oxford University Press.

Tomonaga, M., Imura, T., Mizuno, Y., & Tanaka, M. 2007. Gravity bias in young and adult chimpanzees (Pan troglodytes): tests with a modified opaque-tubes task. Developmental Science, 10: 411–421.

Toulmin, S. 1977. From Form to Function: Philosophy and History of Science in the 1950s and Now. Daedalus, 106: 143–162.

Toulmin, S. 1963. Foresight and Understanding: An Enquiry Into the Aims of Science. New York City, NY: Harper Torchbooks.

Traub, J., & Gardner, H. 1999. A debate on multiple intelligences. The Dana Foundation. Available at: http://www.dana.org/Cerebrum/Default.aspx?id=39332.

Trewavas, A. 2003. Aspects of Plant Intelligence. Annals of Botany, 92: 1–20

Trewavas, A. 2002. Plant intelligence: Mindless mastery. Nature, 415: 841.

Turing, A.M. 1952. Can automatic calculating machines be said to think? BBC Third Programme, 14 and 23 Jan, between M.H.A. Newman, AMT, Sir Geoffrey Jefferson and R.B. Braithwaite. In. B.J. Copeland (Ed.). The essential Turing. Oxford: Oxford University Press: 494–495.

Turing, A.M. 1950. Computing Machinery and Intelligence. Mind, 59: 433–460.

Turing, A.M. 1937. On Computable Numbers, with an Application to the Entscheidungsproblem. Proceedings of the London Mathematical Society, 42: 230–265.

Vaesen, K. 2014. Chimpocentrism and reconstructions of human evolution (a timely reminder). Studies in History and Philosophy of Science Part C: Studies in History and Philosophy of Biological and Biomedical Sciences, 45: 12–21.

Vakoch, D.A. 2011. Communication with extraterrestrial intelligence. Albany, NY: SUNY Press.

Valiant, L. 2013. Probably Approximately Correct. Nature's algorithms for learning and prospering in a complex world. New York City, NY: Basic Books.

Valiant, L. 2003. Three problems in computer science. Journal of the ACM, 50: 96–99.

Vallor, S. 2017. AI and the Automation of Wisdom. In. T.M. Powers (Ed.). Philosophy and Computing. Essays in Epistemology, Philosophy of Mind, Logic, and Ethics. New York City, NY: Springer: 161–178.

Van de Camp, M. 2019. Statussymbole wie Autos und teurer Schmuck sterben aus – in zehn Jahren wird Luxus etwas völlig anderes bedeuten. #Deutschland2030. Interview with Dr. Christian Hugo Hoffmann & Dr. Frank Müller. Business Insider Deutschland. Available at: https://www.businessinsider.de/leben/selbstoptimierung/statussymbole-wie-autos-und-teurer-schmuck-sterben-aus-in-zehn-jahren-wird-luxus-etwas-voellig-anderes-bedeuten/ (29-11-20).

Vardi, M.Y. 2014. Would Turing Have Passed the Turing Test? Communications of the ACM, 57: 5.

Vardi, M.Y. 2012. Artificial intelligence: Past and future. Communications of the ACM, 58: 8–9.

Verdicchio, M. 2017. An Analysis of Machine Ethics from the Perspective of Autonomy. In. T.M. Powers (Ed.). Philosophy and Computing. Essays in Epistemology, Philosophy of Mind, Logic, and Ethics. New York City, NY: Springer: 179–191.

Vernon, P.A., Wickett, J.C., Bazana, B.G., Stelmack, R.M. 2000. The Neuropsychology and Psychophysiology of Human Intelligence. In. R.J. Sternberg (Ed.). Handbook of Intelligence. Cambridge: Cambridge University Press: 245–264.

Vernon, P.A., & Mori, M. 1992. Intelligence, reaction times, and peripheral nerve conduction velocity. Intelligence, 8: 273–288.

Vernon, P. 1950. The structure of human abilities. London: Methuen Books.

Vickrey, C., & Neuringer, A. 2000. Pigeon reaction time, Hick's law, and intelligence. Psychonomic Bulletin and Review, 7: 284–291.

Vinge, V. 2008. Signs of the Singularity. Hints of the singularity's approach can be found in the arguments of its critics. IEEE Spectrum. 01 June. Available at: https://spectrum.ieee.org/biomedical/ethics/signs-of-the-singularity (17-02-21).

Vinge, V. 1993. The Coming Technological Singularity: How to survive in the post-human era. Vision 21: Interdisciplinary Science and Engineering in the Era of Cyberspace, 1: 11–22.

Vinuesa, R., Azizpour, H., Leite, I., et al. 2020. The role of artificial intelligence in achieving the Sustainable Development Goals. Nature Communications, 11: 233.

Visser, B., Ashton, M., & Vernon, P. 2006. Beyond g: putting multiple intelligences theory to the test, Intelligence, 34: 487–502.

Vold, K. 2018. Are 'you' just inside your skin or is your smartphone part of you? Aeon Ideas. 26 February. Available at: https://aeon.co/ideas/are-you-just-inside-your-skin-or-is-your-smartphone-part-of-you (12-12-20).

Von Wright, G.H. 1971. Explanation and understanding. Ithaca, NY: Cornell University Press.

Wagner, R.K. 2000. Practical Intelligence. In: R.J. Sternberg (Ed.). Handbook of Intelligence. Cambridge: Cambridge University Press: 380–395.

Wakefield, J. 2019. The hobbyists competing to make AI human. BBC News. 13 Sept. Available at: https://www.bbc.com/news/technology-49578503 (05-02-21).

Waldmann, M.R., & Mayrhofer, R. 2016. Hybrid causal representations. In: B. Ross (Ed.). The Psychology of Learning and Motivation, 65. New York City, NY: Academic Press: 85–127.

Waldmann, M.R., & Hagmayer, Y. 2013. Causal reasoning. To appear. In: D. Reisberg (Ed.). Oxford Handbook of Cognitive Psychology. New York City, NY: Oxford University Press.

Walmsley J. 2012. Introduction. In: Mind and Machine. Palgrave Philosophy Today. Palgrave Macmillan, London.

Walsh, T. 2017. It's Alive! Artificial Intelligence from the Logic Piano to Killer Robots. Melbourne: La Trobe University Press.

Wang, H. 1996. A Logical Journey. From Gödel to Philosophy, Cambridge, MA: MIT Press.

Ward, T., Bolt, A., Hemmings, N., Carter, S., Sanchez, M., Barreira, R., Noury, S., Anderson, K., Lemmon, J., Coe, J., Trochim, P., Handley, T., & Bolton, A. 2020. Using Unity to Help Solve Intelligence. arXiv:2011.09294.

Wasserman, E.A., & Zentall, T.R. 2006. Comparative cognition: Experimental explorations of animal intelligence. Oxford: Oxford University Press.

Waterhouse, L. 2006. Multiple intelligences, the Mozart effect, and emotional intelligence: a critical review. Educational Psychology, 41: 207–225.

Watt, S. 1996. Naïve psychology and the inverted Turing test. Psycoloquy, 7.

Weaver, W. 1948. Science and Complexity. American Scientist, 36: 536–544.

Wechsler, D. 1958. The measurement and appraisal of adult intelligence. Baltimore: Williams & Wilkins.

Weizenbaum, J. 1976. Computer, Power and Human Reason: From Judgment to Calculation. New York City, NY: H. Freeman.

Weizenbaum, J. 1966. ELIZA – A Computer Program For the Study of Natural Language Communication Between Man And Machine. Communications of the ACM, 9: 36–45.

Wells, M.J. 1966. Learning in the octopus. Symposia of the Society for Experimental Biology, 20: 477–507.

Whitby, B. 1996. Why the Turing test: AI's biggest blind alley. In: P. Millican, &. A. Clark (Eds.). Machines and Thought: The Legacy of Alan Turing. Oxford: Oxford University Press: 53–63.

White, A., & D'Avila Garcez, A.S. 2019. Measurable counterfactual local explanations for any classifier. arXiv:1908.03020.
Whitehead, A.N. 1925/1967. Science and the modern world. New York City, NY: Free Press.
Wickett, J.C., Vernon, P.A., & Lee, D.H. 2000. Relationships between factors of intelligence and brain volume. Personality & Individual Differences, 29: 1095–1122.
Wiener, N. 1961. Cybernetics, or Control and Communication in the Animal and the Machine. Cambridge, MA: MIT Press.
Wilson, S.W. 1991. The animat path to AI. In. J.-A. Meyer & S.W. Wilson (Eds.). From animals to animats. Cambridge, MA: MIT Press: 15–21.
Winograd, T. 1990. Thinking machines: Can there be? Are we? In. D. Partridge, & Y. Wilks (Eds.). The Foundations of Artificial Intelligence: A Sourcebook. Cambridge: Cambridge University Press: 167–189.
Winograd, T. 1972. Understanding Natural Language. San Diego: Academic Press.
Winston, P. 1992. Artificial Intelligence, Reading, MA: Addison-Wesley.
Wissner-Gross, A.D., & Freer, C.E. 2013. Causal entropic forces. Physical review letters, 110: 168702-1–168702-5.
Wittgenstein, L. 1935/1958. The Blue and Brown Books. Oxford: Blackwell Publishers.
Woodward, J. 2011. A Philosopher Looks at Tool Use ad Causal Understanding. In. T. McCormack, C. Hoerl, & S. Butterfill (Eds.). Tool Use and Causal Cognition. Oxford: Oxford University Press: 18–50.
Woodward, J. 2009. Agency and interventionist theories. In. H. Beebee, C. Hitchcock, & P. Menzies (Eds.). The Oxford Handbook of Causation. Oxford. Oxford University Press: 234–262.
Woodward, J. 2007. Interventionist Theories of Causation in Psychological Perspective. In. A. Gopnik & L. Schulz (Eds.). Causal Learning. Psychology, Philosophy, and Computation. Oxford: Oxford University Press: 19–36.
Woodward, J. 2003. Making things happen. A theory of causal explanation. Oxford: Oxford University Press.
Worswick, S. 2018. Mitsuku wins Loebner Prize 2018! Medium. Sept. 13. Available at: https://medium.com/pandorabots-blog/mitsuku-wins-loebner-prize-2018-3e8d98c5f2a7 (05-02-21).
Yablo, S. 1997. Wide Causation. Mind, Causation and the World: Philosophical Perspectives, 11: 225–281.
Yablo, S. 1993. Paradox without self-reference. Analysis, 53: 251–252.
Yampolskiy, R.V. & Fox, J. 2012. Artificial General Intelligence and the Human Mental Model. In. A.H. Eden, J.H. Moor, J.H. Søraker, & E. Steinhart (Eds.). Singularity Hypotheses: A Scientific and Philosophical Assessment, New York, NY: Springer: 129–145.
You, J. 2015. Beyond the Turing test. Science, 347: 116.
Zador, A. 2015. The Connectome as a DNA Sequencing Problem. In. G. Marcus, & J. Freeman (Eds.). The future of the brain. Oxford: Princeton University Press: 40–49.
Zentall, T.R. 2000. Animal intelligence. In. R.J. Sternberg (Ed.). Handbook of Intelligence. Cambridge: Cambridge University Press: 197–215.

About the author

Christian Hugo Hoffmann started this book while working as an Assistant Professor of Finance, which, however, began to look increasingly uninteresting and oppressive. With this book, he returns home to philosophy at the Institute for Technology Assessment and Systems Analysis (ITAS) at the Karlsruhe Institute of Technology (KIT). Apart from being passionate about Artificial Intelligence (AI) in academia, Christian is a tech entrepreneur by heart with three software start-ups in Germany, Switzerland, and Malawi under his belt. Moreover, Christian served as Deputy Director of and Head of AI at the Swiss Fintech Innovation Lab in Zurich, as Director of Startup Grind Geneva, and continues to fulfill his role as start-up coach / judge and mentor in various programs (MassChallenge, Vroom, Kickstart Accelerator), and with involvements in several tech start-ups. You can reach the author at: christian@hoffmann-economics.com.

Index

Agent 27, 102, 104–107, 119–121, 124–126, 128–130, 134, 144–145, 148–149, 152, 163–164, 166, 169, 195, 207, 217, 219–220, 235, 239, 244

AI V, VII, 1–2, 4–6, 9–11, 24, 27–28, 48, 58–74, 76–92, 96–97, 99–102, 104, 107, 111, 114, 116, 121–122, 128, 131, 133, 142–144, 148, 152, 157, 161–163, 165, 167–168, 171, 173–182, 184, 187–188, 190–193, 195, 197–200, 205–211, 213, 215–222, 224–225, 228–239, 241–245, 247, 279

AlphaGo 4, 37, 81, 87, 109, 173–175, 181, 215

Anthropocentrism
– Anthropocentric 11, 59, 142, 162, 169, 187

Artificial animals 9, 40, 47, 59, 61, 77, 83, 90, 160, 170, 242

Artificial general intelligence
– AGI 82, 190

Autonomy
– Autonomous 82, 120–121, 169, 239, 241

Block, Ned 64, 66, 87, 101, 121, 180, 185, 190, 217, 224, 231

Bostrom, Nick 77, 205, 214–216, 219–222, 232

Brain 10, 15, 17–18, 19, 22, 32, 36, 43–47, 55–56, 58–59, 68, 72, 78, 87, 91, 104, 106–107, 159, 175, 185, 215–218, 220, 228, 232

Causal modeling 151

Causality
– Causation 106–109, 111–113, 116, 118–119, 125, 132–133, 135–136, 149, 151, 163–165, 200

Chalmers, David 80, 85, 88, 90, 100, 184, 205, 215–220, 222, 224, 227, 231, 236–237

Chimpocentrism 38, 198

Chinese Room 73, 224, 233–236

Clever Hans 33–34, 36, 38

Complexity
– Complex 18–19, 22, 26, 28, 68, 119, 132, 159, 161, 164–165, 173, 210, 236

Crow
– Crows 49, 53, 77, 91

Cybernetics 28

Dartmouth workshop 4, 67

Deep understanding 131

Dennett, Daniel 10, 37, 50–51, 60, 73–74, 83, 100–101, 108, 130–131, 174–175, 183, 194

Dreyfus, Hubert 2, 68, 224, 229–232, 234

Economics of AI 9, 90

Emotion
– Emotions 30–31, 104

Entrepreneur
– Entrepreneurial VII, 128, 244, 279

Evolution 10–11, 13, 15, 19, 22, 24, 35, 42, 45–46, 51, 54, 66, 73, 77, 87–88, 104, 167, 199, 217–218, 220, 244, 247

Future 27, 30, 50–51, 67, 80, 88, 90, 96, 102, 122, 133, 150, 163, 165, 175, 178, 205, 207, 209, 220–221, 223, 242, 244–245, 247–248

Gärdenfors, Peter 21–22, 53, 68, 83, 125–129, 133–134, 199

Gardner, Howard 28–31, 37, 39–40, 46–47, 57, 91, 95, 97, 118, 140–142, 147, 162, 165, 183, 188, 194, 207

Gödel, Kurt 25, 29, 137, 142, 145, 206, 215, 224–228, 239

Good old-fashioned AI
– GOFAI 67

GPT-3 59, 81, 83–84, 86, 143, 145, 174, 215

Grunwald, Armin VII, 243

Harari, Yuval 5, 11, 19–22, 25, 33, 46, 115, 199

Haugeland, John 10, 58, 67–68, 72–73, 76, 82, 130–131, 174, 179, 183–184, 225, 235

Hoffmann, Christian Hugo VIII, 1–2, 9–10, 24, 28, 33, 39, 60–61, 63–64, 66, 69,

74–75, 77, 84, 87, 99–103, 108, 120, 128, 136, 142, 152, 164, 166, 168, 188, 190, 214, 222, 226–227, 232, 239, 243–244, 279
Hofstadter, Douglas 29, 43, 46, 95, 107, 115, 118–119, 128–130, 134–135, 145, 169, 173–174, 177, 182–184, 218, 226, 228, 232, 236

Intelligence V, VII, 1–2, 3, 4, 5, 6, 7, 9–11, 13, 15, 18–20, 24–48, 53–59, 61–62, 64–68, 72–82, 84, 87–93, 95–97, 99, 101–103, 107–108, 114, 116–121, 124, 126, 128–129, 133–135, 138–140, 142–145, 147–152, 157–158, 160–171, 173, 175–176, 178, 180–188, 190–191, 193–199, 201, 205–207, 209–210, 213–223, 225, 228, 231–232, 235, 237–245, 247–248
Intelligence explosion 88–90, 206, 213, 216, 239
Intervention 107, 112–113, 115, 119, 121, 125–127, 131, 133, 142, 152–153, 163, 169, 218

Kurzweil, Ray 4, 88, 209–210, 212–213, 215

Ladder of causation 107, 109, 112, 114, 116
Learning
– Causal learning 2, 4, 10, 20–21, 22, 27–28, 31, 37–39, 46, 52, 57, 59, 61–64, 68–72, 77, 82–83, 86, 97, 103–104, 107–109, 111, 113–114, 116–119, 121–127, 129, 131, 133–135, 142–143, 148, 150–152, 154, 157, 160, 162–164, 166, 168–170, 173–174, 180, 190, 193, 196, 199–200, 207, 215, 218, 228, 232, 236–239, 242

Marcus, Garry V, 4–5, 15, 17–19, 22, 28, 31–32, 43, 59, 64, 81, 83, 112, 119, 122, 131, 149, 164, 174–175, 179, 190–193, 199–200, 217, 223, 238
Martha 84, 107
Mind 2–3, 6, 9–10, 19, 24, 27–28, 30–31, 37, 43, 46, 54, 60, 63, 67, 73, 83–85, 87, 92, 96, 99, 102, 104, 106, 115, 118,

124–125, 129–130, 137, 147, 149, 157, 162, 164, 174, 178, 185, 187, 191, 214–216, 222, 224–228, 236, 243
Moravec, Hans 12, 53, 82, 209–210, 213–215, 220
Multiple intelligences 29–30, 39–40, 79, 91–92, 95, 118, 147, 162, 183, 207–208, 242
Music
– Musical intelligence 46–47, 142

Neocortex 15, 32, 35–36, 43
Neuroscience 6, 9–10, 11, 18, 29, 78, 96, 104, 107, 243

Octopus
– Octopi VII, 32, 35–36, 38, 53, 92, 128, 142, 147, 164, 198

Pearl, Judea 96, 99, 107–116, 119, 121–123, 125, 129–131, 133, 135, 139, 141, 149, 152–153, 157, 164, 173, 199, 206, 236, 242
Philosophy of AI 6, 9, 90
Prediction machines 87
Psychology 6, 9–10, 30, 74, 78, 96, 104, 107, 118, 122, 143, 162–163, 241, 243–244

Quantum computing
– Quantum computers 213

Radex model 6, 96, 118, 139–140, 145, 150, 166, 242
Robotics 61, 73–74, 76, 148

Searle, John 34, 73, 84–85, 175–176, 178, 197, 205, 207, 224, 233–237
Singularity 6, 88–90, 92, 168, 176, 205–212, 214–216, 219, 238–239, 242
Sternberg, Robert 26–27, 31, 38, 103, 162
Strong AI 5, 84, 86–88, 90, 205–207, 225, 242
Superintelligent AI
– SIAI 207

Syntherion 70, 128
Systems VII, VIII, 1–5, 9, 11, 15, 18, 20, 22, 28, 30, 32–33, 42–43, 54, 58, 61–62, 65, 67, 71–74, 76, 80–82, 84–86, 91–92, 104, 106, 119–124, 128, 132–133, 135, 142–145, 148, 157, 161–169, 174–176, 179, 184, 188, 190, 192–193, 197, 199–201, 206, 209–210, 212–213, 215–216, 219–221, 224–225, 228, 231, 235–238, 241–243, 247
Systems thinking VII, VIII, 28

Technology
– Technological VII, 4, 22, 60, 74, 80, 82, 84, 87–88, 106, 127, 129, 149, 167, 169, 205–206, 217, 219, 244–245
Tools 10, 21, 24, 49, 51, 82, 128, 169, 175, 199–200

Turing, Alan 61, 76, 78, 82, 86, 131, 176–188, 190–191, 193–199, 201, 208, 215, 220, 225, 228, 231, 233–234, 236–237, 242
Turing Test 61, 78, 176–177, 179–188, 190–191, 193–198, 201, 208, 233, 237, 242

Understanding 2–3, 30, 35–37, 41–42, 52, 61, 72, 74, 78, 84, 91, 99, 101–102, 104–105, 112, 116, 123–127, 129, 130–131, 133–135, 139, 161, 164–165, 167, 169, 174–175, 178, 201, 217, 220–221, 224, 230, 233–237, 241, 243–244
Universal taxonomy 119, 150, 153, 163–164, 169, 232, 236, 242

Weak AI 84
Whale
– Whales 36, 42, 44–47

www.ingramcontent.com/pod-product-compliance
Lightning Source LLC
Chambersburg PA
CBHW060351190426
43201CB00044B/1995